AF361407

Phonological Argumentation

Phonological Argumentation

Advances in Optimality Theory

Editors: Ellen Woolford, University of Massachusetts, Amherst, and Armin Mester, University of California, Santa Cruz

Optimality Theory is an exciting new approach to linguistic analysis that originated in phonology but was soon taken up in syntax, morphology, and other fields of linguistics. Optimality Theory presents a clear vision of the universal properties underlying the vast surface typological variety in the world's languages. Cross-linguistic differences once relegated to idiosyncratic language-specific rules can now be understood as the result of different priority rankings among universal, but violable constraints on grammar.

Advances in Optimality Theory is designed to stimulate and promote research in this provocative new framework. It provides a central outlet for the best new work by both established and younger scholars in this rapidly moving field. The series includes studies with a broad typological focus, studies dedicated to the detailed analysis of individual languages, and studies on the nature of Optimality Theory itself. The series publishes theoretical work in the form of monographs and coherent edited collections as well as pedagogical texts and reference texts that promote the dissemination of Optimality Theory.

Consultant Board

Judith Aissen, University of California, Santa Cruz
Daniel Büring, University of California, Los Angeles
Gisbert Fanselow, University of Potsdam
Jane Grimshaw, Rutgers University
Géraldine Legendre, Johns Hopkins University
John J. McCarthy, University of Massachusetts, Amherst
Alan Prince, Rutgers University
Paul Smolensky, Johns Hopkins University
Donca Steriade, MIT, Cambridge, MA
Moira Yip, University College London

Published:
Hidden Generalizations: Phonological Opacity in Optimality Theory
John J. McCarthy
Optimality Theory, Phonological Acquisition and Disorders
Edited by Daniel A. Dinnsen and Judith A. Gierut
Modeling Ungrammaticality in Optimality Theory
Edited by Curt Rice
Conflicts in Interpretation
Petra Hendriks, Helen de Hoop, Irene Krämer, Henriëtte de Swart and Joost Zwarts

Forthcoming:
Understanding Allomorphy: Perspectives from Optimality Theory
Edited by Bernard Tranel
On 'Elsewhere'. Disjunctivity and Blocking in Phonological Theory
Eric Baković
The Phonology of Contrast
Anna Łubowicz
Faithfulness in Phonological Theory
Marc van Oostendorp
Prosody Matters
Essays in Honor of Lisa Selkirk
Edited by Toni Borowsky, Shigeto Kawahara, Takahito Shinya and Mariko Sugahara

Phonological Argumentation
Essays on Evidence and Motivation

Edited by S. Parker

LONDON OAKVILLE

Published by
UK: Equinox Publishing Ltd., 1 Chelsea Manor Studios
Flood Street, London SW3 5SR
USA: DBBC, 28 Main Street, Oakville, CT 06779
www.equinoxpub.com

First published 2009

© Steve Parker and contributors 2009

All rights reserved. No part of this publication may be reproduced or transmitted
in any form or by any means, electronic or mechanical, including photocopying,
recording or any information storage or retrieval system, without prior
permission in writing from the publishers.

British Library Cataloguing-in-Publication Data
A catalogue record for this book is available from the British Library.

ISBN-13   978-1-84553-220-8   (hardback)
            978-1-84553-221-5   (paperback)

Library of Congress Cataloging-in-Publication Data

Phonological argumentation : essays on evidence and motivation / edited
by Steve Parker.
      p. cm. -- (Advances in optimality theory)
  Includes bibliographical references and index.
  ISBN-13: 978-1-84553-220-8 (hb)
  ISBN-13: 978-1-84553-221-5 (pb)
  1. Grammar, Comparative and general--Phonology. 2. Grammar,
Comparative and general--Morphology. 3. Optimality theory (Linguistics)
I. Parker, Stephen G. (Stephen George), 1958-
  P217.P477 2008
  414--dc22
                              2007019454

Typeset by Catchline, Milton Keynes (www.catchline.com)
Printed and bound in Great Britain and the USA

Contents

List of contributors

John Alderete, Department of Linguistics, 8888 University Dr., Simon Fraser University, Burnaby, BC, V5A 1S6, Canada, 778-782-3478, alderete@sfu.ca

Andries W. Coetzee, Department of Linguistics, University of Michigan, 440 Lorch Hall, 611 Tappan St., Ann Arbor, MI, 48109-1220, USA, 734-764-3725, coetzee@umich.edu

Paul de Lacy, Linguistics Department, Rutgers University, 18 Seminary Place, New Brunswick, NJ, 08901, USA, 732-932-1634, delacy@rutgers.edu

Maria Gouskova, Department of Linguistics, New York University, 726 Broadway, 7th floor, New York, NY, 10003, USA, maria.gouskova@nyu.edu

Nancy Hall, Department of Linguistics, California State University Long Beach, 1250 Bellflower Blvd., Long Beach, CA, 90840, USA, 562-985-2656, hall.nancy@gmail.com

Junko Ito, Department of Linguistics, Stevenson Faculty Services, University of California, Santa Cruz, Santa Cruz, CA, 95064, USA, 831-459-3340, ito@ucsc.edu

Ania Łubowicz, University of Southern California, Department of Linguistics, Grace Ford Salvatori 301, Los Angeles, CA, 90089-1693, USA, 213-740-2986, lubowicz@usc.edu

Armin Mester, Department of Linguistics, Stevenson Faculty Services, University of California, Santa Cruz, Santa Cruz, CA, 95064, USA, 831-459-3426, mester@ucsc.edu

Elliott Moreton, Department of Linguistics, Smith Building, Room 104-A, University of North Carolina, Chapel Hill, NC, 27599-3155, USA, moreton@unc.edu

Máire Ní Chiosáin, School of Irish, Celtic Studies, Irish Folklore and Linguistics, John Henry Newman Building, University College Dublin, Belfield, Dublin, 4, Ireland, 353-1-716-8215, maire.nichiosain@ucd.ie

Jaye Padgett, Department of Linguistics, Stevenson Faculty Services, University of California, Santa Cruz, Santa Cruz, CA, 95064, USA, 831-459-3157, padgett@ucsc.edu

Steve Parker, 7500 W. Camp Wisdom Rd., Dallas, TX, 75236, USA, 972-708-7713, steve-monica_parker@sil.org

Joe Pater, Department of Linguistics, 226 South College, University of Massachusetts, 150 Hicks Way, Amherst, MA, 01003-9274, USA, 413-577-1308, pater@linguist.umass.edu

Sam Rosenthall, Department of Linguistics, 331 O'Dowd Hall, Oakland University, Rochester, MI, 48309, USA, 248-370-2163, srosenth@oakland.edu

Jennifer Smith, Department of Linguistics, 309 Smith Building, CB #3155, University of North Carolina, Chapel Hill, NC, 27599-3155, USA, 919-962-1474, jlsmith@unc.cdu

John J. McCarthy

(Picture courtesy of Ben Barnhart; used with permission)

Foreword

In the early 80's John McCarthy gave a talk at UMass Amherst in a workshop on stress and prosodic phonology, organized by me and Alan Prince, who was also on the faculty here at the time. This may have been the first time I'd met John in person, though his renown had preceded him—his thesis and subsequent articles that grew out of it were already defining new areas of research in phonology. I don't remember exactly what John talked about, but I do remember thinking that the scholarship and the argumentation in the talk, and in his work more generally, were superb. More to the point, I realized while listening to him that we had to hire him at UMass. It wasn't any sort of revelation; rather it just seemed obvious to me sitting there in that group of phonologists, in the afternoon light with our backs to the westward windows in some classroom in Machmer Hall, where so many talks in the UMass Linguistics Department have taken place. John McCarthy came to UMass Amherst in 1985. Since that time he has inspired and encouraged countless students. He has been adviser and mentor to some of the finest phonologists of subsequent generations. He is at the heart of the lively community in phonology at UMass, which attracts graduate students and visiting scholars from around the world. I think he has become in the current generation what Morris Halle was for an earlier generation: an admired, committed and enormously influential teacher and the preeminent scholar in his field.

In the mid-80's when John arrived at UMass, I had been struggling for a number of years to find a means of making measurements on a mass of data from phonetic experiments I had conducted on French. Personal computers were just becoming available, and John put together a suite of programs and routines that had been developed at Bell Labs for use on main frame computers that enabled me to pursue this work on a PC in my office. Who would have suspected that this authority on Semitic phonology and morphology and the inventor of C-V tiers and nonconcatenative phonology would be superlative when it came to things computational and phonetic? As a colleague I have felt the greatest admiration for John's research contributions. This has been amplified by amazement at revelations of yet further areas of expertise which I had not known about, and respect and gratitude for his generosity in sharing his knowledge with me and with others. John loves to respond to new intellectual challenges, and is always ready to share the fruits of his discoveries.

The papers in this volume are a reflection of John's work as a teacher, and as a researcher whose ideas have set the agenda for central developments in the field, most recently and most importantly the development of optimality theory. The papers are testimony to the innovative reach of optimality theory and to the depth of explanation that the theory provides. The contributors are all students of John's, almost all of them UMass Ph.D.'s. Each one of these people doubtless has many stories to relate about ways in which John has inspired them or been generous with ideas, or facts, or tools of the trade. The papers speak both to John's influence on the theoretical questions current in the field, and to the craft of argumentation which he has inculcated. I am proud that UMass has been the incubator for scholars making contributions like these, and proud to have been John's colleague in phonology during this time.

Elisabeth Selkirk
Professor and Head
Linguistics Department

Introduction

What this book is about

This is a book about the process of phonological argumentation — that is, demonstrating the validity (or otherwise) of particular phonological analyses. In this book, Optimality Theory (OT) serves as the background. OT is a theory of the cognitive resources devoted to the manipulation of the mental representation of speech sounds. It is currently the most important and widely-practiced theoretical model in the world of formal phonology. Its main premise is that grammars consist of a finite set of universal but violable constraints which are idiosyncratically ranked in each language. Arguing OT involves identifying what the theory claims it does, then probing the properties of that theory. Usually this enterprise involves careful examination of the structure and output of the phonological module, i.e., explaining why sounds pattern the way they do, both in individual languages, and across all languages (typology). The practical side of phonological argumentation is attempting to convince others that one is correct!

How this book is structured

This volume consists of two major sections. Part 1 contains six chapters dealing primarily with the methodology used in motivating the bases of phonological theory. These six papers consider questions such as how constraints are formed and what sort of evidence is relevant in positing them. Part 2 consists of five case studies focusing on particular theoretical issues within OT, usually through selected phenomena in one or more related languages. Hence all five of these final chapters illustrate the kind of argumentation typically proposed in favor of or against specific formal analyses. Within each of these two sections the chapters are alphabetized according to the last name of the (first) author. Here is a synopsis of each paper:

Part 1: Phonological argumentation and the bases of Optimality Theory

Andries Coetzee presents the results of psycholinguistic experiments with speakers of English and Hebrew to motivate his claim that mental grammars are capable of making both categorical and gradient judgments about the wellformedness of hypothetical word-like forms. He proposes a new type of comparative OT tableau to model both kinds of decision-making behavior, which traditional grammars are unable to handle.

Paul de Lacy reviews phonological phenomena which are often presented as evidence for a popular phonological framework. He concludes that the theory does not claim responsibility for many of these phenomena. Based on his work on markedness, he proposes methods to help separate valid from spurious evidence.

Elliott Moreton proposes a stochastic learning algorithm which captures the relative frequency of phonologization effects (Bayesian Constraint Addition). The model is shown to derive the correct results in a simulation of typological patterns involving tones interacting with other tones.

Márie Ní Chiosáin and Jaye Padgett use a systemic approach couched within Dispersion Theory to argue for a principled restriction of the perceptual space of comparison sets which resolves the problem of infinite candidate generation. They apply the theory to Irish dialects in an experiment focusing on historical fortis-lenis contrasts among coronal sonorants.

Joe Pater posits that OT needs both markedness and faithfulness constraints that are lexically indexed to specific morphemes in order to account for non-uniform triggering and blocking in languages like Yine (Piro) and Finnish. He shows that this approach is superior to alternatives in which specific morphemes select rankings of certain constraints (cophonologies), or only faithfulness constraints can be lexically indexed.

Jennifer Smith proposes that Correspondence Theory be extended to include faithfulness relationships between a loanword and the borrower's posited representation of the source-language form, termed the *pLs representation*. Her model of loanword adaptation shows that this process cannot be accounted for only by the grammar of the borrowing language itself, nor by the effects of speech perception alone.

Part 2: Case studies in phonological argumentation

John Alderete compares and contrasts two typical approaches for assigning metrical structure to morphologically complex words: prosodic alignment constraints vs. uniform exponence theory. He applies the two models to the stress systems of five Australian languages and shows that the alignment version avoids several problems inherent in a uniform exponence analysis, such as the need to rank affix-specific faithfulness constraints over root faith.

Maria Gouskova and Nancy Hall examine epenthetic vowels in Lebanese Arabic through acoustic experiments showing that such vowels have phonetic traccs which can help learners distinguish them from underlying vowels. They propose a modified learning strategy based on McCarthy's theory of Candidate Chains that provides a way to model this incomplete neutralization and its opaque interaction with stress assignment.

Junko Ito and Armin Mester review McCarthy's previous proposal for the constraint FINAL-C, based on sandhi processes involving linking and intrusive *r*-liaison in non-rhotic dialects of English. They show that this non-intuitive constraint can be done away with given an enriched view of prosodic constituent structure involving functional morphemes and the onset properties of the maximal prosodic word.

Ania Łubowicz gives evidence that infixes in Palauan and Akkadian are subject to feature cooccurrence restrictions on the root domain, whereas segmentally-identical prefixes are not. In order to account for this asymmetry, she proposes that infixes are structurally incorporated into the root morpheme in the output through a process called morpheme absorption.

Sam Rosenthall relies on a foundational insight of OT — the interaction between ranked and violable constraints — to analyze the intricate morphophonemics of Arabic verb roots containing a glide as one of the radicals. Two separate processes (vowel coalescence and compensatory lengthening) are formally united as resulting from the same subhierarchy of constraints, but only when verb roots are crucially triliteral at the underlying level.

Who this book is for

This collection will be of use to anyone who wishes to engage with current linguistic theory. All those interested in phonology will find this book invaluable, including linguists, psychologists, philosophers, and researchers in allied fields. This volume presupposes a basic background in phonology as well as a working knowledge of OT, so it is not an introductory reader.

Why this book is unique

All of the contributors to this volume have been intimately connected with the program in phonetics and phonology at the University of Massachusetts Amherst. One author (Joe Pater) is currently a professor in the Department of Linguistics there, while the rest are alumni of the graduate school. Consequently, all of us have been directly influenced by John McCarthy, himself one of the major proponents of OT.

Some personal comments about John McCarthy

Paul de Lacy writes: John is a great linguist and a great academic. Putting aside his ground-breaking, highly influential, and numerous theoretical contributions, he is a font of sage advice about teaching, professional development, supervising, publishing, and everything else that an academic has to face day-to-day. I can't think of a better teacher and role model – he practices what he preaches and holds himself to almost unattainably high standards. Equally as important, he showed a great deal of kindness and friendship to me while I was at UMass, and since then. I've only ever seen one kink in John's linguistic armor. After I was at UMass for six months, he turned to me and said, 'I'm only just beginning to understand what you're saying.' This surprised me because in New Zealand the New Zealand accent is renowned for its beauty and clarity, and in its perfection bans coda *r*'s just like John's Bostonian dialect. In any case, for future generations of John's students, I feel compelled to offer some insight into John's method of praising work. John's default word is 'interesting'; it has no semantic content. Confusingly, sometimes it really does mean 'I find this thought-provoking', so I recommend to future students that they ask whether John means '*interesting* interesting', or just 'interesting'. Occasionally John will use other terms, such as the following incisive summary he scrawled boldly on the front page of one of my papers: 'Not a disgrace.' I've printed this as a poster; it hangs proudly in my office.

Maria Gouskova writes: It is hard to think of many modern-day phonologists whose work has been as continually influential and interesting as John's. Because he is such a preeminent researcher, having John as a teacher ought to be more than a little intimidating – but it never is, because he teaches and advises with such warmth and tact. Now that I am a teacher myself, whenever I write comments on a student's paper, I think, is this how John would have put it? But the most fascinating thing about John, to me, is his mind-boggling erudition. John has enriched my mental life with useful information about such disparate topics as the feline critical period for hunting mice, the Stalin-Marr polemic, and the mating and nesting habits of giant swans.

Ania Łubowicz writes: John is a great advisor and teacher. Despite a heavy research load, he always has time for students. Whenever you pass John's office, you can bet there will be a student in there. I can remember when I was that student many times in his office, trying to pull together my ideas for my first Generals Paper. Though I knew what I wanted to write about after listening to a conference presentation, the proposal was far from concrete. John encouraged me to be explicit in my proposal and observations and by doing so, indirectly helped the ideas to grow. He kept me motivated by reading multiple drafts of the paper, responding to frequent email queries and giving invaluable advice on conference presentations and the publication process. And the final result was that the paper was presented at major national and international conferences and published in a major linguistics journal!

Jaye Padgett writes: I arrived at UMass, a new Ph.D. student, in 1985, the same year that John McCarthy arrived there as a faculty member. I liked phonology, but I was planning to become a syntactician. My change of heart was in good part due to John. I was dazzled by the high standards and depth of his work, as I still am today. But it was as much through John's teaching that I was inspired to follow phonology. With his Boston-accented oratory, bobbing up and down on the balls of his feet, his prodigious handouts and spotlight questions, John bordered on fearsome, at least to me. But he brought out what is beautiful and meaningful in theoretical phonology. I had never seen such a convergence of passion, clarity, and penetration in the classroom. To this day John remains the model of a great teacher to me. And some of his exhortations (about writing: 'Jaye, put your cahds on the table') are passed on when I speak to my own students – only without the memorable accent.

Steve Parker writing again: My first personal contact with John McCarthy was back in the late 1980s. I had submitted a squib to *Linguistic Inquiry* at the time when he was in charge of reviewing them. Although my paper was not accepted, his cover letter passing on to me the critical comments of the referees was so positive and encouraging that it took away much of the sting of rejection. This highlights one of his characteristics that I find so admirable: his diplomacy. I can't recall ever seeing him get flustered by a negative question or discussion of his work. Whenever I read a good paper that proposes an interesting new idea, I ask myself, 'Why didn't I think of that?' No one has done that to me more than John has. I'm sure I speak for all of us too in noting how much I've enjoyed his great sense of humor, as well as his highly engaging and entertaining style of teaching. Another anecdote serves to further illustrate why he is so popular with his students. In the spring of 1996 I received word that I had been accepted to begin the program in linguistics at UMass that fall. While I was in the process of deciding whether or not to attend there, I got an e-mail from John mentioning that he had heard about my acceptance and wanted to encourage me to come. That meant a lot to me. In conclusion, John McCarthy, more than perhaps any other phonologist I can think of, epitomizes the concept of a mentor, and is himself a master of the art and science of linguistic argumentation. This volume certainly would not have existed without his input into all of our careers, so we happily dedicate these papers to him as a token of our appreciation.

Acknowledgements

I am indebted to many people for their help during the process of publishing this work. Since its very conception I have benefited especially from the advice and feedback of two colleagues and friends: Maria Gouskova and Paul de Lacy. They selflessly encouraged me every step of the way and made many practical suggestions about the details of contacting authors, soliciting submissions, writing up the book proposal, and the many other hidden tasks of compiling a book like this one. To them I am particularly grateful. I would also like to acknowledge the assistance of a reviewer (whose identity will remain anonymous) as an important source of commentary on the preliminary drafts so as to ensure the quality of the finished product. The series editors, Armin Mester and Ellen Woolford, also helped me at various stages of the project, including the idea of going with Equinox in the first place. Finally, I would like to thank the team at Equinox Publishing for their patient support and technical expertise: Janet Joyce, Valerie Hall, David Graddol, and Tristan Palmer.

Steve Parker
Graduate Institute of Applied Linguistics,
University of North Dakota, and
SIL International
Dallas, Texas, USA
August 2009

Part I

Phonological argumentation and the bases of Optimality Theory

1 Grammar is both categorical and gradient[1]

Andries W. Coetzee

In this paper, I discuss the results of word-likeness rating experiments with Hebrew and English speakers that show that language users use their grammar in a categorical and a gradient manner. In word-likeness rating tasks, subjects make the categorical distinction between grammatical and ungrammatical – they assign all grammatical forms equally high ratings and all ungrammatical forms equally low ratings. However, in comparative word-likeness tasks, subjects are forced to make distinctions between different grammatical or ungrammatical forms. In these experiments, they make finer gradient well-formedness distinctions. This poses a challenge on the one hand to standard derivational models of generative grammar, which can easily account for the categorical distinction between grammatical and ungrammatical, but have more difficulty with the gradient well-formedness distinctions. It also challenges models in which the categorical distinction between grammatical and ungrammatical does not exist, but in which an ungrammatical form is simply a form with very low probability. I show that the inherent comparative character of an OT grammar enables it to model both kinds of behaviors in a straightforward manner.

1 Introduction

There is a growing body of literature showing that phonological grammar influences phonological performance. We know that grammar plays a role in phoneme identification (Coetzee, 2005, 2008; Massaro and Cohen, 1983; Moreton, 2002), the segmentation of speech into words (Kirk, 2001; Suomi et al., 1997), lexical decision (Berent, Shimron and Vaknin, 2001; Coetzee, 2008), word-likeness ratings (Berent, Everett and Shimron, 2001; Frisch and Zawaydeh, 2001), etc. Once we accept that performance reflects the influence of grammar, we can use performance data as a window on what grammar looks like. In this paper, I discuss performance data showing that grammar is categorical and gradient. Grammar must be able to distinguish between grammatical (possible words) and ungrammatical (impossible words). However, grammar must also be able to make gradient well-formedness distinctions within these two sets. In the set of grammatical forms, there are some forms that are 'more' and some that are 'less' grammatical. Similarly, there are 'more' and 'less' ungrammatical forms.[2]

These data speak to the very core of grammar. They show that standard generative models in which grammar is simply a function that maps every input onto its unique grammatical output cannot be entirely correct. This would be equivalent to a grammar that makes only the categorical grammatical/ungrammatical distinction. On the other hand, it also shows that models in which grammaticality is only a value on a continuous scale of probability cannot be correct. We need a model of grammar that can make both the qualitative, categorical distinction between grammatical and ungrammatical, and gradient distinctions within the sets of grammatical and ungrammatical forms. I will show that the connections of Optimality Theory (OT) to standard generative grammar enable OT to draw the distinction between grammatical and ungrammatical in a straightforward manner. However, because of its inherent comparative nature it can also easily model gradient distinctions in well-formedness.

This paper is structured as follows: I start out with a general discussion of the relationship between grammar and word-likeness judgments. The next section discusses the results of word-likeness experiments performed by Berent and colleagues (Berent and Shimron, 1997; Berent, Everett and Shimron, 2001; Berent, Shimron and Vaknin, 2001) with Hebrew speakers. These experiments show that Hebrew speakers categorically distinguish between grammatical and ungrammatical forms in some task conditions, but that they also make gradient well-formedness distinctions in other task conditions. After discussion of the Hebrew experiments, I discuss similar experiments that I conducted with English listeners. These experiments confirm the results of Berent's Hebrew experiments. Once the experimental results have been presented, I develop a straightforward way in which to account for these results within OT. Finally, I show why the results of the experiments are problematic for other grammatical models.

2   Grammar and word-likeness judgments

It is well known that language users have strong intuitions about what counts as a possible word of their language. Although [blɪk] is not an actual word of English, it is perfectly well-formed according to the phonotactics of English. *[knɪk], on the other hand, violates a phonotactic constraint – English does not tolerate [#kn-] word-initially (Chomsky and Halle 1965:101). If these two forms were presented to English speakers in a word-likeness rating task, [blɪk] would receive higher ratings than *[knɪk]. This can be interpreted as evidence for the influence of grammar on word-likeness ratings.

However, there is a confound that sheds doubt on this interpretation. Nonce words that contain phoneme sequences that occur frequently in the lexicon are rated as more word-like than nonce words with less frequent phoneme sequences (Bailey and Hahn, 1998; Hay et al., 2004; Coleman and Pierrehumbert, 1997; etc.). Low ratings for nonce words with phonotactically illegal (and therefore non-occurring) sequences can then be interpreted as the logical extreme of such a frequency bias – a better rating for [blɪk] might simply reflect the fact that [#bl-] has a higher frequency than [#kn-] in the English lexicon.

But there is also experimental evidence showing that grammar does contribute to phonological processing independently from this kind of frequency statistics in the lexicon. In a study of word-likeness ratings in Arabic, Frisch and Zawaydeh (2001) used non-words containing unattested consonant sequences. Half of their stimuli contained consonant sequences that were absent from the lexicon because they violated a systematic phonotactic constraint of Arabic (they contained contiguous homorganic consonants in violation of the Obligatory Contour Principle). The other half contained sequences that they characterize as accidental gaps since none of the sequences belong to a coherent natural class of non-occurring consonant pairs (i.e. there are no phonotactic constraints against them). Both of these kinds of tokens contain non-occurring sequences and therefore do not differ in terms of the phoneme sequence frequency statistics calculated over the lexicon. However, they found that tokens that contained OCP-violating sequences received lower word-likeness ratings than other tokens. Since both of these token types contain non-occurring sequences, this difference cannot originate in lexical statistics. They ascribe the difference to grammar.

Results such as these support the hypothesis that grammar plays a role in word-likeness judgments. If we accept this hypothesis as true, we can look at word-likeness judgments for information on the structure of grammar – this is the topic of the next two sections, where I discuss two kinds of word-likeness judgment tasks. Language users employ the information provided by grammar differently in the two tasks, and consequently treat the same (kind of) token differently. In a 'word-likeness rating' experiment, subjects are presented with one nonce word token at a time, and they have to assign each token a rating from some rating scale. In a 'comparative word-likeness' experiment, subjects are presented with more than one token at a time, and they have to order the tokens according to their word-likeness.

In the experiments that I discuss below, we find evidence for the categorical nature of grammar in the word-likeness rating experiments. All nonce words that are well-formed according to the grammar received relatively high ratings. Consequently, these tokens are not distinguished from each other in terms of their assigned ratings. Similarly, all nonce words that are phonotactically ill-formed received very low ratings and were not distinguished from each other. Although the subjects had a rating scale with several discrete values, they treated the task as an 'accept or reject' task, using basically only two values on the scale. Language users can therefore use the information provided by grammar to make a categorical distinction between grammatical and ungrammatical.

In the comparative word-likeness experiments, we find evidence for the gradient nature of grammar. In these experiments, subjects are sometimes required to compare two grammatical nonce words or two ungrammatical nonce words with each other, and to select the one that is more word-like. In the word-likeness rating task, they might have assigned two grammatical nonce words equally high ratings. But now that option is not available, and we find the following: although two nonce words might both be grammatical, it is possible that one contains a more marked structure and is therefore less well-formed. When forced to choose between two such forms, language users prefer the more well-formed token. The same happens when they are forced to compare two ungrammatical forms. Two forms might both be ungrammatical because they contain marked structures not tolerated in the language. However, one of the forms might contain a more marked structure. When forced to choose between two such nonce words, language users prefer the one that is less ill-formed. In addition to the categorical grammatical/ungrammatical distinction, language users can also make finer gradient distinctions in terms of well-formedness.

In the next two sections, I discuss word-likeness experiments in Hebrew and English that illustrate these two uses of the information provided by grammar. Once the results of the experiments have been presented, I develop a version of OT that can account for the two response strategies.

3   Word-likeness ratings in Hebrew

One of the most striking features of Semitic morphology is the limitation on the distribution of identical consonants in verbal roots (Frisch et al., 2004; Gafos, 2003; Greenberg, 1950; McCarthy, 1986, 1994; Pierrehumbert, 1993; Coetzee and Pater, 2008; etc.). Forms with identical initial consonants are not allowed – *[X-X-Y] is ill-formed. On the other hand, forms with identical final consonants are well-formed – [X-Y-Y] is acceptable.[3] I will refer to *[X-X-Y]-forms as 'initial-geminates', to [X-Y-Y]-forms as 'final-geminates', and to forms with no identical consonants, e.g. [X-Y-Z]-forms, as 'non-geminates'.

Berent and colleagues (Berent, Everett and Shimron, 2001; Berent, Shimron and Vaknin, 2001; Berent and Shimron, 1997) conducted a series of experiments in which they tested whether this restriction plays a role in how Hebrew speakers rate nonce words. In word-likeness rating tasks, they found that Hebrew speakers rated the two kinds of possible words, [X-Y-Z] and [X-Y-Y], equally good and both better than the ungrammatical *[X-X-Y]-forms. However, in comparative word-likeness tasks, their subjects differentiated between the two kinds of grammatical tokens – they preferred the non-geminates over the final-geminates. Although both of these are grammatical, the final geminates contain a marked structure (geminate consonants) absent from the non-geminates. When forced to choose between them, subjects go for the less marked token. I discuss the experiments of Berent and Shimron (1997) as a representative example of these experiments.

3.1   Word-likeness rating[4]

Berent and Shimron (1997) selected 24 root trios. None of the roots corresponded to an existing Hebrew word. One of the members in each trio had three non-identical consonants (henceforth referred to as the 'non-geminate' member). The other members both shared the first two consonants of the non-geminate. One of them doubled the first consonant forming an initial-geminate, and the other doubled the second consonant forming a final-geminate. Each trio had the structure [X-X-Y]~[X-Y-Y]~[X-Y-Z]. Each of these trios was conjugated in three verbal forms. Their stimuli therefore included 72 non-geminate nonce words (24 non-geminate roots conjugated in 3 verbal forms), 72 final-geminate and 72 initial-geminate nonce words. The tokens were randomized, and presented in a written word-likeness rating task to 15 native speakers of Hebrew, all of whom were psychology students at Haifa University in Israel. Subjects had to rate each token on a 5-point scale, with [1] corresponding to a form that is impossible as a word of Hebrew and [5] to a form that is an excellent candidate for a Hebrew word.

Berent and Shimron do not report the average scores assigned to each of the three token types. However, they do report the difference scores – i.e. the difference between the average ratings assigned to each of the three token types.[5] The results of this experiment are summarized in (1), and represented graphically in Figure 1.

(1)   Difference scores in word-likeness rating experiment

Comparison	Example	Difference score	t	df	p
Initial-geminates and non-geminates	*[X-X-Y] [X-Y-Z]	0.881	11.1	46	< 0.001
Initial-geminates and final-geminates	*[X-X-Y] [X-Y-Y]	0.801	10.0	46	< 0.001
Final-geminates and non-geminates	[X-Y-Y] [X-Y-Z]	0.081	[6]		> 0.05

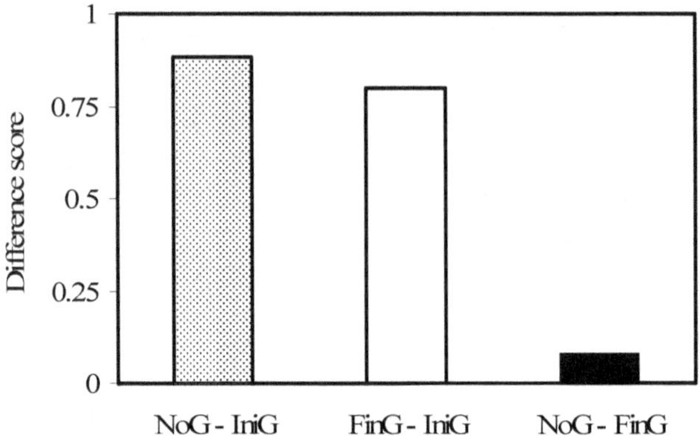

Figure 1: Difference scores in the word-likeness experiment of Berent and Shimron (1997)

3.2   Comparative word-likeness

In a second experiment, Berent and Shimron used the same 24 root trios conjugated in the same three verbal patterns as in the word-likeness rating experiment. They therefore had 72 non-word trios (24 trios conjugated in 3 verbal forms), each trio with a non-geminate, a final-geminate and an initial-geminate. Unlike in the first experiment, where the forms were presented one at a time, the three members of each trio were presented together in the comparative word-likeness experiment. The order among the members of each trio was randomized, and the trios themselves were also randomized. These trios were presented in written form to 18 students from Haifa University, all of whom were native speakers of Hebrew. Their task was to order the members of each trio in terms of its word-likeness. A score of [3] was assigned to the most word-like member, and a score of [1] to the least word-like member. This setup differs from the word-likeness rating experiment by forcing subjects to choose between the two kinds of possible words.

As with the word-likeness rating experiment, Berent and Shimron report only difference scores. Their results are summarized in (2) and represented graphically in Figure 2.

(2)   Difference scores in comparative word-likeness experiment

Comparison	Example	Difference score	t	df	p
Initial-gemination and no-gemination	*[X-X-Y] [X-Y-Z]	1.122	18.6	46	< 0.001
Initial-gemination and final-gemination	*[X-X-Y] [X-Y-Y]	0.682	11.3	46	< 0.001
Final-gemination and no-gemination	[X-Y-Y] [X-Y-Z]	0.44	_[7]		< 0.05

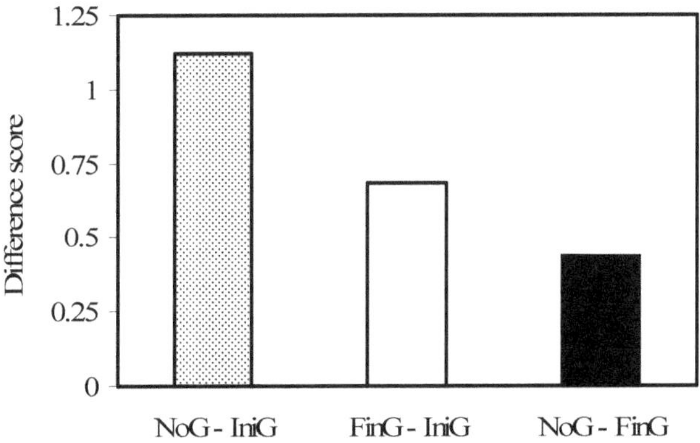

Figure 2: Difference scores in the comparative word-likeness experiment of Berent and Shimron (1997)

In both experiments, their subjects differentiated initial-geminates from non-geminates and final-geminates. This shows that (i) there is a difference between these token types in well-formedness, and (ii) both kinds of tasks are sensitive enough to pick up on this difference. In the comparative word-likeness rating task, the subjects also distinguished between non-geminates and final-geminates, so we know that these two token types also differ in terms of their well-formedness. (See below for the reasons for this difference in well-formedness.) What is interesting is that the subjects did not distinguish between these two token types in the word-likeness rating task, and this in spite of the fact that the word-likeness rating task can detect differences in well-formedness, and that there is a difference in well-formedness between non-geminates and final-geminates. Inspection of Figure 1 will show that there is a small difference between the non-geminates and the final-geminates even in the word-likeness rating task, and that this difference is in the same direction as in the comparative word-likeness rating task. It is possible that this difference between non-geminates and final-geminates would also have reached significance if more data were collected. However, even if that were the case it would still be true that the subjects treat the difference between the ungrammatical tokens (initial-geminates) and grammatical tokens (non-geminates and final-geminates) the same in the two tasks, but they treat the difference between the two kinds of grammatical tokens (non-geminates and final-geminates) differently between the two tasks. The latter difference is significantly decreased in the word-likeness rating task while the former is not.

The results of these two experiments show that language users can use the information provided by grammar in two different ways. In some tasks, they use the information in a categorical manner to distinguish grammatical forms from ungrammatical forms. In other tasks, they use grammar to make finer gradient well-formedness distinctions between different grammatical forms.

4   Word-likeness ratings in English

English restricts the consonants that can co-occur in the onset and coda of a syllable (Fudge, 1969; Davis, 1984). I focus on only one aspect of this restriction here – words of the form [sCVC] are tolerated if both C's are [t], but not if both are [k] or [p] – *state* is a word, but words of the form **skake* and **spape* do not exist in English. Following Davis (1984, 1991), I will interpret the absence of **skake* and **spape* words as evidence that these are not possible words of English (see also Browne, 1981; Clements and Keyser, 1983; Fudge, 1969; Lamontagne, 1993: Chapter 6; etc.). We therefore have a situation very similar to the Hebrew example above – we have a phonotactic constraint that can be used to divide a set of non-words between grammatical forms ([stVt]) and ungrammatical forms (*[skVk] and *[spVp]). However, the situation is also different from the Hebrew example – in English we have two kinds of ungrammatical forms (*[skVk] and *[spVp]) rather than two kinds of grammatical forms as we had in Hebrew.

This makes for an interesting way in which to replicate some of Berent and Shimron's results, and to extend upon their results. If English speakers react the same way as Hebrew speakers, then we would expect them to rate all grammatical forms ([stVt]) high, and all ungrammatical forms (*[skVk] and *[spVp]) low in a word-likeness rating experiment – i.e. we do not expect to see a difference between the two kinds of ungrammatical forms. However, if there is a well-formedness difference between *[spVp]- and *[skVk]-forms, we do expect to see evidence for this difference in a comparative word-likeness experiment. We therefore need to answer the following question: If there is a difference in word-likeness between *[skVk] and *[spVp], which of these two forms will be more and which will be less word-like? There is nothing in the phonological grammar of English that speaks to this question directly. However, there are several pieces of secondary evidence all of which converge on the conclusion that *[spVp] is most likely less well-formed than *[skVk]. I will briefly mention the most important aspects of this evidence here. For a more detailed discussion, see Coetzee (2004:395–8, 403–6).

In general, English restricts the co-occurrence of labials more severely than the co-occurrence of dorsals. There are two kinds of evidence for this. First, there are certain contexts in which two dorsals can occur but two labials cannot: (i) English tolerates words of the form [skVg] but not of the form *[spVb] – e.g. *skag* but **spab*. (ii) English tolerates words of the form [skVXk] where [X] stands for a nasal or a liquid; however, words of the forms *[spVXp] are not tolerated – e.g. *skulk, skunk*, but **spulp, *spump*. (iii) Similarly, English allows words of the form [skGVk] where [G] is a glide, but words of the form *[spGVp] are not tolerated – e.g. *squeak* but **spweep, *spyeep*. The second kind of evidence is not about possible and impossible words, but rather about statistical tendencies in the English lexicon. Berkley (1994, 2000) counted the number of English words with two homorganic consonants separated by at most two segments (i.e. *pop, palm, king, skulk, state, tact*, etc.). She then calculated the number of such words that would have been expected had consonants combined randomly. The ratio of the observed frequency to the expected frequency (O/E) is an index of the degree of over or underrepresentation of each word type. Berkley found that words with two dorsals and words with two labials were both underrepresented (i.e. had O/E-values below 1). However, the O/E-ratio for labials (0.57) was lower than that for dorsals (0.71) This shows that the co-occurrence of labials is more restricted than that of dorsals. See also de Lacy (2002:173 ff.) for arguments that labials are universally more marked than dorsals.

If we assume that the preference for the co-occurrence of dorsals will transfer onto [sCVC]-forms, then, even though both *[skVk] and *[spVp] are ungrammatical, *[skVk] will be more well-formed than *[spVp]. If this is true and if English subjects respond in a manner similar to Hebrew subjects, then English subjects should prefer *[skVk]-forms over *[spVp]-forms in a comparative word-likeness experiment.

I performed a series of experiments with speakers of American English to test these predictions. All the experiments were performed during 2003 at the University of Massachusetts. The rest of this section is dedicated to discussing the design and results of these experiments.

4.1   Word-likeness rating

4.1.1   Design

Subjects. Twenty native speakers of American English were recruited from the undergraduate population at the University of Massachusetts. Most of the subjects grew up in western Massachusetts and were therefore speakers of the same dialect. However, because of exposure to speakers of other dialects, both in their daily lives and on the television and radio, it was not possible to control for differences between subjects in terms of their exposure to different dialects of American English. None of the subjects reported any speech or hearing deficit. Subjects received credit in an introductory linguistics class for their participation.

Token selection. Tokens were selected in three conditions: (i) T~K: 5 non-words each of the form [stVt] and *[skVk]; (ii) T~P: 5 non-words each of the form [stVt] and *[spVp]; (iii) K~P: 5 non-words each of the form *[skVk] and *[spVp]. All tokens were selected to control for the possible influence of lexical statistics on word-likeness rating (see the discussion above). Two kinds of lexical statistics were calculated for each token: lexical neighborhood density (LND) and cumulative bi-phone probability (CBP).[8] The tokens were selected such that the tokens in each condition did not differ in terms of these statistics. If subjects treat these token types differently, the difference can therefore not be ascribed to a difference in these lexical statistics. The actual tokens used and their lexical statistics are included in the appendix.

Recordings. All tokens were read in the frame sentence 'John said ______ again to me.' Tokens were read by a phonetically trained native female speaker of American English. The speaker was in her early twenties, and spoke standard Midwestern American English. She had a clear, native distinction between the vowels in *pin* and *pen*. Each token was recorded 4 times. Recordings were made in a soundproofed booth at the Phonetics Laboratory of the University of Massachusetts. All tokens were excised from the frame sentence, and a single instance of each token was selected for use in the experiment. The instance selected was judged to be the clearest example of the specific token. This judgment was based on impressionistic grounds. All selected instances had released final stops (the release was possible because the word following the token in the frame sentence started with a vowel). This was confirmed by inspection of waveforms and spectrograms of the tokens.

Procedure. There was a total of 24 test-tokens.[9] Each of these tokens was included twice in the stimulus list. To these tokens were added 77 non-word filler items,[10] so that the stimulus list contained a total of 125 tokens. The stimulus list was presented auditorily to subjects twice so that each test-token was presented four times. There was a break of roughly 5 minutes between presentations. The stimulus list was randomized differently on every presentation. After hearing a token, subjects indicated their rating of the token on an answer sheet by circling a number from [1] to [5]. A score of [1] corresponded to a token that was judged as not very well-formed/very unlikely to ever be included in the lexicon of English, and a score of [5] to a token that was judged to be very well-formed/very likely to be included in the lexicon of English. After 5 seconds, the next token was presented. Before the list was presented the first time, 10 filler tokens were presented as practice trials.

4.1.2   Results and discussion

The design of the experiment allows for a comparison of the grammatical forms ([stVt]) with each of the two ungrammatical forms (*[skVk] and *[spVp]), and for a comparison of the two kinds of ungrammatical forms with each other. If the English subjects respond in the same way as the Hebrew subjects, then we would expect the grammatical [stVt]-forms to be rated better than the ungrammatical forms, but we would expect no difference between the two kinds of ungrammatical forms.

Each token was presented four times. The mean score that each subject assigned to each token was calculated. Statistical analyses were performed on these mean scores. The scores were subjected to a 2×3 ANOVA with hypothesized grammatical well-formedness (more well-formed~less well-formed) and condition (K~P, T~K, T~P) as independent variables. The main effects of well-formedness ($F(1, 594) = 109.9, p < 0.001$) and condition ($F(2, 594) = 43.3, p < .001$) were both significant, as well as the interaction between well-formedness and condition ($F(2, 594) = 41.9, p < .001$). The contrasts between the more and less well-formed tokens in each condition were further investigated with one-tailed t-tests. Since three comparisons are made, the critical value for significance is taken to be 0.0167 to control for type 1 errors. These tests returned significant differences for the T~P-condition ($t(198) = 9.1, p < .001$) and T~K-condition ($t(198) = 9.2, p < .001$), but not for the K~P-condition ($t(198) = 0.9, p = .17$). The results are summarized in (3), and portrayed graphically in Figure 3.

(3)   Mean ratings in the three conditions in word-likeness rating experiment

Condition	Token type	Rating
T~P	[stVt]	3.65
	*[spVp]	2.41
T~K	[stVt]	3.64
	*[skVk]	2.43
K~P	*[skVk]	2.52
	*[spVp]	2.41

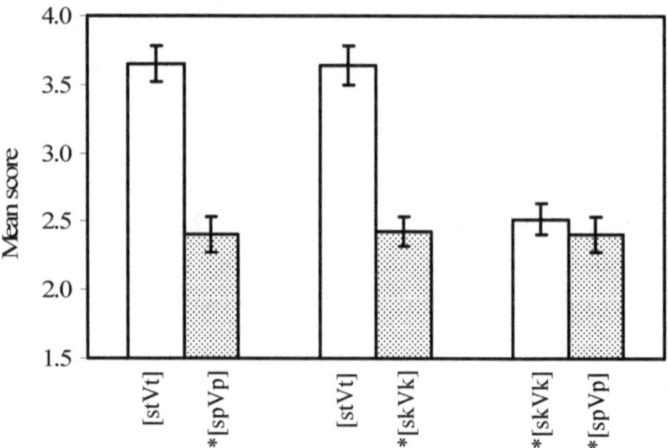

Figure 3: Mean ratings for the three conditions in the English word-likeness rating experiment. Error bars show the 95% confidence intervals.

Like the Hebrew subjects, the English subjects rated grammatical forms better than ungrammatical forms. However, there is no significant difference in the scores of the two kinds of ungrammatical forms. This extends on Berent and Shimron's results. In their experiment, we saw that subjects do not distinguish between different kinds of grammatical forms in a word-likeness rating task. The results of this English experiment show the same for ungrammatical forms.

4.2   Comparative word-likeness

4.2.1   Design

Subjects. The same 20 subjects that took part in the word-likeness rating experiment also took part in the comparative word-likeness experiment.

Token selection. Tokens were selected in three conditions: (i) T~K: 15 non-word pairs of the form [stVt]~*[skVk]; (ii) T~P: 15 non-word pairs of the form [stVt]~*[spVp]; (iii) K~P: 15 non-word pairs of the form *[skVk]~*[spVp]. Tokens were selected such that lexical statistics (CBP and LND) and grammar conflicted in each non-word pair. In the T~K- and T~P-conditions, the LND and CBP of the [stVt]-token was lower than that of the *[skVk]- and *[spVp]-tokens respectively for each token-pair. In the K~P-condition, the lexical statistics of the *[skVk]-token was lower than that of the *[spVp]-token for each token-pair. The expected response pattern based on lexical statistics and that based on grammar are therefore directly opposite. The actual tokens used and their lexical statistics are included in the appendix.

Recordings. Recordings were done in exactly the same manner as for the word-likeness rating experiment.

Procedure. There was a total of 45 test-token pairs – 15 in each condition. I added 45 filler pairs to this. Only non-words were used in the filler pairs.[11] This resulted in a total of 90 token-pairs. Two lists were created from these 90 token-pairs. Each list contained all 90 token-pairs. In List 1, eight out of the fifteen pairs of the T~K-condition had the [stVt]-token first and the *[skVk]-token second. In the other seven token-pairs for this condition, the *[skVk]-token was used first. The same was true for the T~P-pairs and K~P-pairs. In List 2, the order between the members in a token pair was reversed – i.e. if two tokens occurred in the order [Token 1]~[Token 2] in List 1, then they occurred in the order [Token 2]~[Token 1] in List 2. Both lists were presented auditorily to subjects who had to select the member of a pair that they thought to be most word-like. About 5 minutes elapsed between the presentation of the lists. On each presentation of a list, it was randomized differently. Before the list was presented the first time, 10 filler token-pairs were presented as practice trials. Since there is no correct or wrong answer, no feedback was given during the practice trials or during the actual experiment trials.

4.2.2   Results and discussion

Based on the results of Berent and Shimron, and the word-likeness rating experiment discussed above, we expect the subjects to prefer [stVt]-forms over *[skVk]- and *[spVp]-forms. We also expect subjects to make a distinction between *[skVk] and *[spVp] if there is indeed a well-formedness difference between these kinds of forms. As explained earlier, based on general patterns of consonant co-occurrence in English, we expect that *[skVk]-forms are more well-formed than *[spVp]-forms, even if both of these are ungrammatical. We therefore expect that the subjects will prefer *[skVk] more often than *[spVp] when they have to choose between these two forms.

The results of the experiment were scored as follows: each token pair, [Token 1]~[Token 2], was presented twice, so that there are three possible response patterns for each pair. If a subject selected [Token 1] more often than [Token 2], then [Token 1] was assigned a score of [1] for that subject, and [Token 2] was assigned a score of [0]. Conversely, if [Token 2] was selected more often than [Token 1], [Token 2] received a score of [1] and [Token 1] received a score of [0]. If the tokens were selected with equal frequency, both were assigned a score of [1/2] for that subject. These scores were submitted to a 2 × 3 ANOVA with hypothesized grammatical well-formedness and condition as independent variables. A main effect of well-formedness was found

($F(1, 1794) = 68.5$, $p < 0.001$), as well as a significant interaction between well-formedness and condition ($F(2, 1794) = 18.4$, $p < .001$). The contrasts between the more and less well-formed tokens in each condition were further investigated with one-tailed paired sample *t*-tests. As before, I corrected for type 1 errors by dividing the critical *p*-value by the number of comparisons. All three comparisons returned significant results: T~P-condition ($t(299) = 15.4$, $p < .001$), T~K-condition ($t(299) = 11.9$, $p < .001$), and K~P-condition ($t(299) = 2.3$, $p = .01$). The results are summarized in (4), and portrayed graphically in Figure 4.

(4)   Percentage that token type was selected in comparative word-likeness experiment

Condition	Token type	Percentage
T~P	[stVt]	78
	*[spVp]	22
T~K	[stVt]	75
	*[skVk]	25
K~P	*[skVk]	55
	*[spVp]	45

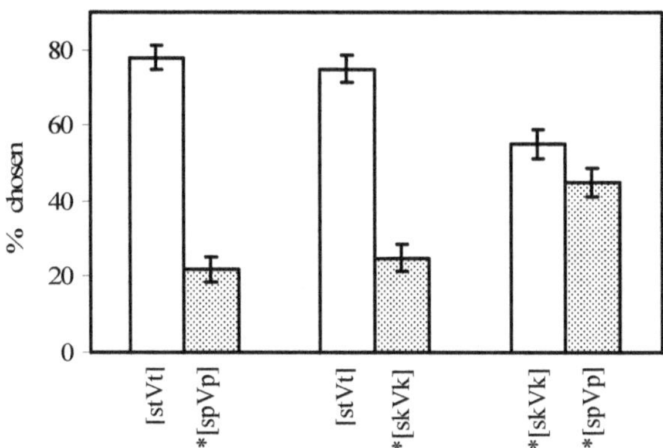

Figure 4: Percentage that token type was selected in the English comparative word-likeness experiment. Error bars show 95% confidence intervals.

These results show that the grammatical [stVt]-forms were preferred over the two types of ungrammatical forms. This replicates the findings of Berent and Shimron for Hebrew and was also expected based on the results of the word-likeness rating experiment discussed above. However, the results of this experiment also extend on those of Berent and Shimron. The English listeners preferred the *[skVk]-forms over *[spVp]-forms, although neither of these are possible words of English. This shows that language users can make finer distinctions within the set of ungrammatical forms in terms of well-formedness.

Taken together, the results of Berent and Shimron on Hebrew and the results on English discussed here, show the following: language users can use the information provided by grammar in both a categorical and in a gradient manner. In task conditions that do not require explicit comparison between forms, language users make only the categorical distinction between grammatical and ungrammatical. However, if task conditions require an explicit comparison between forms, then language users make finer gradient distinctions within the sets of grammatical and ungrammatical forms. We therefore need a theory of grammar that can do both of these things. In the next section, I show how an OT grammar can be used to do just this.

5   An Optimality Theoretic account of categorical and gradient behavior

In this section, I will show that an OT grammar is ideally suited to model both kinds of behavior observed in the experiments discussed above. The following is what happens in a word-likeness rating task: when presented with a non-word, the language user asks the question: is there any possible input that my grammar will map onto this non-word token? An affirmative answer to this question means that the token is a possible word and therefore grammatical. A negative answer means that it is not a possible word and therefore ungrammatical.

The evaluation proceeds differently in a comparative word-likeness task. Now the language user is presented with more than one non-word. The first step is to determine the input for each non-word that would result in the most harmonic mapping onto the non-word. The language user then compares the input~output-mappings for each of the non-word tokens.

5.1   Hebrew

In Hebrew, non-geminates ([X-Y-Z]) and final-geminates ([X-Y-Y]) are grammatical, while initial-geminates (*[X-X-Y]) are ungrammatical. In this section, I first develop an OT account for this, and then show how this OT grammar can be used to explain the results of Berent and Shimron's experiments discussed above.[12]

Following McCarthy (1981, 1986), I assume a distinction between verbal roots and stems. The root is the bare consonantal form stored in the lexicon. The stem is the derived morphological category to which affixes attach, and consists of a combination of the root consonants and the vowels that express the specific conjugational class (*binyan*) of the verb.[13] Also following McCarthy, I will assume that final-geminate verbs are derived from bi-consonantal roots (i.e. /X-Y/ $\rightarrow$ [X-Y-Y] and not /X-Y-Y/ $\rightarrow$ [X-Y-Y]).[14] If these assumptions are made, then there are three questions that still need answering: (i) Why do bi-consonantal roots map onto tri-consonantal forms? Or: why does /X-Y/ not map onto *[X-Y]? (ii) Why do bi-consonantal roots only map onto final-geminates? Or: why does /X-Y/ not map onto *[X-X-Y]? (iii) Under richness of the base, we cannot exclude /X-Y-Y/ and /X-X-Y/ roots from the lexicon. If such roots do (or at least can) exist, then why do final and initial output geminates not originate from these forms? I discuss each of these questions in turn.

Let us first consider the question of why bi-consonantal roots map onto tri-consonantal stems. McCarthy and Prince (1990b) argue that the verbal stem in Semitic languages must end on a consonant (see also Gafos, 1999, 2003). I follow them in assuming the existence of a constraint FINAL-C.

(5) FINAL-C: The verbal stem must end on a consonant.

This is the constraint that is responsible for forcing bi-consonantal roots to map onto tri-consonantal stems. To understand why, we have to consider the vowels that form part of the verbal stem. There are many conjugational classes in Hebrew that are expressed by a bi-vocalic melody. Consider the so-called *piʃel* as example. This conjugational class is characterized by the vocalic melody [i-e]. The stem of a Hebrew verb includes both the root consonants and the vocalic melody – that is, inflectional affixes are attached to the unit comprised of the root plus the vocalic melody. Without augmenting a bi-consonantal root, the stem will end on a vowel – $/X^R\text{-}Y^R$, i-e/ then maps onto $*[|X^RiY^Re|]$.[15, 16] FINAL-C therefore forces the augmentation of bi-consonantal roots by addition of a consonant. The actually observed mapping, $/X^R\text{-}Y^R$, i-e/ $\rightarrow [|X^RiY^ReY|]$, of course violates the faithfulness constraint INTEGRITY (because input /Y/ has two surface correspondents).This gives evidence for the ranking FINAL-C $\gg$ INTEGRITY.

(6) INTEGRITY: Let S_I be the input and S_O the output such that $S_I \mathfrak{R} S_O$. No element of S_I has multiple correspondents in S_O.

For $x \in S_I$ and $w, z \in S_O$, if $x\mathfrak{R}w$ and $x\mathfrak{R}z$, then $w{=}z$ (McCarthy and Prince 1995).

Next consider the question of why bi-consonantal roots map onto final-geminates but never onto initial-geminates. Both $/X^R\text{-}Y^R/ \rightarrow [|X^R\text{-}Y_i^R\text{-}Y_i|]$[17] and $/X^R\text{-}Y^R/ \rightarrow *[|X_i\text{-}X_i^R\text{-}Y^R|]$ satisfy FINAL-C. Why then is the former grammatical but the latter ungrammatical? The difference between these structures is in the alignment of the root and the stem. In the grammatical $[|X^R\text{-}Y_i^R\text{-}Y_i|]$, the root and stem are perfectly aligned at their left edges. However, in the ungrammatical $*[|X_i\text{-}X_i^R\text{-}Y^R|]$, the root and stem are misaligned at their left edges. I argue that it is an alignment constraint that forces the final consonant to spread.

(7) **ALIGN-L**:   The left edge of the root and the left edge of the stem must be aligned.

We now have all the rankings we need to explain why bi-consonantal roots map onto final-geminates. This is illustrated in the tableau in (8). Note that the ranking ALIGN-L relative to the other constraints does not matter.[18]

(8) Bi-consonantal roots map onto final-geminates

$/X^R\text{-}Y^R/$		ALIGN-L	FINAL-C	INTEGRITY
a.	$|X^R\text{-}Y^R|$		*!	
b.	$|X_i\text{-}X_i^R\text{-}Y^R|$	*!		*
c. ☞	$|X^R\text{-}Y_i^R\text{-}Y_i|$			*

Finally, we need to explain why final-geminates and initial-geminates cannot originate from roots with final or initial identical consonants – i.e. why are both $/X^R\text{-}Y^R\text{-}Y^R/ \rightarrow *[|X^R\text{-}Y^R\text{-}Y^R|]$ and $/X^R\text{-}X^R\text{-}Y^R/ \rightarrow *[|X^R\text{-}X^R\text{-}Y^R|]$ ungrammatical? Let us start with initial geminates. The ungrammatical form $*[|X^R\text{-}X^R\text{-}Y^R|]$ has two identical, contiguous consonants in the surface realization of the root. The avoidance of multiple occurrences of identical consonants in some domain can be explained with reference to the Obligatory Contour Principle (OCP) (McCarthy 1986). A version of the OCP indexed to the root is active in the phonology of Hebrew. This version of the OCP is defined in (9). Notice that this is a constraint on the surface realization of the root, and therefore does not place a restriction on possible inputs. In the definition of this constraint, adjacency should be interpreted on the consonantal tier.

(9) **OCP**$_{Root}$:   No contiguous, identical consonants in the surface realization of a root.

To explain the absence of surface forms like $*[|X^R\text{-}X^R\text{-}Y^R|]$, OCP$_{Root}$ has to rank higher than some faithfulness constraint that can be violated in order to avoid violation of OCP$_{Root}$. Since roots like $/X^R\text{-}X^R\text{-}Y^R/$ do not actually exist, there is no evidence for what the relevant faithfulness constraint is. I will assume that one of the identical consonants in the root deletes, earning a violation of MAX-C, to avoid violation of OCP$_{Root}$. Of course, once one of the identical consonants has been deleted, there are only two root consonants left. In order to satisfy the demands of FINAL-C, a third consonant needs to be supplied. We already know that FINAL-C outranks INTEGRITY, and consequently the extra consonant can be supplied by copying the final root consonant. The upshot is that an input like $/X^R\text{-}X^R\text{-}Y^R/$ will map onto the same output as a bi-consonantal input $/X^R\text{-}Y^R/$, i.e. $[|X^R\text{-}Y_i^R\text{-}Y_i|]$. This is shown in the tableau in (10). I do not include the candidate that copies the initial consonant and that is eliminated by ALIGN-L. Since geminate roots do not exist in the Hebrew lexicon, the inputs used in (10) are all hypothetical forms.

(10) $\text{OCP}_{\text{Root}} \gg \{\text{MAX-C}, \text{INTEGRITY}\}$

			OCP_{Root}	FINAL-C	MAX-C	INTEGRITY
$/X^R\text{-}X^R\text{-}Y^R/$	a.	$|X^R\text{-}X^R\text{-}Y^R|$	*!			
	b.	$|X^R\text{-}Y^R|$		*!	*	
	c. ☞	$|X^R\text{-}Y_i^R\text{-}Y_i|$			*	*
$/X^R\text{-}Y^R\text{-}Y^R/$	d.	$|X^R\text{-}Y^R\text{-}Y^R|$	*!			
	e.	$|X^R\text{-}Y^R|$		*!	*	
	f. ☞	$|X^R\text{-}Y_i^R\text{-}Y_i|$			*	*

Of course, if $[|X^R\text{-}X^R\text{-}Y^R|]$ violates OCP_{Root}, then so does $[|X^R\text{-}Y^R\text{-}Y^R|]$. An input root with identical final consonants will therefore be treated in exactly the same way as an input root with identical initial consonants – one of the consonants will delete, and in order to satisfy FINAL-C, the remaining final consonant doubles. This is also shown in the tableau in (10). Note that the faithful but ungrammatical candidate (10d) is phonetically identical to the optimal candidate (10f). The difference between these candidates lies in their hidden morphophonological structure.

There is considerable cross-linguistic evidence that consonantal co-occurrence constraints can apply to different morphological domains – see Tessier (2004b) for a recent review. If OCP_{Root} exists, then a similar constraint indexed to the larger morphological domain of the stem also exists – defined in (11). The last question to answer is where OCP_{Stem} ranks in Hebrew. In order to avoid violation of FINAL-C, Hebrew doubles the second consonant of a bi-consonantal root – see (8) above. In the observed output form, $[|X^R\text{-}Y_i^R\text{-}Y_i|]$, the sequence $[Y_i^R\text{-}Y_i]$ violates OCP_{Stem}. Hebrew therefore also tolerates violation of OCP_{Stem} to avoid a FINAL-C violation, so that OCP_{Stem} must also rank below FINAL-C. This is shown in the tableau in (12).

(11) **OCP_{Stem}:**   No contiguous, identical consonants in the surface realization of a stem.

(12) $\text{FINAL-C} \gg \text{OCP}_{\text{Stem}}$

$/X^R\text{-}Y^R/$		FINAL-C	INTEGRITY	OCP_{Stem}
	$|X^R\text{-}Y^R|$	*!		
☞	$|X^R\text{-}Y_i^R\text{-}Y_i|$		*	*

We now have all the constraints and crucial rankings that we need to account for the distribution of contiguous identical consonants in Hebrew verbs. The tableau in (13) shows how this grammar will deal with the different possible inputs. Note that the ranking of ALIGN-L does not matter in this tableau – every candidate that violates ALIGN-L is harmonically bounded. Also note that because OCP_{Root} and OCP_{Stem} are in a stringency relationship, no ranking can be established between these two constraints with only the phenomena that we have considered above.

In a root with three non-identical consonants, the faithful candidate does not violate any constraints. Unsurprisingly, the faithful candidate (a) is therefore optimal. Now consider the bi-consonantal root input. Faithful (e) fatally violates FINAL-C. Both (f) and (g) satisfy FINAL-C by doubling one of the root consonants, earning them violations of INTEGRITY. However, (g) doubles the initial root consonant so that the root and stem are misaligned at their left edges in this candidate. This earns it a fatal violation of ALIGN-L. Finally, consider roots that contain contiguous identical consonants (either in initial or final position). The faithful candidates of both of these inputs, (h) and (l), fatally violate OCP_{Root}. This violation is avoided by deleting one of the identical consonants. The root is then treated just like a bi-consonantal root – in order to satisfy FINAL-C, the remaining final root consonant doubles.

(13) Basic verbal grammar of Hebrew

Root structure		OCP_{Rt}	AL-L	FIN-C	OCP_{St}	INT	MAX-C
No identical: $/X^R\text{-}Y^R\text{-}Z^R/$	a. ☞ $\lvert X^R\text{-}Y^R\text{-}Z^R\rvert$						
	b. $\lvert X^R\text{-}Y_i^R\text{-}Y_i\rvert$				*!	*!	*!
	c. $\lvert X_i\text{-}X_i^R\text{-}Y^R\rvert$		*!		*	*	*
	d. $\lvert X^R\text{-}Y^R\rvert$			*!			*
Bi-consonantal: $/X^R\text{-}Y^R/$	e. $\lvert X^R\text{-}Y^R\rvert$			*!			
	f. ☞ $\lvert X^R\text{-}Y_i^R\text{-}Y_i\rvert$				*	*	
	g. $\lvert X_i\text{-}X_i^R\text{-}Y^R\rvert$		*!		*	*	
Final identical: $/X^R\text{-}Y^R\text{-}Y^R/$	h. $\lvert X^R\text{-}Y^R\text{-}Y^R\rvert$	*!			*		
	i. $\lvert X^R\text{-}Y^R\rvert$			*!			*
	j. ☞ $\lvert X^R\text{-}Y_i^R\text{-}Y_i\rvert$				*	*	*
	k. $\lvert X_i\text{-}X_i^R\text{-}Y^R\rvert$		*!		*	*	*
Initial identical: $/X^R\text{-}X^R\text{-}Y^R/$	l. $\lvert X^R\text{-}X^R\text{-}Y^R\rvert$	*!			*		
	m. $\lvert X^R\text{-}Y^R\rvert$			*!			*
	n. ☞ $\lvert X^R\text{-}Y_i^R\text{-}Y_i\rvert$				*	*	*
	o. $\lvert X_i\text{-}X_i^R\text{-}Y^R\rvert$		*!		*	*	*

Now that we have a grammar for Hebrew, we can look at the results of Berent and Shimron again. Consider first the results of their word-likeness rating experiment. In this experiment, they found that Hebrew speakers rated the two kinds of grammatical non-words ([X-Y-Z] and [X-Y-Y]) better than the ungrammatical non-words (*[X-X-Y]), but they did not distinguish between the different grammatical non-words. We can explain this as follows: when the subjects are required to rate a single non-word at a time, they determine whether there is at least one input that their grammar can map grammatically onto that non-word. This is equivalent to asking whether the non-word is a possible word or not. If there is an input that would map grammatically onto the non-word, subjects assign it a high score. On the other hand, if there is no such input, subjects assign the non-word a low score.

As the tableau in (13) shows, there is some input that will map onto a non-geminate – namely an input identical to the output. /X-Y-Z/ → [X-Y-Z] is grammatical, and therefore non-geminate non-words are identified as possible words and assigned high scores. Tableau (13) also shows that there are inputs that will be mapped grammatically onto final-geminates. In fact, there are three such inputs, namely /X-Y/, /X-Y-Y/ and /X-X-Y/. Also final-geminates are then identified as possible words and assigned high ratings. The situation with initial-geminates is different. None of the logically possible inputs will be mapped grammatically onto a form such as *[X-X-Y]. This is because both /X-X-Y/ and /X-Y/ are mapped onto final-geminates. Initial-geminates are then identified as impossible words, and assigned low scores.

Now consider the comparative word-likeness experiment. In this experiment, Berent and Shimron found that their subjects imposed the following word-likeness hierarchy on the non-word tokens: non-geminates > final-geminates > initial-geminates. I propose that language users do this as follows: for each of the non-words, they find the input that would most harmonically map onto the non-word. We can identify these inputs in the tableau in (13). For the non-geminate [|X-Y-Z|], this input is obviously $/X^R\text{-}Y^R\text{-}Z^R/$. The input that results in the most harmonic mapping onto a final-geminate is the bi-consonantal root – the mapping $/X^R\text{-}Y^R/ \rightarrow [|X^R\text{-}Y_i^R\text{-}Y_i|]$ violates INTEGRITY and OCP_{Stem}. All other mappings onto a final-geminate violate either a superset of these two constraints or violate high ranking OCP_{Root}. The input that most harmonically maps onto an initial-geminate is either $/X^R\text{-}Y^R/$ or $/X^R\text{-}X^R\text{-}Y^R/$ – the choice depends on the ranking between ALIGN-L and OCP_{Root}, and since neither of these two are violated in Hebrew we cannot determine the ranking between them. For the sake of simplicity, I consider only $/X^R\text{-}X^R\text{-}Y^R/$ in the rest of the discussion. However, the same result would be achieved if $/X^R\text{-}Y^R/$ were used.

Once the input that results in the most harmonic mapping for each non-word has been determined, the language user compares the mappings in a 'comparative tableau', as shown in (14).

(14) Comparing the different non-words in Hebrew

			OCP_{Rt}	AL-L	FIN-C	OCP_{St}	INT	MAX-C
NoG	1	$/X\text{-}Y\text{-}Z/ \rightarrow [|X^R\text{-}Y^R\text{-}Z^R|]$						
FinG	2	$/X\text{-}Y/ \rightarrow [|X^R\text{-}Y_i^R\text{-}Y_i|]$				*	*	
IniG	3	$/X\text{-}X\text{-}Y/ \rightarrow [|X^R\text{-}X^R\text{-}Y^R|]$	*			*		

The comparative tableau in (14) is not an ordinary OT tableau – it does not compare different output candidates for the same input, but rather different input~output-mappings.[19] Rather than the usual pointing hand to indicate the winning candidate, I use Arabic numerals to indicate the order that the grammar imposes on these forms. The non-geminate mapping violates none of the constraints, while the final-geminate mapping violates OCP_{Stem} and INTEGRITY. When these two mappings are compared, the non-geminate mapping is therefore the more well-formed option. Although both of these represent mappings that are possible in Hebrew, they are not equally well-formed. The non-geminate form is perfectly unmarked and perfectly faithful, while the final-geminate is neither perfectly faithful nor unmarked. This corresponds to the way in which Berent and Shimron's subjects responded. When required to compare non-geminates and final-geminates, they preferred the non-geminates over the final-geminates.

The initial-geminate form violates OCP_{Root}. Because of the ranking OCP_{Root} >> INTEGRITY, final-geminates are better than initial-geminates, and this is again how they were rated by the subjects in the experiment.

A note is in order here about how to interpret the tableau in (14). This tableau shows that non-geminates are more well-formed than final-geminates which are again more well-formed than initial-geminates. I claim that the subjects used this information as follows: when asked to choose between a non-geminate and a final-geminate, the subjects are *more likely* to select the non-geminate. In addition to grammar, there are other factors that influence how subjects respond. These other factors include things such as the lexical statistics of tokens (see the earlier discussion), but also things like fatigue, lack of concentration, and individual differences. We can therefore not expect that subjects will *always* act according to the information provided by grammar. However, we can expect that the information provided by grammar will bias their responses.

Since OT already has the ability to compare forms for their relative well-formedness, it is a small change that has to be made to the theory to explain what the subjects do in a comparative word-likeness experiment. Rather than comparing output candidates for the same input, they compare output candidates that do not share the same input.

5.2   English

English allows words of the form [stVt], but not of the form *[skVk] or *[spVp]. In this section, I first develop an OT account to explain this, and then show how this account explains the results of the word-likeness experiments that I discussed earlier.

I assume a markedness constraint against each of the three kinds of tokens considered here, i.e. *stVt, *skVk, and *spVp. These constraints can be viewed as the local conjunction of OCP-type constraints against multiple occurrences [t], [k] or [p] in a single syllable, with a constraint against the sequence [s+stop] (Alderete, 1997; Coetzee, 2004:402–420; Pater and Coetzee, 2005).[20]

It is well established that languages often place restrictions on the occurrence of multiple identical consonants in certain local domains. The Hebrew data discussed just above is an example of this. Similar restrictions also hold in languages as diverse as Arabic (Frisch et al., 2004; McCarthy, 1994), Japanese (Kawahara et al., 2006), Russian (Padgett, 1995), Muna (Coetzee and Pater, 2008), French, Latin and English (Berkley, 2000). In all of these languages, there is evidence that identical (or highly similar) consonants are avoided in some local context. Although there are differences in the details of these restrictions in the different languages, it is clear that there must be a general family of constraints that militate against multiple occurrences of identical (or similar) consonants. I propose that the versions of these constraints stated in (15) are relevant to the restriction in English that is our focus here.[21]

(15) *[t...t]$_\sigma$:   Do not allow a syllable with two [t]'s.
  *[k...k]$_\sigma$:   Do not allow a syllable with two [k]'s.
  *[p...p]$_\sigma$:   Do not allow a syllable with two [p]'s.

There is an extensive literature on the markedness of [s+stop] sequences (Broselow, 1991; Davis, 1984; Hayes, 1985:140–149; Kahn, 1980; Lamontagne, 1993: Chapter 6; Morelli, 1999; Selkirk, 1982; etc.). There are several views on why this sequence is marked. One view considers these structures to be true consonant clusters. If this is the case, then they violate the Sonority Sequencing Principle – sonority falls from [s] to the [stop]. Under another view, these structures are complex segments rather than consonant clusters. This avoids the violation of the SSP. However, if they are complex segments then they are marked per se. Either way, an [s+stop]-sequence is marked. In (16), I formulate a constraint against such sequences.

(16) ***[s+stop]$_\sigma$**: [s] is not allowed to immediately precede a stop in one syllable.

English violates each of the constraints in (15) and (16) individually – this is evidenced by the existence of words such as *sty* (*[s+stop]$_\sigma$), *toot* (*[t...t]$_\sigma$), *cake* (*[k…k]$_\sigma$), and *pop* (*[p…p]$_\sigma$). This means that all of these constraints rank very low in English – so low that they have no discernable effect. What English does not tolerate is the violation of certain combinations of these constraints within a single syllable – specifically, violation of *[s+stop]$_\sigma$ and any of *[k…k]$_\sigma$ or *[p…p]$_\sigma$. OT accounts for the avoidance of the local accumulation of marked structure through local conjunction of markedness constraints (Smolensky, 1995). We can now show that the *sCVC constraints are just the local conjunction of each of the constraints in (15) with the constraint in (16).

(17) *stVt: Do not violate *[s+stop]$_\sigma$ and *[t…t]$_\sigma$ in the same syllable.
   *skVk: Do not violate *[s+stop]$_\sigma$ and *[k…k]$_\sigma$ in the same syllable.
   *spVp: Do not violate *[s+stop]$_\sigma$ and *[p…p]$_\sigma$ in the same syllable.

We know that English tolerates violation of *stVt but not of *skVk or *spVp. This gives evidence for the ranking {*spVp, *skVk} >> Faithfulness >> *stVt. But what about the ranking between *spVp and *skVk? As I have shown above, there are more words in English with two dorsals in one syllable than words with two labials in one syllable. This can be captured by the ranking *[p…p]$_\sigma$ >> *[k…k]$_\sigma$. A question that needs to be answered is how this ranking can be learned. Since English tolerates violation of both these constraints, classical error-driven learning (Tesar and Smolensky, 1998, 2000) cannot be used. Pater (2005) develops an algorithm that can learn rankings from statistical patterns in the lexicon, and that is hence ideally suited for this kind of scenario. When two markedness constraints that are both freely violated in some language have to be ranked, Pater's algorithm ranks higher the constraint that is violated less often. When his algorithm has to rank *[p…p]$_\sigma$ and *[k…k]$_\sigma$, it will hence rank *[p…p]$_\sigma$ higher, since this is the constraint that is violated less often in the English lexicon. Once the ranking *[p…p]$_\sigma$ >> *[k…k]$_\sigma$ has been learned, Ito and Mester's (2003) principle of 'ranking preservation' can be used to infer the ranking *spVp >> *skVk. This principle requires the following: let LC_1 and LC_2 be two constraints formed via local conjunction, and let C_1 be one of the conjuncts of LC_1 and C_2 one of the conjuncts of LC_2. If C_1 >> C_2, then LC_1 >> LC_2. Given that *[p…p]$_\sigma$ and *[k…k]$_\sigma$ are conjuncts of *spVp and *skVk respectively, and given the ranking *[p…p]$_\sigma$ >> *[k…k]$_\sigma$, it follows by ranking preservation that *spVp >> *skVk.

    We now have the following mini-grammar for English: *spVp >> *skVk >> Faithfulness >> *stVt. The tableau in (18) shows that this grammar does correctly predict that [stVt] is a possible word of English while neither *[skVk] nor *[spVp] is. In this tableau, I assume that the relevant faithfulness constraint is IDENT[place]. However, since there are no active alternations in English involving *[spVp] and *[skVk], we cannot know for sure what the constraint should be. It can be any faithfulness constraint that can be violated to avoid violation of *[skVk] and *[spVp].

(18) Mini-grammar of English [sCVC]-forms

		*spVp	*skVk	IDENT[place]	*stVt
/stVt/	☞ stVt				*
	stVk			*!	
/skVk/	skVk		*!		
	☞ skVt				*
/spVp/	spVp	*!			
	☞ spVt				*

This tableau shows that an /stVt/-input will map faithfully onto itself, and therefore [stVt] is correctly predicted as a possible word. However, neither /skVk/ nor /spVp/ maps faithfully onto itself. *[skVk] and *[spVp] are therefore correctly predicted not to be possible words. We now have all the information we need to explain the results of the English experiments discussed above.

Consider first the word-likeness rating experiment. In this experiment, subjects had to rate non-words individually for their word-likeness – i.e. no direct comparison between non-words was required. The results show that the subjects made a categorical distinction between possible and impossible words – the grammatical [stVt] non-words received high scores, and the ungrammatical *[skVk] and *[spVp] forms received low scores but were not distinguished from each other. The subjects used their grammar in the same manner as the subjects in Berent and Shimron's experiment. For each non-word, they determine whether there is an input that will map unto the specific non-word. If such an input exists, the non-word is identified as a possible word, and it receives a good rating. Non-words for which no such input exists are identified as impossible words, and receive low scores.

Now consider the comparative word-likeness experiment. In this experiment, the subjects were required to compare two non-words and to select the one that they deemed most word-like. The results of the experiment show that the subjects rated the non-words as follows: [stVt] > *[skVk] > *[spVp]. They no longer divide the set of non-words into the two categorical classes of grammatical and ungrammatical. Rather, the non-words are now rated gradiently according to their relative well-formedness. The subjects again responded like the subjects in Berent and Shimron's experiment. For each non-word, they first determine the input that would result in the most harmonic mapping onto the non-word. For an [stVt] non-word, this input is obviously /stVt/. Any other input that maps onto [stVt] will violate some faithfulness constraint in addition to *stVt. Similarly, the relevant input for *[skVk] will be /skVk/ – again because any other input will violate a faithfulness constraint in addition to *skVk. With similar reasoning, we can also show that the relevant input for *[spVp] will be /spVp/. Once these inputs have been determined, the subjects compare the three input~output-mappings in a comparative tableau. This comparison is shown in (19).

(19) Comparing non-words in English

		*spVp	*skVk	Faithfulness	*stVt
1	/stVt/ → [stVt]				*
2	/skVk/ → [skVk]		*		
3	/spVp/ → [spVp]	*			

As before, this comparative tableau should be interpreted differently from a standard OT tableau. This is not a production oriented tableau in which different output candidates for the same input are compared. We are not interested in the best candidate, but rather in how all three candidates are related to each other. Since /stVt/ → [stVt] violates the lowest ranking constraint, it is rated best, as indicated by the numeral [1] next to this mapping. Since /spVp/ → [spVp] violates the highest ranking constraint, it is rated worst of all, indicated by the [3] next to this mapping. This corresponds to how the subjects rated these tokens in the comparative word-likeness experiment.

6   Considering alternatives

In the previous sections, I have shown that an OT grammar can account for both the categorical and the gradient response patterns observed in the experiments. In this brief section, I will show that standard generative grammars have no problems in accounting for the categorical grammatical/ungrammatical distinction, but that they are less well-suited to make the finer gradient distinctions between degrees of grammaticality and ungrammaticality. I will also show that models in which well-formedness ratings are a direct reflex of gradient lexical statistics cannot account for the response patterns.

Standard generative models of grammar have no difficulty in differentiating grammatical forms from ungrammatical forms. An ungrammatical form is a form that cannot be generated as grammatical output from any permissible input, and all other forms are grammatical. One reason why some form cannot be generated as a grammatical output is that the input required to derive it is absent from the lexicon because it violates a morpheme structure constraint (MSC). Davis (1984), for instance, claims that *[skVk] and *[spVp] are ungrammatical in English because there is an MSC that bans /skVk/ and /spVp/ from the English lexicon. He defines this MSC as in (20) (Davis, 1984:46). This MSC ensures that [stVt] is grammatical while *[skVk] and *[spVp] are not.

(20)

$$*s \begin{bmatrix} -\text{cont} \\ -\text{cor} \\ \alpha\text{voice} \\ \beta\text{ant} \end{bmatrix} \quad V \quad \begin{bmatrix} -\text{cont} \\ -\text{cor} \\ \alpha\text{voice} \\ \beta\text{ant} \end{bmatrix}$$

While (20) can distinguish between grammatical [stVt] and ungrammatical *[skVk] and *[spVp], it cannot distinguish between *[skVk] and *[spVp] in terms of their relative well-formedness. It is possible to split (20) into separate MSC's for labials and dorsals. *[skVk]-forms and *[spVp]-forms could then be distinguished from each other because they would be ruled out by different MSC's. However, we would still not be able to compare them for their relative well-formedness. To achieve that, we will also have to add comparative powers to the grammar – specifically, we have to impose an ordering between the dorsal-MSC and the labial-MSC such that violating the latter is deemed worse than violating the former. Although a standard generative grammar can in principle derive the well-formedness difference between *[spVp] and *[skVk], it needs to be embellished with special comparative powers to do so. Because OT is by design a comparative theory of grammar based on ranked constraints, the ability to distinguish between *[spVp] and *[skVk] in terms of relative well-formedness follows directly from the basic architecture of the grammar. No additional embellishments are necessary.

Another possible explanation for the response patterns observed in the experiments should be considered, namely the possibility that the results originated not in grammar but rather in statistical patterns from the lexicon. Hay et al. (2004), for instance, argue that 'phonological grammar is a simple projection of the lexical statistics' (p. 59), and moreover that it 'is gradient rather than categorical' (p. 71). The results of the Hebrew and English experiments discussed above support neither of these claims. First, it is clear that the results do not support the claim that well-formedness is (only) gradient. Berent and Shimron found in their experiments that exactly the same tokens are sometimes treated categorically the same, and sometimes gradiently distinguished from each other. The English experiments confirmed this.

Secondly, there is strong evidence that the results of the two sets of experiments cannot be explained solely from the lexical statistics. Consider the Hebrew experiments first. Again, since the same tokens were used in both experiments, the lexical statistics of the tokens in the experiments did not differ. If lexical statistics were responsible for the response patterns, then the subjects should have responded the same in both tasks.

In the design of the English experiments, I controlled specifically for the potential influence of lexical statistics. The tokens were all selected such that the lexical statistics between token types in a condition did not differ, or such that the lexical statistics conflicted with grammar (i.e. if grammar favored x over y, then the lexical statistics favored y over x). If it were lexical statistics that determined the response patterns, then the subjects should either not have distinguished between the token types at all, or if they did make a distinction it should have been the opposite of what would be expected based on grammar alone. The results of the experiments clearly showed that the subjects did distinguish between the token types in well-formedness, and moreover the distinctions they made agreed with grammar and not with the lexical statistics. The response patterns therefore did not originate in the lexical statistics. Regression analyses confirm this. I performed a regression on the response patterns using LND and CBP as the independent variable. The results of these analyses for the two experiments are shown in (21). It is clear that the lexical statistics do not account for a significant part of the variation in the response patterns.

(21) Regression analyses

	LND	CBP
Word-likeness rating	$r^2 = .01$	$r^2 < .01$
Comparative word-likeness	$r^2 = .02$	$r^2 < .01$

The results of the English experiment therefore differ from many results reported in the literature where word-likeness ratings did correspond more significantly with lexical statistics (Bailey and Hahn, 1998; Hay et al., 2004; Coleman and Pierrehumbert, 1997). I cannot offer a clear reason for this difference in the results. However, the results reported in this paper show that the relationship between phonological grammar and the lexicon is more complicated than what is assumed by, for instance, Hay et al. (2004). More research is necessary before we can decide that phonological grammar is only a gradient projection from the lexicon.

7   Conclusion

In this paper, I have discussed data from two sets of word-likeness experiments, showing that humans use their grammar in both categorical and gradient ways. They do have strong intuitions about whether some non-word is a possible word or not (i.e. whether a form is grammatical or not). In task conditions that do not require explicit comparison between forms, the subjects in word-likeness experiments correspond according to these intuitions. This shows that the information provided by grammar can be interpreted in terms of the categorical distinction between grammatical and ungrammatical. But in addition to this distinction, humans can also make more fine grained gradient distinctions between more (im)possible and less (im)possible. They can compare two grammatical forms, and decide which is more word-like. Similarly, they can compare two ungrammatical forms and decide which is more word-like. In task conditions that require subjects to make these kinds of comparisons, they respond along these lines.

If language users can use the information provided by grammar to respond both in categorical and in gradient manners, then grammar should be able to provide both categorical and gradient information. This poses a challenge to standard generative grammar, which was not designed as a comparative theory of grammar. However, because of its inherent comparative nature, OT is perfectly suited for this task. We can make the categorical distinction between grammatical and ungrammatical non-words as follows in an OT grammar: for a non-word, if there is an input that would be mapped grammatically onto the non-word, then the non-word is grammatical (is a possible word of the language). On the other hand, if there is no input that would map onto the non-word, then it is ungrammatical (not a possible word of the language). This is equivalent to what standard generative grammar does – asking whether there is a well-formed derivational history for the non-word. In OT, this is easily done using OT tableaux in the standard manner.

Since an OT grammar is by design comparative, it is also a straightforward matter to get information about the finer gradient well-formedness relationship between non-words. This can be done as follows: for every non-word, determine that input that will map most harmonically onto the specific non-word. Then compare the input~output-mapping for the different non-words in a comparative tableau. In this kind of tableau, EVAL does not compare different output candidates for a single input, but rather input~output-mappings that differ in terms of both input and output.

The results of the experiments also give evidence that phonological grammar is more than a mere projection of lexical statistics. The subjects in the experiments responded in ways that do not support a model where word-likeness is a direct mapping from lexical statistics. Although lexical statistics are gradient and continuous, subjects sometimes responded categorically, grouping together tokens that differ in terms of their lexical statistics. Sometimes the subjects also responded in ways directly opposite to what would have been expected based on the lexical statistics.

Having established that processing data reflect the influence of grammar, and having shown that we can account for this influence in OT, we can now use processing data as a rich and largely untapped source of information about grammatical competence. This opens up many new and interesting research possibilities.

Appendix

Tokens used in English word-likeness rating experiment

T~K-condition

[sTvT]	LND	CBP	[sKvK]	LND	CBP
stʌt	10.65	0.066	skeɪk	26.06	0.186
stɑːt	44.16	0.279	skæk	22.12	0.227
stɔːt	23.06	0.217	skɑːk	18.41	0.219
stʊt	17.06	0.144	skɛk	12.65	0.193
stʌt	42.19	0.219	skɪk	37.31	0.299
Mean	27.424	0.185		23.31	0.225

t-test on LND: $t(8) = .52, p = .62$ *t*-test on CBP: $t(8) = .95, p = .37$

T~P-condition

[sTvT]	LND	CBP	[sPvP]	LND	CBP
stʊt	17.06	0.144	spɑːp	21.41	0.244
stɔɪt	10.65	0.066	spɛp	20.32	0.208
stʌt	42.19	0.219	spɪp	26.69	0.212
stɑːt	44.16	0.279	spæp	17.98	0.201
stɔːt	23.06	0.217	spiːp	27.45	0.213
	27.42	0.185		22.77	0.216

t-test on LND: $t(8) = .67, p = .52$ *t*-test on CBP: $t(8) = .82, p = .44$

K~P-condition

[sKvK]	LND	CBP	[sPvP]	LND	CBP
skaɪk	26.06	0.185	spæp	17.98	0.201
skaʊk	9.95	0.001	spɑːp	21.41	0.244
skiːk	28.63	0.134	spɛp	20.32	0.208
skɔːk	10.04	0.171	spɪp	26.69	0.212
skuːk	12.64	0.193	spiːp	27.45	0.213
	17.46	0.137		22.77	0.216

t-test on LND: $t(8) = 1.18, p = .27$ *t*-test on CBP: $t(8) = 2.18, p = .06$

Tokens used in English comparative word-likeness experiment

T~K-condition

[sTvT]	LND	CBP		[sKvK]	LND	CBP	Diff in LND	Diff in CBP
stɔːt	23.06	0.217		skæk	22.12	0.227	0.94	-0.010
stʊt	17.06	0.144		skɑːk	18.41	0.219	-1.35	-0.075
stɔɪt	10.65	0.066		skɛk	12.65	0.193	-2.00	-0.127
stɔɪt	10.65	0.066		skɑːk	18.41	0.219	-7.76	-0.153
stɔɪt	10.65	0.066		skʌk	19.38	0.183	-8.73	-0.117
stɔɪt	10.65	0.066		skæk	22.12	0.227	-11.47	-0.161
stʊt	17.06	0.144		skeɪk	26.06	0.186	-9.00	-0.042
stʌt	42.19	0.219		skɪk	37.31	0.299	4.88	-0.080
stɔːt	23.06	0.217		skɪk	37.31	0.299	-14.25	-0.082
stʊt	17.06	0.144		skɪk	37.31	0.299	-20.25	-0.155
stʊt	17.06	0.144		skæk	22.12	0.227	-5.06	-0.083
stɔɪt	10.65	0.066		skaɪk	13.89	0.157	-3.24	-0.091
stɔɪt	10.65	0.066		skeɪk	26.06	0.186	-15.41	-0.120
stʊt	17.06	0.144		skɛk	12.65	0.193	4.41	-0.049
stɔɪt	10.65	0.066		skɪk	37.31	0.299	-26.66	-0.233
	16.54	0.122			24.21	0.228		

t-test on LND: *t*(14) = 3.32, *p* =.005   *t*-test on CBP: *t*(14) = 7.26, *p* <.001

T~P-condition

[sTvT]	LND	CBP		[sPvP]	LND	CBP	Diff in LND	Diff in CBP
stɔːt	23.06	0.217		spɪp	26.69	0.212	-3.63	0.005
stɔɪt	10.65	0.066		spʌp	11.38	0.182	-0.73	-0.116
stɔɪt	10.65	0.066		spiːp	27.45	0.213	-16.80	-0.147
stɔɪt	10.65	0.066		spɪp	26.69	0.212	-16.04	-0.146
stɔːt	23.06	0.217		spiːp	27.45	0.213	-4.39	0.004
stɔɪt	10.65	0.066		spɑːp	21.41	0.244	-10.76	-0.178
stɔɪt	10.65	0.066		spæp	17.98	0.201	-7.33	-0.135
stʊt	17.06	0.144		spæp	17.98	0.201	-0.92	-0.057
stʊt	17.06	0.144		spɪp	26.69	0.212	-9.63	-0.068

[sKvK]	LND	CBP		[sPvP]	LND	CBP	Diff in LND	Diff in CBP
stɔɪt	10.65	0.066		speɪp	17.13	0.163	-6.48	-0.097
stɔɪt	10.65	0.066		spep	20.32	0.208	-9.67	-0.142
stʊt	17.06	0.144		spɑ:p	21.41	0.244	-4.35	-0.100
stʊt	17.06	0.144		spi:p	27.45	0.213	-10.39	-0.069
stʊt	17.06	0.144		spep	20.32	0.208	-3.26	-0.064
stʊt	17.06	0.144		spʌp	11.38	0.182	5.68	-0.038
	14.87	0.117			21.45	0.207		

t-test on LND: $t(14) = 4.30$, $p < .001$ *t*-test on CBP: $t(14) = 6.28$, $p < .001$

K~P-condition

[sKvK]	LND	CBP		[sPvP]	LND	CBP	Diff in LND	Diff in CBP
skaʊk	9.95	0.001		spæp	17.98	0.201	-8.03	-0.200
sku:k	12.64	0.193		spæp	17.98	0.201	-5.34	-0.008
skaʊk	9.95	0.001		spɑ:p	21.41	0.244	-11.46	-0.243
sku:k	12.64	0.193		spɑ:p	21.41	0.244	-8.77	-0.051
skʊk	3.86	0.097		spɑ:p	21.41	0.244	-17.55	-0.147
skaʊk	9.95	0.001		spep	20.32	0.208	-10.37	-0.207
sku:k	12.64	0.193		spep	20.32	0.208	-7.68	-0.015
skʊk	3.86	0.097		spep	20.32	0.208	-16.46	-0.111
ski:k	28.63	0.134		spɪp	26.69	0.212	1.94	-0.078
skɔ:k	10.04	0.171		spɪp	26.69	0.212	-16.65	-0.041
skʊk	3.86	0.097		spɪp	26.69	0.212	-22.83	-0.115
skɔ:k	10.04	0.171		spi:p	27.45	0.213	-17.41	-0.042
skʊk	3.86	0.097		spi:p	27.45	0.213	-23.59	-0.116
skaʊk	9.95	0.001		spʌp	11.38	0.182	-1.43	-0.181
sku:k	12.64	0.193		spʌp	11.38	0.182	1.26	0.011
	10.30	0.109			21.26	0.212		

t-test on LND: $t(14) = 5.26$, $p < .001$ *t*-test on CBP: $t(14) = 5.00$, $p < .001$

Notes

1   I would like to express my appreciation to the following people for discussion of earlier versions of this paper: Shigeto Kawahara, John Kingston, Elliott Moreton, and Joe Pater. Also the audiences at GLOW 2004, NELS 36, and at the University of Michigan, New York University, Cornell University, and the University of Maryland gave valuable feedback on this work. Steve Parker, as the editor of this volume, and an anonymous reviewer helped to improve the paper tremendously. Most of all, I would like to extend my gratitude to John McCarthy. Not only was he very involved in the development of this paper, he was also instrumental in every aspect of my development as a linguist. Of course, I take full responsibility for all views expressed here.

2   It is worth remarking that I use the term 'gradient' here differently than, for instance, Boersma (1998) and Flemming (2001) do. My use of the term does not refer to gradient phonetic effects in the realization of categorical phonological categories, and it does not refer to different possible realizations of the same input. I use the term here to refer to gradient well-formedness distinctions that hold between forms that do not share the same input.

3   I use X, Y and Z as variables that range over all of the Hebrew consonants. Real Hebrew words, of course, also contain vowels. Since the vowels are not relevant to the point made here, I abstract away from the vowels.

4   I discuss only the most relevant aspects of the experimental design. Refer to Berent and Shimron (1997) for the full details. For discussion of the lexical statistics of the tokens, see more below.

5   These difference scores were computed as follows (here and in the rest of the paper NoG = no geminate, IniG= initial geminate, and FinG= final geminate) : (i) Difference Score (IniG~FinG) = Mean Score (FinG) – Mean Score (IniG). (ii) Difference Score (IniG~NoG) = Mean Score (NoG) – Mean Score (IniG). (iii) Difference Score (FinG~NoG) = Mean Score (NoG) – Mean Score (FinG).

6   Berent and Shimron do not report the t-statistic for this comparison. They do, however, report that a p-value of larger than 0.05 was obtained for this comparison using the Tukey HSD test.

7   Berent and Shimron do not report the t-score for this comparison. They do report that a p-value of smaller than 0.05 was obtained for this comparison using the Tukey HSD test.

8   The lexical statistics were all calculated from the CELEX database (Baayen et al., 1995). Since the phonetic transcriptions in CELEX reflect British pronunciation, this database was 'Americanized' before the calculations were done. The changes that were made include things such as replacement of [a] with [æ] in words like *half*, addition of [ɹ] in the pronunciation of words like *car*, etc. I am indebted to John Kingston for this.

LND was calculated according to the method used by *inter alia* Vitevitch and Luce (1998, 1999) and Newman et al. (1997). The neighbors of a token are defined as any word that can be formed from the token by substitution, addition or deletion of one phoneme from the token. LND is calculated as follows: (i) Find all the neighbors for a token. (ii) Sum the log frequencies of all the neighbors. The lexical neighborhood density therefore takes into account both the number of neighbors and their frequencies.

To understand how transitional probabilities were calculated, consider the token [skɔk] as an example. For the sequence [sk] we can calculate the probability of an [s] being followed by a [k], and the probability of a [k] being preceded by an [s]. To calculate the probability of [s] being followed by [k]: (i) take the log of the frequency of [s]; (ii) take the log of the frequency of the sequence [sk]; (iii) divide the log frequency of [sk] by the log frequency of [s]. The probability of a [k] being preceded by a [s] can be calculated in a similar manner. The CBP of some token is the product of all the bi-phone probabilities of that token.

9   This number is smaller than the expected number of 30 (3 conditions × 2 token types per condition × 5 tokens per token type), because the same token is sometimes used in two different conditions.

10 The fillers were selected such that approximately an equal number of all tokens were possible words and impossible words. Fillers that represented impossible words violated a constraint on the consonants that co-occur in the onset and coda of a single syllable (Fudge, 1969). They were therefore ill-formed for reasons similar to the ill-formedness of the *[skVk] and *[spVp]-tokens.

11 The fillers in this experiment were selected using the same criteria as in the previous experiment. See previous footnote.

12 I sketch only the outlines of an account here. See Coetzee (2004:348–80) for more detail.

13 The question of whether the root exists as a separate morphological entity has been questioned in recent years. Bat-El (1994), Ussishkin (1999) and Gafos (2003) do not assume the existence of the root. However, see Berent, Everett and Shimron (2001) and Berent, Shimron and Vaknin (2001) for arguments in favor of the root.

14 This assumption is shared by *inter alia* Gafos (1999). Ussishkin (1999) also assumes that geminate verbs derive from bi-consonantal forms. However, for him the bi-consonantal form is not a bare consonantal root but rather an output base that contains consonants and vowels. Gafos (2003) also assumes that geminates derive from bi-consonantal inputs. However, he assumes that the consonant that shows up as geminate on the surface is underlyingly linked to two moras.

15 Stem boundaries are marked by vertical lines |. Superscripted R indicates morphological membership of the root.

16   Other alternatives are ruled out by other high ranking constraints. $[|\text{i.}X^R\text{e}Y^R|]$ and $[|X^R\text{i.e}Y^R|]$ are both ruled out by ONSET. $[|X^R\text{e}Y^R|]$ and $[|X^R\text{i}Y^R|]$ are ruled out by a constraint requiring faithful parsing of the vocalic melody – some version of MAX-V (Gafos, 2003; Ussishkin, 1999).

17   Subscripted *i* represents phonological relatedness.

18   There are several other candidates satisfying FINAL-C and ALIGN-L that are ruled out by high ranking constraints not considered here. First, there is a candidate that supplies the third stem-final consonant by epenthesis rather than copying, i.e. $*[|X^R\text{-}Y^R\text{-}Z|]$. The fact that Hebrew chooses copying over epenthesis, shows that DEP-C >> INTEGRITY. There is also a candidate that copies the initial root consonant to the right and a candidate that copies the final consonant to the left, i.e. $[X_i^R\text{-}X_i\text{-}Y^R]$ and $[X^R\text{-}Y_i\text{-}Y_i^R]$. These candidates are ruled out by a high ranking constraint requiring the surface correspondents of the root to be contiguous, i.e. CONTIGUITY indexed to the root.

19   See Berent and Shimron (1997) for a similar proposal, and Coetzee (2004) for an explicit formalization of an OT model that can do these kinds of comparisons. Sorace and Keller (2005:1516) claim that an OT grammar cannot compare candidates that are derived from different inputs. It is true that this kind of comparison is not usually done in production oriented OT. However, it is untrue that an OT grammar cannot do this. Nothing in the way that EVAL works depends on the origin of the candidates being compared – i.e. it can compare forms that do not share the same input. Even in classic OT, there is acknowledgement that EVAL can do this. In 'lexicon optimization', EVAL compares different possible inputs for a single output (Prince and Smolensky, 1993/2004). The tableau des tableaux introduced by Ito, Mester and Padgett (1995) gives formal expression to this property of EVAL in classical OT. See Coetzee (2004: Chapter 2) for a detailed discussion of this characteristic of EVAL.

20   I give only a very basic motivation for these constraints here. See Coetzee (2004) for a complete discussion and motivation. See Baertsch and Davis (2003) for a very different approach.

21   These constraints are too specific. The domain should probably be defined more broadly – as English also does not allow words of the form $*[\text{spV.pV}]$ or $*[\text{skV.kV}]$. These constraints should also apply to more than just the voiceless stops – since English also does not tolerate $*[\text{slVl}]$, $*[\text{snVn}]$, etc. For more on these kinds of restrictions, see Fudge (1969). For discussion about how to state the domain of these constraints, see Coetzee (2004:420).

2 Phonological evidence[1]

Paul de Lacy

This chapter examines a well-known generative innatist theory of the phonological component and related modules. It asks what this theory identifies as empirical evidence for it, and for which modules. It also identifies predicted ambiguities, where two or more modules influence the same phenomenon. Specific phenomena discussed include alternations, phonotactics, phonetic neutralization, loanword adaptation, and typological frequency.

1   Introduction

Prince (2007) has emphasized that a theory itself is necessarily an object of study. Derived from this point is the theme of this chapter: a theory itself must be examined to determine what is evidence for it.

The past few decades have seen the development of a generative, innatist, modular framework (GIMF) for theories of the cognitive resources used for the production and perception of human speech. Theories of the phonological component (PhC) such as Chomsky and Halle (1968) and Prince and Smolensky (1993/2004) are set within GIMF, as are theories of the phonetic component such as Keating (1988, 1990). GIMF theories share many properties (elaborated in section 2) – so many that it is possible to ask of them as a class: what is the GIMF phonological component responsible for? This question expands to: what does the GIMF PhC generate and influence, and what can interfere with a straightforward relation between PhC representations and their physical realization or perception?

Many empirical phenomena have been argued to provide evidence within GIMF phonological theories; they include phonotactic generalizations, synchronic alternations, free variation, diachronic change, loanword adaptation, language games, first and second language acquisition data, frequency (typological, lexical, text, allophonic), cross-dialect comparisons, and many more. Understanding of the various GIMF modules and mechanisms (phonological, phonetic, perceptual, learning) and of external performance phenomena has developed to such a point that we can now profitably ask: Is the GIMF phonological component entirely, partially, or not at all responsible for these phenomena? How can we tell?

I emphasize that I am not asking whether a particular phenomenon should be the responsibility of *every* theory of the phonological component. I am asking whether a *GIMF* phonological component predicts that it should be responsible; non-GIMF theories need to be examined separately (e.g. non-innatist/functionalist theories – see Gordon 2007 for an overview), and nothing said here necessarily applies to them. Also, there is a wide range of GIMF phonological theories, and many differ on the details of what they are responsible for generating. However, there are properties common to all of them that make generalizations possible.

With a narrower focus, the issue of a GIMF phonological module's responsibility is crucial to theories of markedness. There has been a great deal of disagreement recently about which phenomena are relevant for the concept of markedness (e.g. Blevins 2004, Hume 2004a, de Lacy 2006a, Rice 2007). A great deal of this disagreement can be traced back to fundamentally different conceptions of the properties of the phonological component, and its relation to other modules (or even if there is such a module). This chapter aims to clarify the phonological component's role for the particular framework I work in – GIMF. This framework is discussed in more detail in section 2.

The primary difficulty faced here is that a GIMF phonological component's output can be obscured by other modules and influences. For example, a non-trivial phonetic component (e.g. Keating 1988, 1990, Kingston and Diehl 1994) can obscure differences between phonological symbols (section 4). The perceptual system can also act so that the phonological representation a hearer deduces is different from the speaker's (section 5). External factors can also affect speech sound patterns, especially typological frequency and lexicon content (section 6). Section 7 discusses GIMF theory building and evaluation techniques.

2   The GIMF framework

The framework outlined here is generative, innatist, and modular, with 'non-trivial' modules, explained below (for recent overviews see Harris 2007, Kingston 2007). I reserve the term 'theory' here to refer to theories of particular modules. 'Framework' refers to the theory of modules (i.e. which ones exist, how they relate to each other), and of the core properties shared among modules (e.g. generativist, innatist). The overview is brief because the framework and theories are commonly used; apart from the discussion below, I will assume the reader's familiarity with them.

A symbol manipulation module – the 'phonological component' (PhC) – receives an input from a lexicon (via or at least influenced by a syntactic and/ or morphological component). The PhC effects non-trivial mappings from input to output (Chomsky and Halle 1968, Prince and Smolensky 2004). The output of the PhC is the input for another cognitive component – the 'phonetic component' – which converts it into a different type of representation ('gradient') (Keating 1988, 1990, 1996, Kingston 2007§17.4.3 for an overview). The output of the phonetics is (eventually) realized as movements of articulators and the lungs; the movements cause speech sound. There is also a perceptual mechanism that processes auditory stimuli, converts them into a phonetic representation, and then a phonological one, and matches or converts the phonological representation into lexical items (e.g. see Moreton 2000).

The theory is innatist in that each module comes 'genetically endowed' with primitives – i.e. representations, constraints, input→output derivational mechanisms, and so on. The primitives are not learned. (It is of course worth examining functionalist, non-innatist theories – e.g. Gordon 2007 – to see what they predict to be evidence; the aim here is to focus solely on innatist theories.) For an overview of the innatist approach, see Newmeyer (1998, 2003).

The cognitive modules are 'non-trivial' in the sense that they do not provide a straightforward conversion of input to output. PhCs may differ from language to language so that the same input in different grammars is mapped to different outputs. The same is true for the phonetic component. For example, in some languages the phonological feature [+voice] is phonetically interpreted as voiceless unaspirated but in others as voicing (i.e. as different degrees of Voice Onset Time) (Kingston and Diehl 1994). The physical properties of the articulatory tract may alter the phonetic output; for example, while the phonetic output may call for a drop in F_0, physical restrictions may prevent this from happening if the speaker's pitch production has 'bottomed out'. Of course, each module is limited: not all imaginable unfaithful input→output mappings in the PhC are permitted, and the range of realization of phonological symbols by the phonetic component is restricted (though exactly how limited is debated – SPE cf. Declarative Phonology – Scobbie et al. 1996), and the articulatory tract is sufficiently similar in humans to often make individual physical differences irrelevant. Consequently, production and perception involve the complex interaction of modules in GIMF; the PhC is just one factor of many (Chomsky and Halle 1968:3).

There are some major differences between GIMF and other theories. A competing framework considers the PhC and phonetic component as 'the same' in some sense – for example, they may employ representations with similarly fine distinctions (e.g. Kirchner 1998). Another is to say that the PhC is very unrestricted in what it can generate, and that all observed restrictions follow from transmissibility in learning (perhaps advocated by Evolutionary

Phonology (EP) – Blevins 2004, 2006, cf. de Lacy and Kingston 2006, de Lacy 2006a). Obviously, each theory needs to be separately examined for what it predicts to be evidence for it. The focus here is on the generative, innatist, modular framework outlined above and developed in detail by the cited works.

The model above is incomplete as it does not mention other relevant cognitive modules. These may include a 'paralinguistic' module (e.g. Ladd 1996§1.4), and an 'orthographic' module for conversion of written/typed text to phonological representation. These modules are of course important in a comprehensive examination of the capabilities of the PhC, but will not be discussed here due to lack of space.

Below I will refer to 'evidence' a great deal. 'Evidence' for the PhC refers to an individual's speech sound phenomenon which must be generated by the PhC (i.e. the PhC is 'responsible' for the phenomenon). Such evidence provides a way to determine individual states of the PhC, leading to a theory of all possible states (i.e. a 'phonological theory/theory of the PhC').

3   Phonological responsibility

The aim of the following two sections is to ask what the GIMF PhC is 'responsible' for, what the extent of its responsibility is, and to provide the beginnings of an answer. The point in doing so is not to exhaustively determine the answer, but to illustrate how the theory can be usefully examined in its own right.

While it would be a legitimate strategy to focus on one particular GIMF PhC theory like Optimality Theory, there is no need to – the many GIMF phonological theories proposed so far share many properties that mean they predict similar responsibilities.

GIMF theories are about the cognitive resources of an individual. A particular set of speech-related cognitive modules exists in a particular speaker, and is devoted to a particular grammar. A number of implications about potential evidence for the theory follow from these basic notions. An individual may have several different grammars (i.e. registers, dialects, languages). The theory is about individual grammars, so there is nothing inherent in GIMF theories that requires a ranking in one grammar to imply that some or every other grammar has the same ranking.[2] Similarly, the theory's principles mean that a ranking for one individual cannot be used to determine the ranking of another individual, even if they speak the same dialect. Therefore the only legitimate source of evidence identified by the theory is the output of an individual grammar in an individual speaker.

This restriction on evidence for a PhC theory may seem extreme, and is far from current practice. For example, phonological descriptions often draw on data from several different speakers of a language or dialect, amalgamate their data, and provide a description of the amalgamation. For those interested in the PhC, what's the problem with doing so?[3]

A significant problem is the creation of a 'pseudo-grammar'. Suppose different phenomena from different speakers are combined: S1's assimilation, S2's neutralization, and S3's stress pattern. Does the combination of different aspects of S1, S2, and S3 necessarily create a possible language? The theory does not guarantee this: since the only legitimate object of study is an individual grammar in an individual speaker, the combination of the output of different grammars could create a set of data that no grammar could generate.

Similarly problematic is the 'democratic' method of phonological description. In this approach, data from several speakers is examined, and the majority attestation is chosen as the actual process. For example, suppose of six speakers four have assimilation /nk/ → [ŋk], four have foot-initial aspiration of stops, and three have lenition of /v/→[w] in onsets. The democratic method would provide a ranking that could produce assimilation, stop aspiration, and lenition. However, there is no guarantee that this collection of data is ever possible for an individual speaker: it could be that none of the speakers have all three phenomena together. Consequently, this sort of democratic theorizing is a bad idea; the theory accounts for the grammars of *each* speaker so the only legitimate approach is to provide grammatical descriptions for each speaker.

But is it legitimate to generalize from grammar to grammar if they generate the *same* (or at least very similar) phonological outputs? Suppose there are two speakers S_1 and S_2 and they have the same phonological outputs *and* they have exactly the same linguistic experience: could we conclude they have the same ranking? This issue depends on a theory of learnability (not included in the theoretical package outlined in section 2; see Tesar 2007 for an overview). Because the components allow non-trivial input→output mappings, the theory can allow several different ways to produce the same output. For example, suppose both speakers lack [k] in codas. In OT, the [k] could be potentially eliminated in coda environment through deletion, coalescence /$V_1 k_2$/→[$V_{1,2}$], lenition /Vk/→[Vx], change in place of articulation /Vk/→[Vt͡ʃ], epenthesis /Vk/→[V.ki̠], and so on. If one's theory of learnability forced the speaker to choose the same one of these particular options, then it would be legitimate to say that S_1 and S_2's ranking are the same. However, if the learning process allowed a random choice of rankings that generated the same output, there would be simply no guarantee that one speaker will have the same ranking as another, even though they have exactly the same output. This is one aspect of non-triviality in the PhC: the same phonotactic pattern can often derive from many different inputs via many different derivational routes.

This point is even more extreme in different registers. For example, for an individual speaker of Samoan, his/her 'colloquial' grammar has a [k] where his/her 'formal' grammar has a [t] (Mosel and Hovdhaugen 1993). Can one conclude that /k/→[t] in the formal grammar, or that /t/→[k] in the colloquial grammar? The theory does not commit itself to this assumption. The fact is that there are two different grammars (or at least two different rankings), and potentially two different lexicons. The fact that [tai] 'tide' in formal Samoan is used to express the same meaning as [kai] in colloquial Samoan therefore does not imply that the underlying form is /tai/ in both registers (or /kai/), or that there is a process of /t/→[k] (or /k/→[t]) in one or the other. What is relevant here is a theory of inter-grammar interference: if additional theoretical mechanisms required that all registers have the same lexicon, for example, then it would be possible to use one grammar to provide information about the other. However, the framework outlined above says nothing about such cases except that they are two different grammars, and therefore it is not necessarily legitimate to generalize from one to the other. Of course, it would be ideal to *have* such a theory of between-grammar influence, but the point is that no such theory necessarily *follows* from the basic GIMF principles. Any claim of between-grammar interference therefore needs to be buttressed by a theory of how that interference works.

In short, core properties of GIMF restrict reliable potential evidence for its modules to the speech that is generated by an individual grammar of an individual speaker. Other theories may make other evidence relevant. A theory of between-grammar influence may mean that a ranking or lexical entry for one grammar may be the same for another grammar in the same speaker. A theory of learnability may necessitate that given a particular output a learner will always posit the same ranking (choosing from several potential alternatives). However, GIMF does not guarantee such assumptions, so whenever evidence is adduced that does not derive from a single grammar in a single speaker, further theoretical devices that make the evidence relevant need to be made explicit.

The 'one grammar of one speaker' is an ideal – a way to avoid problems that can be introduced by pooling data of different speakers. However, from a practical point of view many descriptions with such amalgamated data are probably still useful, even more so for descriptions in which variation among speakers is noted. However, unless the issue of data amalgamation is overtly discussed, it introduces an element of uncertainty for the PhC theorist: were patterns found in the minority of speakers ignored? The issue comes up frequently with 'variation': in several cases I have seen recently descriptions are unclear whether variation is truly free (i.e. the variants occur freely in the grammar of an individual speaker) or dialectal (i.e. speakers are internally consistent about the variant they use, but different speakers use different variants).

3.1   Phonotactics

Since the source of evidence for the theory is limited to a single grammar of an individual speaker, one can ask which aspects of the grammar are potentially observable. Given current technology, only the output is visible; even then, the PhC's output isn't directly observable – only sound and articulator movement is detectable, but for the moment it will be naïvely assumed that the phonological output can be unambiguously recovered from any speech output (see section 4 for a rejection of this view). So, the GIMF PhC's output is effectively observable. PhC theories predict that the phonological component is wholly responsible for the distribution of phonological symbols in different environments – i.e. 'phonotactics'.

For example, Hawai'ian permits [p k ʔ] in outputs and no other oral stops, so the PhC must be able to generate this inventory (Pukui and Elbert 1979). The lack of a [t] is very rare (though for similar languages see de Lacy 2006a§1.3.1.1). Nevertheless, its rarity is irrelevant: the PhC must be able to generate a grammar without it because no other cognitive module is capable of doing so. The theory predicts that the PhC must account for all phonotactic patterns; a single valid example is therefore enough to motivate a revision of the theory (a point emphasized by Everett 2003 for metrical theory). Exactly what is meant by 'generate this inventory' differs in specific GIMF PhC theories; in SPE it could be due to restrictions on lexical form (Morpheme Structure Constraints), in OT Richness of the Base requires consideration of the mapping of input /t/ and a constraint-based solution to its lack of attestation (if an 'accidental lexical gap' approach is eliminated).

There are limits on what phonotactics can tell the analyst, but they differ depending on what theory one adopts. In some GIMF PhC theories, phonotactics provide insight into what outputs the PhC must generate, but not necessarily how it generates them. As observed above, a language with no [k] in codas (and no relevant alternations) can achieve this pattern by many different means: deletion, coalescence, change in place or manner, and so on. The rankings and input→output mappings that end up in a lack of output [k] are not directly observable for this phonotactic generalization: only the fact that output [k] is not present is directly detectable; rankings and inputs must be inferred from outputs.

The fact that OT – and SPE, and every other generative theory – can often provide several ways to account for a particular phonotactic pattern is occasionally underappreciated. For example, Lhasa Tibetan allows [m] and no other nasal stop word-finally, though [n] and [ŋ] are allowed elsewhere (Denwood 1999). As there are no alternations to show what happens to word-final /n/, is it reasonable to assume it neutralizes to [m]? No – the theory does not necessarily require that /n/ *must* neutralize: it could delete, coalesce with a preceding vowel /Vn/→[V̄], and so on (see de Lacy 2006a§8.2 for other examples). (This is particularly true for Optimality Theory; for SPE, there may be a morpheme structure constraint that bans /n/ from the lexicon, and/or the choice of possible mappings may be limited by the simplicity principle – Chomsky and Halle 1968:295).

Phonotactics in OT may give some idea as to the input→output mapping and constraint ranking, given certain assumptions (Tesar 2006). If a segment such as [p] is allowed in onsets on the surface, some relevant faithfulness constraint must outrank all markedness constraints against [p] (in onsets) (for a more precise characterization of neutralization rankings, see de Lacy 2002:ch.6). It is less clear what the appearance of [p] tells one about input→output mappings. It is possible that /p/→[p], or it could be that /p/→∅ and /f/→[p] in a chain-shifting fortition process; in principle, either input→output mapping is possible (e.g. McCarthy 2005b). If one adopts a learnability principle whereby a learner always assumes a faithful map in the absence of alternations (an eminently reasonable principle), then non-alternating phonotactics provide evidence for faithful input→output mappings. Certainly, if a language *bans* [p], there is no direct way without an explicit learnability theory of knowing what happens to /p/ apart from the fact that it does not surface as [p].

In short, GIMF PhC theories predict that all phonotactic regularities in every output of every grammar of every individual are valid evidence for the PhC's structure. Phonotactics provides evidence that the PhC must be capable of generating the relevant outputs, but does not necessarily imply any particular input or ranking. Additional theories may change the picture substantially. For example, a particular theory of learning may predict that a speaker will choose a particular input and ranking if they observe a phonotactic pattern like lack of a coda [k] (i.e. perhaps lack of coda [k] always comes about through neutralization). However, unless such a learning theory is identified, phonotactic generalizations do not provide clear evidence in GIMF theories about I→O mappings.

3.2   Alternations

GIMF PhC theories provide a mechanism for relating the outputs of morphologically-related forms – i.e. 'alternations'.[4] The theory imposes one unique input form for any given morpheme (ignoring suppletion for the moment, discussed below). Therefore, differences in the realization of a morpheme in different environments provide evidence for inputs and rankings. It is an absolutely crucial point that no other cognitive module in GIMF is responsible for alternations – the PhC bears all responsibility for generating them (though see section 4 regarding the phonetic module).

As with phonotactics, individual theories differ significantly as to *how much* insight alternations provide. For example, in the Nepalese language Yamphu the morpheme 'daughter-in-law' surfaces as [næmːiʔ] on its own and as [næmːid-æʔ] with the instrumental/ergative (Rutgers 1998). The common part is the morph for 'daughter-in-law' – [næmːiʔ]~[næmːid]. There are two important aspects here: that [ʔ] and its corresponding segment [d] are not identical, and that [næmːi] is identical in both forms.

In both OT and SPE, the input must contain a segment that corresponds to the output [ʔ]/[d]. Therefore, the alternation shows that Yamphu has an input→output mapping that involves feature change: i.e. some input segment /α/ becomes [ʔ] in codas and [d] elsewhere. From this point on, individual theories differ widely as to how much more can be determined.

In classical OT with Richness of the Base, on the basis of this alternation alone the [d]~[ʔ] alternation could indicate that /d/→[ʔ] in codas, or that /ʔ/→[d] in onsets, or both, or that /d/→[ʔ] in codas and /ʔ/→∅ in a chain shift, or that there is a different input segment (/t/→[ʔ] in codas, /t/→[d] intervocalically) (see McCarthy and Wolf 2005 for recent discussion). The theory allows a large range of options from phonotactics and alternations. These options can often be narrowed down by considering more alternations, which may eliminate some possible input→output mappings (not in this case, though). An explicit GIMF-compatible theory of learnability is often necessary to narrow down the options further.

It's worth making a further point about the significance of an explicit learning theory here. The theory does not necessitate that the two forms of 'daughter-in-law' are related by means of an input; it can account for the morphological relatedness by having two phonological forms for the morpheme 'daughter-in-law' – /næmːid/ and /næmːiʔ/; they are mapped faithfully to the output, and the appropriate form is selected by phonological principles (e.g. Mascaró 1996).

So why should the alternation analysis be favoured over the supple-tion analysis? The fact that the [d]~[ʔ] correspondence occurs in dozens of morphemes would heavily bias any reasonable analyst towards adopting an alternation analysis, and so does the fact that [d] never appears in codas, as does the productivity of this alternation. However, nothing in the GIMF PhC theory requires this to be so in the sense that either a suppletion or alternation analysis will equally account for this data. It is perhaps here where a theory of learning is crucial: such a theory needs to impose a bias against learners adopting a suppletive analysis – the learner needs to have an almost pathological desire to analyze different morphs of a morpheme as deriving from the same input, with suppletion only as a last resort. Of course, this is only a description of what a theory of learning needs to do – it requires exact formalization. To summarize, GIMF PhC modules offer two ways of dealing with a morpheme's

morph variation: through alternations and phonologically-conditioned suppletion. Putting aside suppletion, in all extant GIMF PhC theories, alternations
provide insight into underlying forms and constraint rankings/rules.

So far, this chapter has merely discussed what is already commonly
known: that phonotactics and alternations are evidence for theories of the
PhC. However, what's really of importance is to show *why* phonotactics and
alternations are evidence. They're evidence because within GIMF there's no
other module that can generate phonotactic patterns and morpheme alternations.
A practical benefit of asking this question is that it leads to an argumentation
generalization for those who work within a theory that subscribes to a GIMF
framework (e.g. classical/innatist OT, SPE, LPM, etc.). The principle assumes
a 'straightforward' phonetic interpretation where the phonetic translation preserves all phonological distinctions; it will be revised after considering the
phonetic component in this section.

(1) *GIMF PhC I→O argumentation ('straightforward phonetics' version, revised
     below)*

Non-suppletive alternations generated by an individual grammar of an individual speaker provide evidence for input→output mappings (and from these
mappings, for the form of constraints and ranking).

- An 'alternation' of a morpheme refers to different realizations ('morphs')
  of that morpheme in different phonological environments.

Depending on the theory, there may be other ways to determine input→output
mappings apart from (1). Individual theories may allow non-alternating phonotactics to provide evidence for /α/→[β] mappings. However, (1) is what's
common to extant theories committed to GIMF. It is worth noting that arguments for input→output mappings made without the support of alternations are
not uncommon, usually without explicit explanation of how the non-alternating
forms provide evidence for those mappings.

4   Phonetic influence

The GIMF phonetic module is significantly non-trivial: there is no simple 1:1
relation between phonological outputs and their phonetic realization. Multiple
articulatory strategies may be used to realize the same phonological structure, even within the same language (e.g. Kingston 2007 for an overview).
Consequently, synchronic alternations and phonotactics are not always perfect
evidence for phonological structure because the phonetic component(s) may
obscure the observable form of phonological outputs. The idea that the pho-

netic module can obscure phonological form is expressed in GIMF in that (a) phonological representation is distinct from phonetic representation and (b) the phonological output is not straightforwardly recoverable from the phonetic output (e.g. Keating 1988; Kingston 2007).

There has always been recognition of the difficulties that a non-trivial phonetic module poses for recovering phonological structures. For example, Chomsky and Halle (1968:110–111) note that there are both phonological and phonetic 'vowel reduction' processes; the phonological process results in a phonological output with unstressed vowels as [ə], while the phonetic process takes fully specified unstressed vowels and realizes them as more centralized than their stressed counterparts. Similarly, Cho and Keating (2001) identify phonetic fortition processes, while Bye and de Lacy (2008) discuss phonological fortition. Some ways in which phonetic interpretation can obscure the form of phonological outputs are sketched in (2).

(2) *How can phonological structure be obscured?*

   (a) *Phonetic neutralization:* Two different phonological symbols are phonetically realized in the same way (e.g. voiced and voiceless epiglottal plosives both realized as voiceless – Ladefoged and Maddieson 1996).

   (b) *Phonetic non-realization:* A phonological symbol/feature has no phonetic realization (see below).

   (c) *Phonetic epenthesis:* Part of the phonetic output does not stand in a direct relation to any part of the phonological output (e.g. interpolation in intonation, 'intrusive' segments) (e.g. Ali et al. 1979 and many others).

   (d) *Phonetic deletion:* A phonological symbol's phonetic realization is 'overwritten' by other segments' (e.g. overlap – Browman and Goldstein 1995).

   (e) *Phonetic allophony:* A phonological symbol has different phonetic realizations, either in different languages, or in different environments in the same language (e.g. English [voice] – Kingston and Diehl 1994; domain-final lengthening causes duration allophony in vowels).

   (f) *Phonetic transference*: A symbol is not realized where it is specified in the phonological string (e.g. /ʔ/ in Pendau is realized as creaky voice on a preceding vowel – Quick 2004; [voice] in English coda stops is realized as lengthening of the preceding vowel; tone is often realized on segments after its phonological sponsors ('late realization')).

   (g) *Phonetic assimilation:* i.e. anticipatory/perseverative coarticulation.

Foot heads and stress provide a good example of phonetic allophony and non-realization. Foot heads can be realized as any, none, or all of raised F_0 (perhaps in some cases lowered F_0 – Gussenhoven 2004), increased duration, and increased loudness (Hayes 1995§2.1). Cairene Arabic provides a rather remarkable case where the word's head syllable has a phonetic stress realization while other foot heads do not (Allen 1975, McCarthy 1979b, Hayes 1995§4.1.3). The location of main stress can only be identified by building quantity-sensitive trochaic feet from left to right: e.g. [(ˌʔad)(ˌwi.ja)(ˈtu.hu)] 'his drugs (nominative)', [(ˌka.ta) (ˈbi.tu)] 'she wrote it', [(ˈka.ta)ba] 'he wrote', [(ˌʔin)(ˈka.sa)ra] 'it got broken'. Without non-head feet, it would be impossible to predict whether main stress would fall on the penult or antepenult (cf. Crowhurst 1996, de Lacy 1998). However, the phonetic stressing is ‖ʔinkˈasara‖, not *‖ʔˈinkˈasara‖ – syllables that head non-head feet have no phonetic stress realization (‖x‖ indicates the phonetic realization of [x]). Consequently, the phonetic output does not provide direct evidence for foot structure.

Chomsky and Halle (1968:311) identify a case of phonetic neutralization: two different sets of features (i.e. [+anterior, –coronal, +back, +high] and [–anterior, –coronal, +back, +high, +round]) are phonetically realized as labio-velar. As another example, I have argued elsewhere for phonetic neutralization with glottal and velar nasals. There are nasal stops with a phonologically *glottal* Place of Articulation – symbolized as [N] (de Lacy 2002, 2006a,b). However, the [glottal] feature is interpreted as requiring an absence of consonantal constriction downstream from the sound source (de Lacy 2002, 2006b§2.2.1.1; adapting Ohala and Lorentz 1977). It is implemented by making an obstruction at the soft palate, as shown in diagram (3). After Ohala and Lorentz (1977), the diagram shows the airflow through the oral and nasal cavities. The oral cavity is blocked at the velar/uvular region, so air is forced to go through the nasal cavity. The black dots indicate the air's path from the lungs out through the nasal passages.

(3)

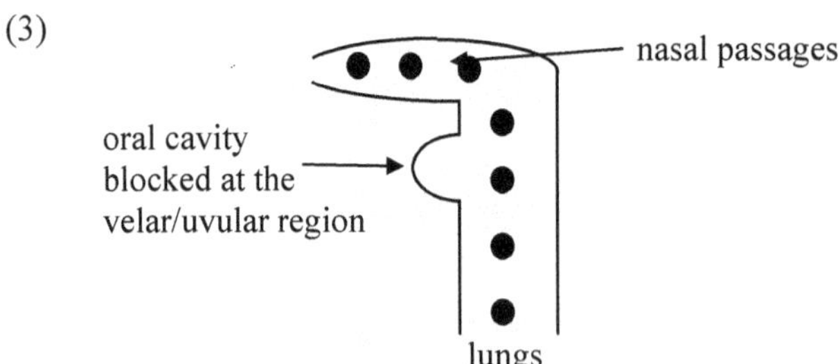

Velar stops are made in much the same way – with a consonantal constriction at the hard palate – but for entirely different reasons: they have an articulatorily-defined target to achieve. Consequently, distinct phonological symbols velar [ŋ]

and glottal [N] are phonetically realized in a similar way: they are phonetically neutralized to ‖ŋ‖.

Consequently, the only evidence that there are phonological glottal nasals is from their effect on other phonological elements. For example, assimilation shows that there are glottal nasal stops in Yamphu. Oral stops become [ʔ] before another glottal: e.g. /mo-dok-ha/ → [modoʔha] 'like those' (p. 48), *[modokha]; /læːt-he-ma/ → [læːʔhema] 'to be able to do' (Rutgers 1998:48). Nasal stops also assimilate to glottals, and the result is glottal [N]: /pen-ʔi/ → [peNʔi] 'he's sitting'; /hen-heː-nd-u-æn-de/ → [heNheːndwende] 'can you open it?' (p. 44). If Yamphu [N] is really velar [ŋ], this assimilation is inexplicable as one would expect stop assimilation to produce a [k] before [ʔ]: i.e. /læːt-he-ma/ → *[læːk.he.ma]. From a broader perspective, assimilation of PoA always results in agreement of PoA features. Therefore, the nasal that appears before [h] in Yamphu must be phonologically [glottal].[5]

[N] behaves like other glottals in triggering processes. Gutturals – glottals, pharyngeals, and uvulars – can force an adjacent vowel to have a retracted tongue root ([RTR]). For example, Arabic verb stems must have a low vowel next to a guttural in the imperfect: e.g. [faʕal]/[ja-fʕal] 'do', *[faʕil] (McCarthy 1994). The generalization holds for uvulars [ʁ χ], pharyngeals [ʕ ħ], and glottals [ʔ h], but not for velars. Similarly, Miogliola's vowels must be RTR when followed by a tautosyllabic moraic glottal nasal [N] (Ghini 2001:ch.4). Coda [N] is usually non-moraic (e.g. [feᵘN] 'fine'), but becomes moraic when a consonant follows (e.g. [feᵘNᵘd͡z]) or after a stressed vowel. The only vowels allowed before moraic [N] are the RTR vowels [ɛ œ a ɔ]; ATR [i y e æ ɑ o u] are not allowed. As velars never cause vowels to lower, it must be the case that Miogliola [N] is post-velar – i.e. glottal.[6]

[N] also alternates with other glottals. For example, [ñ] appears in Aguaruna onsets, but is realized as [N] in codas: [suŋkuN] 'influenza' c.f. [suŋ.ku.ñ̃-ăn] 'influenza+accusative' (Payne 1990: 162). If this [N] is really velar [ŋ], the motivation for the alternation is unclear; alternations involving [h] in other languages produce coronals (e.g. Korean – de Lacy 2006a§3.3.2).

[N] has the same distribution as other glottals. It is common for glottals to be banned from onset position. For example, Chamicuro does not allow [h] in onsets (Parker 1994); Buriat's [N] is allowed only in codas while [n] and [m] appear in onsets (Poppe 1960). If Buriat [N] is actually a velar [ŋ], it is difficult to explain why [k], [g], and [x] can all appear in onset position. In fact, there is no language that bans velars like [k g x ɣ] in onsets but allows them in codas; glottals excepted, every PoA that is allowed in codas is also allowed in onsets (§3.2.3, Goldsmith 1990, Beckman 1998). So, the fact that Buriat's 'ŋ' is only allowed in codas indicates that it is really glottal [N]. Miogliola [N] has the same distribution, consistent with its vowel-lowering behavior mentioned above (Ghini 2001§5.1). Other evidence for the glottal nasal [N] is provided in de Lacy (2006a:39–42).

The implication of phonetic non-realization and neutralization is that the effect of a phonological symbol on its environment plays an essential part in establishing the validity of many phonological arguments. To take an extremely conservative stance, reliance on phonetic realization as evidence for a phonological symbol/mechanism is in many cases inadequate. Of course, specific theories of the phonetic component place strong limits on phonetic realization; [t] cannot be interpreted as ‖m‖ (though cf. Declarative Phonology – Scobbie et al. 1996). Phonetic realization alone can therefore provide a range of possible phonological structures, but to narrow the options down further it is necessary to provide evidence from environmental interaction.

The method of providing evidence for a phonological element from its interaction with other elements is currently sporadic in phonological descriptions and analyses. For example, a large number of descriptions of foot structure rely entirely on phonetic evidence for locating foot heads and not on the foot's effect on other phonological elements (e.g. on vowel allophony, etc.). Relying on speech output alone to provide evidence for a phonological symbol is of course predicted by the theory to be acceptable if it can be shown that no other cognitive component (e.g. none of the processes in (2)) has interfered. Given that it is unknown (at least to me!) whether (2) is exhaustive and what the range of possible realizations of a given segment is, a methodologically conservative approach is to insist that evidence from environmental interaction be provided along with phonetic evidence for any assertion about phonological structure. Again, this is an ideal; in some cases there may be no environmental interactions to bolster the evidence for a particular phonological structure. In such a case, strictly speaking there is no choice but to acknowledge the ambiguity of the evidence.

(4) *GIMF PhC I→O argumentation (revised)*

    (a) To show that /α/→[β], evidence must consist of non-suppletive alternations generated by an individual grammar of an individual speaker.

    (bi) It should be demonstrated that the phonetic module has no (or irrelevant) influence.

    (bii) Evidence from environmental influences should be supplied.

    (c) The implications drawn from phonotactic evidence should be appropriately limited, as determined by the theory (e.g. many different rankings can account for the lack of coda [k] in OT).

A broader implication for the analyst is that the aims of phonological descriptions need to be carefully scrutinized before using them in service of a PhC theory. Many descriptive works do not aim to provide an account of the outputs of an individual grammar of an individual speaker; consequently, for the PhC-theorist translating the grammar's claims into evidence for the PhC is often a non-trivial task.[7] A related implication is that following the principles in (4) rigidly means that the amount of reliable information that the analyst can use is currently *extremely* small: very often descriptions pool information from different speakers, rely entirely on phonetic evidence alone for phonological structures, and make assertions about underlying forms and processes that rely on a particular theory not shared by the analyst.[8]

5   Perceptual influence

The GIMF perceptual process is significantly non-trivial. The speaker's phonological output is translated into phonetic form, converted to articulation, and the resulting sound then passes through the physical medium; the hearer must segment the acoustic signal and match it to phonetic categories, then convert the phonetic categories into a phonological representation, which is then matched with lexical form. So, between the speaker and the hearer lie a number of opportunities for the speaker's phonological output to be obscured to the hearer – i.e. the speaker's phonological output may be inaccurately reconstructed by the hearer. The challenges posed by the perceptual system are clear in loanword adaptation – a commonly used source of evidence for the phonological module.

There has been a recent upsurge in interest in the role of perception on loanword adaptation, including Silverman (1992), Yip (2002), Kenstowicz (2003), Peperkamp and Dupoux (2003), Broselow (2004, 2006), LaCharité and Paradis (2005), C. Ito et al. (2006), Hsieh et al. (2006), Smith (2006b, this volume) and others. This section can't hope to do justice to the proposals and analyses in these articles. Instead, it examines what GIMF with a non-trivial phonetic component says the PhC must and may not be responsible for in loanword adaptation.

Decoding the acoustic signal into a phonetic representation is a non-trivial process that may result in loss (or gain) of information in relation to the speaker's intentions. The hearer must determine which part of the acoustic signal is actually speech, and which aspects of the acoustic signal are significant in phonetic segmentation. Languages may differ in this – some features of the signal may be ignored because they never figure contrastively (with the result that non-native contrasts may be hard or impossible to perceive (e.g. for me the difference between [ɪ] and [ə])). As a practical example, how does a Māori (Polynesian; New Zealand) hearer process the New Zealand English (NZE) phonetic output ||saɪn|| 'sign'? One challenge for the Māori is that ||s|| is not an output of his/her language. The Māori needs to discover the speaker's phonetic intention in producing ||s||, but faced with the fact that ||s|| is not a phonetic realization associated with the Māori's phonetic and perceptual system, it would be consistent with GIMF to expect that only part of ||s|| is treated as salient for speech: i.e. part of the acoustic signal is ignored. The part that is not ignored is sufficiently close to ||h|| that it gets perceived as ||h||. In other words, the hearer's phonetic representation may differ from the speaker's phonetic output as a side effect of focusing on the language-specific significant parts of the speech signal.

Even if the hearer can correctly interpret every aspect of the speaker's phonetic speech output as speech, there is another major hurdle to overcome: the conversion of phonetic into phonological representation. As mentioned above, the same phonological symbol can have a range of phonetic realizations in a particular language, and the realizations of the same phonological symbol may differ. For example, Māori has a range of phonetic realizations of phonological [h], ranging between ||h||, ||x||, and ||ʃ|| (i.e. there's free variation in dorsal-palatal constriction) (Bauer 1993). In contrast, NZE [h] is consistently ||h||. Consequently, if a Māori says ||ʃ||, another Māori will perceive it as ||ʃ|| and then map it to phonological [h]; if a NZE speaker says ||ʃ||, another NZE speaker will map it to [ʃ] because ||ʃ|| is not in the range of phonetic realizations of [h]. However, if a *Māori* hearer perceives NZE ||ʃ||, the Māori perceptual system will map it to [h]. Consequently, NZE [ʃ] is uniformly borrowed as Māori [h]: e.g. NZE [ʃip] 'sheep' ~ Māori [hipi]; NZE [ʃu] 'shoe' ~ Māori [huː].

Another challenge is that the same phonological symbol can be phonetically interpreted in different ways in different languages (Kingston and Diehl 1994). For example, English word-initial [b] (like other word-initial [+voice] stops) is interpreted as voiceless and unaspirated (i.e. ||p||). In contrast, Māori [p] is realized as voiceless unaspirated (||p||) (the same is true for [t] and [k] as ||t|| and ||k||). So, Māori [pɪripɪri] *Acaena anserinifolia* is phonetically realized as ||pɪripɪri||; when English speakers heard ||pɪripɪri||, they converted it to phonological [bɪribɪri] (thus New Zealand English *biddybiddy*).[9] This loanword adaptation of Māori [p] to NZ English [b] is therefore 'pre-phonological' – it is a result of the different mappings between the phonological and phonetic representations in Māori and English.[10]

So, there are many opportunities for pre-phonological adaptation of a speech signal by a hearer. Since the perceptual mechanism can have something to do with loanword adaptation, the remaining issue is *how* responsible the perceptual system can be (something that's not going to be resolved here). After all, the PhC certainly could be responsible for some adaptations – the theory does not prevent the PhC from influencing loanword form: if a loanword is correctly perceived and assigned an input phonological representation that cannot be faithfully produced in the speaker's grammar, the grammar would be responsible for that aspect of the adaptation. The challenge is that until there is a full understanding of the power of the perceptual component to adapt foreign sounds to fit the language's expected sounds, there are very few sure ways to figure out the extent of influence of the PhC on loanword adaptation. However, the theory does provide a couple of ways to tell.

One way is to see what sort of PhC capabilities a particular loanword adaptation would require. In the Māori [p] to NZE [b] adaptation, a phonological account would require a mapping of /p/→[b]. Such across-the-board stop voicing is unknown in synchronic alternations (cf. intervocalic voicing).

Another way is through alternations. For example, NZE [saɪn] 'sign (verb)' was borrowed into Māori as [haina]. Is the appearance of final [a] due to a pre-phonological misanalysis (e.g. Peperkamp and Dupoux 2003), or a phonological process?

Happily, Māori has a number of underlyingly consonant-final roots. For example, /hopuk/ 'catch' surfaces as [hopu] on its own, but as [hopuk-ia] in the passive and [hopuk-aŋa] in the gerund (see de Lacy 2003 and references cited therein). A problem with putative /haɪn/ is immediately apparent: it should undergo *deletion* like other consonant-final roots: i.e. /haɪn/ doesn't map to *[hai].

One way out of this problem is to propose a loanword-specific faithfulness constraint (e.g. loanword-MAX); this constraint would block deletion in loanwords, and so allow epenthesis as a back-up strategy. However, this solution also fails. If the passive suffix is added to /haɪn/, the result would be /haɪn-ia/ → *[hainia]; however, the attested form is [haina-tia] (the [tia] allomorph of the passive is used for long roots with *underlying final vowels* (also the gerund: [haina-taŋa] 'signature', *[hain-aŋa] – Ngata 1993)). It is also not possible to argue that the first adopter of the word had underlying /hain/, and other speakers mislearned it as /haina/: Māori speakers have no difficulty learning underlying consonant-final words, and the very high frequency of passive forms gives them ample opportunity to do so.

'Sign' is merely one example of a general pattern: *all* English consonant-final words borrowed into Māori take the allomorph of the passive and gerund that attaches to underlying vowel-final verbs (Hale 1968, Blevins 1994:41). It is clear from alternations that no English consonant-final word is underlying consonant-final in the Māori lexicon; therefore, there is no evidence that word-final loanword 'epenthesis' is phonological.

To hammer the last nail into the coffin, English words that end in a C_1C_2 are adapted in Maori as C_1V: e.g. NZE [ˈʔiːdʒəpt] 'Egypt' is adapted as MAO ['iːhipa], NZE ['sɜːvənt] ~ Māori ['haːwini], NZE ['tæks] ~ Māori ['taːke]. The perceptual account would say that the Maori perceptually ignore the final consonant: their perceptual mechanism discards the acoustic cues to the final consonant as non-speech or irrelevant speech sound. The phonological account requires a deletion mechanism, with a UR for 'tax' as /tæːks/ (or /taːkh/), while the perceptual account says that it is [taːke]. Again, alternations provide a way to determine the difference. The UR of 'tax' with the passive /taːkh-ia/ should surface as *[taːkehia]; it does not: it takes the form of the passive used with underlying V-final words: [taːke-tia]; [h] does not appear (e.g. [ko toː utu teːnaː i aːhei kia <u>taːketia</u> i muɾi iho i ŋa taŋohaŋa katoa] 'That is your taxable income after all deductions have been made' (Ngata 1993).

The only way to maintain a phonological analysis would be to propose that output-output faithfulness specific to loanwords accounts for their invariant shape under affixation (i.e. loan-OO-FAITH » IO-FAITH » OO-FAITH). However, this analysis predicts that there should be at least *some* language in which alternations show that the underlying form of loanwords has the same shape as the source language form (i.e. IO-FAITH » loan-OO-FAITH, OO-FAITH); this would show that the phonological component is crucial in loanword adaptation. I have been unable to find clear cases so far, suggesting that the majority of loanword adaptation is due to perceptual mechanisms.

One final alternative to consider is that the Māori speaker does not store the perceived form [haɪn] as /haɪn/, but instead passes it through the phonological system and lexically stores the output. The problem with this approach is as noted above: the phonological component would generate *[hai] from input /haɪn/, not the attested [haina].

To summarize, GIMF with a non-trivial perceptual system and phonetic module predicts that the phonological component is not responsible for all loanword adaptation. GIMF predicts that it *is* responsible for alternations, so the way to show that the phonological component has determined the form of loanword adaptations is through alternations. Although GIMF predicts that the PhC *could* be responsible for some loanword adaptations, the current limited understanding of the extent to which the perceptual mechanisms may influence loanword form means that it would be reasonable to err on the side of caution in the sense that every claim that loanword adaptation is due to phonological mechanisms should ideally be accompanied by an alternation of a loanword to verify its underlying form. A little less stringently, if no phonetic/perceptual motivation for a particular loanword adaptation can be found, then there's the beginning of an argument that the PhC must be responsible; however, the clincher would be providing an alternation.

The influence of the perceptual system is also relevant in diachronic change and language acquisition. Proto-Eastern Polynesian *t became Hawai'ian [k] (Clark 1976), but does this mean that there was a speaker who had /t/→[k]? By no means: the sound change could have been actuated through a misperception (e.g. Blevins 2004, Ohala 1983). At the time of the *t→k change, pre-Hawai'ian had the stops [p t ?]. If there was variation in phonetic realization of the coronal stop between ‖t‖ and ‖k‖, the sound change could have been a matter of the learner analyzing the phonetic symbol behind the variation as [k] rather than [t]. The fact that a speaker has α and a learner β does not necessarily mean – in the theory – that the learner has /α/→[β]. In fact, it is telling that there is *no* case of synchronic neutralization in which /t/→[k], eliminating the possibility of an account that relies on the PhC (de Lacy 2006a).

There are probably cognitive modules other than the perceptual system that could influence speech sound. For example, a 'paralinguistic' module could alter the phonetic output to signal emotion by altering pitch range, vowel length, degree of VOT, and so on; see Ladd (1996§1.4) for discussion. There may also be a symbol manipulation module that is used in language games to alter phonological structure in fairly unconstrained ways (as in games which reverse the order of segments – a process not attested in other morphological/ phonological processes). No doubt an orthographic module relates lexical items to the hand movements that produce text (through writing/typing). The issue, of course, is one of responsibility: a theory of the PhC will identify which phenomena it is responsible for, but other cognitive components may also influence those phenomena. Consequently, only after examining other cognitive components is it clear what the 'extent' of the PhC's responsibility for particular phenomena is.

The immediate methodological implication is that using loanword adaptation to argue for GIMF PhC mechanisms is a non-trivial and challenging task. To be sure that a particular adaptation is due to the phonological component, it must be shown that it is not a pre-phonological adaptation.

6   External influences

Typological frequency is often used to motivate proposals about GIMF PhCs. Two types of frequency must be distinguished here (as in traditional work on universals): absolute (implicational) universals and universal tendencies. An absolute universal is all or nothing: α is either present or absent in every language; absolute implicational universals work the same way: if α is present then so is β in every language (e.g. if a language has a default epenthesis of stops, it will be [?] or [t] – de Lacy 2006a:79–109). Universal tendencies are just that: if a language has α it may also often have β, but sometimes may not (e.g. if a language has a [g] it will also probably have a [b], but a few [g d] and [g] inventories exist – see below). The discussion below focuses first on universal tendencies because they illustrate most clearly the role of external influences.

Many GIMF theories of markedness have interpreted the universal tendency that [t] is very common in segmental inventories to mean that the PhC favors [t] over other stops. In representational approaches, [t]'s high frequency has been taken to mean that it is representationally less complex than other segments (Paradis and Prunet 1991); in constraint-based theories of markedness, [t]'s violations are always less significant (through fixed ranking of *k, *p above *t), or a proper subset of other consonant's violations. However, what is the extent of the GIMF PhC's responsibility for typological frequency? Are other modules and factors involved?

Certainly, external factors *can* influence language typology. War, pestilence, and plague can affect populations, and even wipe out entire languages (e.g. the genocide of various Native American populations in the 19th and early 20th centuries – Brown 1970); a result is a loss of linguistic diversity. Similarly, invasion increases language contact, and borrowing can reduce typological diversity. For example, the Pacific nation of Tonga invaded a number of Pacific islands in the 18th century. Through language contact it left behind its stress system so that the number of languages with strictly right-aligned trochees (e.g. [ma(áma)], [pa(káta)]) increased relative to those with non-strictly right-aligned trochees (e.g. [(máa)ma], [pa(káta)]) (e.g. Pukapuka – Salisbury 1993). One would hope that such external effects could be minimized by taking a genetically diverse sample with a large number of languages. However, there is no guarantee this is the case. The world's languages are very closely related (most are Austronesian, Niger-Congo, and Indo-European), and there is no reason to think that their precursors represented a well distributed sampling of possible grammars.

Another important influence is diachronic change. Some languages are not possible to actuate or transmit for functional reasons. For example, no language has just one consonant and one vowel – such a language would be communicatively impossible for many reasons (e.g. memory limitations would prevent hearers from distinguishing a word with 12 syllables from one with 13, etc.). No language uses every symbol in the IPA chart – such a language would make grotesquely inefficient use of its segmental resources.

As Blevins (2004) and others have observed recently, pressures in diachronic change can also favor some types of language over others. Blevins observes that [g] is more perceptually confusable than [b] and [d]; there are also production and aerodynamic difficulties with [g] (Ferguson 1975, Ohala 1983; velars induce a strong build-up of intraoral pressure which inhibits voicing).

Consequently, if any voiced stop is to be altered through misperception (or to avoid excessive articulatory effort) by a learner, it's likely to be [g]. The typological result is that of the voiced stops, [g] is the most likely one to be missing in a language. So, there is no need to appeal to properties of the GIMF PhC to account for the lack of desirability of [g] in inventories.

It's clear that typological frequency can be influenced by factors other than the PhC. So what aspect of typological frequency is the PhC responsible for? Continuing with the focus on voiced stops, what is definitely relevant for the PhC is the fact that *all* imaginable voiced stop inventories exist (limiting to just [b d g]):

(5) *Voiced stop inventories (limited to [b d g])*

g	b	d	Languages
✓	✓	✓	Nhanda (Blevins 2001), Catalan (Wheeler 2005)
✓	✓		Tigak (Beaumont 1979)
✓		✓	Wapishana (Tracy 1972), Ayutla Mixtec (Pankratz and Pike 1967)
	✓	✓	Sioux Valley (Santee) (Shaw 1980:17), Xavanté Macro-Jê (Rodrigues 1999a)
✓			Makurap (Rodrigues 1999b:112ff)
	✓		Koasati (Kimball 1991)
		✓	Diyari (Austin 1981), Nambiquara (Kroeker 1972)
			(No voiced stops) Māori (Bauer 1993)

GIMF PhCs are responsible for phonotactic outputs of this kind (see section 3.1), so it must be the case that the PhC can *generate* each type of voiced stop inventory. The ability to generate attested languages is the minimum required of the PhC. Is it also the maximum required? Does the PhC have *anything* to do with inventory tendencies?

It is not obvious that it must. The GIMF PhC generates the phonological part of grammars, but does not inherently make any claim about the frequency of those grammars in languages. It is quite possible that the PhC has nothing at all to say about universal tendencies – pattern frequency is entirely determined by external factors and pressures in diachronic change, as outlined above.

Consequently, a challenge for those who wish to use universal tendencies to determine properties of the PhC is that all external factors and diachronic influences must be eliminated from the tendency under examination. This is an immensely difficult issue because it is hard to measure the potential influence of some of the external factors above – it requires knowing a great deal about a language's social history. There is also no guarantee that the languages attested in the world represent an even distribution of all possibly generable languages. The ancestors of current languages may have represented only a small and skewed range of possible languages, but their influence is still felt. Consequently, getting a typologically diverse sample of languages is no guarantee that the PhC's capabilities are represented in any reasonably distributed way.

However, Elliott Moreton's recent work (2007, this volume; Moreton and Thomas 2007) provides a potential way forward. Moreton constructed artificial languages with different phonological processes which have phonetic motivations of equal magnitude. He then determined how easy the two languages were to learn. People were able to learn (i.e. have judgments about) one language much more easily than the other. Since the languages had no 'ancestry', and their phonetic precursors were identical, the learning bias must be due to cognitive (i.e. PhC) effects. The general strategy employed by Moreton is what is needed to determine the cognitive contribution to universal tendencies – i.e. eliminate the effects of language change, performance, and non-phonological modules; whatever's left must be due to the PhC.

Unfortunately, there are uncertainties with the approach used by Moreton. Moreton (p.c.) observes that it is as yet unclear how lab-based learning of artificial languages relates to learning of natural languages. The learners are adults, not pre-critical period children, and unlike natural languages the artificial languages have no semantic content (like glossolalia – de Lacy to appear). The relation between the natural-language-learning process and the artificial-language-learning process may be a complex one. In any case, Moreton's approach is significant: it offers the promise of being able to eliminate external factors that cannot be easily (or ever) eliminated when dealing with actual language typology.

Moreton's work makes it even more imperative to eliminate all PhC-external influences on typological frequency before attempting to evaluate the PhC's role. A statement like '[t] is present in 98% of currently attested languages' is worthless in judging the PhC's capabilities unless the effects of PhC-external influences are taken into account. In this case, there are clear functional biases towards [t] involving ease of articulation and perceptibility. Once these PhC-external biases are considered, there may be no role for the PhC to play; it might even be possible that [t] is *under*represented!

By no means am I suggesting that the PhC could not be adapted to influence typological frequency. The PhC *could* be adapted to have influence on universal tendencies. Purely formal biases could be introduced into the learning process to favor the actuation or transmission of some grammars over others. Moreton

(2007) proposes a method of doing so (also see Coetzee 2002). What I am merely pointing out is that at the moment typological frequency is not straightforward evidence for the PhC's structure. How do we tell what the cognitive contribution to typological frequency is, given that external factors interfere so significantly? If Moreton's approach can be perfected, it will provide a way to tell. At the moment, however, it's impossible to be sure. For example, while functional factors make one expect fewer languages with [g] than with [b], once those factors are eliminated is [g] actually *more* frequent than one would expect, relative to [b]? If so, then there's room for a cognitive explanation; at the moment, we don't know whether there's anything for the PhC to account for.

Absolute universals are slightly easier to deal with. If a particular pattern is never present (or always present – e.g. CV syllables), it is possible in some cases to determine whether the PhC is responsible. If α never occurs but there are good 'diachronic' motivations for its occurrence (e.g. good reasons to actuate it), then the PhC must be responsible for its absence. This point has been argued for the unattested epenthetic [k] (de Lacy and Kingston 2006), lack of 'selective' coda stop devoicing (de Lacy 2006b), lack of stress systems with attraction to schwa (Kiparsky 2008), lack of word-final obstruent voicing (Kiparsky 2006), absence of stress systems attracted to low tone or higher vowels (de Lacy 2006b), and lack of systems in which vowel height is affected by consonant voicing (Moreton 2007). In all of these cases, there are good functional reasons for actuating such a process in diachronic change, yet they do not occur. In at least some of the cases, it has been shown that there was a series of diachronic changes that made actuation of the property almost inevitable, yet the property did not develop.

Of course, if there *is* a good diachronic reason why a phenomenon may never occur, it is then hard to argue that the PhC prevents it from happening. For example, Myers (2002) argues that clusters of a nasal stop followed by a voiceless consonant are never altered by epenthesis because there is no robust phonetic motivation that would cause the cluster to be misperceived with an intervening vowel, and thereby actuate a sound change. In this case, it is not easy to determine whether the PhC also actively prevents epenthesis as a response to NC̥ clusters. Of course, it is not necessarily the case that the PhC *allows* epenthesis in this situation (cf. Blevins 2004:237; de Lacy and Kingston 2006§4), but it is not obvious that the *lack* of NC̥ epenthesis is something the PhC's must account for.

To summarize, it is by no means straightforward to argue from typological frequency facts to a claim about the GIMF PhC. External factors and the learning process significantly obscure the cognitive contribution. In some cases with absolute universals, the external factors can be mitigated. With universal tendencies the challenge is much greater. Consequently, many arguments from typological frequency for the PhC must be treated with keen scepticism as they frequently fail to take external factors into account. The way forward is for every typological frequency fact to try to eliminate external influences, and see what is left for the PhC to account for. Moreton's work may open up a new way forward in this regard.

The discussion above has focused on typological frequency, but there are many other types of tendency. For example, 'corpus frequency' is about how frequently a particular sound pattern shows up in a selection of spontaneous speech; 'lexical frequency' is about sound patterns in a person's lexicon, and so on. Many of the same issues with typological frequency arise with these other types of frequency. Altshuler (2006) provides an example from Osage. Osage has lexical stress: some words have primary stress on the initial syllable while others have it on the pen-initial: e.g. [bága] 'burr' cf. [nã:xó] 'break by foot'. Altshuler (p.c.) reports that there are more initial-stressed words in the Osage lexicon than ones with peninitial stress. From this fact, a common conclusion would be that the words with peninitial stress (i.e. the less frequent ones) have underlying (lexical) stress. However, there is nothing inherent in GIMF theories of the PhC that leads to this conclusion. The PhC theories must account for both stress patterns: i.e. that words with initial stress and peninitial stress are generated. There are two ways to deal with this pattern (apart from lexically-specific constraint rankings): either default stress is initial and all peninitial stresses are lexical, or default stress is peninitial and all initial stresses are lexical (in OT the fact that default stress is initial does not prevent there from being lexical items with underlying stress on the initial vowel). As it turns out, Altshuler argues that other phonological processes show that default stress is peninitial, and so initial stress is marked lexically.

7   Evidence in GIMF theories of the PhC

In some analyses, a 'data-oriented' approach is taken: a speech sound phenomenon is identified and the PhC is assumed to be responsible, so a PhC theory is proposed. In many cases, the assumption is benign in that the PhC theory being used demonstrably (or at least reasonably) *is* responsible. However, a danger is that the analyst could be trying to use a GIMF PhC theory to account for data that some other module (or external effects) is entirely or partially responsible for. Another subtler problem is that the data-oriented approach guarantees that some PhC capabilities will be extremely hard – perhaps impossible – to discover because no analysis has either encountered the relevant phenomenon or on encountering it thought to ascribe it to the PhC.

Some examples of the dangers of the data-oriented approach to theory building are found in work on markedness. A frequent strategy since the Prague School (e.g. Trubetzkoy 1939) and Greenberg's typological work has been to compile cases that have similar tendencies in terms of sound patterns then provide a theory to account for them. For those whose aim is data collection – i.e. taxonomy (e.g. Greenberg 1966) – this approach makes perfect sense. However, for those interested in identifying data that can provide insight into the adequacy of a GIMF theory of the PhC, the data-oriented approach is fraught with danger: it employs an assumption that apparent similarities in phenomena necessarily have a single common source – i.e. the PhC.

7.1   Labial unmarkedness

For a recent example, I focus on labial unmarkedness: the idea that labials can be the least marked of all major Place of Articulation features, at least in some languages. This discussion here focuses on Hume (2003) (hereafter 'H'); the proposal is also advocated in Hume and Tserdanelis (2002). An important caveat: H's theoretical assumptions may not necessarily be set within GIMF. Hume's later and developing work (2004a, 2006) assumes a non-GIMF approach to phonology and phonetics. Consequently, the following should be read as the evaluation of a GIMF version of H, not necessarily of H itself.

What does it mean for a feature to be 'unmarked' in terms of the PhC? Work within Optimality Theory over the past several years has equated markedness with constraint violation profiles. So the claim that [labial] is the least marked PoA in a particular language is formalized by having a constraint C (or constraints) that favor [labial] over other PoA features, and no constraint that favors another PoA feature over [labial] outranks C. In more concrete terms, labial unmarkedness could be expressed as a ranking ‖ *dorsal, *coronal, *glottal » *labial ‖, ignoring other labial-favoring and -disfavoring constraints.

H presents an archetypal markedness argument for labial unmarkedness. A number of diagnostics that are traditionally accepted as giving insight into markedness are applied to the question of whether labial can ever be the least marked PoA in a language. Some of the diagnostics H discusses are summarized in (6). The references in square brackets are my own: they agree with the claim the particular phenomenon gives insight into markedness. H also discusses deletion and syllabification; for relevant evaluation see de Lacy (2006§8.2.3, 8.7.2).

(6) *Hume's (2003) diagnostics for labial unmarkedness*

    (a) Labials are *acoustically less salient* than other PoAs in English (Miller and
          Nicely 1955) and Japanese (Sekiyama and Tohkura 1991)
          [Battistella 1990, Jun 1995]

    (b) Labials are almost as *typologically frequent* as coronals (Maddieson 1992)
          [Greenberg 1966]

    (c) The labial [m] is *more frequent* in Sri Lankan Portuguese Creole words than [n]
          [Greenberg 1966]

    (d) The labial [m] can *appear in more environments* in Sri Lankan Portuguese
          Creole than [n]

    (e) Labial stops are *acquired* before other segments in language acquisition
          [Jakobson 1941, 1949]

    (f) Labials are the sole *undergoers of assimilation* in Sri Lankan Portuguese
          Creole
          [Kiparsky 1982, Mohanan 1993, Jun 1995, Rice 1999]

    (g) Labials can be the *sole segment in a language's coda*
          [Rice 1999]

For present purposes, the central question is whether any GIMF PhC theory is necessarily responsible for the phenomena in (6). There are a group of diagnostics which are simply outside the purview of a theory of Competence: (6a) refers to 'acoustic salience', a concept which is definable within the perceptual modules but not within the PhC; (6b,c,d) are statements about frequency whose relation to the PhC is currently unclear (see section 6); and (6e) is about order of language acquisition, which can be affected by Performance concerns (e.g. labial articulation is more visible than other articulations, so may be easier for the learner to identify).

There are some phenomena that the PhC *does* predict that it's responsible for – i.e. alternations and phonotactics. These include (6f) and (g). (6f) is about alternations: it refers to assimilation; if it is shown that the assimilation is not due to phonetic coarticulation then the phonological issue is valid. (6g) is about phonotactic distribution; if it is demonstrated that there is a language with a coda segment that is phonologically labial, the generalization is valid.

In short, worrying about what the theory predicts is relevant has cut down the potential evidence for labial unmarkedness from 7 to 2 items. One can now ask if (6f) and (g) are really evidence for labial unmarkedness (i.e. for a ranking like *dors, *cor, *glottal » *labial). This is the point at which specific theories of the PhC must be consulted (e.g. de Lacy 2006a§8.2.3). (6g) is unlikely to be a relevant indicator in any PhC theory because it is a phonotactic generalization and does not involve alternations – there is therefore no way of knowing what happens to other nasals, so /m/'s relation to /n/ and /ŋ/ is indeterminable. As an interesting aside, the PhC theory in de Lacy (2006a) predicts that the synchronic alternations of epenthesis and positional neutralization do provide evidence for markedness. However, no language has context-insensitive epenthesis of a labial (except perhaps for [w]), and none has neutralization (with alternations) to labials (de Lacy 2002, 2006a). de Lacy (2006a) also argues that (6f) is not relevant because assimilation is adversely affected by faithfulness.

The surprising result is that in the light of GIMF, the items in (6) are at best superficially related: the PhC is not responsible for all – or even most – of them. However, here is where the methodological danger is at its most extreme: the phenomena in (6) all superficially *look* like they have something in common: i.e. labial sounds and phonological symbols that are phonetically realized as labial are 'preferred' over other PoAs. The vague commonality could lead analysts to attempt to provide a theory to account for them all. However, this is no more legitimate than randomly choosing *any* subset of (6) and providing a theory for them: the selection of data is not driven by a theory, but rather by intuition.

This point may seem to be an overstated – even unfair – criticism. After all, doesn't the clustering of similar phenomena make it at least *likely* that there's a unified explanation behind them all? There is no doubt that intuitions and hunches like this play an important role in any scientific investigation. However, once intuited, they deserve careful scrutiny because they're not derived from the principles of one's theory. For (6), the phenomena look similar because the different modules that are responsible for them happen to agree on some things: labials happen to be easy to perceive, easy to produce, and stable in diachronic transmission. In contrast, I've argued elsewhere that they are *never* the least marked major place of articulation in any phonological component (de Lacy 2006a). So, the 'labial markedness facts' above illustrate well how non-PhC modules and external effects may favor a sound pattern while the PhC does not.

Tradition is also an acute problem for theories of markedness. Greenberg's oft-cited work on markedness had a taxonomic aim; there was no cognitive theory underlying the taxonomy, so language-related phenomena were not organized on a cognitive basis. However, Greenberg's work has often been adopted wholesale into generative theories with the unfortunate assumption that all his observations and taxonomies are relevant to the grammatical competence. However, from the point of view of GIMF, the phenomena used in Greenberg's work have a variety of sources: the PhC, the phonetic component, the perceptual system, and external influences. The same point has been made for many other traditional terms. Archangeli and Pulleyblank (2007) observe that the traditional term 'harmony' is unlikely to refer to any single formal phenomenon; also see Bye and de Lacy (2008) for 'fortition' and 'lenition', and Gussenhoven (2007) for 'lexical tone' and 'intonation'.

Of course, it's usual – perhaps inevitable – practice to collect data from a variety of phenomena and try and give a unified explanation for it. However, the examples above illustrate the sort of dangers that arise. Without an analysis of the resulting PhC theory and its related modules, there is an acute danger that too much is being asked of it.

A similar issue has arisen recently in terms of theories of free variation (see Anttila 2007 for an overview). Theories differ as to *how much* they should account for. Many recent free variation theories agree that the PhC should be able to generate the free variants of a wordform (Anttila 2007). Theories differ as to whether they should also account for the *relative* frequency of the wordforms (Coetzee 2004, 2006), or the *absolute* frequency of a wordform (as in Stochastic OT – Boersma 1998). Is a theory that provides a way for the PhC to accurately generate grammars in which one of two free variants occurs 92% of the time better than one that only accounts for the relative frequency of wordforms, which are in turn surely better than those theories that merely generate the free variants? By no means. To show that a theory that only generates free variants and says nothing about their relative or absolute frequency is clearly wrong, it is necessary to show that there is no other cognitive module or external influence that could also provide an account (e.g. could variability in phonetic coarticulation be responsible for some variation?, etc.). Coetzee (2006) puts this point succinctly: 'If grammar [i.e. the PhC] accounts perfectly for the observed frequencies, it actually accounts for more than its fair share of the variation. The close fit that is sometimes observed between observed and predicted frequencies in these models can then be a liability rather than an asset... The grammar is but one of the things that determine the frequency of variants.' In short, ignoring the limitations of the PhC and the responsibility of other modules can be a great liability – it can lead to proposing unnecessary PhC mechanisms.

7.2   Evaluation

A problem similar to the one encountered above arises in theory evaluation. It's a common technique to identify a phenomenon and see whether a particular PhC theory can account for it. Usually this technique is used to compare PhC theories with the point being that one PhC theory can account for the data while another cannot. Is this a valid evaluation method?

Yes, but only under two conditions. One is that it must be demonstrated that the GIMF PhC theory that is being evaluated predicts that it is responsible for the phenomenon, rather than some other module. If so, then the theory must be examined as to the 'extent' of its responsibility: i.e. are there any other cognitive modules or even external influences that could also account for/influence the data?

These points will be illustrated by examining a critique in Blevins (2006), a synopsis of Evolutionary Phonology (EP – Blevins 2004). EP is a theory of language transmissibility: i.e. why some sound patterns are more likely to survive inter-generational transmission intact, while others rarely survive. EP provides a way to think about typological frequency, such as why so few languages lack a [t] (i.e. because [t] is very stable in transmission as it is unlikely to be altered/misperceived), why final devoicing is common, and so on. Blevins (2006) contrasts EP with Optimality Theory, but the evaluation could equally be applied to any GIMF PhC theory.[11]

(7) *Evaluation of Optimality Theory*

> 'However, what Optimality theory fails to account for is why certain sound patterns, like final devoicing, are very common, while others, like final voicing, are rare. Factorial typologies, like generative feature/rule schemas, provide a vocabulary for describing sound patterns and alternations, but they offer little of predictive value when we ask why a particular sound pattern occurs where and when it does.' (Blevins 2006§3.1)

The critique in (7) is missing a link in its argumentation. It does not show that OT predicts that the PhC *should* be responsible for typological frequency generalizations like the ones cited. It also does not show why OT should account for diachronic actuation (i.e. why a 'sound pattern occurs where and when it does'). In short, it is not enough to criticize a theory by showing that it fails to account for a phenomenon P; it must be shown that the theory predicts that it is responsible for P.

On a related point, it is not an easy task to argue that if the PhC *could* account for a phenomenon P it must do so. It is necessary to ask how other modules or external effects influence P. If there is a residue of P that must be accounted for by the PhC, then an argument can be made for altering the PhC to account for that 'residue' of P. As a quick example, many languages have neutralization of nasal place of articulation to (what emerges as phonetically) velar or uvular. GIMF PhCs are capable of dealing with alternations, but *must* it be responsible in this particular instance? Certainly, no other module can effect unfaithful mappings from inputs to outputs, but is the PhC responsible for the output being velar or uvular? As discussed in section 4, the phonetic component can interpret [glottal] in nasals as velar/uvular, so in this case while the PhC module is responsible for an unfaithful input→output mapping (i.e. neutralization), it is not responsible for the interpretation of phonological [glottal] and velar/uvular. If one wishes to argue that the PhC is responsible for the velar/uvular articulation, it must be shown that the output sound is phonologically [dorsal], and is not a phonological [glottal] that has been interpreted as velar/uvular by the phonetic component (cf., e.g., Howe 2004). In an ideal world: it is not enough to show that the PhC *could* be responsible, it must be demonstrated that no other module or external influence could be responsible *and* that the PhC predicts that it is responsible. Of course, demonstrating responsibility is a big challenge, and may seem to simply lead to a lot of qualifications before anything is asserted about the PhC (or any other module). This is probably true (see below for an example), but it's not obvious that careful qualification of the validity of one's reasoning is a bad idea.

I mentioned at the beginning of this chapter that the usual data-oriented approach means that the analyst may miss phenomena that the theory is responsible for simply because he/she has not yet encountered them. Alan Prince (p.c.) observes that this problem arises clearly with 'data-driven typologies': when a slew of (intuitively) related data is collected, and then a theory is provided to account for it. The theory-builder might receive hints and inspiration from looking at the data, but without then examining the theory in its own right for what it predicts should exist, there is great danger. This danger is evident in some analyses that propose constraints. For example, Lombardi (2003) argues for a set of constraints to account for the set of epenthetic segments she identifies; however, when other constraints (i.e. the theory *in toto*) are considered, the number of epenthetic segments predicted increase significantly (de Lacy 2006a§7.2). As argued above, it is not enough to collect data, hope that it is all due to a single mechanism or module, and propose mechanisms to deal with it. It is necessary to examine a theory for what it predicts it is responsible for, and seek out the data it predicts should and should not exist.

I am concerned that the preceding discussion might be read as an exhortation to do nothing: if one is faced with a speech sound phenomenon that no theory accounts for, or that more than one module could account for, what can one do?

Luckily, this issue is becoming less and less of an issue as theories of the various GIMF modules and understanding of learnability, perception, and external effects has increased significantly. However, until a comprehensive Theory of Every(speech-sound)thing is developed, it will always be a potential problem for theories of the PhC.

A first step is to be sure that the theories of speech-related cognitive modules (i.e. phonetics, perceptual mechanisms, etc.) and related external effects have been adequately examined. Understanding of speech-related modules and mechanisms has advanced enough now that they can be seriously examined in relation to many speech sound phenomena. In some cases, inadequate examination has persisted until quite recently. Typological frequency is a relevant case: it has been common to ascribe the frequent appearance of [t] in languages as evidence for a PhC mechanism that favored coronals over other places of articulation. The contribution of its ease of actuation and transmission in diachronic change to understanding typological frequency has only recently received serious attention, even though the pressures involved have been understood for some time (e.g. Ohala 1983).

The step above would identify modules that could be responsible for the phenomenon and those that could not. It has been good practice to acknowledge such discoveries, as Chomsky and Halle (1968:11) do:

> Since other aspects of performance have not been systematically
> studied, our attempt to delimit the boundary of underlying competence
> by providing specific rules for vowel reduction must be taken as quite
> tentative. When a theory of performance ultimately emerges, we may find
> that some of the facts we are attempting to explain do not really belong to
> grammar but instead fall under the theory of performance.

This acknowledgement is different from acknowledging the possibility that *anything* could be responsible. Chomsky and Halle identify *particular* sources of potential explanation here (i.e. in slightly updated vocabulary – the phonological and phonetic modules). The GIMF theory will more often than not exclude some modules as sources of potential explanation. The value of giving disclaimers – i.e. of identifying potentially responsible modules as in the quote above – is that it provides an easy way to re-evaluate old proposals as theories progress, just as Chomsky and Halle's acknowledgement underscores the point that their theory does not *exclude* the possibility for a phonetic module to produce the effect observed as 'vowel reduction'. To put this point another way, proposing a PhC mechanism to deal with a particular phenomenon without acknowledging the role of other modules makes an implicit claim about responsibility: i.e. that no other module could have any effect (e.g. see Coetzee's critique of free variation theories above). For example, if a PhC theory accounts for typological frequency within a high degree of accuracy, it makes the implicit claim that external effects, learning, and diachronic change can have *no* (discernible) effect. If this is indeed the claim, then acknowledging it is crucial.

The final step is to modify the GIMF theory of the PhC. At this point, the GIMF theories need to be re-examined to see what they predict their modules are responsible for.

A final issue: are all GIMF theories of the PhC immune from criticism?[12] Are theories of the PhC free to pick and choose what they can handle easily and simply exclude any potential counterevidence as falling outside their domain of responsibility? By no means. The discussion in this chapter has simply enlarged the domain of consideration from the PhC alone to the GIMF modules that interact in the speech sound cognitive system. Every speech sound phenomenon must be accounted for somewhere within this system (or through external effects as discussed in section 6). If it can be demonstrated that the PhC is the only possible module that could be responsible for a particular phenomenon, then it must be responsible. If other modules necessarily influence a certain phenomenon, then the PhC is necessarily not the sole source of explanation for that phenomenon.

If one's current PhC theory cannot account for a particular phenomenon, then either the PhC theory must be changed or it must be shown that some other module is responsible. Given advances in the understanding of GIMF modules other than the PhC, this enlarged focus is a necessity.

So, suppose someone points out that a PhC theory cannot account for a phenomenon P. Either the theory is wrong, or another module is responsible for P. If it can be shown that no other module could be responsible, then the PhC theory is wrong. Otherwise the theory is only potentially wrong; there is then a burden to show that some non-PhC module is responsible for P.

8   Conclusion

This chapter has examined a well developed generative framework and asked what it predicts its phonological module is responsible for. It is clear that the phonotactics and alternations of a single grammar of a single speaker are crucial evidence for the structure of the PhC. However, even this 'best evidence' can be obscured by the effects of other cognitive modules such as the phonetic component and the paralinguistic module. 'External' factors (e.g. influences on learning, the physical structure of the articulatory tract) can further obscure the effect of the phonological output on speech sound.

Recent consideration of the role of non-phonological modules has cast doubt on the relevance of a variety of phenomena for phonology. This is clear for loanword analysis, where a great deal of adaptation may be due to perceptual mechanisms, and perhaps also for some aspects of language games, which often show symbol-manipulation that is not observed in natural language.

The influence of external factors means that it is extremely difficult to show that typological frequency necessarily must be explained by the PhC. Many sound-related phenomena were not discussed in detail here, but require the same sort of evaluation, including diachronic sound changes, speech sound regularities in first- and second-language acquisition and aphasia, lexical and corpus frequency, and so on.

In terms of theory-building and -evaluation, the implications identified here are that the technique of identifying a set of data and then finding a theory to account for it, or evaluating a theory with respect to it, poses dangers. In terms of evaluation, it is not adequate to identify data and evaluate whether a theory can or cannot account for it; it is essential to show that a theory predicts that it should account for a set of data before evaluating it with respect to that data. In GIMF, it is also necessary to show that no other module could be responsible for (aspects of) the data.

Methodologically, the implications place a huge demand on the GIMF PhC analyst. Every description must focus on an individual grammar of an individual speaker unless additional theories of inter-grammar interaction are made explicit; data must therefore be controlled for dialect and register. It is not enough to rely on phonetic realization to argue for a particular phonological structure/segment; the effect of the structure/segment on its environment should also be examined so as to eliminate the obscuring effects of phonetic interpretation. Nonetheless, I doubt that this chapter has added anything that is not already known to phonological analysts working within GIMF: many of the results are accepted as methodologically good principles of analysis anyway. However, the aim here has been to show *why* they are methodologically good principles – they are so because of what the theory claims it is responsible for.

Finally, the focus here has been on GIMF. The conclusions reached here may not have any relevance to non-GIMF theories; this is an issue that needs to be taken up with each separate framework.

Notes

1   My thanks to an anonymous reviewer, Steven Parker, and Bruce Tesar for detailed comments, to Daniel Altshuler, Lee Bickmore, Chuck Cairns, Marcel den Dikken, Janet Fodor, Catherine Kitto, and Robert Vago for their comments, and to audiences at CUNY, UPenn, Johns Hopkins, and Rutgers for their feedback on the talk version of this chapter. See http://ling.rutgers.edu/~delacy for materials relating to this chapter.

2   I will assume Optimality Theory's formalism here; the same arguments in general form apply to SPE or any other generative theory that fits the framework in section 2.

3   I am not criticizing the practices of descriptive linguistics here. Problems only arise when it is assumed that the concerns of descriptive linguistics (e.g. taxonomy) are the same as those of the PhC-linguist (i.e. cognition).

4   I am using the term 'alternation' here to refer to any pair of morphologically related forms that give insight into the input, as determined by a particular theory (e.g. OT, SPE). Alternations have been contrasted with 'automatic phonological processes', also called 'allophony'. In Prague School phonology, SPE, underspecification theory, and their successors, non-alternating allophony also gives insight into underlying forms through requirements of simplicity and economy of representation. This is not the case in OT: e.g. there is no reason to conclude that English [kʰæt] is underlying /kæt/ rather than /kʰæt/ (see Prince and Smolensky 1993/2004 on Lexicon Optimization). At this level of detail, individual GIMF PhC theories must be consulted for what they predict to be relevant in determining underlying forms. However, they all share enough properties so that useful generalizations can be made.

5   Could this assimilation be analyzed as having [ŋ] (not [N]), with /n/→ŋ/_? because [ŋ] is the closest thing to a glottal the language has? If so, one would expect a similar situation in some language involving stops: i.e. /at-ha/ → [akha] if [ʔ] was banned. I don't know of any case like this or of any analogous example involving major Place of Articulation. In all cases I have seen, place assimilation results in agreement of major place features.

6   An alternative analysis is that [N] nasalizes the preceding vowel, and nasal vowels must be [–high]. However, Ghini does not report any such nasalization, and vowels do not lower before other nasals (e.g. [ɪŋ.d͡ʒénw] 'naïve', *[ɪŋ.d͡ʒɛ́nw]).

7   I'm not implying that it *should* be the aim of a descriptive work to provide evidence for the PhC. It should be the job of a PhC-theorist to show that all descriptive work appealed to really provides evidence, as defined by the particular theory being used.

8   I have not discussed the effect of the physical structure of the articulatory apparatus and its obscuring influence on speech sound. For example, the articulators responsible for F_0 modulation cannot keep up with phonetic specifications in fast speech; consequently, F_0 may not reach the depths of a low target between two high targets (e.g. Myers 1999 and others). So, the physical apparatus may obscure phonological outputs.

9   Other early borrowings reflect the /p/→[b] borrowing: e.g. ['pakaɾu] 'broken' > NZE [ˌbʌɡəˈɹu], ['puːhoi] {placename} > early NZE ['bu(w)ai]. The influence of missionaries, orthography and an upsurge in public interest in Māori pronunciation has overwritten some of the early loans: e.g. [puːhoi] is now said ['pʰuhoi] (note the medial [h] in an unstressed syllable – a phonotactic impossibility in native NZE words). Standardization of loanwords by a panel of experts makes recent adaptations close to worthless as giving insight into cognitive processes.

10   As expected, all NZE word-initial phonological [b] (phonetic ‖p‖) were adopted as Māori [p] (phonetic ‖p‖), as both are voiceless unaspirated (e.g. [ˈpia] < NZE [ˈbiə] 'beer', [ˈpaki] < NZE [ˈbʌgi] 'buggy'). NZE [pʰ] (phonetic ‖pʰ‖) was borrowed as Māori [p] (phonetic ‖p‖), too.

11   I cite Blevins (2007) merely for convenience; I have seen and heard the view echoed many times that generative theories fail because they do not account for various types of frequency generalizations, in particular when comparing formalist/innatist with functionalist theories.

12   My thanks to an anonymous reviewer for raising this issue.

3 Underphonologization and modularity bias[1]

Elliott Moreton

The most straightforward theory of how phonologization interacts with Universal Grammar to determine typology is that UG defines the cognitively possible grammars ('hard' typology), while phonologization determines how frequent they are ('soft' typology). This paper argues instead that some soft typology has a cognitive source, and proposes a formal explanation. Phonological patterns relating tone to tone are shown to be more common than those relating tone to voicing and aspiration (20 families on 5 continents versus 8 families on 4 continents). This soft typological fact cannot be derived from differential robustness of the phonetic precursors, which have similar magnitude (survey of 26 studies of 17 languages). A learning algorithm is proposed in which the learner chooses between Optimality-Theoretic constraint sets based on how probable they make the training data ('Bayesian Constraint Addition'). This biases the learner towards phonologizing processes driven by 'modular' markedness constraints, i.e., ones that interact with few other constraints. Its application to the tone case is illustrated by simulation, and compared with alternatives.

1   Introduction

Why are some phonological patterns common, while others are rare or nonexistent? As languages are continually changing and mutating into new languages, it must be the case that some patterns are likelier than others to be innovated or retained in the face of language change. Discussion has centered on a single important typological fact: 'phonetic naturalness', the tendency for phonological patterns to look like exaggerated versions of subtle phonetic interactions. Two main factors have been identified as favoring the innovation and retention of 'natural' patterns.

One factor is *analytic bias* (Steriade, 2002; Wilson, 2003), cognitive propensities which are hypothesized to make some patterns difficult or impossible to acquire, even from perfect training data. Optimality Theory, and other work in the generative tradition of Universal Grammar, has focused almost exclusively on analytic bias as an explanation for typology in general, and for the 'naturalness' bias in particular (e.g., Chomsky and Halle, 1968: 4, 251, 296–297; McCarthy, 1988; Prince and Smolensky, 1993/2004; Archangeli and Pulleyblank, 1994: 391–395; Hayes et al., 2004).

The other factor is *phonetic precursor robustness*. The hypothesis is that phonological patterns are innovated when phonetic precursors, such as coarticulation, are mis- or re-interpreted as phonological ('phonologized', Hyman, 1976). If some precursors are less subtle or more frequent than others, we will see analogous biases in phonological typology, even if the cognitive system supporting phonology is relatively unrestricted as to the patterns it can acquire (e.g., Ohala 1990, 2005; Hale and Reiss 2000; Hume and Johnson 2001; Blevins 2004:19–21, 41, 281–285).

An adequate theory of typology will have to recognize diachronic filtering caused by asymmetries in both analytic bias and precursor robustness. The simplest theory of their interaction is that the analytic bias delimits the cognitively possible grammars ('hard' typology), while precursor robustness determines their frequency ('soft' typology) (Hyman, 2001; Myers, 2002). This paper argues that some soft typological facts are actually due to analytic bias. There are two sides to the argument, one empirical, one theoretical.

Empirically, it is shown that the typological frequency of a phonological pattern cannot in general be predicted from precursor robustness – that there exist cases of what I will call 'underphonologization', i.e., situations in which two phonetic patterns of similar magnitude correspond to phonological patterns of very different frequency (a phenomenon first noted by Hombert et al., 1979). Specifically, phonological interaction is more common between two tones than between a tone and consonant voicing, even though the phonetic precursors have acoustical effects of the same size. Hence, some soft phonological typology is not just the imprint of phonetic typology.

The theoretical goal is to show how analytic bias can account for the tone generalization. Since the precursors are equally robust, learners must tend to notice tone-tone covariation and overlook consonant-tone covariation. The hypothesis is that the noticing is done by an Optimality-Theoretic grammar, and that the grammar is better at noticing a pattern that is 'modular', in the sense that the markedness constraint driving it interacts with few other constraints. Modularity bias emerges when a learner chooses between possible constraint sets based on how probable they make the observed data.

The paper is organized as follows: Section 2 shows that phonological interactions between two tones outnumber those between a tone and the voicing, aspiration, or fortis-lenis status of a preceding consonant. Section 3 shows that their phonetic precursors are equally robust. Section 4 presents the learning algorithm and illustrates its application. Discussion is in Section 5.

2   Tone-tone patterns outnumber voice-tone patterns

The cases studied here are the phonologization of tone patterns from phonetic F_0 coarticulation, and that of consonant-tone patterns from the phonetic interaction between F_0 and the obstruent features of voicing, aspiration, and fortis/lenis status—collectively referred to here as 'Voicing'. These two cases were identified from a wider preliminary search for potential instances of underphonologization. A focused survey was then undertaken to test the hypothesis that dependencies between tone height in adjacent syllables (tone-tone patterns or 'TTP') occurred more frequently than dependencies between tone height and the Voicing of a preceding obstruent ('VTP').

Cases of TTP and VTP were located by searching (1) the collection of language-description books held by the University of North Carolina at Chapel Hill and written in Western European languages, (2) print and on-line journals focused on language description, such as *Oceanic Linguistics*, (3) general works on tonal phonology, such as Bradshaw (1999) and the XTONE Project (http: // xtone.linguistics.berkeley.edu), and (4) the World Wide Web, using the Google search engine to search on the string consisting of *tones* plus the name of each language family listed in *Ethnologue* (Gordon, 2005). The resulting sample was therefore unsystematic, but broad, and there is no *a priori* reason to expect it to be biased as between TTP and VTP. (It is certainly not exhaustive, but that is in the nature of samples.)

The following selection criteria were applied.

1. The search was restricted to patterns which resembled stylized versions of the phonetic effects of tone-tone and consonant-tone coarticulation, i.e., dependencies between the height of adjacent tones, and between the Voicing of an obstruent and the height of a following tone. This excluded, for example, the devoicing that occurs *after* a falling tone in Kiowa (Kiowa-Tanoan family; Watkins, 1984: 40–41).

2. The sample was limited to languages in which both TTP and VTP had the opportunity to occur, i.e., tone languages described as having a voicing, aspiration, or fortis-lenis contrast in obstruents. This eliminated a number of languages, mostly in South America and Oceania, which have tone-tone dependencies but only one series of oral stops or fricatives, such as Telefol (Trans-New Guinea; Healey, 1964). The same criterion excluded Yabem (Austronesian; Dempwolff, 1939 [2005]), in which voicing is entirely predictable from tone and hence is non-contrastive.

3. The Voicing contrast had to be free of confounding phonetic factors. For example, Kewa (Trans-New Guinea; Franklin, 1971) and Iau (Geelvink Bay; Bateman, 1990) have stop voicing which is inseparable from nasaliza-

tion, while Wuming Zhuang (Tai-Kadai; Snyder and Lu, 1997) confounds voicing with preglottalization.

4. As a way of insuring that patterns were phonological rather than phonetic, the pattern was required to neutralize a contrast found elsewhere in the language. Thus, static phonotactic patterns and morphophonemic alternations qualified, but allophonic alternations did not. The falling tone of the Yeneseian language Ket, for instance, begins perceptibly higher when the syllable onset contains a voiceless consonant (Werner, 1997: 21–23), but the pattern does not qualify because the difference is subphonemic.

5. Alternations limited to specific morphemes did not qualify; e.g., the tone assimilations and dissimilations in the noun-class suffixes of Heiltsuk (Wakashan; Kortlandt, 1975).

6. Languages in the survey must have been described from work with living speakers, rather than reconstructed, as reconstructions can be contaminated by theoretical bias (Maddieson, 1976).

Finally, the survey counted language families, defined as top-level categories in *Ethnologue* (Gordon, 2005), rather than individual languages, to prevent cases of common inheritance from being counted twice. The rationale is that, by counting the different language families in which living languages exhibit TTP and VTP, we are counting *surviving independent innovations* of the two pattern types, and thereby approximating an answer to the question of whether one of them is more likely to be innovated or retained. The results are given in (1) and (2). Italics indicate non-primary sources.

(1) Tone-tone patterns: 20 *Ethnologue* families, 5 continents.

    (a) *Africa*

        (i) *Afro-Asiatic*: Gashua Bade: H→L in L_|H, where | is a clitic- or PPh-boundary (Schuh, 2002). Voicing contrast.

        (ii) *Khoisan*: ‖Ani: Verbs have HH, HL, LH, but not LL (Vossen, 1997: 97–100). Voicing and aspiration contrasts.

        (iii) *Nilo-Saharan*: Zarma: In NP, VP, and between subject and verb, L→H in H_L. HLL is unattested in lexical items (Tersis, 1972: 25–27, 80–81). Voicing contrast.

        (iv) *Niger-Congo*: Tsonga: When an H-toned prefix is added to a word with only L tones, all tones but the last become H (Baumbach, 1987: 46–47). Voicing and aspiration contrast.

(b) *Asia*

(i) *Austro-Asiatic*: Bugan: Progressive tone assimilation across word boundaries (Li, 1996). Voicing and aspiration contrast.

(ii) *Indo-European*: Chakma: A suffix with H tone causes an H-toned monosyllabic root to become L-toned (Huziwara, 2003; p.c., 2005). Voicing contrast.

(iii) *Sino-Tibetan*: Many examples in Chinese languages (*Chen, 2000*). Voicing contrast.

(iv) *Hmong-Mien*: Hmong Daw: High-level and high-falling tones trigger neutralizing process in other tones. Many lexical exceptions (Downer, 1967). Aspiration contrast.

(v) *Tai-Kadai*: Lue: Low-falling tone becomes mid-level after mid-level tone (Hudak, 1996: xx–xxiii). Voicing and aspiration contrasts.

(c) *Central and North America*

(i) *Caddoan*: Caddo: High tone spreads left across an intervening sonorant (Chafe, 1976: 62; Melnar, 2004: 207). Voicing contrast.

(ii) *Huavean*: San Mateo Huave: Rightward spreading of H tone within phrases (Stairs Kreger and Scharfe de Stairs, 1981; *Noyer, 1991*). Voicing contrast.

(iii) *Iroquoian*: Oklahoma Cherokee: Except at the right edge of a word, H tones occur in pairs (H on V:, or LH on V: followed by HL on V:, or LH on V: followed by H on V), but odd numbers of L tones are possible (Wright, 1996). Voicing contrast.

(iv) *Kiowa-Tanoan*: Kiowa: H and HL lower to L following HL (Watkins, 1984: 30). Voicing and aspiration contrast.

(v) *Na-Dene*: Dakelh/Carrier: Disyllabic nouns can have LH, HL, or HH, but not *LL. (Gessner, 2003: 111–127). Aspiration contrast in stops, voicing contrast in fricatives.

(vi) *Oto-Manguean*: Zapotec: Three contrastive level tones, but disyllabic morphemes don't have final high tone. Some low tones become mid before mid and high tones, between and within words; some mid tones become high in a more complicated tonal context (Pike, 1948). Fortis-lenis contrast.

(d) *South America*

    (i) *Andoke*: Andoke: High tone becomes low between two high tones. This is explicitly characterized as neutralizing (Landaburu, 1979: 50). Voicing contrast.

    (ii) *Creole* (English-based): Saramaccan: In certain syntactic contexts, a series of Ls between two Hs becomes H, neutralizing the contrast between, e.g., /H LHL H/ and /H HLL H/. Some lexically marked Ls resist sandhi (Ham, 1999). Voicing contrast.

    (iii) *Tukanoan*: Barasana: Bimoraic morphemes can have H or HL tone pattern. An HL root or suffix suppresses H tone on a following suffix (Gomez-Imbert and Kenstowicz, 2000). Voicing contrast.

    (iv) *Witotoan*: Bora: Successive H tones are allowed, but adjacent L tones are possible only at the end of a tonal domain. The L tones of some suffixes can cause the deletion of root L tones (Weber and Thiesen, 2001). Fortis-lenis contrast.

(e) *Oceania*

    (i) *Sko*: Skou: A word-tone system with three tones, H, L, and HL. Overwriting in compounds: second element wins unless it is L (Donohue, 2003: 339–342). Voicing contrast restricted to p/b.

(2) Tone-voice and tone-aspiration patterns: 8 *Ethnologue* families, 4 continents.

(a) *Africa*

    (i) *Afro-Asiatic*: Lamang: Syllables beginning with voiced obstruents have L tones; other syllables contrast L and H (Wolff, 1983: 66–69).

    (ii) *Niger-Congo*: Ewe: H-tone nominal stem (CV) has voiceless obstruent or sonorant C. Non-H-tone nominal stem (CV) has voiced obstruent. This restriction does not apply to CV verbals (Ansre, 1961: 26–32, 36).

(b) *Asia*

    (i) *Austro-Asiatic*: Bolyu: High and low tone registers contrast after voiceless stops, and voiceless and aspirated stops contrast before low-register tones, but high-register tones do not occur after aspirated stops (Edmondson and Gregerson, 1996).

    (ii) *Hmong-Mien*: Highland Yao: Aspirated initials occur only with higher tones, while unaspirated ones occur with all tones (Downer, 1961).

(iii) *Sino-Tibetan*: Wuyi: Spreading of high-register tones causes devoicing of intervening voiced obstruents (*Yip, 1995: 485–487*).

(iv) *Tai-Kadai*: Mulao: Aspirated initial stops occur only with higher tones, while unaspirated ones occur with all tones (Wang and Zheng, 1993: 14).

(c) *North America*

(i) *Na-Dene*: Dakelh/Carrier. Disyllabic nouns have three tone patterns: LH, HL, and (less frequently) HH. Some trigger tone sandhi (lowering of surface H tone on a following word in certain syntactic contexts); these are analyzed as having an underlying H tone. HL sandhi triggers can have either a fortis or a lenis onset in the first syllable. LH sandhi triggers only have lenis onsets (Gessner, 2003: 202–217).

(d) *Oceania*

(i) *Sko*: Skou: H/L contrast neutralized to phonetic mid tone in syllables with voiced-obstruent onsets. Voicing contrast before falling tone (Donohue, 2003: 350–352).

The survey found TTP in 20 families, and VTP in 8. Since the number of relevant *Ethnologue* families is large (114 top-level categories for oral natural language, plus 30 language isolates and 78 'unclassified' languages), we can model the survey process as a detector counting events emitted at random by two different Poisson processes, and test whether their parameters differ by using Poisson regression.[2] Assuming independence between families, TTP occur significantly more often in this sample than VTP ($p = .029$), indicating that TTP are either innovated more often or lost less often. This finding is surprising in view of two other facts. First, phonologization can create TTP only in a tone language, whereas VTP can also arise in non-tonal languages undergoing tonogenesis (Svantesson, 1989). Second, VTP relate (phonetically-) adjacent elements in the same syllable, while TTP relate (phonetically-) distant elements in different syllables. This could work against TTP, since distant dependencies are in general less salient than close ones (Moreton and Amano, 1999; Newport and Aslin, 2004; Creel et al., 2004). The next section investigates whether the preponderance of TTP over VTP can be explained by differing precursor robustness.

3   Tone-tone and voice-tone precursors

The less phonetic interaction there is between X and Y, the fewer opportunities there are for the listener to misinterpret phonetic covariation as phonological, and hence the less often the X-Y pattern should become phonologized (Ohala, 1994; Kavitskaya, 2002: 123–133; Barnes, 2002: 151–159; Myers, 2002; Blevins, 2004: 108–109). If this explanation applies to the typology of tone patterns, it must be true that, across a wide range of languages, the phonetic precursor of tone-tone patterns must be substantially larger than that of the consonant-tone patterns. It is assumed here that the TTP precursor is F_0 coarticulation between tones, and that the VTP precursor is the perturbation of F_0 by the laryngeal features of the preceding consonant – a widespread but still incompletely understood process (for reviews, see Kingston and Diehl, 1994; Jansen, 2004: 52–53)

For the TTP precursor, the literature was searched for studies where vowel F_0 was measured in the context of neighboring tones and reported in physical units such as Hertz. Only tonal languages could be used, since no others could provide a neighboring tone. For each study, the context deemed likeliest to raise the target tone was designated the 'Raising' context. E.g., if the study measured a [33] target tone in the contexts [44_], [35_], and [21_], the [35_] context was the Raising context, because the author's description implied that this context had the highest F_0 adjacent to the target tone. A 'Lowering' context was likewise designated. The effect of context was defined to be the target F_0 in the Raising context, divided by that in the Lowering context. This procedure automatically normalizes for inter-speaker differences in F_0 range. If the study measured target F_0 at more than one point, the point closest to the context was used. If the study used multiple target tones, effects were computed for each target, then averaged together within each speaker, and then averaged across speakers. Studies which did not allow these computations were not used: those which did not provide comparable contexts (e.g., Odé, 2002), used non-physical units (e.g., Abramson, 1971), or reported only the difference between the two contexts (e.g., Gandour et al., 1994).

A similar procedure was followed for interaction between F_0 and Voicing of the preceding consonant. This phonetic effect can occur in both tonal and non-tonal languages, and can serve as a phonetic precursor of tone rules in both (Svantesson, 1989; Svantesson and House, 2006), so the survey included both tonal and non-tonal languages. The voiceless, aspirated, or fortis consonant was deemed the Raising context (Hombert et al., 1979). Two measurement points in the target tone were collected, when available: the onset of voicing, and a second point at least 40 ms later.

Figure 1 shows the results. Each plotting code represents one study. The vertical axis shows the effect. A value of 1.0 means the context had no effect; larger values mean that F_0 was higher in the Raising context.

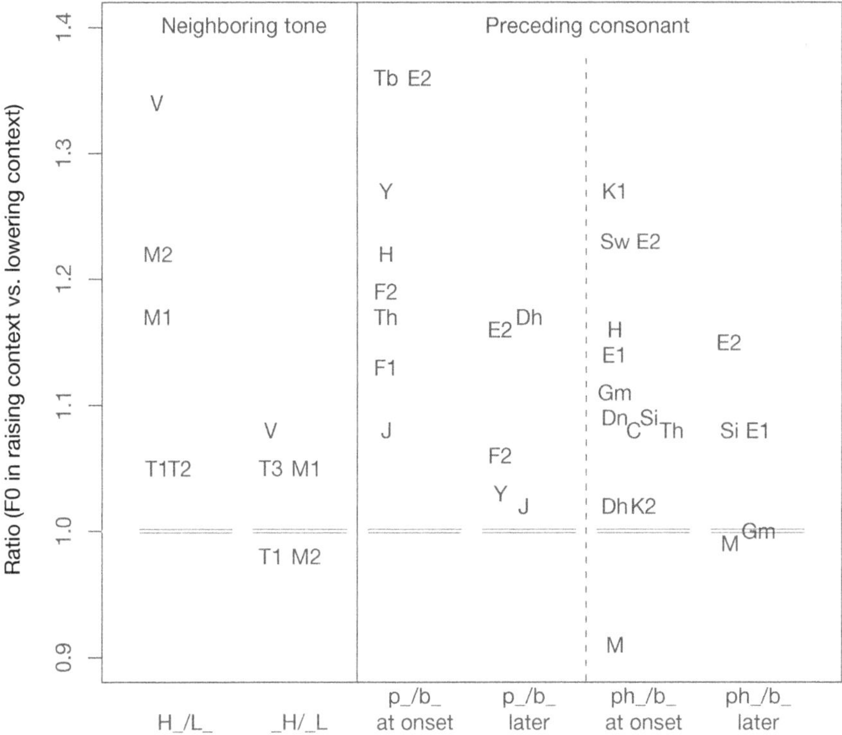

Figure 1: Effects of context on F_0
Each plotting code represents one study. 'H' and 'L' represent higher and lower tone contexts; 'ph', 'p', and 'b' represent voiceless aspirated, voiceless, and voiced consonantal contexts.

(3) Key to Figure 1.

    (a) Effect of tonal context (in tone letters; 1 is lowest, 5 highest):

        (M1) *Mandarin* 2 speakers. /pa pa pa/. All tones in 35_ vs. 0_, at onset: 1.17. In _35 vs. _0, at offset: 1.05 (Shen, 1990, Figure 1).

        (M2) *Mandarin* 8 speakers. /mama/ in frame sentence. 55_, 35_ vs. 21_, 51_: 1.22. _55, _51 vs. _35, _21: .98 (Xu 1997, Figures 4 and 7).

(T1)   *Taiwanese* 1 speaker. Unchecked tones in _55 vs. _21, at offset: 1.05. In 55_ vs. 21_, at onset: .98 (Chang, 1988, Tables 6 and 7).

(T2)   *Taiwanese* 6 speakers. /do/ in carrier sentence after context /si_/. Average of all tones in 55_ vs. 21_: 1.05 (Lin, 1988, Table 2.7).

(T3)   *Taiwanese* 4 speakers. /kau/ with 55, 33, 24, 21, or 51 in frame sentence. _55 vs. _21, at offset: 1.05 (Peng, 1997, Figures 2–5).

(V)   *Vietnamese* 1 speaker. Modal tones, high vs. low preceding context, onset: 1.34; following, offset: 1.08 (Han and Kim, 1974, Figure 2).

(b) Effects of preceding consonant voicing:

(Dh)   *Dakelh (Carrier)* 2 speakers; monosyllabic nouns (all H tone) in 4 different morphological and prosodic contexts; 204 items for Speaker A, 98 for Speaker C. Measured average F_0 for entire vowel. Initial voiceless fricatives vs. voiced fricatives: 1.17 (Gessner, 2003: 175–177).

(E2)   *English* 5 speakers, /sp st sk/ vs. /b d g/ in 'symmetrical CVC syllables' (e.g., /spip/, /bib/); frame sentence. Average across 5 vowels, measured at first glottal pulse after release: 1.36; measured at 5th glottal pulse (= about 40 ms): 1.16 (Ohde, 1984).

(F1)   *French.* 1 speaker. 4 CVC minimal pairs in frame sentence, /p t k/ vs. /b d g/. Average across three vowels (/i a u/) measured at voicing onset, ratio = 1.13 (Fischer-Jørgensen, 1972: 173–174).

(F2)   *French* 5 speakers, 18 CV syllables, /p t/ vs. /b d/. Average across 3 vowels (/i a u/), measured at voicing onset; ratio = 1.19 (Serniclaes, 1992, Table 2.5); measured 40 ms after release, 1.06 (Serniclaes, 1992, Figure 2.4).

(H)   *Hindi* 1 speaker; trisyllabic nonsense phrases /t^{h}ikiCi/ in isolation, where C is one of /p t/ vs. /b d/; likewise /CiCi/, /Ci/, /iCi/. Measured 3 pitch periods at release for /b d/, at voicing onset for /p t/: 1.22 (Kagaya and Hirose, 1975, Table II).

(J)   *Japanese* 3 speakers. Disyllables /kVCV/, where C was /p t k/ vs. /b d g/, identical vowels, initial accent; frame sentence. Average across /e a o/, measured at voicing onset: 1.08; at vowel steady-state: 1.02 (Kawahara, 2005, Figures 20 and 21).

(Tb) *Lhasa Tibetan* 1 speaker, /pa/ vs. /ba/, frame sentence. Measured at oral release; ratio = 1.36 (Kjellin, 1977). (Possibly phonological.)

(Th) *Thai* 1 speaker; CVV syllables, C was /p t/ vs. /b d/. Average across 4 tones (HIGH excluded because of gap in table) and 3 vowels, measured at onset: 1.17 (Gandour, 1974, Table III).

(Y) *Yoruba* 2 speakers, /k/ vs. /g/. Average across 3 tones (H/M/L), measured at voicing onset; ratio = 1.27; 40 ms later: 1.03 (Hombert et al., 1979, Figure 3).

(c) Effects of preceding consonant aspiration:

(C) *Cantonese* 3 speakers, /pʰei55/ vs. /pei55/, frame sentence. Measured at voicing onset: 1.08 (Zee, 1980, Table I).

(Dn) *Danish* 6 speakers; 2-syllable words in frame sentence; initial /ph th kh/ vs. /p t k/. Measured at start of following vowel: 1.09 (Jeel, 1975, Table I).

(Dh) *Dakelh (Carrier)* See (b) for circumstances. Initial voiceless aspirated vs. voiceless unaspirated: 1.02 (Gessner, 2003: 175–177).

(E1) *English* 5 speakers, /pʰ tʰ kʰ/ vs. /b d g/ before /i/; frame sentence. Measured at voicing onset: 1.14; 40 ms later: 1.08 (Hombert et al., 1979, Figure 1).

(E2) *English* 5 speakers, /ph th kh/ vs. /b d g/ in 'symmetrical CVC syllables' (e.g., /phip/, /bib/); frame sentence. Average across 5 vowels, measured at first glottal pulse after release: 1.23; at 5th glottal pulse (= about 40 ms): 1.15 (Ohde, 1984, Figure 5).

(Gm) *German* 1 speaker; /t/ vs. /d/ between stressed /ai/ and an unstressed schwa or syllabic /n/. Words read in isolation, in a monotone. Measured at release: 1.11; 'later': 1.00 (Kohler, 1982, Table I).

(H) *Hindi* See (b) for circumstances. Measured 3 pitch periods at release for /b d/, at voicing onset for /pʰ tʰ/: 1.16 (Kagaya and Hirose, 1975, Table II).

(K1) *Korean* 2 speakers; 1400 tokens. /pʰ tʰ kʰ/ vs. /p t k/. Measured at voice onset: 1.27 (Han and Weitzman, 1970, Table II).

(K2) *Korean* 2 speakers, nonsense words /CV/ and /VCV/. /pʰ tʰ kʰ/ vs. /p t k/. Measured near voice onset: 1.02 (Kagaya, 1974, Table II).

(M)   *Mandarin* 7 speakers, /tʰa/ vs. /ta/, with all four tones; /pha35/ sub-
       stituted for meaningless /tha35/. Real disyllabic words, with target
       in first or second syllable; all possible surface tone combinations.
       Measured at 1st glottal pulse, overall average: .91; 40 ms later: .99
       (Xu and Xu, 2003, Figure 7).

(Si)   *SiSwati* 4 speakers. 8 real-word CVX stimuli, /pʰ/ vs /ɓ/. Measured
       at vowel onset: 1.09; 40 ms later: 1.08 (Wright and Shryock, 1993,
       Figure 1).

(Sw)   *Swedish* 3 speakers; th_t vs. d_d, long vs. short low vowel; second
       consonant short iff vowel long; frame sentence. Mean of short and
       long vowels; measured at onset of vowel: 1.23 (Löfqvist, 1975,
       Table X).

(Th)   *Thai* See (b) for circumstances. /ph th/ vs. /b d/, measured at onset:
       1.08 (Gandour, 1974, Table III)

Pairwise comparisons between each tone condition and each of the consonant
conditions were carried out using a linear mixed-effects model with Language
as a random effect. Only two of the 8 comparisons reached significance at the
5% level (uncorrected for multiple comparisons). The effect of following tone
was significantly smaller than that of the voiced/unvoiced status of a preceding
obstruent measured at voicing onset (means of 1.20 and 1.03, respectively; p
= .0091), whereas the effect of preceding tone was significantly greater than
that of the aspirated/unaspirated status of a preceding obstruent measured at
voicing onset (means of 1.24 and 1.03; p = .0159).

The survey does not support the hypothesis that phonetic tone-tone interaction is greater than Voicing-tone interaction; rather, the two effects are of
about the same size. Thus, the different frequency of TTP and VTP cannot
be explained by differences in precursor robustness. When vowel height is
substituted for tone height, a similar picture emerges: height-height patterns
are more common than height-Voicing patterns, but vowel F1 is less affected
by other vowels than by consonant laryngeal features (Moreton 2007).

4   Modularity bias via Bayesian Constraint Addition

With precursor robustness eliminated as an explanation, it is the turn of analytic
bias. Why are Voicing-tone and Voicing-height patterns underphonologized
relative to tone-tone and height-height patterns? It will not do to say that the
latter are more 'salient' (e.g., because of their featural symmetry) and stop there,

for that merely restates the problem. The formal challenge lies in *deriving* the greater salience from constraint interaction.

This section presents an explicit model of how a Speaker's phonetic precursor becomes phonologized as an optional (probabilistic) phonological process by a misperceiving Learner. The key assumptions are that markedness constraints have to be added to the ranking before they can be ranked, and that the Learner decides whether to add or not based on which choice makes the observed training data more probable ('Bayesian Constraint Addition', BCA). It is shown that BCA automatically disfavors adding markedness constraints that interact with many other constraints. A consequence is that it discourages interaction between phonological subsystems, and thus favors tone-tone interactions over voice-tone interactions.

Background assumptions are stated in Section 4.1. The learning component is presented in Section 4.2, and a simulation of the tone facts in Section 4.3. Discussion of nonstandard assumptions, and predictions, is in Section 4.4. The model is meant only to show that 'soft' analytic bias, in which some patterns are discouraged but not forbidden, can be derived from constraint interaction, and so it has been made as simple as possible. Embedding the concept in a realistic model of acquisition and phonologization is left for future research.

4.1   Background assumptions

Underlying and surface representations are restricted to words of the form *maCaC*, where each vowel bears either H or L tone, each C is [b] or [p], and [m] is an irrelevant sonorant. Thus, every word has equal numbers of tones and obstruents, one tone-tone sequence, and one obstruent-tone sequence. The Speaker's lexicon contains all 16 possibilities, which are produced with equal frequency:

(4)   *mápáp, mápàp, màpáp, màpàp,*
     mápáb, mápàb, màpáb, màpàb,
     mábáp, mábàp, màbáp, màbàp,
     mábáb, mábàb, màbáb, màbàb,

The Speaker's grammar is fully faithful, so that the 16 forms in (4) occur with equal frequency as phonological surface representations. These undergo some phonetically-biased coarticulatory distortion in transmission to the Learner. The Learner is able to compensate for (i.e., undo) most of it, but some coarticulated tokens are misperceived as different from the Speaker's phonological surface representation.

As in Prince and Tesar (1999), the Learner is assumed to be acquiring only surface distributions, not yet a lexicon. Ignorant of the actual contents of the lexicon, this Learner (unlike Prince and Tesar's) assumes correctly that all 16 possible inputs are equally likely, and that any observed inequality among surface forms is due to unfaithful mapping caused by ranked constraints.

We will compare two different cases of phonologization. In the 'LH condition', tonal coarticulation becomes phonologized as rightward L-tone spreading. In the 'bH condition', the phonetic lowering effect of a voiced obstruent becomes a process lowering /H/ after /b/. Both tone and voice are assumed to be privative (H and [voice]). The analysis of vowel harmony proposed by Pulleyblank (2004) is adapted to tone spreading:

(5) Constraints for tone spreading (after Pulleyblank, 2004).

    (a) Max-H: 'Don't delete an H tone.' Give one mark for each underlyingly H-toned vowel with no H-toned surface correspondent.

    (b) *LH: 'No LH tone sequences.' Give one mark for each H tone in the next syllable following an L tone.

These constraints allow only two grammars, distinguished by their effect on /LH/:

(6) (a) Faithful realization

/LH/		Max-H	*LH
☞	LH		*
	LL	*!	

(7) Righward L-tone spreading

b. /LH/		*LH	Max-H
	LH	*!	
☞	LL		*

Analogous constraints are assumed to be involved in lowering H after /b/:

(8) Additional constraints for post-/b/ lowering

    (a) Max-Voice: 'Don't delete a [voice] feature'. * = underlying voiced segment without a voiced surface correspondent.

    (b) *bH: 'No bH sequences.' * = a H tone following a voiced obstruent

Since both Max-Voice and Max-H are relevant, there are three possible grammars, with different effects on /bH/:

(9) (a) Faithful realization

/bH/		Max-Voice	Max-H	*bH
☞	bH			*
	bL		*!	
	pH	*!		

(b) Post-/b/ lowering

/bH/		*bH	Max-Voice	Max-H
	bH	*!		
☞	bL			*
	pH		*!	

(c) Pre-/H/ devoicing

/bH/		*bH	Max-H	Max-Voice
	bH	*!		
	bL		*!	
☞	pH			*

Finally, in order to allow a probabilistic phonetic precursor to be phonologized as a probabilistic phonological process, constraint rankings are continuous. The rank of a constraint specifies the mean position where it will be observed when the grammar is consulted in any particular case (Nagy and Reynolds, 1997; Boersma, 1998: 269–273; Boersma and Hayes, 2001).

4.2 Bayesian Constraint Addition

Crucially, *LH and *bH are off-stage in the Learner's initial state, and must be added to the set of ranked constraints in response to the corpus of perceived training data D. The Learner compares two hypotheses. H_0 is that the constraint set is what the Learner previously thought it was, while H_1 is that it also contains the new constraint. To decide between the two hypotheses, the Learner compares how probable each one is given D. Bayes's Rule prescribes how to do this (MacKay, 2003: 48–57):

$$(10)\quad \frac{P(H_1 \mid D)}{P(H_0 \mid D)} = \frac{P(D \mid H_1)P(H_1)/P(D)}{P(D \mid H_0)P(H_0)/P(D)}$$

$$= \frac{P(D \mid H_1)P(H_1)}{P(D \mid H_0)P(H_0)}$$

Before hearing the data, the Learner estimates that H_0 is true with probability $P(H_0)$, and H_1 with probability $P(H_1)$. The ratio of these probabilities, $P(H_1)/P(H_0)$, reflects the Learner's prior bias towards one or the other hypothesis. To keep things simple, the Learner is assumed to be initially unbiased, so that the ratio is 1. When the data arrives, the original estimate is multiplied by $P(D \mid H_1)/P(D \mid H_0)$, the ratio of how likely D is if H_1 is true to how likely D is if H_0 is true. The result is the Learner's new estimate of the relative probability of H_0 and H_1. ($P(D)$, the Learner's prior estimate of how probable the data itself is, cancels out in the numerator and denominator.)

Now suppose D exhibits a pattern that is inconsistent with any ranking under H_0, but consistent with some rankings under H_1. The Learner has to choose between two improbable coincidences. Is the Speaker's constraint set the one described by H_0, and the 'pattern' merely a statistical fluke? Or is the constraint set the one described by H_1, whose constraints just happen to be ranked exactly right? The key point is: The plausibility of H_1 as an explanation for the pattern depends on how many *other* patterns H_1 allows. If the observed pattern is a one-in-ten coincidence under H_1, then H_1 is a better alternative to H_0 than if the pattern is only a one-in-ten-thousand coincidence. The more distinct patterns H_1 allows, the smaller $P(D \mid H_1)$, and hence, by (10), the smaller $P(H_1 \mid D)$, i.e., the less credence the Learner places in H_1. This effect has been termed the 'Bayesian Occam's Razor', since it penalizes less-restrictive hypotheses (MacKay, 2003: 343ff.).

The connection to modularity is that modular constraint sets make for more-restrictive hypotheses. Suppose a (discretely-ranked) constraint set contains two types of constraint, m involving only tone, and n involving only segments. The set is modular: Rankings within each subsystem matter (they potentially change the underlying-to-surface mapping), but rankings of tonal constraints with respect to segmental constraints do not. There are *(m+n)!* ways to rank the entire set, but actually there are at most *m!n!* distinct grammars. If a new tonal constraint is added, the number of potentially distinct grammars increases slightly, to at most *(m+1)!n!*. But if a new tone-segment constraint is added, the wall of separation between the modules collapses, and the number of potentially distinct grammars can soar above *(m+n)!*.[3] Adding a non-modular constraint causes a steeper increase in the number of different grammars, reduces $P(D \mid H_1)$ more, and so incurs a stronger penalty from the Razor.

Continuous ranking amplifies this effect. For the Learner to recognize whether some H tones are turning into L, what matters is the perceived proportion of four word types. In the LH condition, those types are HH, HL, LH, and LL; in the bH condition, they are pH, pL, bH, and bL. If r is the rate at which the Speaker's intended productions are misperceived, then the frequencies of these types in D are as shown in the 'Perceived' column of Table 1:

Table 1 Corpus frequencies, actual and predicted. See text below for explanation of *p*, *q*, and *s*.

| | | *D* | Predicted by Learner's hypotheses | | |
| | | | H_0:
No change | H_1:
New constraint needed | |
Word type	Intended by Speaker	Perceived by Learner		LH condition	bH condition
HH, pH	$\dfrac{1}{4}$	$\dfrac{1}{4}$	$\dfrac{1}{4}$	$\dfrac{1}{4}$	$\dfrac{1}{4}(1+s_{a,\beta})$
HL, pL	$\dfrac{1}{4}$	$\dfrac{1}{4}$	$\dfrac{1}{4}$	$\dfrac{1}{4}$	$\dfrac{1}{4}$
LH, bH	$\dfrac{1}{4}$	$\dfrac{1}{4}(1-r)$	$\dfrac{1}{4}$	$\dfrac{1}{4}(1-p_\alpha)$	$\dfrac{1}{4}(1-q_{\alpha,\beta}-s_{\alpha,\beta})$
LL, bL	$\dfrac{1}{4}$	$\dfrac{1}{4}(1+r)$	$\dfrac{1}{4}$	$\dfrac{1}{4}(1+p_\alpha)$	$\dfrac{1}{4}(1+q_{\alpha,\beta})$

In either condition, the Learner has two hypotheses. H_0 is that the grammar contains only MAX-VOICE and MAX-H. It predicts that the four categories occur with frequency 1/4. The more the observed deviation from equal proportions in D, the more improbable is H_0. H_1 differs depending on condition.

In the LH condition, H_1 says that the constraint set is {MAX-VOICE, MAX-H, *LH}. Under H_1(LH) the grammar has one genuinely adjustable parameter, α, the ranking distance between the *LH and MAX-H. Changing α changes p_α = P(*LH >> MAX-H | H_1(LH), α). The distance β between *LH and MAX-VOICE can also be adjusted, but that has no effect on the output of the grammar, because the two constraints do not interact. By setting α so that p_α = r, the H_1(LH) grammar can be made to match D, while the H_0(LH) grammar cannot. This is shown in Figure 2.

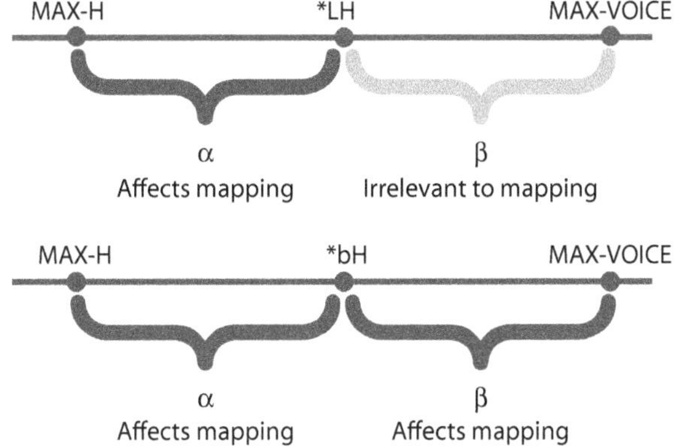

Figure 2: H_1(LH) and H_1(bH) nominally have two adjustable ranking parameters. However, adjusting β in H_1(LH) has no effect on the input-output map.

In the bH condition, H_1 says that the constraint set is {MAX-VOICE, MAX-H, *bH}. Unlike H_1(LH), H_1(bH) gives the grammar two genuinely adjustable parameters. Both α and β matter, since *bH interacts with both MAX-H and MAX-VOICE. The extra degree of freedom allows for more distributions among the four categories than in the LH condition, as shown in the last column of Table 1. Matching the Speaker's data requires setting α and β so that $q_{\alpha,\beta} = r$ and $s_{\alpha,\beta} = 0$. Again, H_0(bH) cannot be adjusted to fit the data.

In both conditions, the Learner is confronted with the same distribution. The data slightly mismatches H_0, to the same degree in the LH and bH conditions. H_1(LH) and H_1(bH) can accommodate the data, but H_1(bH) needs finer tuning to do so, as two parameters have to be set properly rather than just one. The data is therefore deemed less likely (more of a coincidence) by H_1(bH) than by H_1(LH). As a result, H_1(LH) is a better alternative to H_0(LH) than H_1(bH) is to H_0(bH).

4.3   Simulation

To make the discussion entirely concrete, let r be set arbitrarily to $1/15$. We need to specify how the probabilities p, q, and s are related to the ranking distances α and β. Following Boersma (1998; Boersma and Hayes, 2001), each time the grammar is consulted, normally-distributed noise is added to each constraint's fixed position to determine its observed position. The observed distance between two constraints is thus the difference between two independent normal distributions with equal variance, and hence is itself normally distributed. For H_1, then, we can adopt a scale on which the markedness constraint is always observed at 0, while the observed positions of MAX-H and MAX-VOICE are normally distributed with means of α and β and standard deviation of 1.[4] (For H_0, the rankings are irrelevant.) The Learner initially assumes that all possible rankings are equally probable (i.e., a uniform prior distribution for α and β, reflecting the Learner's complete ignorance).

For any corpus D, the probability of D under a hypothesis is just the product of the probabilities assigned to each word of D by that hypothesis. Table 1 shows that, for H_0(LH) or H_0(bH), the probability is always $1/4$. Hence, if there are N tokens in D, then

$$(11) \quad P(D \mid H_0(LH)) = P(D \mid H_0(bH)) = \left(\frac{1}{4}\right)^N$$

In the LH condition, let n_{HH}, n_{HL}, n_{LH} and n_{LL} be the number of words in each category in D. Then for a given α,

(12) $\quad P(D \mid H_1(LH),\alpha) = \left(\dfrac{1}{4}\right)^{n_{HH}} \left(\dfrac{1}{4}\right)^{n_{HL}} \left(\dfrac{1}{4}(1-p_\alpha)\right)^{n_{LH}} \left(\dfrac{1}{4}(1+p_\alpha)\right)^{n_{LL}}$

The probability of D under $H_1(LH)$ is obtained by integrating (12), times the probability density at each α, over all α. Likewise, in the bH condition, for given α and β,

(13) $\quad P(D \mid H_1(bH),\alpha,\beta) = \left(\dfrac{1}{4}(1+s_{\alpha,\beta})\right)^{n_{pH}} \left(\dfrac{1}{4}\right)^{n_{pL}} \left(\dfrac{1}{4}(1-q_{\alpha,\beta}-s_{\alpha,\beta})\right)^{n_{bH}} \left(\dfrac{1}{4}(1+q_{\alpha,\beta})\right)^{n_{bL}}$

with $P(D \mid H_0(bH))$ obtained by integrating (13), times the probability density at each $(\alpha, \beta,)$, over all α and β. For practical reasons, the integrals were approximated by discretizing α and β as a grid of points spaced 0.1 units apart in the region $[-4, 4] \times [-4, 4]$. These limits allow p_α, $q_{\alpha,\beta}$, and $s_{\alpha,\beta}$ to vary from $< .0001$ to $> .9999$. Random corpora D of size N ranging from 0 to 3000 were simulated using R (R Development Core Team, 2005). The resulting likelihood ratios were logit-transformed and plotted to produce Figure 3.

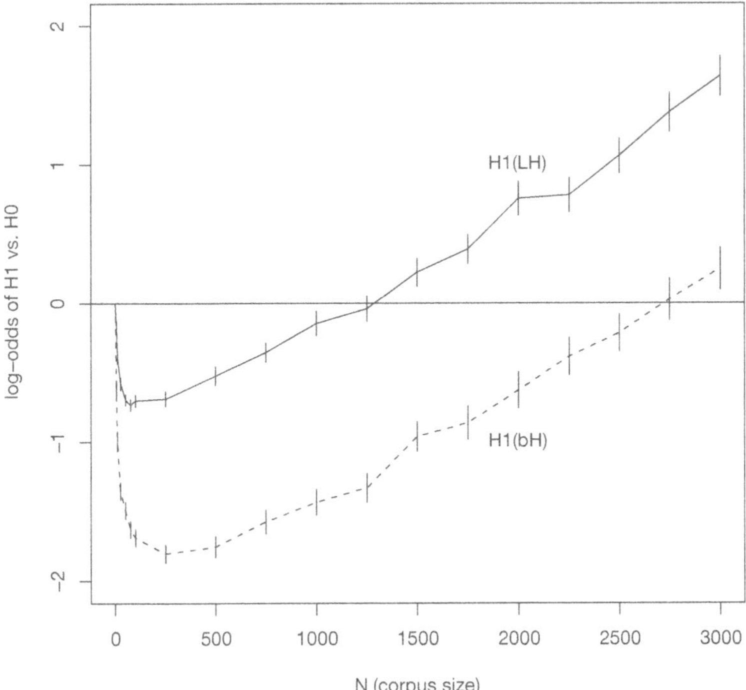

Figure 3: Simulation results. Solid curve: LH. Dashed curve: bH. Log-odds of 0 means that the Learner assigns equal probability to H_0 and H_1. Positive values favor H_1. Bars show 95% t confidence intervals around mean of 1000 runs of the simulation.

The solid curve shows the LH condition. Initially, the log-odds is near 0, because with little data the Learner can't tell whether D is more consistent with either hypothesis. (We can't tell whether a coin is unfair by tossing it three times.) As more data arrives, it becomes clear that only a very specific tuning of $H_1(LH)$ can match it, and the Bayesian Occam's Razor begins to cut against $H_1(LH)$. The log-odds drops rapidly. But as even more data arrives, and the Learner gets better estimates of the frequencies of the four word categories, it becomes clear that, while the data is consistent only with a very specific tuning of $H_1(LH)$, it is not consistent at all with $H_0(LH)$. The log-odds begins to rise. After about 1250 words, the Learner is again equipoised between $H_0(LH)$ and $H_1(LH)$. Thereafter, the preference for $H_1(LH)$ increases without bound.

In the bH condition (dashed curve), H_0 is the same. However, $H_1(bH)$ requires an even more specific tuning to match the data, since both α *and* β have to be just right. This incurs a greater penalty from the Razor. Any criterion set by the Learner for accepting a new constraint will therefore be met sooner in the LH than the bH condition.

This concludes the demonstration that BCA can delay phonologization of a non-modular pattern. In a human learner, the delay would increase the chance that the end of acquisition would intercept phonologization, and so would reduce the typological frequency of the pattern.

4.4   Comments on the model

Despite the term 'constraint addition', it is enough that certain constraints initially be unable to dominate any other constraint, and remain so until the learner explicitly grants permission. These constraints may begin in a separate stratum at the bottom. Alternatively, they may be created by local conjunction (Smolensky, 1996), inductive grounding (Hayes, 1999), or constraint schemata (Smith, 2004), and literally added to the constraint set.

Continuous ranking is not in principle necessary, but it provides two crucial services which are otherwise hard to come by. (1) For BCA to be effective, there has to be a *large* difference between the number of grammars available under $H_1(LH)$ and $H_1(bH)$. Their discrete versions afford just 2 and 3 grammars respectively, but this difference is greatly amplified by gradience. Larger constraint sets may have a similar effect; however, early trials with four and five discretely-ranked constraints have not been encouraging. (2) A subtle phonetic effect that turns *some* LH's into LL's cannot fool a discrete learner into thinking that the correct grammar bans *all* LH's. This is a problem that has to be faced by any theory of misperceptive sound change: Misperception affects one utterance at a time, while sound change affects the whole grammar.

Continuous rankings solve the problem by allowing the first generation to innovate an optional phonological process rather than leap directly to a categorical one. If we suppose that this generation also retains the phonetic precursor, then their speech contains even fewer surface LH's than their parents', since some are changed to LL by the phonology and others by the phonetics. The second generation, learning from this input, will add *LH earlier and rank it higher than the first. Repeated cycles will lead to a near-categorical grammar with high-ranked *LH.[5]

Modularity bias overlaps with the *SPE* evaluation metric (bias against multiple features) and Feature Geometry (bias against cross-tier interaction), but differs empirically from both. *SPE* counts features without regard to their content, so that a rule involving [+nasal] and [–nasal] is just as costly as one involving [+nasal] and [–high] (Chomsky and Halle, 1968: 334–335). Feature Geometry treats all single operations alike, so that a rule spreading [+anterior] is just as complex as one spreading [C-place] (Clements and Hume, 1995: 250). Modularity bias would favor the first of each pair of examples.

The BCA account of modularity bias predicts, uniquely, that the *second* constraint linking domains X and Y is easier to acquire than the first, because the damage is already done. It also predicts rapid acquisition of constraints linking phonology with morphology, since there are no purely morphological constraints for them to interact with. Indeed, morphological conditioning seems common, especially in the complex or unnatural processes most plausibly attributed to language-particular induced constraints (see, e.g., the discussion of Lardil Free-V in Prince and Smolensky, 1993/2004). BCA may also apply to constraints phonologized from the learner's own phonetics (Hayes, 1999, Smith, 2004). Macken (1995: 690–691) notes that child phonology abounds in consonant- and vowel-harmony processes, but that 'none of the primary rules of acquisition and few of the other attested rules in the first year or two (ages one to three) show interactions between consonants and vowels.'

5   General discussion

The hypothesis that causes and effects line up in a simple way, pairing hard typology with Universal Grammar and soft typology with other factors affecting language change (Hyman, 2001; see also Myers, 2002) is probably too strong. We have seen that at least one soft generalization, the preponderance of tone-tone over consonant-tone patterns, cannot be explained by the likeliest diachronic factor, precursor robustness. The same holds for height-height and height-voice interactions. These generalizations, and others involving modularity bias, can be derived from constraint interaction if the learner chooses among constraint sets based on how probable they make the observed data. What are the alternatives?

Anttila (1995; Anttila and Cho, 2004) has used *combinatorial bias,* which occurs when the mapping /A/→[B] is generated by more rankings than /A/→[C]. If all rankings are equally probable, then /A/→[B] is predicted to occur more often than /A/→[C]. Originally applied to within-language variation, this idea has been extended to typology by Coetzee (2002). Here, though, it leads in the wrong direction. A language lacking [LH] must rank *LH over MAX-H. A language lacking [bH] needs only to have *bH dominate *at least one* of MAX-H and MAX-VOICE. Hence [bH]-less languages should outnumber [LH]-less ones. Generally, the more features appear in a markedness constraint, the more ways there are to satisfy it. Combinatorial bias thus favors processes triggered by featurally *complex* markedness constraints.

Another possibility is *initial-state bias.* Many OT learning algorithms require that markedness initially dominate faithfulness (Gnanadesikan, 1995; Smolensky, 1996). This creates a bias towards grammars which allow fewer surface forms, but not towards modular processes. The problem is the same as before: To block the effect of *LH, *LH must be demoted below MAX-H. To block that of *bH, *bH must be demoted below *both* MAX-H *and* MAX-VOICE. Less-modular markedness constraints are harder to deactivate, since deactivating them requires more changes relative to the initial state. If distance from the initial state is what determines typological frequency, then the initial M » F hypothesis is wrong, and some constraints are initially either bottom-ranked or outside the ranking entirely (just as in BCA).

BCA is thus the only proposal on offer that derives modularity bias (or featural-simplicity bias) from constraint interaction. A still-viable alternative explanation of the tone and height facts is that non-grammatical perceptual effects may skew the training data before it reaches the learner's pattern-finding mechanisms. For example, compensation for coarticulation may affect a shorter time window than coarticulation itself does, so that compensation fails more often for TT than CT interactions. This may be true *instead of* or *in addition to* analytic bias. The issue will only be settled in the lab. For instance, the existence of an analytic bias in favor of modularity is supported by the finding that English-speaking adults trained on non-coarticulated $C_1V_1C_2V_2$ stimuli in an artificial-language paradigm learned to recognize height agreement between V_1 and V_2, and voice agreement between C_1 and C_2, better than height-voice agreement between V_1 and C_2 (Moreton, 2007).

Cognition and phonetics interact to determine typology in ways more complicated (and interesting) than has been generally acknowledged. Further progress will require a better quantitative understanding of the typology of phonetic precursors, and of the differential receptiveness of learners to different patterns.

Notes

1   Several people have contributed to this paper, including Andries Coetzee, Paul de Lacy, Shigeto Kawahara, Paul Kiparsky, John McCarthy, Steve Parker, Joe Pater, Jennifer L. Smith, Paul Smolensky, and Anne-Michelle Tessier. It also owes much to Adam Albright and Josh Tenenbaum's 2005 Linguistic Institute class. Thanks are due to Chris Wiesen for statistical advice. Statistics, graphs, and simulations used R 2.2.1 (R Development Core Team 2005). Errors or omissions are solely the author's. This version is current as of January 26, 2007.

2   I am indebted for this suggestion to Chris Wiesen of the Odum Institute for Research in Social Science at the University of North Carolina at Chapel Hill.

3   These worst-case scenarios require artificial construction. Linguistically-plausible constraints would probably lead to much smaller numbers in all three instances.

4   This is an approximation, as it ignores the covariance between the two ranking distances MAX-H to *bH, and MAX-VOICE to *bH. For example, if all three constraints are ranked equally, the true P(MAX-H $\gg$ MAX-VOICE $\gg$ *bH) is 1/6, as all 6 rankings are equally probable, but the approximation makes it 1/8 (= P(MAX-H $\gg$*bH) P(MAX-VOICE $\gg$*bH) P(MAX-H $\gg$ MAX-VOICE | MAX-H, MAX-VOICE $\gg$*bH)). Without this approximation, however, the simulation would run 81 times slower.

5   The prediction is that a new phonological process should grow gradually out of its phonetic precursor, rather than appearing all at once. Such a pattern has been observed (Moreton and Thomas 2007), but could also be due to growth in the precursor itself.

4 Contrast, comparison sets, and the perceptual space[1]

Máire Ní Chiosáin and Jaye Padgett

In recent years a number of researchers have argued that, in order to adequately explain contrast and its effects, phonology must be systemic: evaluation of a form cannot occur in isolation from unrelated contrasting forms, but must take such forms – what we call a 'comparison set' – into account. This presents a formal and empirical challenge for systemic approaches. This paper explores the comparison set within the general approach of dispersion theory, focusing on two matters: the 'problem of infinity' and idealization. A further challenge for the theory, though one shared by many non-systemic approaches too, involves substantiating claims about perceptual distance that underpin the approach. Our discussion of the latter issue focuses on secondary palatalization contrasts in onset versus coda position, with perceptual data from Irish. Our overall goal in this paper is to clarify the nature of these challenges and to outline our own approach to them.

1   Introduction

In the past ten years a number of works have pursued a *systemic* approach to contrast in phonology. According to this approach, the goodness of a form must be judged with respect to other forms with which it contrasts (Flemming 1995/2002, Bradley 2001, Ní Chiosáin and Padgett 2001, Łubowicz 2003, Padgett 2003a,b, to appear a, Sanders 2003, Flemming 2004, Bradley and Delforge 2006, Ito and Mester 2007c, Padgett and Zygis 2007). Because it is inspired in part by the phonetic work of Lindblom (1986, 1990), Flemming (1995/2002) dubbed one version of this general approach *dispersion theory*.

In dispersion theory (DT), contrast exerts an influence on grammaticality in two ways. First, there are constraints that require a given form to be sufficiently perceptually distinct from other contrasting output forms. In the work of Flemming (1995/2002, 2004) these are referred to as Minimal Distance (MinDist) constraints. MinDist constraints are relativized to a particular dimension of contrast, such as vowel color (roughly second formant value, implemented by backness and roundness gestures). We can conceive of such a dimension of contrast as a scale of perceptual distance, as shown in (1). A constraint $\text{MinDist}_{\text{Col}}=n$ requires that potential minimal pairs[2] differing in color (such as [bit] and [but]) differ by at least n on this scale. For dimensions of contrast like this allowing more than a binary distinction, a family of constraints is posited, as in (2). The ranking shown is taken to be universal, since contrasts like [i,y] are inherently more confusable than those like [i,u].[3]

(1)   Vowel color scale (high vowels)

    i   y   ɨ   ɯ u

    1   2   3   4   5

(2)   Minimal distance constraints for color

$\text{MinDist}_{\text{Col}}=1 \gg \text{MinDist}_{\text{Col}}=2 \gg \text{MinDist}_{\text{Col}}=3 \gg \text{MinDist}_{\text{Col}}=4 \gg \text{MinDist}_{\text{Col}}=5$

Second, there are constraints requiring that contrasts themselves be maintained. (It would be possible to vacuously satisfy MinDist constraints by neutralizing, for example, /bit/ and /but/ to [bit].) Padgett (2003a,b, to appear a) argues that, in addition to standard faithfulness (as in McCarthy and Prince 1995), the theory should incorporate the constraint *Merge:

(3)   *Merge: No word of the output has multiple correspondents in the input.

One argument for systemic constraints like these comes from a 'postvelar fronting' sound change that affected East Slavic roughly between the twelfth and fourteenth centuries (Padgett 2003a). The vowel /ɨ/ fronted to [i] after velar consonants, as shown below. (Palatalization before front vowels was a general requirement.) Two questions can be asked about postvelar fronting: (a) why did it occur, and (b) why did it occur only after velars?

(4)   Russian postvelar fronting

kɨjev   >   kʲiev   'Kiev'

gɨbʲelʲ   >   gʲibʲelʲ   'ruin/death'

xɨtrɨj   >   xʲitrɨj   'clever'

According to the analysis in Padgett (2003a), fronting occurred because [i] versus [u] is a perceptually better contrast than [ɨ] versus [u]. This can be seen in the tableau below. The set of forms in the input and candidate outputs are viewed as idealized representations of a language. In East Slavic at the time postvelar fronting occurred, velars did not occur before [i], because an earlier sound change had mutated velars before [i] to palatoalveolars. Hence the gap in the set of forms where [kʲi] should be. The [p]-initial forms stand in for consonants of non-velar place of articulation, all of which could occur before [i]. The constraint $\text{MinDist}_{\text{Col}}{\geq}4$ penalizes every pair of forms like [pʲi] versus [pɨ], potential minimal pairs differing only in vowel color, if they do not differ at least as much as [i] versus [u] do.

(See (1).) Due to postvelar fronting, candidate (5b) has one fewer violation of this constraint than (5a) does. ([kʲi] versus [ku] is a better contrast than [ki] versus [ku] is.) Obligatory palatalization before front vowels is assumed in this tableau.

As for the second question, fronting is argued to have occurred only following velars because in any other context it would have been neutralizing. Candidate (5c) shows this: /pɨ/ has fronted to [pʲi], violating *MERGE. (Its derivational history can be traced by the numerical subscripts, which refer to entire forms like [pu].) Because there were no words having velars before [i], postvelar fronting did not violate *MERGE. Given a ranking *MERGE >> MINDIST$_{Col}$≥4, (5c) is avoided even though it is superior in maintaining perceptually distinct color contrasts.

(5)   Analysis of postvelar fronting

	pʲi₁ pɨ₂ pu₃ kɨ₅ ku₆ tʃʲi₄	*MERGE	MINDIST$_{Col}$ ≥4	IDENT$_{Col}$
a.	pʲi pɨ pu kɨ ku tʃʲi		***!	
b. ☞	pʲi pɨ pu kʲi₅ ku tʃʲi		**	*
c.	pʲi₁,₂ pu kʲi₅ ku tʃʲi	*!		**

The analysis of postvelar fronting makes clear how it can be useful to appeal to systemic constraints, constraints regulating the perceptual distance of contrast and the occurrence of neutralization. And the works cited at the outset demonstrate that there are many such facts requiring appeal to these systemic notions. Yet systemic approaches to phonology such as DT raise formal and empirical challenges. One obvious challenge involves substantiating claims about perceptual distance that undergird systemic accounts. There is still a great deal we do not know about the perceptual organization of speech sounds. Another challenge involves how one determines what might be called the 'comparison set'. If the goodness of a form depends on its relationship to other contrasting forms, then how are we to decide exactly *which* other forms matter? Our goal in this paper is to clarify the nature of these challenges and to discuss our approach to them.

2   Comparison sets

A general challenge for systemic approaches to phonology is the challenge of the comparison set: if the realization of a form like Irish [pʲɔːn] 'pen' depends in part on the existence of contrasting forms like [pɔːn] 'pawnshop' (see section 3), then how do we decide exactly *which* other forms matter in this way?[4] If [pɔːn] has such a bearing on [pʲɔːn], do [dˠinʲɪ] 'people', or [tʲaŋgolˠiəxt] 'linguistics'? Where does it end, and how can we know? Since the set of possible forms is infinite, this is no trivial problem. We divide this challenge into two parts, the 'problem of infinity', and a discussion of idealization.

2.1   The problem of infinity

Ní Chiosáin and Padgett (2001) and Padgett (2003a,b, to appear a) assume that inputs and candidate outputs in DT are entire *languages*, in this respect following Flemming (1999). If we view a language as a set of possible words (putting aside phrases), then we could restate this assumption in the following way: the input to an optimality theoretic tableau is the set of all possible words (effectively the entire 'rich base'), while a candidate output is some subset (proper or not) of this set. However, analysts cannot grapple with entire languages at one time. For the purposes of analysis, Ní Chiosáin and Padgett (2001) and Padgett (2003a,b, to appear a) employ a strategy of severe idealization, discussed further below.

Though the use of idealization seems reasonable, the assumption we are abstracting away from – that inputs and outputs are languages – raises questions. A worry for this assumption arises from the fact that the set of all possible words is infinite. It is infinite, even assuming that the number of features, and therefore of segment types, is finite, because words can be indefinitely long. If a candidate language can contain an infinite number of forms, then it can violate a given constraint an infinite number of times. This is of concern because it can undermine crucial constraint comparisons.[5]

Consider for example the analysis of postvelar fronting in (5). In that analysis *MERGE outranks MINDIST≥4, and this explains why fronting occurs only following velars. The tableau in (7) repeats (5), but now considers the implications of infinite sets of forms. (Forms with [tʃ] have been omitted to ease reading the tableau.) Next to forms like [pʲi] and [ku] there are possible forms such as [pʲila] and [kula], as well as [pʲilala] and [kulala], and so on. Once all of these forms are counted, it can be seen that (7a) and (7b) will each incur an infinite number of MINDIST violations (one for [pʲi] versus [pɨ], another for [pʲila] versus [pɨla], etc.), and (7c) an infinite number of *MERGE violations (one for [pʲi$_{1,2}$], another for [pʲila$_{1,2}$], etc.).

The algorithm given by Prince and Smolensky (1993/2004) for determining the relative harmony of two candidates for a constraint C has two parts:

(6) Relative harmony of candidates A and B with respect to constraint C
   (a) if candidate A has no violations of C and candidate B has some violations, eliminate B;
   (b) otherwise, remove one violation mark from each candidate and try (a) again.

(6b) applies recursively until either A or B is eliminated, or there are no more violations to compare. For two candidates that have infinite violations, the problem arises in the case of (6b).

With *MERGE >> MinDist≥4, we can still eliminate (7c) by clause (6a), because (7a) and (7b) have no violations of *MERGE. The problem is the comparison between (7a) and (7b), which in (5) are distinguished by the number of MinDist violations. The intuition we want to capture is that faithful (7a) is worse than (7b) because it has more MinDist violations, since postvelar fronting has not occurred. But if both candidates have an infinite number of MinDist violations that must be assessed, we cannot make this distinction using (6b). Without this distinction, candidate (7a) will (incorrectly) win.

(7) Postvelar fronting with infinite constraint violation

				*MERGE	MinDist$_{Col}$ ≥4	IDENT$_{Col}$
	pʲi$_1$ pɨ$_2$ pu$_3$ kɨ$_4$ ku$_5$ pʲila$_6$ pɨla$_7$ pula$_8$ kɨla$_9$ kula$_{10}$ (etc...)						
a. ☞	pʲi$_1$ pɨ$_2$ pu$_3$ kɨ$_4$ ku$_5$ pʲila$_6$ pɨla$_7$ pula$_8$ kɨla$_9$ kula$_{10}$ (etc...)					∞	
b. ⊗	pʲi$_1$ pɨ$_2$ pu$_3$ kʲi$_4$ ku$_5$ pʲila$_6$ pɨla$_7$ pula$_8$ kʲila$_9$ kula$_{10}$ (etc...)					∞	∞!
c.	pʲi$_{1,2}$ pu$_3$ kʲi$_4$ ku$_5$ pʲila$_{6,7}$ pula$_8$ kʲila$_9$ kula$_{10}$ (etc...)				∞!		∞

However, as Abby Kaplan (p.c.) points out to us, the issue exemplified by (7) is not one of formal intractability. The infinities in question are enumerable, and it is easy to show that the MINDIST$_{Col}$ violations of (7b) are a subset of those of (7a): (7a) has *one* MINDIST$_{Col}$≥4 violation involving velars for every two involving labials, while (7b) has *none*. For many if not all cases where infinite violations are being compared, a superset-subset relationship of this sort might be demonstrable. Seen in this way, this infinite comparison is not so far removed from (6) as it might appear: the point of (6) is to eliminate the candidate having the superset of violations! Though it would require an elaboration of (6) to accommodate comparing infinite violations as in (7), we see no obvious reason why this could not be done. However, in the spirit of exploration we discuss here means by which candidates might be restricted to finiteness.

Working within a framework called *contrast preservation theory* (which she abbreviates PC theory), Łubowicz (2003) proposes one way to guarantee a finite comparison set: the set is defined in relation to a given input I under consideration, and the length of forms included in the set is limited by the length of I. [6] Specifically, the input comparison set consists of all forms that can be derived by the following operations (which may be combined): (a) replacing any segments of I with any one segment each, (b) deleting any segments of I, or (c) inserting any one segment before or after any segments of I. Candidate outputs consist of forms that are a subset (proper or not) of these input forms, as in DT. The possibilities for the input are illustrated schematically in (8), for the Irish form /pɔːn/ 'pawnshop'. Replacing one original segment gives for example (8a). In (8b), a segment has been replaced, but also two have been added. Example (8c) combines all three operations. In effect, this comparison set is defined as a kind of 'neighborhood' around W, in the sense familiar from psycholinguistics, except that it is a maximally inclusive neighborhood: all forms of length n share the same comparison set. And as is usual in systemic theories, this set includes all possible words, not just existing lexical items.

(8)   Deriving a comparison set (Łubowicz 2003)

	p		ɔː		n		
a.	p		ʌː		n		pʌːn
b.	p	l	ʌː		n	ə	plʌːnə
c.	m	ɑ			k		mɑk

Because only one segment can be inserted into any 'slot' to the left or right of an original segment, the number of forms in this comparison set is finite. In fact, it is all forms of length $2n+1$ or less, where n is the length of I. Though finite, this set can be very large. For a three-segment form I like /pɔːn/ (where $2n+1 = 7$), assuming for discussion that the number of segment types available universally is 100 (though this is too low), the set includes $100^7 + 100^6 + ... + 100^1$ forms. Łubowicz's actual analyses therefore employ severe idealization, as those of Ní Chiosáin and Padgett (2001) and Padgett (2003a,b, to appear a) do.

As noted, one property of this approach to determining a comparison set is that it is done relative to a designated form I, 'the form of interest', e.g. /pɔːn/. This property in turn entails variability in the content of that set. If form I consists of three segments like /pɔːn/, the comparison set consists of all possible words of length 0–7 segments; for a 4-segment I like /dʸinʲɪ/ 'people' the set includes the same forms plus forms of length 8–9 segments; and so on. This variability in the formal characterization of the comparison set may not be desirable.[7] For this reason and for the sake of simplicity we suggest a different means to achieve finiteness: impose an absolute upper limit on the length of forms that can be admitted into the set of candidate outputs. Assuming this limit is universal and inviolable, it should take the form of a restriction on OT's Gen function. The set of inputs therefore remains infinite, but Gen filters out forms beyond a certain length, so that each output candidate is necessarily a set of forms that is finite in number. A limit on the length of forms can reasonably be motivated by the increasing processing difficulty of longer forms.

It is worth mentioning one other conceivable approach to the problem of infinity: take the object of evaluation in DT to be *inventories*: for example, the input is the set of all possible segment types, and output candidates are subsets of this set. (The work of Flemming 1995/2002, 2004 often presents in this way, though this seems to be an expository strategy rather than a theoretical claim.) Inventories are by nature finite, and inventories of *segments* are much smaller than sets of possible words, even for modest-length words. If comparison sets are inventories, however, they cannot in fact be inventories of segments. To see this, consider first postvelar fronting once again. The explanation for fronting after velars (and not after labials, for example) is the prior lack of forms like *$kʲi$. This is not a gap in the inventory of *segments* but in the inventory of something larger, such as syllables. Similarly, Ní Chiosáin and Padgett (2001) and Padgett (2003b) argue for a systemic account of the realization of palatalization and velarization on consonants, in which the quality of the following vowel plays a key role. The analysis requires comparing sequences like [bʲi] and [bʸi]. Łubowicz (2003) also motivates analyses that make sense only when sequences of vowel and consonant are compared. If such analyses are to be possible, then the inventory in question can consist of units no smaller than the syllable (or perhaps the demisyllable, Fujimura 1979).

It is not clear, however, that even a syllable-like constituent is large enough to permit systemic explanations of phonological patterns. For example, Sanders (2003) argues that word-level nasal harmony in Tuyuca is motivated by constraints requiring two words to differ in nasality by as many segments as possible. Padgett (to appear a) proposes a DT analysis of rhotic distribution in Catalan which requires comparison of phrase-level forms like *mà restà* 'the hand remained' and *mar està* 'the sea is'. More generally, it is desirable to pursue a theory in which phonological effects of all sorts – including harmonies, stress and segment interactions, etc. – can be explored with the benefit of systemic principles where they seem beneficial. For these reasons, we advocate an approach to systemic phonology in which the objects of analysis are the same as for other theories of phonology: words and phrases. Avoiding the issues that arise when candidate sets are infinite – assuming they should be avoided – therefore requires imposing length limits on this set of forms, as discussed above.

2.2   Idealization

In previous works we have discussed the role of idealization in systemic phonology, and argued that systemic theories are no different from others in their need for idealization (Ní Chiosáin and Padgett 2001, Padgett 2003a,b, to appear a). Here we discuss some concrete strategies for idealizing, and argue that idealization involves making explicit one's analytical premises.

The puzzle that leads to idealization is not hard to see: given the vast number of possible forms – even if it is finite – how are we to determine the relevance of these forms to a particular form, or set of forms, under consideration? Taking up the example from the introduction, suppose we are interested in the palatalization contrast seen in Irish [pʲɔːn] 'pen' versus [pɔːn] 'pawnshop'. What forms need to be taken into consideration for such an analysis? This group of forms is what we mean by 'comparison set'.

Idealization involves reducing the set of relevant forms to a small number which *represent* or exemplify only those factors considered to be relevant for an analysis. For example, though words might be of great length, length per se (as opposed to prosodic factors like position with respect to stress, word-initial or -final position, etc.) seems to have only a modest bearing on phonology. That is, processes like flapping, vowel reduction, voicing assimilation, etc., do not greatly depend on word length. This means that we can often restrict an analysis to forms of only one or two syllables in length, and assume that the results generalize to larger words.

Within these parameters, further progress in idealizing is made by paying attention to what phonological factors seem to be independent of each other.

For example, there is little or no evidence that word-final obstruent voicing ever depends on the quality of a preceding vowel, or that stress assignment depends on consonantal place of articulation. The independence of such factors is judged normally from known phonological patterns themselves, though perceptual studies can in principle lend support. Note that the question of what matters is a *substantive* one whose answer will depend on the phenomenon under consideration. Further, it is by nature *empirical* and therefore subject to revision as we make discoveries. For these reasons, we do not think there can be a formal procedure for determining an idealization, any more than there can be a formal procedure to tell us what candidates and constraints to include in any standard OT tableau (see below). Rather, such decisions must be up to the experience and ingenuity of the analyst.

Consonantal palatalization is perhaps a relatively challenging case, because the occurrence of palatalization is known to depend on at least position (e.g., preconsonantal, word-final, etc.), place of articulation of the consonant in question, and quality of the neighboring vowel (Takatori 1997, Ní Chiosáin and Padgett 2001, Padgett 2001, Kochetov 2002, Padgett 2003b). Further, palatalization contrasts can in fact involve palatalized, plain, and velarized consonantal realizations, depending especially on vowel context. Even limiting ourselves to word-initial versus -final position, three places of articulation, and five vowel qualities, this might seem to suggest considera-tion of at least 135 forms: the 45 shown in (9), and analogous forms having coronals and velars.

(9)   Idealized comparison set for palatalization contrast (labials only)

pip	pipʲ	pipˠ	pʲip	pʲipʲ	pʲipˠ	pˠip	pˠipʲ	pˠipˠ
pep	pepʲ	pepˠ	pʲep	pʲepʲ	pʲepˠ	pˠep	pˠepʲ	pˠepˠ
pap	papʲ	papˠ	pʲap	pʲapʲ	pʲapˠ	pˠap	pˠapʲ	pˠapˠ
pop	popʲ	popˠ	pʲop	pʲopʲ	pʲopˠ	pˠop	pˠopʲ	pˠopˠ
pup	pupʲ	pupˠ	pʲup	pʲupʲ	pʲupˠ	pˠup	pˠupʲ	pˠupˠ

However, we need not consider all of these forms simultaneously, in one OT tableau, because some of the factors at work are plausibly independent of others. The realization of palatalization on labials, for example, possibly does not depend on the realization of palatalization on coronals or velars in the same language. Therefore we can construct separate tableaux for each place of articulation. Likewise, the realization of palatalization on initial consonants is plausibly independent of that on final consonants. Therefore, instead of one tableau with all of the forms in (9), we can construct two with only the 15 forms each in (10). We have already pared things down to a somewhat manageable size. An analysis will consist of one constraint ranking, and six tableaux ((10)a,b * three places of articulation), each having subsets of the forms in (10a), or (10b), etc.

(10) Revised comparison set for palatalization contrast (labials only)

	a.				b.		
	pi	pʲi	pˠi		ip	ipʲ	ipˠ
	pe	pʲe	pˠe		ep	epʲ	epˠ
	pa	pʲa	pˠa		ap	apʲ	apˠ
	po	pʲo	pˠo		op	opʲ	opˠ
	pu	pʲu	pˠu		up	upʲ	upˠ

We may well go still further, though. It is not obvious that the realization of palatalization before one vowel depends on its realization before another vowel. If we assume it does not, then we can employ one tableau for the series [pi, pʲi, pˠi], another for [pe, pʲe, pˠe], and so on (see for example Ní Chiosáin and Padgett 2001, Padgett 2003b).

Idealization of this sort is desirable because it makes analyses manageable. It is *defensible* to the extent we are correct in assuming that ignored factors do not matter. As we have noted in other works, idealization occurs in any linguistic analysis (as well as in other scientific fields), where it is desirable and defensible for the same reasons; it is not a new feature of systemic theories. What is new here is rather (1) the more *obvious* need to idealize when doing systemic phonology, since we must take contrasting forms into consideration, and (2) the need to be *explicit* about how we idealize in order to be clear on what the input is, and what candidate outputs are.

Lurking behind this discussion of idealization is the worry, which some may feel when encountering systemic theories, that formal rigor or clarity of predictions has been compromised. For example, we might ask how safe the postvelar result is, given its dependence on idealization. It is clear how the analysis works in (5) given the forms entertained in the idealization, but one can imagine other forms *not* entertained that might undermine the explanation. For example, though fronting has improved the contrast between /kɨ/ and /ku/, it has presumably worsened that between /kɨ/ and /kʲe/, since [kʲi] is closer to [kʲe] than [kɨ] is. Perhaps including /kʲe/ within the idealization, along with pertinent perceptual distance constraints, would change the result.

Though this is a real concern, it is not at all particular to systemic theories. Consider the standard OT tableau in (11i), for example, which presents an analysis of regressive voicing assimilation making use of constraints familiar from the literature on assimilation and positional faithfulness (e.g., Lombardi 1999, Padgett to appear b). Candidate (11)ib wins as desired. But this result can be undermined by candidates we have failed to consider, such as (11)iid), which would win given the current constraints.

(11) (i) Idealization in standard OT

/akba/		SPREAD(voi)	IDENT_Ons(voi)	IDENT(voi)
a.	akba	*!		
b. ☞	agba			*
c.	akpa		*!	*

(ii) Result undermined given new candidates, e.g.,

d.	akəba		

The possibility of such dark horse candidates is painfully familiar to anyone who has worked in OT. In the case of (11), obvious solutions to the analytical problem come to mind, e.g., introduce a high-ranking faithfulness constraint against vowel insertion. (Similarly, the worry about [kʲi] versus [kʲe] could be addressed by assuming that MINDIST for vowel height is low-ranked.) But this should not obscure the underlying point: for any analysis, it is always possible that a candidate not considered exists, one which might undermine the analysis presented and may even be very hard to handle were it discovered. There is nothing in the formalism of OT that helps us with this problem. To put it differently, even the most precisely formalized analysis in OT is only as good as the assumptions that go into it, in particular the constraints and candidates that constitute the premises of the analysis. And this is simply a version of a more general fact of life for theorists of any sort: no matter how precisely formalized and internally coherent an analysis is, it is subject to defeat once underlying assumptions are shifted.

Bringing the point back to the specifics of DT, the point is that an idealization is not merely an analytical convenience. Rather, it represents an explicit claim about the premises of an analysis, that is, about what matters and what does not matter in analyzing the phenomenon in question. DT does not differ in employing idealization, only in the degree to which idealization is made apparent.

3   Perceptual distance and phonology

In the past decade or so a good deal of work has emerged motivating the use of perceptual features and perceptual explanations in phonology (besides work in DT, see especially Steriade 1997, Boersma 1998, Steriade 2001a). In all of these works, the perceptual distance of contrasts is a foundational notion.

The vowel color scale seen in (1) is repeated here as an example. The idea of perceptual distance of course implies a perceptual space (what Steriade 2001a calls a 'P-map').

(12) Vowel color scale (high vowels)

   i   y   ɨ   ɰ   u
   1   2   3   4   5

The use of perceptual distance plays a key role in the realms of both markedness and faithfulness. Its use in markedness is clear in DT (see the introduction, and below), and it is implicit in the theory of licensing by cue (Steriade 1997). As for faithfulness, Steriade (2001a,b) argues convincingly that perceptual distance of input-output mappings is important to resolving the 'too many solutions' problem in phonology (compare Wilson 2001, for whom the use of perceptual distance is also key). The theory of positional faithfulness (Casali 1996/1998, 1997, Beckman 1997–1998) also draws implicitly on the notion of perceptual distance, since it is motivated in part by the claim that contrasts are better realized in certain strong positions. Since the perceptual space has become fundamental to so much explanation in phonology, it is likely that perceptual studies will occupy an increasingly important place in the theory. (Two recent works combining perceptual studies with phonological theory are Kochetov 2002, and Kawahara 2006.) Drawing on our own work (Ní Chiosáin and Padgett 2007), we illustrate here the use of perceptual data to inform phonological analysis. The empirical focus is on secondary palatalization contrasts in onset versus coda position, with perceptual data from Irish.

Recent cross-linguistic surveys (Takatori 1997, Kochetov 2002) have established some typological implications concerning secondary palatalization contrasts (e.g., [pʲa] versus [pa]). For example, syllable-final contrasts imply syllable-initial contrasts, and contrasts in labials imply also contrasts in dentals. Kochetov (2002), on the basis of articulatory, acoustic and perceptual studies of palatalization in Russian, argues that these asymmetries follow from perceptual biases.[8] To put it simply, the more marked contrasts are those that are perceptually more difficult to discern. For example, Kochetov argues that a language like Bulgarian, having only onset palatalization, lost the coda contrast historically due to its perceptual weakness.

It is well known that listeners can find it challenging to perceive phonemic contrasts that do not exist in their language. For this reason, it would not do to test the perceptual claim about onset versus coda palatalization only on speakers of Bulgarian. The problem is one of circularity: we would like to argue that Bulgarian lacks the coda contrast because that contrast is perceptually difficult; but in Bulgarian the coda contrast may be perceptually difficult in any case *because* it does not exist. To avoid this circularity, we can test the perceptual claim against languages which have a palatalization contrast in both onset and coda position. If we find an asymmetry in such cases, we can plausibly claim that there is a language-independent perceptual bias, and that this bias is itself the cause of markedness asymmetries. Russian is such a language, and so is Irish.

Traditionally, the consonant system of Irish is divided into two opposing sub-systems, the 'slender' (palatalized/plain) consonants and the 'broad' (velarized/labialized/plain) consonants. The phonemic oppositions, given below, are usually represented as palatalized/nonpalatalized; the phonetic realizations, however, vary according to place of articulation and environment.[9]

(13) Irish phoneme inventory

	Labial		Coronal		Dorsal		Glottal
Voiceless stop	p	pʲ	t	tʲ	k	kʲ	
Voiced stop	b	bʲ	d	dʲ	g	gʲ	
Voiceless fricative	f	fʲ	s	ʃ	x	xʲ	h
Voiced fricative	v	vʲ			ɣ	ɣʲ	
Nasal	m	mʲ	n	nʲ	ŋ	ŋʲ	
Liquid			l	lʲ			
			r	rʲ			

Examples of contrastive palatalization in Irish are given in (14a) (onset), (14b) (coda), and (14c), where (final) palatalization encodes grammatical categories such as plural and genitive.

(14) Palatalization contrasts in Irish[10]

a.	boːn	'white'		bʲoːn	'peak'	
	poːn	'pawnshop'		pʲoːn	'pen'	
b.	broːd	'drizzle'		broːdʲ	'neck, throat'	
	skoːl	'supernatural being' (m sg)		skoːlʲ	'shadow' (f sg)	
c.	kat	'cat' (sg)		katʲ	'cat' (pl)	
	boːd	'boat' (nom sg/gen pl)		boːdʲ	'boat' (nom pl/gen sg)	

We carried out an AX discrimination ('same-different') task involving pairs of words like *poːn-pʲoːn, rap-rapʲ*. The factors manipulated were syllable position (initial versus final), voicing, and place of articulation (labial versus coronal), though only syllable position is discussed here. The vowel in the stimuli was always [a] or [ɔː]. Stimuli were recorded by a native speaker of Irish, and were

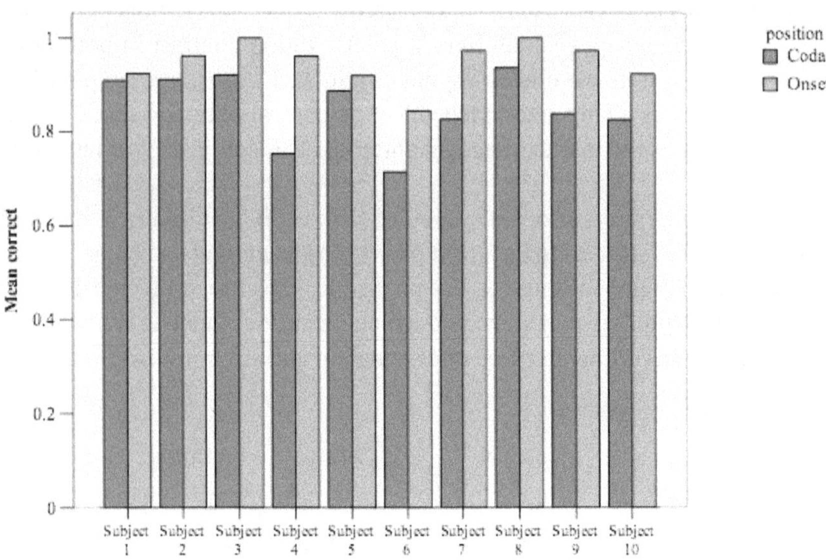

Figure 4.1: Mean correct 'different' responses: coda vs. onset (by subject)

in most cases real words, though a few were nonce words. Subjects were 10 native Irish speakers of Connaught Irish (West Galway).[11] Figures 4.1 and 4.2 show the difference in correct responses between coda (84%) and onset (94%) positions (F(1, 9) =12.30, p = .007). That is, subjects were better at distinguishing pairs like *pɔːn-pʲɔːn* than pairs like *rap-rapʲ*.

Our results are similar to Kochetov's in motivating a perceptual disparity between onset and coda palatalization contrasts. Results like these can be used to motivate a dispersion-theoretic analysis of the onset-coda asymmetry. In particular, they indicate that there is an asymmetry in perceptual distance like that given schematically in (15).

(15) Perceptual distance asymmetry between onset and coda palatalization contrast

    pa.................... pʲa   'Onset palatalization distance'
    ap.............apʲ   'Coda palatalization distance'

The Minimal Distance constraints of DT refer to disparities in perceptual distance like this. Since the details of the perceptual space for palatalization are not as well understood as those of the space for vowels – for example, how close in absolute terms are different units like [ap] and [apʲ], what is the shape and dimensionality of this space – we do not try to formalize them here. In particular, rather than use a numbered scale as in (12), we refer directly to

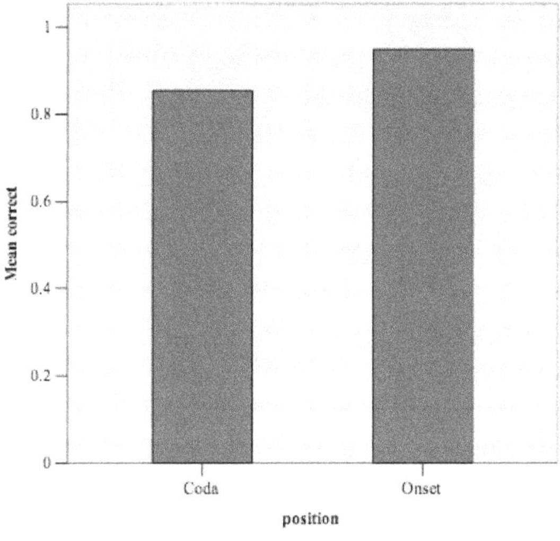

Figure 4.2: Mean correct 'different' responses: coda vs. onset (all subjects)

'onset palatalization distance' and 'coda palatalization distance' in the constraint formulations. What we *can* infer from our results is the relevance of this distinction. It can be encoded via the constraints, and fixed universal ranking, shown in (16).[12] (However, since all the contrasts we consider here meet the constraint $\text{MinDist}_{\text{Coda-Pal}}$, this constraint is not shown in the tableaux below.)

(16) Minimal distance constraints for palatalization

    a. $\text{MinDist}_{\text{X-Pal}}$:   Potential minimal pairs differing in secondary palatalization differ at least as much as C versus C^{j} in position X do.

    b. $\text{MinDist}_{\text{Coda-Pal}} \gg \text{MinDist}_{\text{Onset-Pal}}$

Neutralization of a palatalization contrast in the coda, as in Bulgarian (see Kochetov 2002), is captured by the ranking shown in (17). Candidate (17)a includes a pair of forms $(\text{ap}_3\text{-ap}^{\text{j}}_4)$ that violates $\text{MinDist}_{\text{Onset-Pal}}$. It violates this constraint because the contrast in coda palatalization in [ap] versus [ap^{j}] is not as good as an onset palatalization contrast. Candidates (17)b–d satisfy this constraint vacuously by coda neutralization. Of the latter forms, (17)d neutralizes more than is necessary. Candidates (17)b, c differ in whether neutralization is to the marked or unmarked (as judged by *C^{j}, a constraint with articulatory motivation), with the unmarked outcome favored.

(17) Neutralization of the coda contrast (as in Bulgarian)

	pa_1 p^ja_2 ap_3 $ap^j{}_4$	MinDist$_{Onset-Pal}$	*Merge	*C^j
a.	pa_1 p^ja_2 ap_3 $ap^j{}_4$	*!		**
b. ☞	pa_1 p^ja_2 $ap_{3,4}$		*	*
c.	pa_1 p^ja_2 $ap^j{}_{3,4}$		*	**!
d.	$pa_{1,2}$ $ap_{3,4}$		**!	

In the case of languages like Irish and Russian, where the palatalization contrast in coda position is maintained, *Merge outranks the perceptual MinDist constraint (as well as the articulatory *C^j), as shown below.

(18) No neutralization (as in Irish)

	pa_1 p^ja_2 ap_3 $ap^j{}_4$	*Merge	MinDist$_{Onset-Pal}$	*C^j
a. ☞	pa_1 p^ja_2 ap_3 $ap^j{}_4$		*	**
b.	pa_1 p^ja_2 $ap_{3,4}$	*!		*
c.	pa_1 p^ja_2 $ap^j{}_{3,4}$	*!		**
d.	$pa_{1,2}$ $ap_{3,4}$	*!*		

As the reader can verify, ranking *C^j at the top will predict a language with no palatalization contrast, as in English.

Recalling section 2, the analysis above exemplifies the role of idealization in systemic phonology. For the purposes of this analysis, it has been assumed that everything but onset versus coda position of a plain versus palatalization contrast can be ignored. Hence the input is always the same, the four forms [pa, p^{j}a, ap, ap^j] representative of all that is assumed to matter. Outputs are always subsets of this input (proper or not). In many cases, ignoring other factors is justified by our (relative) confidence that they never have any bearing on the facts at hand. In this case, we have also abstracted away from some factors that likely *do* matter to a full analysis of the onset-coda asymmetry, such as quality of the neighboring vowel, and place of articulation of the consonant. Therefore, though the analysis given is formally unproblematic, it is indeed an idealization.

Returning to the main issue here, we conclude this section by discussing a major challenge for the program of building phonological explanations on perceptual studies. This challenge follows from the language-particularity of perception already mentioned. It has long been known that speech perception is shaped by linguistic experience (see Strange 1995 for an overview of research). For example, German speakers have more difficulty distinguishing [ɛ] from [æ] than English speakers do (Barry 1989); English distinguishes these sounds as phonemes, while German does not. Further, 'reorganization' of perception based on native contrasts begins within the first year of life (Kuhl 1991, Best 1994). Since the point of dispersion theory, licensing by cue theory, and related work is to harness the perceptual space to *explain* phonological patterns – including systems of contrast – these facts raise crucial questions: to what extent does a language-independent perceptual map exist, and how we can get information about it? Is there, after all, any language-independent answer to the question of how perceptually distinct [ap] is from [apʲ]?

Johnson (2004) and Huang (2004) discuss this issue, as well as the question whether choosing the right experimental method can help disentangle language-particular perception from a hypothesized universal perceptual map, assuming the latter exists. Building on earlier observations that different experimental tasks can elicit so-called 'phonetic' versus 'auditory' perception, these works explore the effect of tasks carrying a low-memory load and emphasizing fast responses. Such tasks might favor the 'auditory' perception mode and, to the extent that low-level auditory processing is not language-particular, therefore tell us something about the universal perceptual space. An example of such a task is an AX (same-different) discrimination task, in which the interstimulus interval is very short (allowing listeners to judge based on auditory memory traces rather than recall of categories), the same two stimulus types are compared within blocks, and fast responses are encouraged (reaction times are measured). The Irish perceptual data described above was gathered by such a task. In an experiment with a similar design comparing Polish and English speakers' ability to discriminate among Polish sibilants, Zygis and Padgett (to appear) find that, while Polish and English speakers differ notably in errors made, the patterns revealed by reaction times are more similar. Still, the prospects of a universal perceptual space remain unclear. On the other hand, the increasing reliance of phonological theories on perceptual distance claims gives us a compelling reason to pursue research into the perceptual space in spite of the challenges.

4   Conclusion

Since candidate outputs in dispersion theory are sets of forms, they can each contain infinite forms and therefore trigger infinite violations. The relative harmony of candidates having infinite violations can in principle be evaluated assuming that violations are countably infinite and that violations due to one candidate can be shown to be a subset of those due to another. However, this represents a qualitative elaboration over the current algorithm in optimality theory for determining candidate harmony. Should we wish to avoid moving in this direction, then we must impose limits on the length of possible words entertained by OT, in order to avoid infinite constraint violations. We have made no claims about what such a length limit should be, since the precise answer does not affect the basic point. In any case, explicit idealizations must play a key role in systemic theories. This is not a formal issue, in our view, but a specific version of a more general methodological issue confronting all theories.

Perceptual distance, and a hypothesized universal perceptual map, are notions that undergird a great deal of current phonological theory, particularly OT. They play a key role in dispersion theory, licensing by cue theory, positional faithfulness, and accounts of the 'too many solutions problem'. Perceptual studies are therefore likely to become a more important source of evidence for phonological claims. Though this will be a challenging research program, it is an exciting one for phonology.

Notes

1   This research was supported by faculty research funds granted by the University of California, Santa Cruz, and by the Forschungsinstitut für Geistes- und Sozialwissenschaften, Universität Siegen. We are grateful to Adam Albright, Abby Kaplan, Ania Łubowicz, Steve Parker, Ruth Kramer, and Kie Zuraw for comments that improved this paper.

2   A 'potential minimal pair' is a pair of output forms all of whose corresponding segments but one are identical. See Padgett (2003a,c).

3   Compare Flemming (1995/2002, 2004) to Padgett (1997) and Ní Chiosáin and Padgett (2001) for somewhat different approaches to constraints in DT. The discussion in this paper combines aspects of both.

4   The Irish forms here and elsewhere in the paper are representative of western dialects of Irish.

5   Thanks to John McCarthy and Alan Prince for bringing this issue to our attention.

6   See Tessier (2004a) for another proposal for deriving a finite comparison set for any input *I*, based on the constraint rankings of a language.

7   Abby Kaplan (p.c.) notes that it entails a surprising 'observer-dependence': if the 'form of interest' is (for example) [pɔːn], then hypothetical [pɔːnlala] will not be included in the comparison set; however, the comparison set for [pɔːnlala] *will* include [pɔːn]!

8   'Syllable-initial and -final' are approximations to a truth that is more nuanced and dependent on precise phonetic context, a fact we abstract away from here.

9   Palatalization usually involves a raised-fronted dorsum and, in some dialects, a palatal off-glide preceding back long-vowels. Velarized consonants involve a retracted dorsum, though in some cases the secondary articulation is more accurately characterized as uvularization, (e.g., Ní Chasaide 1999 on Doirí Beaga Irish, a northern dialect). Broad labials preceding certain front vowels are frequently labialized (e.g., Quiggin 1906 on northern Irish dialects, Ní Chasaide 1999).

10   Abbreviations are as follows: m(asculine), f(eminine), s(in)g(ular), pl(ural), nom(inative), gen(itive).

11   For details about the experiment see Ní Chiosáin and Padgett (2007).

12   Kochetov (2002) couches his account in terms of positional faithfulness theory. He also argues that the implied rankings are inferred by learners based on the perceptual disparity, rather than being universally given.

5 Morpheme-specific phonology: Constraint indexation and inconsistency resolution[1]

Joe Pater

This paper argues that exceptions and other instances of morpheme-specific phonology are best analyzed in Optimality Theory (OT) in terms of lexically indexed markedness and faithfulness constraints. This approach is shown to capture locality restrictions, distinctions between exceptional and truly impossible patterns, distinctions between blocking and triggering, and distinctions between variation and exceptionality. It is contrasted with other OT analyses of exceptions, in particular those that disallow lexically indexed markedness constraints and those that invoke lexically specified rankings (that is, cophonologies). The data discussed are from Assamese, Finnish and Yine (formerly Piro). A learnability account of the genesis of lexically indexed constraints is also provided, in which indexation is used to resolve inconsistency detected by Tesar and Smolensky's (1998, 2000) Recursive Constraint Demotion algorithm.

1   Introduction

Morphemes often behave differently phonologically in ways that cannot be explained purely phonologically: one morpheme undergoes or triggers a process while another morpheme fails to undergo or trigger that process, even though the two are in all relevant respects indistinguishable. Syncope in Yine (formerly known as Piro; Matteson 1965, Kisseberth 1970, Lin 1997) provides an example of such morpheme-specific phonology. Morphemes differ in whether they cause the preceding vowel to delete (/heta+nu/ [hetanu] 'going to see' vs. /heta+lu/ [hetlu] 'see it'), and in whether they undergo deletion themselves (/meyi+wa+lu/ [meyiwlu] 'celebration' vs. /heta+wa+lu/ [hetawalu] 'going to see him yet'). As the behavior of the homophonous pair of /-wa/ morphemes illustrates, morphemes that fail to condition syncope can differ in whether they undergo the process.

The distinction between exceptional triggering and blocking exemplified by Yine is captured straightforwardly in Optimality Theory (OT) if markedness and faithfulness constraints can be lexically indexed (Pater 2000). Morphemes that trigger a process are indexed for the application of a lexically specific markedness constraint, and morphemes that block a process are indexed for the application of a lexically specific faithfulness constraint. However, this distinction is not expressed in either of two alternative approaches to exceptionality in OT: a theory in which morphemes select constraint rankings (the 'cophonology' approach; e.g. Anttila 2002, Inkelas and Zoll 2003), or a theory in which only faithfulness constraints can be lexically indexed (e.g. Fukazawa 1999, Ito and Mester 1999b, 2001). These three theories of exceptionality are introduced in section 1 of the paper. Section 2 shows how indexation of markedness and faithfulness constraints deals with the Yine data, and discusses the difficulties faced by the alternatives.

Anttila (2002) uses data from Finnish /a+i/ allomorphy to argue for a version of the cophonology approach. In this theory, morphemes can only be specified for rankings that are left unspecified in a partially ordered grammar. In the third section of the paper, I show that the types of patterns Anttila captures with this approach can in fact be straightforwardly analyzed with indexed constraints. In addition, I show that constraint indexation captures generalizations that escape the partial ordering theory of cophonologies. One generalization is that the Finnish alternation applies only to a string that includes a portion of the exceptional morpheme. A simple locality convention for the interpretation of indexed constraints accounts for this restriction, and similar ones in other languages, and rules out a range of implausible non-local morpheme-specific processes. This locality restriction is unstateable under the cophonology approach, or under the faithfulness-only indexation theory. A second type of generalization involves distinctions between variation and exceptionality, which are conflated in the partial ordering/cophonology theory, but which can be separated if exceptionality involves indexation.

Section 4 provides a learnability account that uses the inconsistency detection properties of the Recursive Constraint Demotion Algorithm (Tesar and Smolensky 1998, 2000, Tesar 1998, Prince 2003) to trigger the creation of indexed constraints. This account of the genesis of indexed constraints resolves the incongruity of having morpheme-specific constraints in a theory that assumes constraint universality, and also ensures that learners will seek a phonological generalization before resorting to an analysis in terms of exceptionality. In section 5 representational approaches to exceptionality are briefly discussed, with a focus on learnability considerations. Section 6 further discusses the power of the indexation and cophonology approaches, and section 7 concludes.

2   Yine syncope and constraint indexation

2.1   Constraint indexation and cophonologies

Morphologically indexed constraints make their first appearance in the foundational work on Optimality Theory. Prince and Smolensky (1993/2004) propose Edgemost constraints that apply to specific morphemes in order to distinguish prefixes, suffixes, and edge-oriented infixes from one another. McCarthy and Prince (1993a) reformulate Edgemost constraints in terms of Generalized Alignment, which they also use for cases of prosodic subcategorization, in which a morpheme is placed next to an instance of a prosodic category.

Fukazawa (1999), Ito and Mester (1999b, 2001), Kraska-Szlenk (1997, 1999) and Pater (2000) extend morphological indexation from Alignment to other constraints. Under this view, a single constraint can be multiply instantiated in a constraint hierarchy, and each instantiation may be indexed to apply to a particular set of lexical items. These indexed constraints are universal markedness and faithfulness constraints whose application is relativized to a set of lexical items (cf. the 'parochial' constraints in Hammond 1995 and Green 2005, which are not markedness constraints, since they can demand marked structures, and are not faithfulness constraints, since they apply directly to surface representations; see Russell 1995 and Golston 1996 for related proposals).

To take a simple hypothetical example, a language might have coda deletion (e.g. 1a,b), which is blocked in some lexical items (e.g. 1c):

(1)   a.   /pak/   → [pa]   /pak+a/   → [paka]
      b.   /lot/   → [lo]   /lot+a/   → [lota]
      c.   /tak/   → [tak]   /tak+a/   → [taka]

Coda deletion requires a ranking of NoCoda >> Max. The exceptional items are targeted by a morphologically indexed Max constraint. This version of Max (Max-L) ranks above NoCoda, and applies only to those lexical items indexed for its application (here with an 'L' for 'lexical').

(2)   Grammar: Max-L >> NoCoda >> Max
      Lexicon: /pak/ /lot/ /tak$_L$/

The tableaux in (3) show the results of applying this grammar to a form that lacks the index (/pak/), and one that bears it (/tak$_L$/).

(3)

Input	Output	Max-L	NoCoda	Max
pak	pak		* !	
	☞ pa			*
tak$_L$	☞ tak		*	
	ta	* !		*

An important attribute of this approach to morpheme-specific phonology is that it captures the distinction between an exceptional form and an impossible one. Let us further assume that onset clusters are entirely absent from our hypothetical language. *COMPLEX ('no consonant clusters') would dominate MAX-L, since there is no evidence to contradict the default Markedness >> Faithfulness ranking (Smolensky 1996, Hayes 2004, Prince and Tesar 2004). If under Richness of the Base (Prince and Smolensky 1993/2004) an underlying form with a cluster is given a lexical diacritic, the cluster is reduced, as shown in (4). This is not to say a language could not have both exceptional codas and clusters, but rather that in the absence of evidence of a structure, a learner creates a grammar that rules it out completely.

(4)

Input	Output	*COMPLEX	MAX-L	NOCODA	MAX
CCV	CCV	*!			
	☞ CV				*
CCV$_L$	CCV	*!			
	☞ CV		*		*

A closely related approach to morpheme-specific phonology is that of cophonology theory (Kirchner 1993, Nouveau 1994, Ito and Mester 1995a,b, Orgun 1996, Inkelas 1999, Anttila 2002, Inkelas and Zoll 2003, Caballero 2005 and Zamma 2005). In this view, a grammar has only a single instantiation of each constraint, but individual morphemes can demand a different ranking of some of them. The term 'cophonology' might appear to imply a formalization in which morphemes that are subject to different rankings are submitted to entirely different grammars. I will retain this term, but will adopt a notation similar to that of Anttila (2002), in which there is a single constraint hierarchy, and morphemes impose rankings of only a subset of the constraints.

Our hypothetical example could be analyzed in cophonology theory with a grammatical hierarchy of *COMPLEX, NOCODA >> MAX, and with exceptional lexical items selecting the reverse ranking of MAX and NOCODA. The exceptional ranking is included as part of the lexical entry for the morpheme.

(5)   Grammar: *COMPLEX, NOCODA >> MAX
       Lexicon: /pak/ /lot/ /tak$_{Max>>NoCoda}$/

Input	Output	*COMPLEX	NOCODA	MAX
pak	pak		*!	
	☞ pa			*

Input	Output	*COMPLEX	MAX	NOCODA
tak$_{Max>>NoCoda}$	☞ tak			*
	ta		*!	

Without further elaboration, this theory cannot express the distinction between exceptional and impossible patterns. If lexical items are specified for constraint rankings, then by Richness of the Base any constraint ranking should be available for lexical specification. Returning to our example of a language that has exceptional codas but bans consonant clusters, nothing would rule out the specification of a lexical item for the reverse ranking of *COMPLEX and MAX, as illustrated in the following Richness of the Base tableau:

(6)

Input	Output	*COMPLEX	NOCODA	MAX
CCV	CCV	*!		
	☞ CV			*

Input	Output	MAX	NOCODA	*COMPLEX
CCV$_{\text{Max}>>\text{*Complex}}$	☞ CCV			*
	CV	*!		

To overcome this sort of problem, Anttila (2002) extends the partial ordering theory of variation to morpheme-specific phonology. Under the Subregularity Interpretation (Anttila 2002: 22), only pairs of constraints whose ranking is unspecified in the grammar can have lexically specified rankings. Our hypothetical language would have a ranking of *COMPLEX over MAX, and the ranking of NOCODA would be left unspecified. Lexical items are then specified for a ranking of the conflicting constraints, here MAX and NOCODA.

(7)　Grammar:　　*COMPLEX >> MAX
　　　　　　　　No CODA
　　Lexicon:　　/pak$_{\text{NoCoda}>>\text{Max}}$/ /lot$_{\text{NoCoda}>>\text{Max}}$/ /tak$_{\text{Max}>>\text{NoCoda}}$/

At first glance, this analysis seems to be a notational variant of the constraint indexation analysis. However, there are two differences that we can see even in this simple example.

First, indexed constraints account for impossible patterns in the way that is standard in OT: by using the grammar, constructed on the basis of positive evidence, to filter out a rich base. On the other hand, the partial ordering/ cophonology theory adds a stipulation that lexical rankings are limited to those that are unspecified in the grammar.

The second difference stems from the fact that in the partial ordering theory all lexical items must be specified for a ranking of the grammatically unranked constraints. If a lexical item were left unspecified, then it would show variation, with a ranking chosen randomly each time it is submitted to the grammar. Anttila (2002) presents this connection between variation and exceptionality as a positive attribute of the model, but there are clearly many cases of exceptionality without accompanying variation, and variation without exceptionality. This is evident in that in lexical phonology, variation is seen as a characteristic of post-lexical rules, and exceptionality of lexical rules (see e.g. Kaisse and Shaw 1985). In section 3.2, I will show that this conflation of variation and exceptionality leads to missed generalizations in the Finnish data Anttila (2002) analyzes. However, the problem goes far beyond the Finnish case, since the partial ordering/cophonology model predicts that all variation should be accompanied by exceptionality, and vice versa (see Anttila 2002: 29 for some discussion).

A further difference between lexical rankings and indexed constraints is that only the latter can distinguish between a lexically indexed markedness constraint, which produces exceptional triggering of a process, and a lexically indexed faithfulness constraint, which produces exceptional blocking. This distinction is also unavailable to a theory in which only faithfulness constraints can be indexed (e.g. Fukazawa 1999, Ito and Mester 1999b, 2001, Kraska-Szlenk 1997, 1999). In the next section, I show that the distinction between exceptional blocking and triggering is necessary to capture the facts of Yine syncope.

2.2   Yine and indexed constraints

Kisseberth (1970) draws attention to Yine syncope, as described in Matteson (1965), for its implications for a theory of exceptions in rule-based phonology. Unless indicated otherwise, the examples here are ones Kisseberth supplies. The forms in (8) show syncope applying before the nominalizing suffixes /-lu/ and /-nu/ ([ru] in (8c) is an allomorph of /-lu/; /nu/ is used for abstract nouns as in (8d)), before the indirective suffix /-ya/ (8e), and before the third person singular pronominal suffix /-lu/ (8f).

(8)   a.   /yimaka+lu/   [yimaklu]   'teaching'
      b.   /kama+lu/   [kamlu]   'handicraft'
      c.   /kakonu+lu/   [kakonru]   'a shelter in which a hunter hides'
      d.   /hata+nu/   [hatnu]   'light, shining'
      e.   /heta+ya/   [hetya]   'see there'
      f.   /heta+lu/   [hetlu]   'see it'

As the examples in (9) illustrate, syncope fails to apply before the verbal theme formative /-ta/, the anticipatory suffix /-nu/, and the intransitive verb theme suffix /-wa/.

(9)   /meyi+ta/   [meyita]   'to celebrate'
      /hata+ta/   [hatata]   'to illuminate'
      /heta+nu/   [hetanu]   'going to see'
      /meyi+wa+ta/   [meyiwata]   'to celebrate' (Matteson: 303)

All of the suffixes that fail to trigger syncope in (9) do undergo it when placed before one of the syncope-triggering suffixes, as the examples in (10) show.

(10) /meyi+wa+lu/   [meyiwlu]   'celebration'
     /heta+nu+lu/   [hetanru]   'going to see him'
     /yona+ta+na+wa/   [yonatnawa]   'to paint oneself'

However, there is a further 'exceptional' suffix /-wa/ ('yet, still') which neither conditions syncope nor undergoes it:

(11) /heta+wa+lu/   [hetawalu]   'going to see him yet'
     /n+hiʃinika+wa+lu/ [nuʃinikawalu] 'I'm still thinking about it' (Matteson: 74)

There is no phonological property that distinguishes the morphemes that trigger syncope from those that do not: the homophones with the shape /-nu/ fall into the two classes. Similarly, morphemes that block syncope and those that do not have no distinguishing property, as clearly illustrated by the two morphemes /-wa/. There is also no apparent morphosyntactic distinction between the different classes of morpheme, and no restriction that triggers must appear closer to the root than non-triggers (or vice versa), as might be expected under an interpretation of the data in terms of lexical or prosodic phonology. In her grammar, Matteson (1965) treats the distinction between triggers and non-triggers as idiosyncratic.

To deal with the Yine data, Kisseberth (1970: 57) proposes a theory of exceptionality in which lexical items are categorized as 'either undergoing a rule or not, and as either serving as the context for a rule or not' (see Zonneveld 1978, 1985 for further discussion and a critique). This distinction is expressed naturally in a version of OT with indexed markedness and faithfulness constraints.

As the constraint driving syncope, I will make use of an Alignment constraint requiring a suffix to follow a consonant (cf. Lin 1997).[2] 'Suffix' in (12) is a convenient cover term for the set of morphemes that follow the root.

(12) ALIGN-SUF-C Align(Suffix, L, C, R)
     The left edge of a suffix coincides with the right edge of a consonant

The motivation for this constraint may be to phonologically mark morphological boundaries; the onset of a suffix-initial consonant could well be more prominent when it is preceded by a consonant than when it is preceded by a vowel. Yine syncope does not seem to be driven by a STRESS-TO-WEIGHT constraint (see Gouskova 2003 on prosodically driven syncope); it also occurs before bisyllabic suffixes, in which case the resulting CVC would occupy a stressless syllable, given Yine's pattern of penultimate main stress and clash-avoiding secondary stress.

The ranking ALIGN-SUF-C >> MAX produces vowel deletion, as shown in the tableau in (13):

(13)

Input	Output	ALIGN-SUF-C	MAX
heta+ya	hetaya	* !	
	☞ hetya		*

To distinguish the suffixes that trigger syncope from the non-triggers, the suffixal argument of the ALIGN constraint that dominates MAX is indexed to the set of morphemes that trigger syncope. The general ALIGN constraint rests beneath MAX. The result is shown in (14), which includes in the lexicon all of the suffixes found in examples (8) – (11) above.

(14) Grammar: ALIGN-SUF(L)-C >> MAX >> ALIGN-SUF-C

Lexicon: /-lu$_L$/ /-nu$_L$/ /-lu$_L$/ /-ya$_L$/ /-ta/ /-nu/ /-wa/ /-wa/

Input	Output	ALIGN-SUF(L)-C	MAX	ALIGN-SUF-C
heta+ya$_L$	hetaya	* !		*
	☞ hetya		*	
heta+wa	☞ hetawa			*
	hetwa		* !	

Similarly, to distinguish the suffixes that undergo syncope from those that don't, MAX appears in both a lexically indexed and a general version. The lexically indexed version ranks above the indexed markedness constraint; the general one ranks beneath it. The index for MAX is given as 'L2', and for ALIGN as 'L1'.

(15) Grammar: MAX-L2 >> ALIGN-SUF(L1)-C >> MAX >> ALIGN-SUF-C

Lexicon: /-lu$_{L1}$/ /-nu$_{L1}$/ /-lu$_{L1}$/ /-ya$_{L1}$/ /-ta/ /-nu/ /-wa/ /-wa$_{L2}$/

Input	Output	MAX-L2	ALIGN-SUF(L1)-C	MAX
heta+nu+lu$_{L1}$	hetanulu		* !	
	☞ hetanru			*
heta+wa$_{L2}$+lu$_{L1}$	☞ hetawalu		*	
	hetawlu	* !		*

Syncope is also blocked when it would create a triconsonantal cluster (Matteson 1965: 36, Lin 1997), which indicates that a constraint against such clusters dominates the indexed alignment constraint. I will use the simple constraint *CCC for this purpose; see Lin (1997: 420) for an alternative formulation. The result of this ranking is shown in (16), with an example Matteson (1965: 36) glosses as 'she washes it'.

(16)

Input	Output	*CCC	ALIGN-SUF(L1)-C
terka+lu$_{L1}$	terklu	* !	
	☞ terkalu		*

A hierarchy for Yine syncope that incorporates indexed markedness and faithfulness constraints is thus as in (17).

(17) *CCC, MAX-L2 >> ALIGN-SUF(L1)-C >> MAX >> ALIGN-SUF-C

This analysis distinguishes morpheme-specific triggering from morpheme-specific blocking, and also accounts for phonological blocking.

2.3   Yine and cophonologies

In a cophonological analysis of Yine, morphemes would select rankings between the markedness constraint causing syncope and the conflicting faithfulness constraint. Under this approach, a morpheme causing syncope could be distinguished from one that does not as follows (compare 14):

(18)

Input	Output	ALIGN-SUF-C	MAX
heta+ya	hetaya	* !	
	☞ hetya		*
Input	Output	MAX	ALIGN-SUF-C
heta+wa	☞ hetawa		*
	hetwa	* !	

One issue is the determination of the outcome with morphemes that demand opposite rankings of the constraints. In /heta+nu+lu/ [hetanru], for example, /-nu/ requires MAX >> ALIGN-SUF-C to block deletion in the stem-final syllable, while /-lu/ requires ALIGN-SUF-C >> MAX to force deletion in /-nu/. However, given some kind of cyclic evaluation, which Lin (1997) argues is independently necessary for Yine, the outcome for /heta+nu/ could be calculated before, and independently of, the outcome for the entire string (see Orgun 1996 and Inkelas and Zoll 2005 on cyclicity and cophonologies). This is not a complete solution, since the syncope-producing constraint must also be limited to apply only to the environment of the outermost suffix of the complete /heta+nu+lu/ (perhaps using bracket erasure), but the problem does seem resolvable.

The more serious problem is how to distinguish the two forms of /-wa/ noted by Kisseberth (1970) and discussed in section 2.2. Both suffixes fail to trigger syncope, which should indicate that MAX dominates the markedness constraint. The problem is that only one of the suffixes fails to undergo syncope: in constrast to the /-wa/ meaning 'yet, still' in [hetawalu], the intransitive verb theme suffix in /meyi+wa+lu/ does syncopate ([meyiwlu]). As it stands, the account predicts that both should block (or that both should undergo, if the following suffix determines the ranking, as in the cyclic account mooted in the last paragraph). In other words, cophonology theory fails to distinguish morpheme-specific triggering from morpheme-specific blocking. This is an instance of a more general locality problem for cophonologies: when morphemes impose a ranking on the grammar, they do not specify where in the string that ranking should apply. When /-wa/ demands a ranking MAX >> ALIGN-SUF-C, it does not specify whether that ranking stops /-wa/, the preceding syllable, or some other syllable from undergoing syncope.

3   Finnish /a+i/ allomorphy

3.1   Locality and *[ai]

Anttila (2002) presents a pair of morphologically conditioned alternations in Finnish as providing evidence for a choice of lexical rankings over indexed constraints. In this section, I discuss the constraint that triggers these alterna-tions and show that constraint indexation allows for an analysis of the local nature of this and other cases of exceptional triggering. I also show that extant versions of cophonology theory and faithfulness-only indexation fail to capture such locality effects. Except where indicated, all of the data come from Anttila (2002), who based his study on an electronic version of a dictionary of Modern Finnish (Sadeniemi 1973).

The alternations affect a stem-final low vowel /a/ that precedes one of two homophonous suffixes /-i-/, which indicate either past or plural. The /a/ either deletes, or mutates to [o]. The examples in (19) show that the choice between the alternations is sometimes lexically determined; the stems are identical in all relevant phonological respects, yet one undergoes final vowel mutation (19a), one undergoes final vowel deletion (19b), and one varies between mutation and deletion (19c).

(19) a.   /tavara+i+ssa/ [tavaroissa]   'thing (plural-inessive)'
     b.   /jumala+i+ssa/ [jumalissa]   'God (plural-inessive)'
     c.   /itara+i+ssa/   [itaroissa] ~ [itarissa] 'stingy (plural-inessive)'

The alternations do not apply stem internally (20a), nor do they apply in all derived environments; (20b) is an example of non-application with the conditional suffix /-isi/ (Arto Anttila p.c.).

(20) a.   /taitta-i/   [taittoi] ~ [taitti] *[toittoi] *[titti]   'break (past)'
    b.   /anta-isi/   [antaisi]   'give (conditional)'

Anttila's (2002) analysis focuses on the interplay between morphological and phonological conditioning in the choice between mutation and deletion, and does not include the constraint that drives the alternation. To penalize the [ai] sequence in the appropriate morphological context, we can index the relevant constraint to the plural and past tense morphemes. For expository ease, I will adopt the straightforward but stipulative *[ai] as the active constraint. The indexed version of the constraint ranks above MAX and IDENT, while the general version of it ranks beneath the faithfulness constraints. The past and the plural /-i-/ are both indexed for the application of the specific constraint:

(21) Grammar: *[ai]$_L$ >> MAX, IDENT >> *[ai]
    Lexicon: /-i-/$_L$ /-i-/$_L$ /-isi-/ /taitta/

In the analysis of Yine, the indexed markedness constraint was an ALIGN constraint that provides an argument for the suffix. As such, the alignment constraint automatically specifies the context in which it applies. The following schema specifies how other indexed constraints assess violation marks:

(22) *X$_L$
    Assign a violation mark to any instance of X that contains a phonological
      exponent of a morpheme specified as L

This formulation serves as a locality convention for indexed constraints: they apply if and only if the locus of violation contains some portion of the indexed morpheme. Note especially that 'phonological exponent' in (22) is fulfilled by any subpart of the morpheme; there is no requirement that the entire morpheme be contained within the scope of the constraint. The locality convention in (22) also provides an explicit formulation of how a constraint indexed to a general morphological category applies: *X$_{SUFFIX}$, for example, would apply to all instances of X that include an element of a suffix (see Pater 2006 for an application to derived environment effects). Along these lines, the Finnish *[ai] constraint could also have been specified to apply to Plural and Past tense morphemes.

The following tableau shows how the ranking in (21) applies to /taitta-i/:

(23)

Input	Output	*[ai]$_L$	Max	Ident	*[ai]
/taitta-i$_L$/	taittai	* !			**
	☞ taitti		*		*
	☞ taittoi			*	*
	titti		** !		
	toittoi			** !	

The indexed constraint *[ai]$_L$ assigns a violation only to an [ai] sequence containing the indexed morpheme /-i/ and not to the root internal one. Because the indexed constraint does not apply to the root-internal [ai] sequence, the faithfulness constraints protect it. Because the ranking between Max and Ident is unspecified, either deletion or mutation of the stem-final vowel can emerge as the optimal outcome (see Casali 1997 on constraints that block changes to the suffix-initial vowel). Section 3.4 shows how the choice between deletion and mutation is made for stems that allow only one outcome. But first, I will provide another example of a case of exceptional triggering that is similarly local and discuss the locality problems faced by alternative theories.

3.2   Exceptional triggering in Assamese

Mahanta (2007) provides an example of local exceptional triggering in Assamese [ATR] harmony. In this language, [+ATR] spreads regressively from the high vowels [i] and [u], yielding an allophonic alternation in the mid vowels, which appear as [+ATR] [e] and [o] when they precede [+ATR] vowels, and as [-ATR] [ɛ] and [ɔ] elsewhere. Underlying [-ATR] [ʊ] also neutralizes with [+ATR] [u] when it precedes a [+ATR] vowel. Harmony is iterative, in that the targets of harmony spread [+ATR] to preceding vowels. Iterativity is illustrated in examples (24a–c), where harmony is triggered by the [+ATR] vowels in the initial position of the suffixes /-iya/ and /-uwa/.

(24) a.   [bɔyɔx] 'age'   [boyoxiya] 'aged'
  b.   [tɔlɔt] 'below'   [tolotiya] 'subordinate'
  c.   [gʊbɔr] 'dung'   [guboruwa] 'fly (with dung-like smell)'

The low [-ATR] vowel [a] is normally opaque to vowel harmony, as shown in examples (25a) and (25b); the /-i/ suffix regularly triggers harmony in other [-ATR] vowels.

(25) a.   [kɔpah] 'cotton'   [kɔpahi] 'made of cotton'
  b.   [zɔkar] 'shake'   [zɔkari] 'shake' (infinitive)

The exceptional triggering pattern arises when the morphemes /-iya/ and /-uwa/ in (24) are added to stems whose final vowel is [ɑ]. With these morphemes, /ɑ/ raises to a mid [+ATR] vowel, usually [o] (26a–g), except when [e] precedes, in which case /ɑ/ also surfaces as [e] (26h–i). In examples (26e–i), we see again that harmony is iterative; the raised /ɑ/ yields the regular harmony pattern to its left.

(26) a. [sɑl]   'roof'   [soliya]   'roof'
     b. [dɑl]   'branch'   [doliya]   'branch-ed'
     c. [dʰɑr]   'debt'   [dʰoruwa]   'debtor'
     d. [mɑr]   'beat' (verb)   [moruwa]   'beat' (causative)
     e. [bɔzɑr]   'marketplace'   [bozoruwa]   'cheap'
     f. [kɔpɑl]   'destiny'   [kopoliya]   'destined'
     g. [gʊlɑp]   'rose'   [gulopiya]   'pink'
     h. [ɛŋɑr]   'charcoal'   [eŋeruwa]   'black as charcoal'
     i. [dʰɛmɑli]   'play/amusing'   [dʰemeliya] 'playful/amusing'

The local nature of the exceptional triggering pattern is shown in the following examples, in which non-stem-final /ɑ/ fails to raise.

(27) a. [patɔl]   'light'   [patoliya]   'lightly'
     b. [apɔd]   'danger'   [apodiya]   'in danger'
     c. [abɔtɔr]   'bad time'   [abotoriya] 'bad timed'
     d. [alɑx]   'luxury'   [aloxuwa]   'pampered'
     e. [adʰa]   'half'   [adʰoruwa]   'halved'

Mahanta's analysis involves a lexically indexed version of the following constraint, whose definition I have slightly elaborated:

(28) *[-ATR][+ATR]
     Assign a violation mark to the minimal string containing a [-ATR] vowel
        followed by a [+ATR] vowel

'Minimal' in this definition refers to the smallest string of segments that contains the specified sequence, and which would fail to contain the sequence if a segment were removed. This is included to make explicit the locus of violation (thanks to Colin Wilson for related discussion). The indexed constraint would then be formulated as in (29).

(29) *[-ATR][+ATR]$_L$
     Assign a violation mark to the minimal string containing a [-ATR] vowel
        followed by a [+ATR] vowel, if that string contains a phonological exponent of
        a morpheme indexed as L

As Mahanta shows, a ranking in which these constraints straddle a faithfulness constraint generates /ɑ/ raising only in the immediate context of the exceptional morpheme:

(30)

Input	Output	*[-ATR][+ATR]$_L$	Ident-Low	*[-ATR][+ATR]
/alax-uwa$_L$/	alax-uwa	*!		*
	☞ alox-uwa		*	*
	olox-uwa		**!	

For further details of the analysis, see Mahanta (2007).

In the Assamese example, the indexed constraint is well-motivated both in the phonology of the language and cross-linguistically. It is only the ranking that is exceptional. The locality of the exceptional pattern provides strong support for the claim that indexed constraints are interpreted as in (22) (see Finley 2006 for further discussion of locality in exceptional vowel harmony).

There are some instances of exceptional triggering in which the exceptional pattern is perpetuated beyond the purely local environment (thanks to Matt Wolf for discussion). Terena, for example, has iterative nasal spreading in the context of the first person morpheme (Bendor-Samuel 1960), but no nasal harmony elsewhere. All cases of this type, however, seem to involve a 'floating feature', that is, a morpheme that is realized only as a featural change on the stem. McCarthy (2003b: 204) uses comparative markedness to analyze a tonal pattern of this type in which a floating feature docks and triggers iterative spreading. Interestingly, comparative markedness can only generate iterative spreading (it would fail to capture a case like Assamese exceptional triggering), and indexed markedness can only generate non-iterative spreading (that is, where the spreading is exceptional). Why the scenarios traditionally described in terms of floating features should be associated with the constraint generating iterative spreading, and the ones that involve triggering by context should involve indexed markedness or the like, is a question for further research.

3.3   The challenge of local exceptional triggering

In this section, I discuss the challenges posed by local exceptional triggering for cophonology theory and for indexed faithfulness theory, using the Finnish case to illustrate. Recall that /-i-/, but not /-isi-/, triggers mutation. A cophonology analysis would allow /-i-/ and /-isi-/ to select different rankings of *[ai] and the faithfulness constraints:

(31) a.   /-i-/   *[ai] >> Max, Ident
     b.   /-isi-/   Max, Ident >> *[ai]

An indexed faithfulness analysis would also leave the *[ai] constraint in its general form, but have faithfulness constraints indexed to morphemes that do not trigger the alternation:

(32) Grammar: Max_L, Ident_L >> *[ai] >> Max, Ident
     Lexicon: /-i-/ /-i-/ /-isi-/$_L$

It is not clear, on either account, how to deal with a form like /taitta-i/, in which one /ai/ sequence undergoes the alternation, and the other one does not. In the cophonology analysis, we might put /taitta/ in the list of morphemes with the FAITH >> MARK ranking:

(33) a.   /-i-/   *[ai] >> Max, Ident
     b.   /-isi-/ /taitta/   Max, Ident >> *[ai]

But which ranking should /taitta-i/ select? Either ranking will yield the wrong result: either both /ai/ sequences will surface, or neither will.

In the morpheme-specific faithfulness account, we could similarly index /taitta/ to the faithfulness constraints:

(34) Grammar: Max_L, Ident_L >> *[ai] >> Max, Ident
     Lexicon: /-i-/ /-i-/ /-isi-/$_L$ /taitta/$_L$

The problem here is that this would protect both instances of /a/, rather than just the second one.

A possible solution for the Finnish case would be to relativize *[ai] to the derived context. With this constraint, which I will label *[a+i], analyses are available in either framework; (35) sketches the lexical ranking analysis, and (36) the indexed faithfulness one.

(35) a.   /-i-/ /taitta/   *[a+i] >> Max, Ident
     b.   /-isi-/   Max, Ident >> *[a+i]

(36) Grammar: Max_L, Ident_L >> *[a+i] >> Max, Ident
     Lexicon: /-i-/ /-i-/ /-isi-/$_L$ /taitta/

One issue with this approach is that it requires an additional theory of derived environment effects: with morpheme-specific constraints, these are captured by simply indexing a constraint to a general morphological category (see Pater 2006). A bigger issue is that this solution does not address the general locality problem for morpheme-specific phonology (see Horwood 1999 and Wolf 2006 for discussion of locality problems in the Antifaithfulness theory of Alderete 2001 and the Realize Morpheme theory of Kurisu 2001).

For the analyses of Finnish in (35) and (36) to be successful, a certain amount of non-locality must be countenanced. The morpheme that fails to trigger (/-isi-/) must demand higher faithfulness not for itself, but for the immediately adjacent segment, so that the stem-final /a/ neither mutates nor deletes. A similar scenario will obtain for any situation in which triggering morphemes must be distinguished from non-triggers, and the alternation takes place outside of the morpheme; the Assamese case discussed in the previous section provides another clear example. The problem is in defining how much non-locality is allowed.

If the ranking introduced by a morpheme holds over the entire string, clearly undesirable results follow (see also Horwood 1999). For example, a language could have a general ranking ONSET >> DEP, which produces epenthesis in vowel-initial stems. If a suffix could introduce a DEP >> ONSET ranking that holds over the entire string, then epenthesis would be blocked word-initially only in the presence of that suffix, as in (37), where /ba/ is the exceptional morpheme.

(37) /amana/   [ʔamana]   /amana+da/ [ʔamanada]
     /amana+ba/ [amanaba]

A legion of similarly implausible cases could be constructed; I leave this to the reader's imagination.

Kiparsky (1993), Inkelas (2000), Mascaró (2003) and Kurisu (2006) discuss several cases in which affixation has effects that are somewhat similar to (37); it leads to a change that is not phonologically conditioned by the affix, and occurs at a distance. In Catalan, for example, exceptions to unstressed vowel deletion are regularized in derivation (e.g. the exceptional unreduced [e] of [tótem] 'totem' is lost in [tutəmízmə]). As Kiparsky (1993) notes, this can be characterized as the loss of exception features in the derived form. Note that this is different in at least two ways from the hypothetical example in (37), in which derivation *induces* exceptionality, and only one morpheme introduces the exceptional alternation. Possible analyses for cases of the Catalan type include an exceptionality analogue of bracket erasure, or indexation of faithfulness to a category that identifies the bare stem but not the derived one. It does not seem that the full power of cophonology theory is needed (cf. Inkelas 2000), since this would also generate unattested cases like those in (37).

A position between the extremes of the ranking holding only of the morpheme itself, and of it holding for the whole string, is that it holds of a string that contains some portion of that morpheme. This restriction is straightforwardly captured by the interpretive schema for indexed constraints in (22). In this theory, an indexed constraint cannot have the unattested long-distance triggering effect shown in (37). If indexation were limited to faithfulness constraints, it is difficult how to see how the intended restriction could be stated. It would also be difficult to formalize in cophonology theory, especially since it is taken as a fundamental and distinguishing assumption of the cophonology program that phonological constraints are not specified for morphological context:

> All constraints are fully general, but morphological class or lexical class are potentially associated with distinct rankings of those constraints. (Inkelas and Zoll 2003: 1)

> The alternative [to indexed constraints – JP] is to keep phonological constraints purely phonological, but posit a range of distinct COPHONOLOGIES, that is, different constraint rankings for different morphological categories. (Anttila 2002: 2)

3.4   Morphological and phonological conditions on repair choice

Anttila (2002) shows that both morphological idiosyncrasy and the phonological environment can affect the choice of mutation or deletion as the repair for *[ai]. He uses the partial ordering/lexical ranking theory to analyze the interplay between morphological and phonological conditioning. Here I replicate a portion of Anttila's analysis with indexed constraints to show that they are capable of expressing these sorts of generalizations. I also provide an analysis of generalizations that can be captured with indexed constraints, but not under partial ordering/cophonology theory.

As mentioned in section 3.1, stems of the same phonological shape can show three patterns. They can either select mutation, deletion, or vary between the two. The examples are repeated in (38).

(38) a.   /tavara+i+ssa/   [tavaroissa]   'thing (plural-inessive)'
     b.   /jumala+i+ssa/   [jumalissa]   'God (plural-inessive)'
     c.   /itara+i+ssa/   [itaroissa] ~ [itarissa]   'stingy (plural-inessive)'

I will follow Anttila (1997, 2002) in analyzing variation as the result of conflicting constraints being unranked with one another, with a ranking being randomly selected each time the grammar derives an output. However, it is worth noting that the present account of morpheme-specific phonology is compatible with other approaches to variation, including that of Boersma and Hayes (2001).

The grammar in (39) deals with the three stem types. The general MAX and IDENT are left unranked, so that unindexed stems show variation. Morpheme-specific versions of the constraints are ranked above the general ones; stems indexed to one of them will show consistent deletion or mutation.

(39) Grammar: *[ai]-L1 >> MAX-L2, IDENT-L3 >> MAX, IDENT >> *[ai]
     Lexicon: /-i-/$_{L1}$ /-i-/$_{L1}$ /-isi-/ /tavara/$_{L2}$ /jumala/$_{L3}$ /itara/

The result of applying this grammar to each of the three stem types is shown in (40). The unindexed stem shows variation (two optimal candidates in this tableau), while the indexed stems show either mutation or deletion, depending on whether they are indexed to MAX or IDENT.

(40)

Input	Output	*[ai]-L1	MAX-L2	IDENT-L3	MAX	IDENT
/itara-i_{L1}-ssa/	itaraissa	* !				
	☞ itarissa				*	
	☞ itaroissa					*
/tavara$_{L2}$-i_{L1}-ssa/	tavaraissa	* !				
	tavarissa		* !		*	
	☞ tavaroissa					*
/jumala$_{L3}$-i_{L1}-ssa/	jumalaissa	* !				
	☞ jumalissa				*	
	jumaloissa			* !		*

Antilla (2002) presents data showing that in some phonological contexts, not all these options are observed. With stems that consist of an even number of syllables (the stems in (40) are trisyllables), the generalization he uncovers is relatively straightforward: mutation occurs unless the preceding vowel is round, in which case deletion occurs instead. Anttila analyzes deletion after round vowels as an effect of an OCP constraint against a sequence of round vowels, which is violated when mutation creates an [o]. Since Finnish constructs trochees from left-to-right, Anttila (2002: 17) derives the syllable count generalization by restricting the constraint to the foot-internal context. To rule out mutation for this type of stem, Anttila ranks OCP/V[rd]$_\Phi$ above MAX (which he labels *DEL). In his account, the presence of this ranking in the grammar bans lexical items from choosing the reverse order of the constraints. We can achieve the same effect with morpheme-specific constraints by ranking OCP/V[rd]$_\Phi$ above the indexed version of MAX:

(41) OCP/V[rd]$_\Phi$, IDENT-L3 >> MAX-L2 >> MAX, IDENT

With this ranking, even if a lexical item with a final round vowel is indexed to lexically specific MAX, it will undergo deletion rather than mutation, since mutation conflicts with OCP/V[rd]$_\Phi$. The difference between disyllabic and trisyllabic stems is demonstrated in the following Richness of the Base tableaux, in which foot boundaries are indicated by parentheses. These tableaux show the result of indexation to MAX-L2 for both stem shapes. In disyllabic forms, where OCP/V[rd]$_\Phi$ applies, mutation is ruled out, even with this indexation. In trisyllabic forms, mutation does occur with indexation. Hypothetical forms are used in both cases; Anttila (2002: 10) states that 1/3 of the forms like /itota/ undergo categorical mutation, though he does not provide any examples.

(42)

Input	Output	OCP/V[rd]$_\Phi$	IDENT-L3	MAX-L2	MAX	IDENT
/tota$_{L2}$-i$_{L1}$/	☞ (toti)			*	*	
	(totoi)	* !				*
/itota$_{L2}$-i$_{L1}$/	(ito)ti			* !	*	
	☞ (ito)(toi)					*

The other side of this even-numbered stem generalization, that mutation applies in the absence of a preceding round vowel, is not dealt with in Anttila's (2002) analysis. As it stands, the analysis predicts that these stems should behave just like trisyllables of the same phonological shape. To some extent, this is borne out: as the example /taitta-i/ [taitt-oi] ~ [taitt-i] discussed in the last section shows, this side of the generalization is not iron-clad. Anttila (2002: 5) cites Karlsson (1982) as noting approximately 35 verb stems with variation in this context. However, unlike the trisyllabic stems, none of this type undergo categorical deletion.

To generate the default pattern of mutation, we need a constraint that applies to even-numbered stems, but not odd-numbered ones; ranking MAX over IDENT will not suffice. Drawing on Anttila's proposal that foot structure is responsible for syllable count generalizations, we can note that in the bare form of an odd-numbered stem the final syllable will be unparsed. Given a faithfulness relation between the stem and the suffixed form (see esp. Baković's 2000 elaboration of Benua's 1997/2000 proposal), a MAX constraint that protects only footed segments will target the final vowels of only even-numbered stems. This constraint, which I will label OO-MAX$_\Phi$, ranks above the general form of IDENT, but beneath OCP/V[rd]$_\Phi$, so that deletion still occurs with a preceding round vowel, as in /tota-i/ [toti] (see (42)). To allow for variation between mutation and deletion in exceptional cases like /taitta-i/, the lexically specific version of IDENT ranks evenly with OO-MAX$_\Phi$. The tableaux in (43) demonstrate the results of these rankings for an unindexed disyllabic stem (/pala/ 'burn'; Anttila 2002: 3) and an indexed one (/taitta/ from (20)), along with an indexed trisyllabic stem (/jumala+i+ssa/ 'God' (plural-inessive)).

(43)

Input	Output	OO-Max$_\Phi$	Ident-L3	Max-L2	Max	Ident
/taitta$_{L3}$-i$_{L1}$/	☞ taitti	*			*	
	☞ taittoi		*			*
/pala-i$_{L1}$/	pali	* !			*	
	☞ paloi					*
/jumala$_{L3}$-i$_{L1}$-ssa/	☞ jumalissa				*	
	jumaloissa		* !			*

Because the final vowel of the trisyllabic stem /jumala/ lies outside of a foot in the base form and is hence not subject to OO-Max$_\Phi$, indexing it to Ident-L3 will categorically result in deletion. And as the tableaux in (40) show, indexation of a trisyllable to Max-L2 chooses consistent mutation, while lack of indexation produces variation. For disyllables like /taitta/ and /pala/, however, the options in (43) are the only available ones; consistent deletion requires a preceding round vowel.

This analysis cannot be translated into Anttila's (2002) theory. As noted above, because the partial ordering/lexical ranking theory allows lexical rankings to fix only grammatically unordered constraints, exceptionality and variation are conflated. To get variation for /taitta-i/, in partial ordering/lexical ranking theory the constraints picking mutation and deletion would have to be unranked. But if they are unranked, then stems should be able to select a ranking of the constraint picking deletion over the one preferring mutation, resulting in the unattested pattern of consistent mutation in this environment. See Pater (2006) for discussion of further generalizations in the Finnish data that cannot be expressed with cophonologies.

4   Constraint indexation as inconsistency resolution

In this section I propose an account of creation of lexically indexed constraints in terms of inconsistency resolution, and show that it can handle the Yine case, in which both faithfulness and markedness constraints must be appropriately indexed (see also Winslow 2003, Pater 2004, 2006, Becker 2006b and Tessier 2006 on indexation as inconsistency resolution, as well as Ota 2004 for discussion of Japanese postnasal voicing in similar terms).

As Tesar, Alderete, Horwood, Merchant, Nishitani and Prince (2003) point out in the context of lexical stress, exceptions to patterns of phonological alternation give rise to an inconsistent set of data, which can be detected by Tesar and Smolensky's (1998) Constraint Demotion Algorithm (CDA; see Tesar 1998, Prince 2003, McCarthy 2005b, and Tesar and Prince 2007 for other applications of inconsistency detection). This is illustrated by the set of winner-loser pairs (Prince 2003) for the hypothetical language discussed in section 2.1.

(44)

Input	**W ~ L**	NoCoda	Max
pak	pa ~ pak	W	L
lok	lo ~ lok	W	L
tak	tak ~ ta	L	W

Each row of the table presents the optimal form, or 'winner', paired with a suboptimal competitor or 'loser'. For each pair, the W's and L's in the constraint columns indicate whether a constraint prefers the winner or loser. A constraint ranking will correctly choose the winner if and only if every constraint preferring the loser is dominated by some constraint preferring the winner. The winner-loser pairs in (44) impose incompatible requirements on the ranking; /pak/ → [pa] requires NoCoda >> Max, and /tak/ → [ta] requires Max >> NoCoda. The CDA will fail to rank these constraints, and 'declare inconsistency' (Prince 2003).

The recursive version of the CDA (RCD; Tesar and Smolensky 1998, 2000) is a particularly useful tool in diagnosing the locus of inconsistency. It starts by identifying all of the constraints that prefer only winners (that is, that prefer the winner or prefer neither the winner or the loser), and installs them in a stratum. It then eliminates all of the winner-loser pairs from the dataset in which the just-installed constraints prefer the winner (since the optimality of the winner is now guaranteed), and goes on to construct the next stratum in the same fashion. The procedure stops when all of the data are eliminated, or when no constraints prefer only winners. In the latter case, the residue of the dataset contains inconsistency (unless none of the constraints assign Ws to the remaining pairs, in which case the constraint set is inadequate for some other reason).

What happens after RCD detects inconsistency? For lexical stress, Tesar et al. (2003) propose that the lexical representation is altered, the winner-loser pairs are updated, and constraint demotion restarts. It is unlikely, however, that all instances of morpheme-specific alternation can be dealt with in terms of differences in lexical representation. And even in those cases in which a structural account is available, the search space of possible lexical changes is extremely large. Tesar et al. (2003) abstract from this problem by only considering changes in underlying stress, but if lexical 'surgery' is disconnected from constraint ranking, it is not at all clear how the pattern of constraint violations can guide the change in underlying representation (see further section 5).

Here I suggest instead that when the constraint demotion algorithm can no longer find constraints that favor only winners, it seeks a constraint that favors only winners *for all instances of some morpheme*. It then ranks that constraint, indexed to all of the morphemes for which it favors only winners. In the simple case in (44), there are two such constraints: MAX and NoCODA. It is perhaps inconsequential which is chosen, since an indexed version of either one will allow inconsistency to be resolved. If, however, it is taken as a goal to lexically index the smaller set of forms (i.e. the 'exceptional' ones), then a bias to a smaller set of indexed morphemes could be built in (see Winslow 2003, Pater 2004, and the Appendix), thus choosing MAX to be the indexed constraint, as in (2) above.

The Yine case is more interesting in that the correct choice between constraints must be made for each morpheme in order to get the right results. For example, the following data must lead to morpheme-specific ALIGN for /-lu/ and morpheme-specific MAX for /-wa/, and no marking for the other morphemes.

(45) /heta+lu/   [hetlu]   'see it'

    /heta+nu/   [hetanu]   'going to see'

    /heta+nu+lu/   [hetanru]   'going to see him'

    /heta+wa+lu/   [hetawalu]   'going to see him yet'

When learning commences, there are only unindexed versions of the constraints:

(46) ALIGN-SUF-C, MAX

In (47) we see that the winner-loser pairs are inconsistent with one another.

(47)

Input	**W ~ L**	MAX	ALIGN-SUF-C
heta+lu	hetlu ~ hetalu	L (heta)	W (lu)
heta+nu	hetanu ~ hetnu	W (heta)	L (nu)
heta+wa+lu	hetawalu ~ hetawlu	W (wa)	L (lu)
heta+nu+lu	hetanlu ~ hetanulu	L (nu)	W (lu)

In this table, the relevant morpheme is indicated alongside the W and L marks. This information is needed to correctly identify the locus of inconsistency. A more explicit statement of the inconsistency resolution routine that makes use of this information appears in (48).

(48) i.   Clone a constraint that prefers only Ws in all instances of some morpheme

    ii. Index it to every morpheme for which it prefers only Ws

In the first step, we can only index MAX for /-wa/ – MAX prefers Ls and Ws for /heta/, and ALIGN-SUF-C prefers Ls and Ws for /lu/.

(49)

Input	W ~ L	Max	Align-Suf-C	Max-L1
heta+lu	hetlu ~ hetalu	L	W	
heta+nu	hetanu ~ hetnu	W	L	
heta+wa$_{L1}$+lu	hetawalu ~ hetawlu	W	L	W
heta+nu+lu	hetanlu ~ hetanulu	L	W	

Since Max-L1 prefers only winners, RCD places it in the first stratum. Since RCD eliminates winner-loser pairs after installing a constraint preferring the winner, the third pair of table (49) is removed, yielding the following partial hierarchy and table:

(50) Max-L1 >>

Input	W ~ L	Max	Align-Suf-C
heta+lu	hetlu ~ hetalu	L	W
heta+nu	hetanu ~ hetnu	W	L
heta+nu+lu	hetanlu ~ hetanulu	L	W

In the above set of winner-loser pairs Align-Suf-C now assigns only Ws for /lu/; Max continues to assign a W and an L to /heta/. Table (51) shows the result of cloning and indexation:

(51) Max-L1 >>

Input	W ~ L	Max	Align-Suf-C	Align-Suf-C-L2
heta+lu$_{L2}$	hetlu ~ hetalu	L	W	W
heta+nu	hetanu ~ hetnu	W	L	
heta+nu+lu$_{L2}$	hetanlu ~ hetanulu	L	W	W

The RCD's stratum formation and winner-loser pair elimination now yields (52):

(52) Max-L1 >> Align-Suf(L2)-C

Input	W ~ L	Max	Align-Suf-C
heta+nu	hetanu ~ hetnu	W	L

RCD's next two iterations place all of the constraints in the hierarchy:

(53) Max-L1 >> Align-Suf-C-L2 >> Max >> Align-Suf-C

The ranking of the constraint *CCC will be established straightforwardly, given forms like /terkalu/ [terkalu] *[terklu], which show that *CCC dominates Align-Suf-C:

(54)	Input	W ~ L	*CCC	Align-Suf-C-L2
	terka+lu$_{L2}$	terkalu ~ terklu	W	L

In fact, except for the special circumstances discussed in Lin (1997), from which I abstract here, *CCC is unviolated in Yine.[3] Thus, *CCC would be installed in the first step of the constraint demotion algorithm, since it prefers only winners, and the winner-loser pair in (54) would be immediately eliminated from consideration. The grammar constructed for Yine by RCD with inconsistency resolution would thus be as in (55).

(55) *CCC >> Max-L1 >> Align-Suf-C-L2 >> Max >> Align-Suf-C

The ranking of *CCC raises an important point. Given morphologically indexed faithfulness constraints, one might worry that the learner wouldn't bother with the phonological generalization at all. In the present case, why doesn't the learner just index /terka/ to Max, and treat this as another morphological exception? The answer lies in the way that this modified RCDA works. RCD seeks to deal with the data in terms of a constraint ranking. Only when inconsistency prevents this from happening are indexed constraints created. In the case of forms like /terkalu/, the winner-loser pair in (54) will already have been eliminated from consideration by the ranking of *CCC before inconsistency resolution applies; the phonological explanation takes precedence over the lexical one (see also Tesar et al. 2003).

The prioritization of ranking over indexation is not in itself sufficient for the learner to capture all generalizations in patterns of alternation (note that this proposal is not meant to handle exceptions to phonotactic generalizations; see Pater 2005, Albright 2006, Coetzee and Pater 2008 and Hayes and Wilson 2008 for recent discussion of the learning of gradient phonotactics). At the end of learning, there will be a set of indexed morphemes over which there may be both phonological and morphological generalizations that are not yet expressed. The phonological generalizations would be those that cannot be captured by the posited universal constraint set (see Becker 2006b for related discussion). The morphological generalizations would be ones in which morphemes of a particular lexical or morpho-syntactic class pattern together (see e.g. Ito and Mester 1995a,b, and 1999b on lexical strata, and Smith 1997 on noun faithfulness). For the latter, it may be that learners are biased to index constraints to information already present in the lexicon, since this would avoid the postulation of an arbitrary diacritic, and would presumably render the lexical encoding more robust (see Anttila 2002 on the emergence of morphological conditioning of exceptionality).

There are several other ways in which this learning proposal may be profitably developed. Here the data were presented to the learner all at once; an on-line learner would be more realistic (see Tesar 1998 and subsequent work on how inconsistency can be detected by an on-line learner). The implementation of this proposal in such terms would be straightforward; the only difference would be that the learner might clone more constraints than it would if it had access to all of the data. Another extension would be to variation. As Tessier (2006) discusses in detail, an alternative OT learning model that handles variation, the GLA of Boersma (1998) and Boersma and Hayes (2001), does not deal with the full range of patterns of exception, even with the supplementary proposals of Zuraw (2000). As Andries Coetzee (p.c.) has pointed out to me, one way of extending the current theoretical model to variation would be to treat a morpheme that displays variation as one that bears multiple indices. This may lead to a fairly simple elaboration of the learning model (see Tessier 2006 for an alternative). And finally, the procedure for selecting a constraint to clone likely needs to be further specified; see the Appendix for discussion.

5   Representational approaches to exceptionality

The lexical idiosyncrasies of Yine syncope could be reanalyzed in representational terms, without recourse to the lexical diacritics that indexed constraints require. Matteson's (1965: 36) convention for notating non-triggering morphemes in fact suggests such an analysis: that they possess an unspecified vocalic position (e.g. /-Vta/), whose presence blocks the application of syncope (see Wolf 2006 on how to derive this sort of blocking in OT). For the morpheme that fails to undergo deletion, one might lexically specify some aspect of syllable structure (e.g. a mora), which is protected by a faithfulness constraint (e.g. MAX-M; see Inkelas, Orgun and Zoll 1997 and Inkelas 2000 for related proposals).

The main challenge for such an analysis is to specify how a learner would arrive at the representations needed to make it work. The most difficult cases are ones where the feature that must be specified in the non-alternating forms is not the only feature that changes in the alternating form. Taking the Yine example of exceptional blocking of syncope, it is not just the vocalic mora that is variably present in surface allomorphs of alternating vowels, but the entire vowel. For the analysis mentioned in the above paragraph to work, the learner must somehow be guided to choose the mora as the element to specify in non-alternating /-wa/, and leave absent from the alternating form. Presumably, the guide would be the presence of a faithfulness constraint that specifically targets the mora, and can protect it from deletion. While it is plausible that a learner might restructure an underlying representation so that it allows a constraint to choose the correct output, no extant learnability proposal allows for this. The process of surgery, as Tesar et al. (2003) term it, is grammar-blind. Inkelas

(1994) proposes a version of lexicon optimization (Prince and Smolensky 1993/2004) that leads to underspecified representations. However, as Bruce Tesar (p.c.) notes, this proposal assumes the existence of a constraint ranking; it has yet to be incorporated into a learning model that also acquires a ranking. One might also limit the representational search space; see Tesar (2006) on contrast analysis. Ultimately, the success of learnability proposals, rather than some unstated aesthetic principle, should choose between representational and diacritic approaches to exceptionality, insofar as they can handle the same range of data. Since the pattern of constraint violations directly guides the required adjustment to the system in the inconsistency resolution account of constraint indexation, this seems a particularly promising approach.

The empirical scope of various approaches to exceptionality remains to be determined. It is unclear whether all cases of exceptionality can, or should, be given a diacritic treatment (see also Ito and Mester 2001, Albright 2002, and Becker 2004 for recent arguments for diacritic analyses; cf. Inkelas et al. 1997 on Turkish, though see Becker 2006b). Instances where the markedness motivation for the alternation has disappeared, as in many cases of mutation (see Wolf 2006), seem particularly amenable to a representational analysis. And of course, non-surface-true underlying forms are required to deal with opacity (see McCarthy 2005b). However, it is equally unclear whether a representational account of morpheme-specific phonology can be made fully general. It should be noted that even proponents of representational approaches in OT see a role for morpheme-specific constraints or rankings (see e.g. Inkelas 1999, Kager 2008).

As well as clarifying the relative scope of purely diacritic and structural approaches, further research should cast light on the viability of various intermediate positions (e.g. indexation limited to a subset of markedness constraints, or structural hypotheses limited to surface observable forms), and of alternative analyses of exceptionality like Alderete's (2001) Antifaithfulness theory, the Realize Morpheme theory of Kurisu (2001) and others, Kager's (2008) extension of allomorphy theory, and Zuraw's (2000) extension of Boersma (1998) and Boersma and Hayes' (2001) stochastic OT (see also Hayes and Londe 2006).

6   On the power of diacritic theories

It is most likely that representational and diacritic theories of exceptionality do not overlap completely in the set of attested phenomena that they can account for, and so the challenge will be to parcel out the explanatory burden appropriately. However, the three diacritic theories discussed in this paper do account for essentially the same phenomena, and so we can ask which of them seems most likely to account for all and only the attested types of exceptionality and of other morpheme-specific phonology. In earlier parts of the paper I have advanced specific arguments in favor of constraint indexation; here I attempt to address the more general question of whether the theories differ in the extent to which they allow different phonological patterns to co-exist in a single language.

It might seem obvious that a theory that allows both markedness and faithfulness constraints to be indexed is more powerful than one that allows only faithfulness indexation. However, since most phonological processes involve crucial rankings between markedness and faithfulness constraints, it is somewhat difficult to find phenomena that cannot be analyzed in terms of faithfulness indexation (for attested cases that argue for markedness indexation, see Pater 2000, 2006, Ota 2004, and Flack 2007b; see also Gelbart 2005). Inkelas and Zoll (2003) provide a cogent demonstration that the restriction of indexation to faithfulness does not impose substantial limits on the set of patterns that can co-exist in a language. I know of just two problems. Indexed markedness constraints can produce the unattested templatic backcopying pattern that McCarthy and Prince (1995, 1999) avoid by eliminating templates from prosodic morphology (see Flack 2007b; cf. Inkelas and Zoll 2005, Gouskova 2006). The other major worry with indexed markedness constraints is that if they can be relativized to a category like Root, then they can subvert a fixed Root-Faith >> Affix-Faith meta-ranking (McCarthy and Prince 1995), and produce a language that that neutralizes contrasts root-internally, but not in affixes (see Albright 2004, Tessier 2004b, Beechey 2005, Urbanczyk 2006 for related discussion). How these issues are best addressed is a matter for further research; completely ruling out markedness indexation does not seem to be a viable approach.

Most versions of cophonology theory can express the same sorts of morphologically specific ranking reversals as a theory with indexation of both markedness and faithfulness constraints. Anttila's (2002) partial ordering/ cophonology theory also seems nearly, if not completely equivalent. Insofar as there is no restriction on how many constraints can be left unordered, this theory does not impose any restrictions on what rankings can co-exist in a language. The only exception is that it cannot express the equivalent of the following type of indexed constraint grammar, where the lexically specific version of the constraint is separated by more than one stratum from its general counterpart:

(56) Con1-L >> Con2 >> Con3 >> Con1

As far as I know, the empirical force of this restriction has yet to be demonstrated.

Since all of the diacritic theories seem to allow an extremely wide range of rankings to co-exist in a single language, an obvious question is why we don't find languages that mix very different properties together. The main issue with this line of objection is that it's difficult to measure heterogeneity: how does one quantify the attested phonological differences between morphemes that we do find in a single language, versus those that do not co-exist? However, it does seem that languages maintain a certain degree of homogeneity, for example by regularizing exceptional patterns over time. This would receive a relatively natural explanation in indexation theory, if one assumes that constraint clones and indices add complexity to the system that is sometimes eliminated over the course of time.

7   Conclusions

In this paper, I have shown that several considerations favor a theory of morpheme-specific phonology with indexed markedness and faithfulness constraints over either a theory with only indexed faithfulness constraints, or cophonology theory. Unlike these alternatives, it allows for a distinction between exceptional triggering and blocking, which was shown to be neces-sary to analyze the Yine data. Given the locality convention introduced here, indexed markedness constraints allow for a straightforward analysis of the locus of Finnish /ai/ allomorphy and Assamese exceptional ATR harmony, and also resolve general locality problems for morpheme-specific phonology. And finally, indexed constraints allow for distinctions between exceptional and impossible patterns, and between exceptionality and variation.

I have also provided a learnability account in which indexed constraints are created to deal with inconsistency in the learning data. This is a relatively straightforward extension of Tesar and Smolensky's (1998, 2000) RCDA, and avoids some of the issues faced by learnability analyses posited for representa-tional theories of exceptionality. In addition, this learnability proposal provides an explicit resolution of an apparent theoretical incongruity. The existence of morpheme-specific constraints is sometimes seen as incompatible with a theory in which constraints are universal (see e.g. Green 2005): is the Tagalog con-straint ALIGN([UM]AF, L, STEM, L) proposed by McCarthy and Prince (1993a) present in all grammars? Under this proposal, morpheme-specific constraints are constructed from universal constraints in the course of learning.

Appendix: Analyzing Inconsistency

The learnability proposal in sec. 4 remains to be fully elaborated and implemented. The main issue that arises is how to choose between constraints to clone when more than one is selected by the criterion in (48i.), repeated in (A1i.).

(A1) i. Clone a constraint that prefers only Ws in all instances of some morpheme
    ii. Index the cloned constraint to every morpheme for which it prefers only Ws

Recursive Constraint Demotion (RCD) will usually winnow down the constraint set considerably by the time inconsistency is encountered. However, as members of the Rutgers Optimality Research Group have pointed out to me, RCD may stall at a point when constraints not involved in the inconsistency pattern remain to be installed. Such a situation is illustrated schematically in (A2):

(A2)

Winner~Loser	Con1	Con2	Con3	Con4
a~b	W	L		
c~d	L	W	L	
e~f			W	L

The problem for the constraint indexation proposal is the following. Assuming that the inputs underlying 'a~b', 'c~d', and 'e~f' are all separate morphemes, Con1, Con2 and Con3 could all be cloned under the definition in (A1), but cloning Con3 would not resolve inconsistency. One possibility would be to simply allow the learner to choose randomly, since it would eventually find a useful constraint to clone. However, a guided approach is likely preferable. Here I address only the problem of finding useful constraints; see Becker (2006b) and Pater (2006; sec. 3.3) on choosing between useful constraints to ensure restrictiveness. Before proceeding, I should emphasize that the analysis of inconsistency is important not only for this learnability proposal, but more generally for diagnosing the source of failure when a constraint set fails to capture a data pattern.

The task of identifying the locus of inconsistency is complicated by the fact that more than two constraints, and more than two winner-loser pairs, can be involved in creating an inconsistent pattern of W and L marks. The following table illustrates.

(A3)

Winner~Loser	Con1	Con2	Con3
a~b	W	L	
c~d		W	L
e~f	L		W

The pattern of marks in (A3) can be extended to create an 'irreducibly inconsistent system' (IIS; van Loon 1981) with a set of winner-loser pairs of any size. IIS is a term used in the analysis of inconsistent systems in Linear Programming; see Potts et al. (2009) on the connection between Linear Programming and the constraint demotion algorithm. A definition adapted to OT from Chinneck and Dravnieks (1991) appears in (A4) (readers that consult the original definition should note that the term 'constraint' in Linear Programming refers to a linear inequality, not a constraint in the linguistic sense).

(A4) *Irreducibly Inconsistent System (in OT)*
  An irreducibly inconsistent system is a minimal inconsistent set of Winner-Loser pairs, that is, an inconsistent set that becomes consistent when one Winner-Loser pair is removed.

To find an IIS, one can apply Chinneck and Dravnieks' (1991) technique of Deletion Filtering, in which the following procedure is applied to each Winner-Loser pair until they are all tested (see Chinneck and Dravnieks for a proof that Deletion Filtering yields an IIS):

(A5) *Deletion Filtering (in OT)*
  i. Temporarily remove a Winner-Loser pair from the inconsistent set
  ii. If the remaining set is consistent, return the Winner-Loser pair to the set; if the remaining set in inconsistent, remove the Winner-Loser pair permanently

This procedure would eliminate the final row of the table in (A2), leaving W marks only in the columns of the constraints involved in the inconsistency pattern, thus providing the desired input for (A1).

However, it may be that the goals of finding useful constraints to clone, and of analyzing inconsistent OT systems for other purposes, do not require this brute force method. The procedure I term Analytic Filtering (A6) takes as its first step the elimination of constraints that cannot be contributing to inconsistency (many other such constraints – those that prefer only winners – would have already been installed by RCD). The second step pares down the resulting winner-loser set. Analytic Filtering reduces the table in (A2) to an IIS containing just the first two winner-loser pairs, and will leave the table in (A3) untouched.

(A6) *Analytic Filtering*
  i. Remove constraint columns containing only Ls
  ii. Remove Winner-Loser pair rows containing only Ws

Though Deletion Filtering and Analytic Filtering yield similar results for cases (A2) and (A3), there are at least two ways in which the results of these two procedures will diverge. Analytic Filtering will not eliminate Winner-Loser pairs that duplicate the same portion of a pattern of inconsistency, as in (A7). Since either of the last rows could be removed without yielding a consistent set, this is not yet an IIS.

(A7)

Winner~Loser	CoN1	CoN2
a~b	W	L
c~d	L	W
e~f	L	W

Another situation in which Analytic Filtering will fail to yield an IIS is when there are multiple patterns of inconsistency in the residue of RCD, as in the following example:

(A8)

Winner~Loser	CoN1	CoN2	CoN3
a~b	W	L	
c~d	L	W	L
e~f		L	W

Here either the first or third row would have to be removed to yield an IIS.

It is not clear that the further reduction performed by Deletion Filtering in these cases is either necessary, or useful, for an OT learner or analyst. For example, if it is taken as a goal to index the smallest set of morphemes, then the information that CoN1 assigns Ws to fewer morphemes than CoN2 in (A7) is crucial, and would be lost through Deletion Filtering. And if it is taken as a goal to clone the smallest number of constraints, then (A8) contains the information that CoN2 participates in both patterns of inconsistency, which would also be lost after Deletion Filtering. However, other cases of inconsistency may well be better analyzed using Deletion Filtering or some other method; how to best perform inconsistency analysis in OT remains an open research question.

Notes

1   Acknowledgements: From the time I was a visiting graduate student at UMass through the last decade as his colleague, I have benefited greatly from John McCarthy's generosity of spirit and intellect. Discussion in Ling 730 (UMass, Fall 2004), co-taught with John McCarthy, and Ling 606 (UMass, Spring 2005) contributed much to the development of the material herein. For helpful comments in those classes and elsewhere, I thank Eric Baković, Michael Becker, Adrian Brasonoveau, Andries Coetzee, Naz Merchant, Alan Prince, Bruce Tesar, and Matt Wolf. I am especially grateful to Arto Anttila for discussion of Finnish, to John McCarthy, Anne-Michelle Tessier and Nicholas Winslow for extensive discussion of the learnability proposal, and to Sara Finley, Kathryn Flack, Maria Gouskova, Peter Jurgec, Shigeto Kawahara, Michael Key, Shakuntala Mahanta, Marc van Oostendorp, Steve Parker, Kathryn Pruitt, and Hideki Zamma for comments on a draft of the paper.

2   Lin's (1997) syncope constraint requires the stem to end in a consonant. Lin does not analyze the absence of syncope in unsuffixed stems, or with non-triggering suffixes. Under the locality condition discussed in section 2, the scope of the indexed constraint must include the triggering morpheme; Lin's constraint would not meet this criterion. One might also invoke an Alignment constraint that requires a suffix to follow a heavy syllable; Matteson (1965: 24) describes post-vocalic consonants as variably closing the preceding syllable (cf. Lin 1997: 425). However, in deference to Matteson's claim that pre-consonantal consonants are invariably syllabic, I retain the formulation in (12).

3   These special circumstances are in the context of an opaque interaction in which vowel deletion feeds consonant deletion and compensatory lengthening, as well in as clusters incorporating a mono-consonantal affix.

6 Source similarity in loanword adaptation: Correspondence Theory and the posited source-language representation[1]

Jennifer L. Smith

Source-similarity effects in loanword adaptation are formalized in Correspondence Theory (McCarthy and Prince, 1995). A correspondence relation holds between the loanword and the *pLs representation,* the borrower's posited representation of the source-language form; including the pLs representation in the model allows a consistent account of the interaction between phonological adaptation processes and factors such as perception and orthography. Empirical support is provided for the Correspondence Theory approach, which predicts multiple phonological adaptation strategies for loanwords.

1   Introduction

Evidence from loanword adaptation (LWA) has been influential in phonological argumentation, especially in constraint-based frameworks. LWA is the process of taking a form from the source language (Ls) and incorporating it into the borrowing language (Lb), performed by an Lb speaker with at least limited exposure to Ls. This paper contributes to debates about the nature of LWA and its relationship to phonology, perception, and other factors.

One position supported here is that *LWA cannot be attributed to the Lb-internal phonological grammar alone.* Certainly, Lb constraints are involved in LWA. Loanwords are typically adapted to comply with certain Lb phonotactic restrictions, so some of the constraints that enforce phonotactics in non-loans also affect loanwords (Yip, 1993; Paradis and LaCharité, 1997; Broselow, 2000; Jacobs and Gussenhoven, 2000). However, there are aspects of LWA that the Lb-internal grammar cannot account for. For example, some languages have a loanword-specific adaptation strategy that differs from default Lb-internal phonological processes (Section 3).

This paper also demonstrates that *LWA cannot be attributed to speech perception alone.* Again, this is not to deny that perception affects LWA. Perceptual similarity can influence the choice of adaptation strategy (Yip, 2002; Kang, 2003). Moreover, some adaptation 'repairs' arise when Lb listeners misperceive Ls forms (Silverman, 1992; Peperkamp and Dupoux, 2003). However, examples presented here show that LWA processes cannot all be reduced to misperception. In Japanese (Section 3), the pLs representation sometimes contains Lb-illicit segments contributed by orthographic information. These segments trigger epenthesis, but the epenthesis cannot have a perceptual basis since the triggering segments have no perceptual basis. In Finnish, Hmong, and Sranan (Section 4), highly salient segments undergo deletion in LWA, despite phonological evidence that they are perceived. As misperception cannot account for these epenthesis and deletion effects, they must be part of the phonological (production) grammar.

Section 2 develops a formal model of LWA, extending the insights of recent work applying Correspondence Theory (McCarthy and Prince, 1995) to source-similarity effects like those responsible for LWA-specific phonological processes. An explicit proposal is made concerning the Ls-based phonological string that stands in correspondence with the adapted loanword. This string, the *posited Ls (pLs) representation,* is part of the Lb speaker's phonological system, serving as a repository for all information the Lb speaker has about the Ls form. The pLs representation allows for a consistent formal treatment of effects on LWA by perception, orthography, knowledge of Ls grammar, and other factors (Section 3). Additional support for a correspondence-based approach to LWA comes from the fact that *multiple strategies* are available for adapting loanwords (Sections 3–4), as expected given a full set of rankable Ls-Lb faithfulness constraints. Conclusions and implications for LWA and phonological argumentation are discussed in Section 5.

2   Modeling adaptation

This section presents the SB-correspondence model of LWA:[2] The SB (Ls-to-Lb) correspondence relation (Section 2.1) holds between an Lb loanword and the pLs representation of its source form (Section 2.2). The predictions of the model are compared to those of other approaches in Section 2.3, setting the stage for the analyses in Sections 3–4.

2.1   Source similarity as correspondence

Certain aspects of LWA require a mechanism beyond the non-loan Lb phonology. This is true for cases of *importation,* where Lb-illicit structures persist in loanwords even though they would be actively avoided in non-loans (Haugen, 1950; Karvonen, 1998; Smith, 2006a). Another adaptation-specific effect is seen when loanwords surface unfaithfully in order to conform to Lb phonotactics, but the adaptation strategy used differs from the default non-loan phonological process (Yip, 2002; Kenstowicz and Suchato, 2006; Smith, 2006b; see Section 3).

Loanwords differ from non-loans in another respect as well: They have Ls source forms, to which they often remain similar after adaptation, within phonological or sociolinguistic limits (Haugen, 1950: 216; Kim, 1982: 446; Lovins, 1975: 38). A formal appeal to source similarity can account for many of the aspects of LWA that go beyond Lb-internal phonology, including the preservation of Lb-illicit structures and the existence of adaptation-specific strategies.[3]

Within Optimality Theory (OT; Prince and Smolensky, 1993/2004), the dominant framework for modeling similarity between two representations is Correspondence Theory (McCarthy and Prince, 1995). Faithfulness constraints demand identity, along some phonological dimension, between elements of phonological strings that stand in a *correspondence relation.*

(1)   Given two strings S_1 and S_2, **correspondence** is a relation $\Re$ from the elements of S_1 to those of S_2. Elements $\alpha \in S_1$ and $\beta \in S_2$ are referred to as **correspondents** of one another when $\alpha\Re\beta$. (McCarthy and Prince, 1995: 262; original emphasis)

Correspondence relations have been proposed for various S_1-S_2 pairs, including input-output and base-reduplicant (McCarthy and Prince, 1995), output-(derivationally related) output (Benua, 1997), and segments showing long-distance featural agreement (S. Rose and Walker, 2004). A faithfulness constraint such as MAX 'No deletion: Every segment of S_1 has a correspondent in S_2' (McCarthy and Prince, 1995: 264) has an instantiation for each correspondence relation, giving MAX-IO, MAX-BR, MAX-OO, etc. Each version of MAX is a distinct constraint, separately rankable from the others. Thus, a language can prohibit the deletion of underlying segments (MAX-IO ranked high) while tolerating imperfect copying in reduplication (MAX-BR ranked low).

Because Correspondence Theory is designed to model phonological similarity, it is straightforward to formalize loanword-source similarity effects by defining a new correspondence relation. When faithfulness constraints on this correspondence relation are ranked high, Ls characteristics persist in Lb loanwords even when they would not survive in the Lb-internal phonology. Proposals to extend Correspondence Theory to loanword-source similarity include Kawu (1999), Kang (2003), Adler (2006), Kenstowicz and Suchato (2006), Y. Rose and Demuth (2006), and Smith (2006a,b); Alber and Plag (2001: 820) invoke an output-output correspondence relation for source-similarity effects in a creole. However, prior accounts have typically not been explicit about the nature of the source-language form involved in the relation.

Here, the correspondence relation involved in LWA is formalized as the *SB correspondence (SBcorr)* relation, which relates the Lb loanword, not to the Ls underlying form or surface form directly, but to the pLs representation.

2.2   The pLs representation

The *pLs representation* is the Lb speaker's posited representation of a loanword's Ls form. Formally, the pLs representation is a necessary component of the SBcorr model. Any string standing in correspondence must be phonologically represented by the Lb speaker. Therefore, a source-similarity correspondence relation cannot directly involve a physical Ls surface form, unfiltered by the Lb speaker's perceptual system and (meta)linguistic knowledge. Conceptually, the pLs form represents the Lb speaker's awareness that a word from another linguistic system is being borrowed. It is formally distinct from an underlying representation; it is an Ls model for the Lb loanword, not a lexical entry in Lb (although during the adaptation process, the pLs form may determine the input for the IO relation as well; see Section 3.2).

The representations and correspondence relations involved in LWA are summarized in (2). As the diagram suggests, the role of the pLs representation (demarcated '|...|') is similar to that of the morphological base in an output-output relation (Benua, 1997).

(2)   Correspondence relations in LWA

	Lb speaker's phonological system	/input/
		↕ *IOcorr relation*
Information about Ls form →	|pLs representation|	↔ *SBcorr relation* [output]

The pLs representation provides a way to reconcile prior proposals about factors that can influence the outcome of LWA. For example, discussions of loanword phonology sometimes debate whether Lb speakers are sensitive to 'phonological' (Hyman, 1970; Paradis and LaCharité, 1997, 2001; LaCharité and Paradis, 2005) or 'phonetic' (Silverman, 1992; Yip, 2002) aspects of Ls forms. Realistically, both types of influence can occur (see also Kang, 2003; Y.

Rose and Demuth, 2006). Depending on the kind of exposure Lb speakers have to Ls, multiple sources of information may contribute to the pLs representation (3).

(3) Potential influences on the pLs representation

<table>
<tr><td>
• perceptual information
• orthographic information
• explicit knowledge of Ls grammar
• ...
</td><td>→</td><td>|pLs representation|</td></tr>
</table>

When spoken language serves as the input to LWA, the Lb speaker obtains information about the Ls form through speech perception; this information is then encoded in the pLs representation. Aspects of the Ls form that are veridically perceived make the pLs form similar to the Ls surface form, creating the potential for phonetic-level perceptual similarity effects in LWA (Yip, 2002; Kang, 2003). On the other hand, the perception of a non-native form may be distorted by the native speech-perception system's inventory of segments (Werker and Tees, 1984) or prosodic structures (Dupoux, Kakehi, Hirose, Pallier, and Mehler, 1999). Accordingly, several researchers have proposed that 'repairs' to loanwords are partly (Silverman, 1992; Yip, 2002) or wholly (Peperkamp and Dupoux, 2003) caused by phonotactically driven misperception of Ls forms. Sections 3–4 show that LWA cannot be entirely reduced to misperception. Still, in cases where perceptual distortion occurs, it is the pLs representation that formally models those effects, sometimes serving as the starting point for further—phonological—adaptation processes.[4]

Orthography is another factor that can influence an Lb speaker's knowledge of an Ls form (Haugen, 1950; Lovins, 1975; Dohlus, 2005; Vendelin and Peperkamp, 2006). The written form of an Ls word may provide clues to its phonological or phonetic content that the Lb speaker would not have perceived auditorily, so access to orthographic information can make the pLs representation more like the actual Ls form than an auditory borrowing would have been. Conversely, an orthographic representation can also be misinterpreted by the Lb speaker, causing the pLs representation to contain entirely different segmental categories from the Ls surface form, as with [u] for expected *[a] in Japanese [buza:] < English *buzzer* (Miura, 1993: 126).

Other sources of information may also affect the pLs representation. Yip (2002) speculates that Cantonese speakers assign Lb vowel categories in loanwords from English partly based on visual information about lip rounding and jaw height. Additionally, many cases of borrowing involve at least some degree of bilingualism on the part of Lb speakers; explicit knowledge of Ls phonology (Paradis and LaCharité, 1997) or morphology and syntax (Silverman, 1992: 292) can influence adaptation.

Under the model of LWA presented here, the pLs representation is a unified repository for the Lb speaker's knowledge of the Ls form, even when multiple sources of information contribute to that knowledge.

2.3   Predictions of the SBcorr model

In the SBcorr model, source-similarity constraints are faithfulness constraints on a new correspondence relation. This relation involves the pLs representation, which allows multiple sources of information about the Ls form to be involved in similarity effects. Taken together, these characteristics make predictions that distinguish the SBcorr model from other approaches to LWA.

2.3.1   Loanword-specific adaptation strategies

Including loanword-specific faithfulness constraints in the SBcorr model predicts that adaptation and the default Lb phonology need not invoke the same phonological processes. The strategy used to avoid a markedness violation depends on the ranking among faithfulness constraints, and including SBcorr constraints creates the potential for different rankings on the SBcorr and IOcorr relations (Section 3). This prediction distinguishes the SBcorr model from models in which LWA is driven entirely by the Lb-internal phonology, with no loanword-specific phonological apparatus (Jacobs and Gussenhoven, 2000; Broselow, 2000).[5] Languages with LWA-specific phonological processes have been identified, including Korean (Kim, 1982; Kang, 2003), Swahili (Kraska-Szlenk, 1999), Maori (Yip, 2002), and Thai (Kenstowicz and Suchato, 2006). The case of Japanese (Peperkamp, 2004; Smith, 2006b) is discussed in Section 3.

2.3.2   Flexibility of adaptation strategies

The SBcorr model formalizes source-similarity constraints in Correspondence Theory, a general approach to faithfulness constraints. SBcorr constraints, like all faithfulness constraints, are violable and may be differently ranked in different languages. This predicts that all types of phonological processes are available for adapting loanwords, not only the cross-linguistically common epenthesis strategy. The SBcorr model therefore differs from approaches to LWA that restrict the range of available adaptation strategies, such as those that encode the epenthesis preference into the formal model of LWA (Paradis and LaCharité, 1997, 2001; Karvonen, 1998; Yip, 2002), and those that link all adaptation effects directly to perceptual distortion (Peperkamp and Dupoux, 2003; Peperkamp, 2004).

Section 4 presents cases of LWA that involve deletion of [s] and other highly perceptually salient segments. It is not plausible for the deletion of such salient segments to stem from misperception (a claim that is reinforced by phonological or phonetic evidence from each language discussed). Thus, misperception cannot be the only factor at work in LWA in general, nor can misperception be the only explanation for deletion in adaptation. A phonological model of LWA is necessary, and it must allow deletion as well as epenthesis. Such flexibility in phonological adaptation strategies is strong evidence in favor of the Correspondence Theory approach. (See Kenstowicz and Suchato, 2006: 936 for related discussion; on factorial typology and the cross-linguistic epenthesis preference, see Section 5.2.)

3 Orthographic influence and loanword-specific adaptation strategies in Japanese

According to the SBcorr model, LWA involves more than an input-output mapping in the Lb grammar. The Lb speaker also sets up a pLs representation and establishes SBcorr constraints that demand phonological similarity to that representation. This section demonstrates the SBcorr model as applied to Japanese loanwords from English. Japanese has a loanword-specific adaptation strategy, which motivates the distinction between SBcorr and IOcorr constraints (Smith, 2006b). Japanese also shows that the pLs representation can be influenced by orthography as well as by perception.

In the non-loan phonology of Japanese, unsyllabifiable consonants are avoided through deletion, not epenthesis (McCawley, 1968), as seen in morphological alternations like /kak+rɯ/ → [ka.k_ɯ] 'write-NONPAST'; this indicates that DEP-IO dominates MAX-IO. However, loanwords typically undergo epenthesis, and epenthesis-based adaptation is highly productive.

(4) Epenthesis in Japanese loanwords (Arakawa, 1977; Smith, 2006b)

    ɡɯ.ɾi.se.ɾiN   < English   [ɡl]*ycerine*

    po.ket.to   *pocke*[t]

    dʒit.taː.baɡ.ɡɯ   *jitterbu*[ɡ]

Before addressing these examples in a phonological model of LWA (Section 3.2), it is necessary to confirm that they show *phonological* unfaithful mappings rather than perceptual distortion (Section 3.1). Japanese-speaking listeners have difficulty distinguishing certain $[VC_1.C_2V]$ / $[V.C_1ɯ.C_2V]$ nonce pairs in which C_1C_2 is an illegal coda-onset sequence (Dupoux et al., 1999), so some inserted vowels in Japanese loanwords may arise from misperception. However (contra Peperkamp and Dupoux, 2003), this cannot be true for all epenthetic vowels. Some Japanese loanwords are adapted from a pLs representation in which consonants that trigger epenthesis are present for orthographic, not perceptual, reasons. Epenthesis triggered by such consonants cannot arise from misperception; it must reflect an unfaithful phonological mapping.

3.1   Orthographic influence on the pLs representation

Evidence that some consonants in pLs representations come from orthography is provided by Japanese loanwords with doublet forms that show deletion instead of the more widespread epenthesis; compare (4) and (5).

(5)   Deletion in Japanese loanwords (Ichikawa, 1929; Arakawa, 1977; Smith, 2006b)

_ɾi.sɯ.ɾiN   < English [gl]*ycerine*
pok.ke_   *pocke*[t]
dʒi.ɾɯ.ba_   *jitterbu*[g]

For such doublets, it can often be shown that the deletion loanword is an auditory borrowing, while the epenthesis loanword has been borrowed under heavy orthographic influence. For example, deletion loans are more likely to have [ɯ] for English unstressed vowels, while their epenthesis doublets tend to have 'spelling pronunciation' vowels; compare [ɾi.sɯ.ɾiN] and [gɯ.ɾi.se. ɾiN] < *glycerine*. Also, deletion loans are more likely to have [ɾ] for American English flapped /t,d/, as in [dʒi.ɾɯ.ba] versus [dʒit.taː.bag.gɯ] < *jitterbug*. (See Smith, 2006b for additional examples and discussion.)

The fact that deletion tends to correlate with other evidence of auditory borrowing indicates that for these doublets, it is deletion, not epenthesis, that results from perceptual assimilation. With an auditory loanword, a Japanese Lb speaker may not perceive certain non-salient consonants (and certainly would not 'perceive' the underlying representation of a reduced vowel). On the other hand, when Ls orthography is available, it gives the Lb speaker information about codas, consonant clusters, and non-reduced forms of vowels, which are used to establish the segmental content of the pLs form (see Dohlus, 2005; Vendelin and Peperkamp, 2006 on the use of orthography to determine vowel categories in adaptation). So the pLs representation of *jitterbug* as an orthographic loanword is something like |dʒɪtɚˈbʌg|, while the pLs representation of the auditory version is something like |dʒɪɾəbʌ|.[6]

LWA in Japanese is overwhelmingly based on written materials (Lovins, 1975; Miura, 1993). Therefore, acknowledging orthographic influence on the pLs form accounts for the striking prevalence of epenthesis in the face of perceptual deletion, and the pervasive 'phonemic' treatment of reduced vowels and /t,d/ in flapping contexts, in loanwords from English. This is not to say that perceptual epenthesis never occurs for Japanese speakers; the deletion misperceptions discussed above are in different phonological environments than the epenthesis misperceptions of Dupoux et al. (1999), and perceptual epenthesis has been experimentally confirmed in other languages (e.g., Kabak, 2003). The point here is that many Japanese pLs representations contain unsyllabifiable consonants that do not trigger perceptual epenthesis—or undergo perceptual deletion—because those pLs representations have been established wholly or partly on the basis of orthography. This confirms that the epenthesis triggered by such unsyllabifiable consonants is phonological. (See Shinohara, 2000, for additional evidence that some epenthesis in Japanese LWA is phonological, because it interacts with other phonological processes such as accent assignment.)

3.2   The SBcorr model and loanword-specific adaptation strategies

The epenthesis strategy used in adapting a Japanese pLs form with unsyllabifiable consonants, such as |ɡɹiseɾiɴ| or |dʒɪtəˑbʌɡ|, differs from the default non-loan phonological process, which is deletion. The existence of a loanword-specific adaptation strategy shows that certain SBcorr constraints outrank the relevant IOcorr constraints, allowing a different unfaithful mapping to be chosen just in case a pLs form exists. (Non-loans, which have no associated pLs representation, vacuously satisfy SBcorr constraints, so only IOcorr constraints apply to them.)

Here is what happens when a Japanese speaker, having established a pLs representation like |ɡɹiseɾiɴ|, goes on to adapt the form as a loanword. I assume that formally, LWA differs from an ordinary pass through the phonological production grammar only by including a pLs representation. This accounts for the fact that many aspects of the Lb-internal phonology are also relevant for LWA, as when Lb phonotactic restrictions drive adaptation; one example from Japanese is *COMPLEXONSET (Prince and Smolensky, 1993/2004), penalizing onset clusters, which is respected in loanwords like [ɡɯ.ɹiseɾiɴ] (*[ɡɹiseɾiɴ]).

If LWA involves a superset of the mechanisms involved in the Lb-internal phonology, then there must be an IOcorr relationship in addition to the language-contact-driven SBcorr relationship. But what determines the 'input' form, since by definition the loanword has not yet been adapted, and so has no lexical entry in Lb? By analogy to OT models of L1 phonological acquisition, where the learner's input is the same as the adult output (Tesar and Smolensky, 2000), I suggest that the Lb adapter copies the pLs representation to create an input form.[7]

Thus, LWA for (orthographic) English *glycerine* in Japanese involves the pLs form |ɡɾiseɾiɴ|, which is related to the output by SBcorr constraints, and the (identical) input form /ɡɾiseɾiɴ/, which is related to the output by IOcorr constraints.

(6)   Epenthesis in adaptation

/ɡɾiseɾiɴ/ pLs: |ɡɾiseɾiɴ|	Max- SB	*Comp Ons	Dep- SB	Dep- IO	Max- IO
☞ (a) **ɡɯ.ɾi**.se.ɾiɴ			*	*	
(b) _ɾi.se.ɾiɴ	*!				*
(c) **ɡɾi**.se.ɾiɴ		*!			

The choice of epenthesis (a) over deletion (b) shows that some Max constraint prevails. However, Max-IO cannot be the high-ranked constraint; non-loans avoid unsyllabifiable consonants by deletion, giving Dep-IO >> Max-IO. Because the epenthesis strategy is specific to LWA, it must be Max-SB that dominates Dep-SB (and Dep-IO). Finally, because complex onsets are avoided both in LWA (c) and in the non-loan phonology, *ComplexOnset must dominate at least Dep-SB and Max-IO.

(7)   Ranking for LWA-specific epenthesis in Japanese

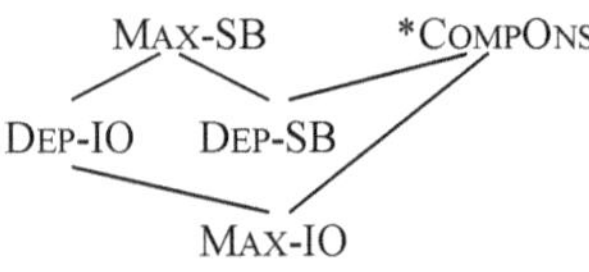

In a language with an adaptation-specific phonological process, like Japanese, at least one SBcorr constraint must outrank at least one IOcorr constraint. The existence of such languages therefore motivates the inclusion of the SB correspondence relation in the model. Languages without adaptation-specific strategies can be modeled as well: If all SBcorr constraints are crucially dominated, then LWA involves the same unfaithful mappings as the non-loan phonology.

4   Flexibility of adaptation strategies

Cross-linguistically, epenthesis is extremely common in LWA (Paradis and LaCharité, 1997). However, the SBcorr model predicts that other unfaithful mappings should also be available. To confirm this prediction, it is necessary to find languages with non-epenthesis adaptation strategies that are phonological processes, not effects of perceptual distortion.

This section examines LWA in Finnish, Hmong, and Sranan, in which adaptation strategies include deletion of [s]. Voiceless stridents are highly salient (Wright, 2004), so [s] deletion is not plausible as a misperception 'repair.' Moreover, each of these languages has /s/ in its inventory, so these [s]-deletion cases are not exceptions facilitated by the unavailability of a sufficiently similar segment in Lb (as proposed by Adler, 2006 for Hawai'ian).

4.1   Finnish

In Finnish non-loan phonology, there are restrictions on syllable structure (Hakulinen, 1961; Karlsson, 1983; Sherer, 1994; Karvonen, 1998). Onset clusters are prohibited. Codas are allowed, but word-final codas must be coronal (Hakulinen, 1961: 8), and medial codas are subject to a syllable-contact restriction against obstruent codas followed by sonorant onsets (Sherer, 1994: 118). The native segmental inventory includes one coronal sibilant, symbolized /s/; its realization varies between [s] and [ʃ], depending somewhat on vowel context (Hakulinen, 1961: 9–10; Karlsson, 1983: 17).

The prohibition on word-initial clusters in Finnish drives adaptation (although less-nativized loanwords show faithful importation of #(C)CC). Initial clusters are avoided by deletion of all but the pre-vocalic C (Campbell, 1998: 62). This pattern includes [#sC] clusters, which undergo deletion of [s]. Many of the loanwords showing [s] deletion are older loans from Swedish or Slavic, but [s]-deletion cases are also reported by Kolehmainen (1937) in loanwords specific to the Finnish community in the US. The US Finnish loanwords are described as 'a large and increasing number' of items (Kolehmainen, 1937: 62), which suggests that borrowing and adaptation were ongoing when these loanwords were recorded.

(8)   [#sC] clusters: [s]-deletion

    (a)   Finnish (Luthy, 1973: 6–7; Campbell 1998: 62)

puola	< Swedish [sp]*ole*	'spool'
tuoli	[st]*ol*	'chair'
tykki	[st]*ycke*	'cannon'
koulu	[sk]*ola*	'school'
räätäli	[skr]*addare*	'tailor'
ruuvi	[skr]*uv*	'screw'
nikkari	[sn]*ickare*	'carpenter'

    (b)   US Finnish (Kolehmainen, 1937: 63)

toori	< English [st]*ore*	
touvi	[st]*ove*	

In addition to the general perceptual salience of stridents, it is highly unlikely that the stridents in the forms in (8) are imperceptible to Lb speakers, since stridents in other contexts—including word-initial and pre-C contexts—survive.

(9)   Stridents adapted as [s(s)] (Kolehmainen, 1937: 62)

s̠aitvooki	< English [s]*idewalk*
pas̠ketti	*ba*[s]*ket*
kis̠ti	*ki*[tʃ]*en*
haus̠s̠i	*hou*[s]*e*
luns̠s̠i	*lun*[tʃ]

It is true that the cases of [s] in (9) are all adjacent to a vowel on at least one side, which differs from the #_C cases in (8). However, sibilants have robust internal cues (Wright, 2004), so detection of their presence is not as dependent on vowel transitions as is the case for other obstruents. Moreover, the fact that faithful importation of [#sC] forms occurs in less nativized loanwords also suggests that the [s] in such constructions is perceptible. Kolehmainen (1937: 63) gives US Finnish *skeptikko* (< English *skeptic*); additional examples are provided by Luthy (1973) and Karvonen (1998).

Further evidence that deletion in Finnish LWA is phonological is the fact that this adaptation strategy is specific to word-initial position. In other contexts, unsyllabifiable consonants are avoided through epenthesis, often of [i]. For example, if an obstruent-sonorant (TR) sequence between vowels is treated unfaithfully, the output is [VT$\underline{V}$RV] with epenthesis, not *[VT_V] or *[V_RV] with deletion.

(10) Epenthesis in illegitimate medial clusters

   (a)   Medial TR clusters: epenthesis (Kolehmainen, 1937: 62)

äp̠y.liä	< English *apple* (+ *ä* PARTITIVE)
pet̠i.ruuma	*bedroom*[8]

   (b)   Compare medial TT, RR, RT clusters (Kolehmainen, 1937: 62)

skep.tikko	< English *skeptic*
kis̠.ti	*kitchen*
pas̠.ketti	*basket*
far̠.mari	*farmer*
kän̠.tiä	*candy* (+ *ä* PARTITIVE)
jaar̠.ti	*yard* 'lawn'

The unfaithful mapping in [VTRV] forms is driven by *COMPLEXONSET (Prince and Smolensky, 1993/2004), which disallows onset clusters, and SYLLABLECONTACT (Bat-El, 1996), which penalizes a sonority rise across a syllable boundary.

Epenthesis is also found in word-final position. Finnish and US Finnish loanwords nearly always end in a vowel, often [i], even when the final consonant of the Ls form is a phonotactically permissible final coda (Kolehmainen, 1937: 63; Hakulinen, 1961: 19; Karvonen, 1998: 30; Kiparsky, 2003: 147).

(11) Final codas: epenthesis (Kolehmainen, 1937: 62)

saitvooki	< English *sidewalk*
jaarti	*yard 'lawn'*
pasketti	*basket*
farmari	*farmer*

Kiparsky (2003: 146) attributes final epenthesis in loanwords to STEMCONSTRAINT, a markedness constraint requiring stems (although not words) to end in a vowel. This constraint would be satisfied equally well by deletion of the final consonant, but epenthesis is the chosen adaptation strategy.[9]

Thus, for both medial obstruent-sonorant clusters and word-final consonants, epenthesis is the preferred LWA process. US Finnish *petiruuma* 'bedroom' exemplifies the constraint rankings that produce this result.

(12) Epenthesis

/petruum/ pLs: |petruum|	*COMP ONS	SYLL CONTACT	STEM CONSTR	MAX-SB	DEP-SB
☞ (a) ˈpe.**ti.ruu.ma**					**
(b) ˈpe.**truu.ma**	*!				*
(c) ˈ**pet.ruu.ma**		*!			*
(d) ˈpe_.ruu.ma				*!	*
(e) ˈpe.ti.**ruum**			*!		*
(f) ˈpe.ti.ruu_				*!	*

The choice of candidate (a) over candidates (b) and (c) shows that epenthesis into the [tr] sequence is preferred over an onset cluster (b) and a coda-onset sequence with rising sonority (c). This motivates the ranking {*COMPONS, SYLLCONTACT} >> DEP-SB. The choice of (a) over (e) shows that epenthesis after word-final [m] is preferred to a faithful consonant-final form, which motivates STEMCONSTR >> DEP-SB. Finally, the choice of (a) over (d, f) shows that epenthesis, not deletion, is the preferred adaptation strategy, so MAX-SB dominates DEP-SB (and DEP-IO).

(13) Interim ranking

{*COMPONS, SYLLCONTACT, STEMCONSTR, MAX-SB} >> DEP-SB

But if epenthesis is the preferred strategy in Finnish LWA, then why do #CC clusters undergo deletion? As argued above, deletion cannot stem from failure to perceive the word-initial consonant, as even highly salient [s] is affected. On the other hand, there is a *phonological* explanation for why epenthesis has a different status for #CC cases. Finnish has initial stress, so if the leftmost vowel were epenthetic, main stress would fall on an epenthetic vowel—a configuration that is avoided in a number of languages (Alderete, 1999a; Gouskova and Hall, this volume). Additionally, deletion in #CC is not specific to [s], which further supports the phonological character of this adaptation strategy. The examples of word-initial cluster simplification that he provides happen to involve [#sC] clusters, but Kolehmainen (1937: 63) explicitly refers to '[t]he rule that *no word can begin with two consonants* without dropping one or more letters' [emphasis added]. Examples of (older) Finnish loanwords in which non-[s] clusters are adapted by deletion of the first consonant are given in (14) for comparison.

(14) Initial #CC: deletion (Luthy, 1973: 6; Campbell, 1998: 62)

_risti	'cross'	< Old Russian	[kr]*istĭ*
_lukkari	'chorister'	< Swedish	[kl]*ackare*
_luostari	'monastery'		[kl]*oster*
_lyijy	'lead (carbon)'		[bl]*y*
_rouva	'lady, Mrs.'		[fr]*u*
_ranska	'French'		[fr]*anska*

Formally, stress[10] on an epenthetic vowel is penalized by the constraint HEAD-DEP (Alderete, 1999a; there is no evidence to determine whether the HEAD-DEP constraint at work here is on the SB or IO relation, so the correspondence relation is left unspecified). The ranking of HEAD-DEP with respect to the constraints introduced above is exemplified with US Finnish *toori* 'store'.

(15) Deletion in #CC clusters

/stoor/ pLs: |stoor|	*COMP ONS	SYLL CONTACT	STEM CONSTR	HEAD-DEP	MAX-SB	DEP-SB
☞ (a) 'too.ri					*	*
(b) 'stoo.ri	*!					*
(c) 'si.too.ri				*!		**
(d) 'is.too.ri				*!		**
(e) 'toor			*!		*	
(f) 'too					**!	

The initial [st] sequence undergoes deletion[11] (a), not epenthesis (c,d), showing that HEAD-DEP dominates MAX-SB (and MAX-IO). The onset cluster is avoided (b), so *COMPONS dominates MAX-SB (and MAX-IO). However, only word-initial clusters trigger deletion (f); when HEAD-DEP is not at stake, the ranking of MAX-SB >> DEP-SB motivated in (12) leads to epenthesis.

(16) Ranking for Finnish LWA

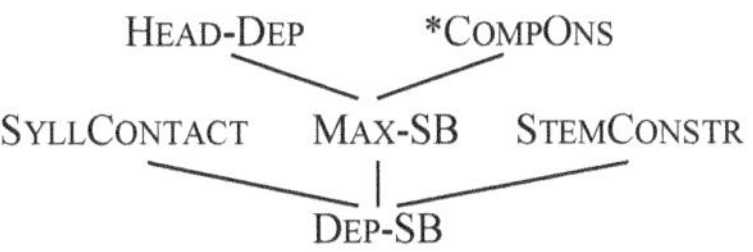

In conclusion, the deletion of initial [s] in Finnish LWA is phonological. Evidence against a misperception account includes both the general salience of [s] and the fact that [s] deletion is grammatically determined, driven by a constraint against stressed epenthetic vowels. This result supports the SBcorr model, which predicts that phonological deletion is possible in LWA.

4.2   Hmong

Another language in which LWA involves deletion of [s] is (White) Hmong (Golston and Yang, 2001). In fact, unusually from a cross-linguistic perspective, deletion is the default adaptation strategy in Hmong (Golston and Yang, 2001: 50). Hmong has strict CV(V) syllable structure, but a large consonant inventory that includes affricates and prenasalized and laterally released stops. As in Finnish, [s] deletion occurs despite the inclusion of [s] in the native inventory. Ls [s] in onset position is typically borrowed as [s], confirming the general perceptibility of this segment to Hmong speakers.

(17) [s] in onset position (Golston and Yang, 2001: 48, 49, 53)

sà.lɔ̀.mɔ̃̀	< French	[s]*alomon* 'Solomon'
sì.dáɨ	< English	[s]*edar*
să.lă		[s]*alad*
pě.sî		*Pep*[s]*i*

Ls codas, including [s], are avoided by deletion.

(18) [s] codas: deletion (Golston and Yang, 2001: 40, 46, 49, 53)

kʰǐ_.mǎ_	< English	*Chri*[s]*tma*[s]
ᵐbǎ_		*bu*[s]
ᵑgě_		*ga*[s]
ʔɔ.fí_		*offi*[s]
ⁿdʒû_		*jui*[s]
ʔâì_		*ice* ([s])
pù.lǐ_		*poli*[s]

Golston and Yang (2001: 51) propose a phonological account of deletion adaptations for Ls codas, in which NoCoda (Prince and Smolensky, 1993/2004) and Dep(-SB, in terms of the SBcorr model) are ranked over Max(-SB). The alternative would be a misperception account, according to which Hmong speakers do not perceive Ls consonants, including [s], in coda position; if this were the case, there would be no evidence for phonological deletion in Hmong LWA. However, beyond the general argument that [s] is too salient not to be perceived, there is additional evidence against a misperception account of coda [s] deletion in Hmong LWA: [#sC] clusters are adapted, not by deletion, but by epenthesis.

(19) [#sC] clusters: epenthesis (Golston and Yang, 2001: 48, 53)
    sì.tŭ.pe̞   < English [st]*upid*
    sàɨ.kû   [sk]*ool*

Golston and Yang (2001) do not present any other examples of Hmong loanwords with onset clusters in the Ls forms, so it is unclear whether epenthesis occurs in all onset clusters, is restricted to word-initial onset clusters, or affects [#sC] clusters only. It would also be important to determine whether this epenthesis pattern is phonological or is the result of perceptual distortion adding a nucleus to the pLs representation (although the highly salient [aɨ] diphthong in the adapted form of *school* in (19) is not suggestive of perceptual epenthesis). Crucially, however, these [#sC] cases show that [s] is perceptible word-initially before a consonant, a context very similar to the V_.C (coda) context where [s] deletion occurs.[12]

4.3 Sranan

A third example of adaptation by deletion involving Ls [s] is found in Sranan (Alber and Plag, 2001). Sranan is a creole, and the morphemes of interest here have source forms in the lexifier language, English. Arguably, the same phonological and perceptual factors that are involved in borrowing a loanword are also involved in lexifying a creole, so it is still appropriate to speak of phonological adaptation with reference to an Ls surface form and a pLs representation.

In Sranan, Ls [#sC] clusters are avoided by [s] deletion when C is an obstruent.

(20) [#s]+obstruent: [s]-deletion (Alber and Plag, 2001: 815)

_*piki*	< English [sp]*eak*
_*pramaseti*	[sp]*ermaceti*
_*pori*	[sp]*oil*
_*tan*	[st]*and*
_*tori*	[st]*ory*
_*tranga*	[st]*rong*
_*krebi*	[sk]*rape*
_*kweri*	[sk]*uare*
_*krasi*	[sk]*ratch*

Here again, it is unlikely that the [s] deletion in (20) is caused by failure to perceive this segment. Instances of [s] from other phonological contexts in Ls forms are adapted faithfully or trigger epenthesis, as seen in (21).

(21) Examples retaining [s] (Alber and Plag, 2001: 816)

masra	< English *ma*[s]*ter*
nasi	*na*[s]*ty*
sisa	[s]*i*[s]*ter*
fosi	*fir*[s]*t*
hesi	*ha*[s]*te*

The choice between deletion (including [s]) as in (20) and other strategies as in (21) is driven by the phonological constraint ranking. For details, see Alber and Plag (2001: 826–7); in brief, deletion of initial [s] is driven by a contiguity constraint that is also responsible for other patterns in the data, such as the treatment of word-final consonants. Once again, it cannot be the case that [s] in Ls forms is generally imperceptible to Lb speakers. Instead, deletion of [s] is enforced by the phonological grammar of LWA.

4.4   Conclusions: deletion of highly perceptible segments

Finnish, Hmong, and Sranan provide examples of [s], a highly perceptible segment, undergoing adaptation by deletion (see also Shinohara, 2006: 1061 on [s] deletion in Marshallese LWA). These examples show that not all instances of deletion in LWA can be attributed to Lb speakers' failure to perceive Ls segments. Jacobs and Gussenhoven (2000: 198) include [s] deletion in Hawai'ian loanword adaptation as part of their argument that perceptual factors are *never* relevant in LWA. As discussed in Section 2.2 above, the SBcorr model does not take that position; there is significant evidence that perceptual factors, including phonotactically driven misperception, do play a role in LWA. However, the [s]-deletion cases demonstrate that misperception cannot be the *only* explanation for deletion in adaptation. These cases also serve as a counterexample to Adler's (2006: 1041) proposal that [s] deletion is only possible in LWA when Lb lacks strident fricatives, since Finnish, Hmong, and Sranan all have /s/ in their inventories.

Other examples of non-perceptual deletion in adaptation include post-tonic syllables in Huave (Ls=Spanish; Davidson and Noyer, 1997) and liquids in Cantonese (Ls=English; Silverman, 1992). In Huave, an SBcorr constraint (in current terms) preserving stress location, plus constraints on stress placement and foot form, drive deletion of entire syllables: Ls ['i.ga.do] → Lb ['ik] 'liver' (Davidson and Noyer, 1997: 68–70). It is unlikely that a whole [...VCV] sequence would fail to be perceived.[13] In Cantonese, the [pr] cluster is avoided by deletion in *printer,* but by epenthesis in *print,* because of word-minimality effects (Silverman, 1992: 290); since deletion is sensitive to non-local phonological factors, it is phonological, not perceptual.

These deletion cases confirm that even segments that persist into the pLs representation are potentially subject to phonological deletion. Therefore, a phonological model of LWA must allow for flexibility of adaptation strategies. This supports the SBcorr model, in which SB faithfulness constraints may be ranked differently in different languages.

5   Further implications

The findings discussed above, and the SBcorr model that they support, have additional implications for LWA and for phonological theory more generally.

5.1   The non-universality of source-similarity constraints

Using Correspondence Theory to model source-similarity constraints means that such constraints need not be universally present. SBcorr constraints are added to a speaker's grammar only if the speaker establishes an SB correspondence relation, preparing to adapt an Ls form.

There are precedents for recognizing different numbers of correspondence relations in different grammars. Urbanczyk (1995: 505) demonstrates that a language may include multiple reduplicative morphemes with distinct base-reduplicant (BR) correspondence relations, and distinct rankings for BR_icorr and BR_jcorr constraints. Similarly, Benua (1997: 25) allows for multiple output-output (OO) correspondence relations. In principle, there is no upper bound on the number of reduplicative morphemes or levels of 'cyclic' affixes in a language. This requires that additional sets of BRcorr or OOcorr constraints be generated when needed. Correspondence Theory permits this, since each constraint type, such as MAX or DEP, is defined as a general schema (McCarthy and Prince, 1995: 264), to be relativized to any pair of strings S_1-S_2. We can assume that positing a new correspondence relation automatically invokes a set of faithfulness constraints on that relation. Therefore, general schemas for correspondence constraints are part of the universal constraint set, but the particular correspondence relations that determine concrete faithfulness constraints may differ by language. Accordingly, there are no SBcorr constraints in an Lb speaker's grammar until an SBcorr relation is established; then, a set of SB faithfulness constraints is supplied. Non-correspondence formalisms for source-similarity constraints would require either universally present loanword-specific constraints, or a novel mechanism for adding loanword-specific constraints to the grammar when needed.

Once SBcorr constraints are invoked, they must be ranked. But when rankings involved in adaptation are not attested in the Lb-internal phonology, how are they learned (Golston and Yang, 2001; Broselow, 2004; Kenstowicz and Suchato, 2006)? The SBcorr model provides a useful perspective on this problem. When a native speaker establishes an SBcorr relation, the pre-existing Lb ranking is unchanged except for the addition of SBcorr constraints. These new constraints can be arbitrarily ranked by the individual speaker; alternatively, the speaker can learn the Lb adaptation *conventions* and thus which SBcorr constraints are ranked high (similar to learning a language game). Indeed, adaptation strategies are often variable for early loanwords, later becoming highly conventionalized (Haugen, 1950). In any case, whether a speaker chooses to preserve certain Ls characteristics, or learns particular source-similarity effects from the community's adaptation conventions, the relevant SBcorr constraints will be ranked above any competing constraints. Further research is needed to determine how the SBcorr constraints that are not active in LWA are handled. They may be ranked by default, perhaps below relevant markedness constraints (Prince and Tesar, 2004) or below IOcorr constraints.

5.2   Factorial typology and the epenthesis preference in LWA

The SBcorr model predicts that LWA may involve unfaithful mappings besides epenthesis, because it includes a full set of faithfulness constraints (McCarthy and Prince, 1995: 370–372), any of which can be ranked low enough to be violated. The languages in Section 4 confirm that epenthesis is not the only option, because they use deletion, violating MAX-SB. Violations of other SBcorr constraints are attested as well. The violation of IDENT[*Feature*]-SB constraints would result in featural changes, which are common in LWA; misperception can distort feature values (Werker and Tees, 1984), but Lb-illicit segments can also be veridically perceived (Kabak, 2003), so some feature-change effects are probably phonological. Adaptation strategies violating UNIFORMITY-SB (coalescence) and INTEGRITY-SB (diphthongization) also seem to occur (Hyman, 1970; Lovins, 1975; but see Paradis and Prunet, 2000). Finally, faithfulness constraints on string edges (ANCHOR-SB) and string-element adjacency (CONTIGUITY-SB) are frequently violated when epenthesis or deletion occurs.

On the other hand, metathesis (violating LINEARITY-SB) is exceedingly rare in LWA (Gouskova, 2001; LaCharité and Paradis, 2005). Gouskova (2001: 183) suggests that this might be related to the strong cross-linguistic epenthesis preference in LWA (Paradis and LaCharité, 1997). Neither the avoidance of metathesis, nor the general epenthesis preference, is predicted by the SBcorr model. Some models of LWA build the epenthesis preference directly into the grammar (Paradis and LaCharité, 1997; Karvonen, 1998; Yip, 2002). However, such an approach is problematic for those languages that do use deletion in LWA. Moreover, deletion is more common than epenthesis in diachronic change (Crowley, 1997: 42) and child language acquisition (Bernhardt and Stemberger, 1998), suggesting that epenthesis is not a general default.

An alternative explanation for the epenthesis preference is that it is sociolinguistic. Sociolinguistic factors are known to influence LWA. For example, greater and lesser degrees of nativization (i.e., different constraint rankings) sometimes correlate with attitudes toward native and foreign cultures, or with the degree of cultural integration of the loanword's referent (Luthy, 1973: 12; Lovins, 1975: 6, 38; Mosel, 2004). The fact that LWA can become conventionalized (Haugen, 1950: 217; Hyman, 1970: notes 6–7; Lovins, 1975: 38) shows that a particular SBcorr ranking can spread through the Lb community. Epenthesis, deletion, and featural change all have the same *formal* status, being faithfulness violations, but it seems that people find a loanword to be more similar to its source when it includes all of the Ls material (deletion dispreferred), in the original order (metathesis dispreferred), even if this leads to unfaithfulness in the form of epenthesis (Lovins, 1975: 38; Gouskova, 2001: 183). Access to Ls orthography may strengthen this reluctance to 'leave things out' of loanwords, as pidgins and creoles seem less biased toward epenthesis strategies (Alber and Plag, 2001). Thus, the SBcorr model predicts that the anti-deletion constraint MAX-SB has no special *phonological* status in LWA; cross-linguistically, this constraint tends to be ranked high, perhaps for sociolinguistic reasons, but this is not required.

5.3   LWA and phonological argumentation

If LWA involved no mechanisms beyond the Lb-internal phonology, then the contribution of adaptation evidence to phonological argumentation would be straightforward (see, e.g., Hyman, 1970). However, both LWA-specific constraints and extra-phonological factors such as perception and orthography are relevant for adaptation as well, and this has certain implications. Before adaptation processes can be used as phonological evidence, it must be established that they are indeed phonological unfaithful mappings (see also de Lacy, this volume). Moreover, the fact that SBcorr constraints are involved in adaptation means that Lb-internal 'hidden rankings' cannot conclusively be established on loanword evidence alone. On the other hand, evidence from adaptation can shed light on the architecture of the phonological system, as when Lovins (1975: 32) uses LWA to argue against highly abstract URs, or when constraint-based frameworks are shown to require fewer loanword-specific mechanisms than rule-based frameworks (Yip, 1993; Paradis and LaCharité, 1997; Broselow, 2000; Jacobs and Gussenhoven, 2000; Golston and Yang, 2001).

For example, the use of a correspondence relation, distinct from the IOcorr relation, to model source-similarity effects supports the inclusion of multiple correspondence relations in the grammar, which has implications for the treatment of cyclic or output-output effects in morphological derivation (Smith, 2006a).

The flexibility of adaptation strategies for loanwords also has implications for Correspondence Theory. Precisely how many different adaptation strategies are predicted depends on whether faithfulness constraints can be ranked in any order (McCarthy and Prince, 1995), or whether faithfulness constraints whose violations are more perceptually salient are necessarily higher ranked (as in the original P-map model of Steriade, 2001a; see also Adler, 2006). The [s]-deletion cases in Section 4 show that, whatever role perceptual salience plays in Correspondence Theory, it cannot fix constraint rankings absolutely (a point also made by Steriade, 2004)—the phonological grammar must be free to choose something other than the perceptually minimal adaptation strategy, or salient segments like [s] would never be deleted.

In conclusion, although loanword adaptation provides less direct evidence about the grammar of individual languages than was once hoped, it still contributes to a broader understanding of universal grammar and phonological theory.

Notes

1   Many thanks for comments and discussion to Tuuli Adams, Misha Becker, Lisa Davidson, Maria Gouskova, Dan Karvonen, Shigeto Kawahara, Tomoyuki Kubo, Craig Melchert, Jeff Mielke, David Mora-Marín, John McCarthy, Elliott Moreton, Steve Parker, Paul Roberge, Kevin Roon, Jason Shaw, John Singler, Donca Steriade, Tim Vance, Natasha Warner, Andy Wedel, Adam Werle, and audiences at UNC-CH, University of Arizona, and Kyushu University.

2   Modeling adaptation is distinct from modeling the synchronic phonological system of a language whose lexicon includes etymological loanwords (adapted and imported by previous Lb speakers). If an etymological loanword was nativized during adaptation, it has become an Lb lexeme that conforms to Lb phonotactics. Subsequent Lb learners of this lexeme (not from Ls speakers) have no motivation to assume an Ls-like form and recapitulate the adaptation process. Alternatively, if an etymological loanword was not fully nativized during adaptation, then it has become an Lb lexeme with 'foreign' characteristics. Such lexemes may cause Lb learners to develop a stratified lexicon (Fukazawa, Kitahara, and Ota, 1998; Ito and Mester, 1999b; Ota, 2004; Pater, 2005) or to reanalyze the core Lb grammar (Rice, 2006), but these consequences are distinct from the original process of adapting loanwords.

3   Proposals have also been made for adaptation-specific or loanword-specific markedness constraints (Karvonen, 1998; Pater, 2004). A related scenario is one in which a language has a stratified lexicon (caused by the presence of etymological loanwords), but the least-marked stratum is not the one containing the native lexemes, but rather one containing a particular set of loanwords (Kawahara, Nishimura, and Ono, 2003). Examining the interaction between source-similarity constraints and loanword-specific markedness effects is left for future research.

4   Yip (2006: 951) proposes a 'non-native percept' as an intermediate stage between the 'perceptual module' and the 'L1 grammar' in LWA. This is similar to the role played by the pLs representation in the model proposed here, but the pLs representation incorporates additional factors beyond speech perception.

5   Models such as those of Broselow (2004) and Peperkamp (2004) acknowledge LWA-specific *effects*, but attribute them to factors outside the production grammar.

6   This paper is concerned mainly with epenthesis and deletion, so the *segmental* categories shown in pLs representations are intended as plausible approximations. For example, it remains to be determined whether English [ɪ] is assimilated to Japanese [i] by perceptual distortion (Werker and Tees, 1984) and/or grapheme-to-phoneme conversion (Vendelin and Peperkamp, 2006), or whether [ɪ] persists into the pLs representation, subsequently to be mapped to [i] in the phonology; similarly for, e.g., stop voicing in Finnish (Section 4.1).

7   A conceivable alternative is that there is no input in LWA, only a pLs form; IOcorr constraints would be vacuously satisfied during LWA, and would not be crucially ranked with SBcorr constraints. But even under this assumption, a distinction between IOcorr and SBcorr constraints is necessary in order to account for loanword-specific adaptation strategies and the maintenance of Lb-illicit structures in loanwords.

8   Although Ls *bed+room* is a compound, it is unlikely that Lb *petiruuma* reflects the Ls morphological structure (*peti+ruuma*). A short word with a final stop like Ls *bed* would typically have the final stop geminated, i.e., *petti* (Karvonen, 1998). Therefore, the [i] in *petiruuma* is classified as a case of medial epenthesis, not final epenthesis as in (11).

9   Kolehmainen's (1937: 62) list includes one form in which a final C has apparently been avoided through deletion: *kisti_* < *kitchen*. This might reflect failure to perceive the word-final [n] in the English source form, and therefore the absence of |n| in the pLs representation, but further investigation is needed.

10   Finnish has secondary stress, so the relevant HEAD-DEP constraint may refer to the head of the prosodic word rather than to all prosodic heads.

11   The winning deletion candidate is [_toori], not *[s_oori]; in Finnish LWA, #CC clusters undergo deletion of the first C, not the second. This might be due to a high-ranking CONTIGUITY constraint, penalizing deletion not at an edge (McCarthy and Prince, 1995), or it might have to do with preferential preservation of a consonant in the context _V as opposed to the context _C (Steriade, 2008).

12   There are some differences in perceptibility between the two contexts, but each has advantages. Word-initial position is attentionally privileged in speech perception (Marslen-Wilson, 1984), but post-vocalic position generally provides better cues to consonant identification (Wright, 2004).

13   Broselow (2004: 8) proposes that Huave speakers perceive the Ls stress and assign a word boundary after the stress foot, which causes them to disregard subsequent segments. On this view, Huave truncation becomes a case of misperception. But this does not explain why Huave speakers fail to borrow the whole 'phrase' corresponding to the Ls form. (Compare Golston and Yang, 2001: 55 on the phrase-like status of polysyllabic loanwords in Hmong.)

Part II

Case studies in phonological argumentation

7 Exploring recursivity, stringency, and gradience in the Pama-Nyungan stress continuum[1]

John Alderete

This chapter reviews contemporary approaches to the morphological influences on stress in certain Pama-Nyungan languages, including Diyari, Dyirbal, and Warlpiri. To account for the variation found in these languages, nine different theories are developed that differ in the constraints responsible for edge effects in stress and the alignment of morphological and prosodic structure. The factorial typologies of each theory are analyzed and shown to support three conclusions concerning the analysis of morphological stress in particular and the nature of constraints in general. First, stringency or 'special-general' relations between two morpho-prosodic alignment constraints are necessary because theories without these stringency relations either do not describe all of the data or predict the existence of rather implausible stress patterns. Second, while some constraints that require gradient constraint evaluation can (and indeed must) be dispensed with, it appears that gradiently assessed constraints like AllFeetLeft are still necessary. Third, there is both theoretical and empirical support for the recursive prosodic word analysis of (McCarthy and Prince, 1994). This analysis is also shown to make predictions about logically possible systems that may be explored in future work.

1 Introduction

When more than one theory is consistent with the data at hand, what is the next step in an investigation? While some observations can be made by scrutinizing formalisms, most linguists agree that the only successful way to make the next step is to study the inherent assumptions of each theory and vigorously explore their consequences. One of the things that distinguishes research in Optimality Theory ((Prince and Smolensky, 1993/2004), (McCarthy and Prince, 1995)) from other research paradigms is that its central tenets actually require a deep understanding of the consequences of theory. Optimality Theory (OT) is inherently typological because the well-formedness constraints that are at the heart of any OT theory do more than provide an analysis of a particular phenomenon in a particular language. Through ranking permutation, these constraints make direct predictions about the ways in which a given phenomenon can vary cross-linguistically. The typological predictions of an OT theory are established in a factorial typology, the set of grammars that result from all possible orderings of the assumed constraints. Factorial typologies are extremely powerful tools when applied to the job of comparing theories because they enable the researcher to probe theoretical consequences in vivid detail.

This chapter illustrates the validity of this approach by reviewing and extending theories of the morphological influences on stress in some Pama-Nyungan languages. The focus of this investigation is on three topical issues in phonological theory, given below, which identify some of the core assumptions that distinguish prior work on this problem.

- *Recursive prosodic word aligned with morphology* ((McCarthy and Prince, 1994), (Kager, 1997), cf., (Crowhurst, 1994), (Berry, 1996)): should the impact of morphology on the prosodic system be accounted for with alignment constraints that require a recursive prosodic word?

- *Stringent constraint relations* (see (Prince, 1997)): do the constraints that require alignment of morphological and prosodic categories stand in a special-general relation?

- *Gradient constraints* ((Alber, 2005), cf., (Kager, 2005), (McCarthy, 2003c)): are constraints that require gradient constraint evaluation, like ALLFEETLEFT, necessary for the Pama-Nyungan stress continuum?

A comparison of nine distinct theories (i.e., fragments of *CON*, the universal constraint set, that produce a factorial typology) supports the following conclusions. First, stringent constraint relations are necessary in the Pama-Nyungan stress continuum, because theories without stringency relations for certain constraints either do not describe all of the data or predict the existence of rather implausible stress patterns. Second, while some constraints that require gradient constraint evaluation can, and indeed must, be dispensed with, it appears that ALLFEETLEFT is still necessary, because an alternative that removes this constraint overgenerates. Third, there is both theoretical and empirical support for recursivity, and this assumption also makes predictions about logically possible systems that may be explored in future work. Finally, the chapter constitutes an extended argument for using factorial typology as a research tool, because it allows for penetrating theory comparison and also identifies clear directions for future research.

2   Background

To understand the morphological influences on stress, it is necessary to establish some background on the morphologies of the languages under analysis. The continuum of morphological effects discussed below is represented by four Pama-Nyungan (PN) languages: Diyari, Dyirbal, Pintupi, and Warlpiri.[2] The morphological template given below, adapted from (Austin, 1981) and (Dixon, 1980), accounts for the principal morphological structures discussed here, namely inflected nouns and verbs.

(1)   Morphological frame: Root (+ Derivational suffix(es)) + Inflection

As illustrated by the examples in appendix B, all of the languages are non-prefixing and nouns and verbs have an obligatory inflection (which may be null in nouns). Both nouns and verbs may have one or more derivational suffixes. PN languages, including Dyirbal and Warlpiri, may also have conjugation classes marked by certain consonants associated with stems (cf., Indo-European theme vowels). The history of these consonants seems to point to a re-analysis of stem-final consonants as part of the ending (Dixon, 1980). In any case, they are not systematic in the languages discussed here, so they are not included in the above template.

All four PN languages also have a common stress rule in mono-morphemic words.

(2)   Basic stress pattern in mono-morphemic words (see references cited above)

Main stress on the first syllable and alternating stress on every nonfinal odd syllable.

Following (Hayes, 1995) for Pintupi, this pattern can be treated straight-forwardly as a case of left-to-right syllabic trochees, with no provision for degenerate feet. In OT terms, left-to-right iterative foot parsing and the absence of degenerate feet follow from ranking FOOTBINARITY above PARSESYLLABLE, which in turn dominates ALLFEETLEFT (McCarthy and Prince, 1993). In other words, feet must be binary, so unpaired final syllables are unfooted, and the imperative to foot syllables, embodied in PARSESYLLABLE, requires iterative footing. These rankings will be assumed throughout, and the last two con-straints, PARSESYLLABLE and ALLFEETLEFT, will be integrated with theories of morphological stress in sections 3–4.

The impact of morphology on metrical stress can be observed by comparing the following patterns, which are exemplified in appendix B. The schemata below include a three-syllable root and two slots for mono- and disyllabic suffixes. The root is always first (because these languages are non-prefixing) and separated from the following suffixes by '|'. Two suffixes are separated by '-', a convention used throughout. '(o o)' indicates a metrical stress foot.

(3) Morphological influences on foot parsing

Inputs	Diyari	Dyirbal	Warlpiri	Pintupi
a. /ooo|o/	(oo)o|o	(oo)(o|o)	(oo)(o|o)	(oo)(o|o)
b. /ooo|oo/	(oo)o|(oo)	(oo)o|(oo)	(oo)o|(oo)	(oo)(o|o)o
c. /ooo|o-o/	(oo)o|o-o	(oo)o|(o-o)	(oo)o|(o-o)	(oo)(o|o)-o
d. /ooo|o-oo/	(oo)o|o-(oo)	(oo)o|(o-o)o	(oo)(o|o)-(oo)	(oo)(o|o)-(oo)
e. /ooo|oo-o/	(oo)o|(oo)-o	(oo)o|(oo)-o	(oo)o|(oo)-o	(oo)(o|o)(o-o)
f. /ooo|oo-oo/	(oo)o|(oo)-(oo)	(oo)o|(oo)-(oo)	(oo)o|(oo)-(oo)	(oo)(o|o)(o-o)o
	Each morph-eme stressed separately	*Root|af juncture never crossed, except (a)*	*Root|af juncture crossed under duress*	*No morpho-logical influence*

The organization of data in this table, adapted from (Kenstowicz, 1997), makes a crucial assumption, namely that these languages are placed on a continuum. Diyari, on one extreme, shows the strongest influence from morphology. Feet never cross a morpheme boundary, either at the root|affix boundary or between two suffixes. This observation led (Poser, 1989) to conclude that each morpheme is stressed separately, i.e., each morpheme constitutes a separate domain for laying down binary feet. Pintupi, at the opposite pole, shows no influence from morphology on this continuum: poly-morphemic and mono-morphemic words follow the basic stress pattern. Dyirbal, on the other hand, shows an intermediate effect: feet may cross a morpheme boundary, e.g., [(oo)o|(o-o)]. But, with one exception (3a), foot parsing in Dyirbal restarts at the root|affix juncture, showing that this juncture is important. Warlpiri shows a further step towards Pintupi, because it allows crossing at the root|affix boundary in (3d). This boundary crossing seems to be done only under duress, however, because Warlpiri shows a preference for complete footing in some words with even number syllables (3d) and not others (3e). Given this continuum, what is the nature of the morphological influences in PN such that they are felt strongest in Diyari, to a lesser degree in Dyirbal and Warlpiri, and not at all in Pintupi?[3] An empirical point in the description of Dyirbal needs to be addressed before discussing prior research. In all previous theoretical treatments of Dyirbal, excluding (Berry, 1996), the pattern in (3a) has been erroneously treated as [(oo)o|o], apparently due to a misclassification of data in (Dixon, 1972). The generalization that these analysts work with is one in which the root|affix boundary is never crossed at all in Dyirbal; but this generalization is not true in (3a) (R.M.W. Dixon, personal communication). The analyses discussed below have been adapted to the correct description of Dyirbal.

Prior research on PN morphological stress can be divided into two classes: those that account for poly-morphemic forms by relating them back to a morphological 'base', and those that account for the influence with simultaneous reference to morphology and prosody. The former class was inaugurated in (Poser, 1989), which proposed a cyclic analysis where degenerate feet are built (and later deleted) over final unpaired syllables in successive cycles, effectively restarting footing with the addition of new suffixes. This analysis was later extended in (Halle and Kenstowicz, 1991). In more recent work, (Kenstowicz, 1997) and (Pensalfini, 1999) propose an OT version of this approach, appealing to Uniform Exponence constraints to model the cyclic effects and eliminating the need for degenerate feet.

The focus of the theory-testing below, however, will be on the simultaneous reference theories, because they are similar enough to be compared efficiently, and, more importantly, they relate to the topical issues in phonology laid out in the introduction. Within this class of theories, there are two subclasses of theories: a recursive analysis, proposed originally in (McCarthy and Prince, 1994) for Diyari and extended in (Kager, 1997), and a nonrecursive analysis proposed independently in (Crowhurst, 1994) and (Berry, 1996). The analysis of Ngalakgan in (Baker, 1999) is also notable because it deals with a set of stress patterns similar to Warlpiri, and it is also nonrecursive, though it specifically rejects the use of alignment constraints.

The chief difference between these two approaches has to do with how feet are prevented from straddling morpheme boundaries. In the recursive approach, straddling feet are prohibited as an indirect effect of prosodic closure (described in detail below), while the nonrecursive approach bans it directly with two constraints, TAUTOMORPHEMICFOOT and ALIGNLEFT(MORPHEME, FOOT) (all constraints are defined in appendix A). TAUTOMORPHEMICFOOT prohibits feet that straddle a morpheme boundary by requiring both branches of a foot to dominate segments in the same morpheme. It is top-ranked in Diyari and fully accounts for the morphological effect on stress in this language. For the intermediate effects in languages like Dyirbal, ALIGNLEFT(MORPHEME, FOOT) is proposed as a way of motivating foot parsing to align with the onset of each new morpheme, as shown below with an effect of minimal violation.

(4)   Morphological effect without prosodic closure (after (Crowhurst, 1994))

/ooo|o-o/	ALIGNLEFT(MORPH, FT)	ALLFTLEFT	TAUTOMORPHFT
☞ (ó o) o | (ó – o)	*	***	*
(ó o) (ó | o) – o	**!	**	*

The recursive analysis does not directly relate foot structure and morpheme boundaries, but rather proposes that limitations on feet come from the prosodic closure of morphological constituents. In particular, an alignment constraint, ALIGNRIGHT(STEM, PRWD), requires the right edge of all stems to line up with the right edge of some prosodic word (PrWd). An assumed recursive stem in poly-morphemic words therefore requires a recursive prosodic word. This recursive structure restricts foot structure in suffixes because the over-arching assumptions in prosodic layering do not allow disyllabic feet that cross the stem|affix boundary to satisfy ALIGNRIGHTSTEM. Further, foot binarity prevents stress via degenerate feet. The effect of recursivity is illustrated in the tableau below for Diyari, which separates prosodic and morphological structure for readability (see also (Kager, 1997) for a parallel effect in Sibutu Sama prefixed structures).

(5)   Recursive PrWd in Diyari produces prosodic closure

/ooo | o/	ALIGNRT(STEM, PRWD)	PARSESYLL	NONRECUR(PRWD)
☞ $\{\{(x.)\,.\,\}_{PrWd}\cdot\}_{PrWd}$ $[[\,\acute{o}\,o\,o\,]_{Stem}\,o\,]_{Stem}$		**	*
$\{(x.)(x\quad.)\}_{PrWd}$ $[[\,\acute{o}\,o\,\grave{o}\,]_{Stem}\,o\,]_{Stem}$	*!		

One advantage of the recursive analysis is that it relates the morphological stress effects in PN to other types of prosodic closure, like syllabification effects in Axininca Campa (McCarthy and Prince, 1994). The same alignment constraints are responsible for rather different phenomena. The analysis is problematized somewhat, however, by the morphology of PN languages. Traditional morphological analysis distinguishes roots from a root plus a derivational affix in e.g., $[[[root] + affix\,]_{Stem} + inflection]_{Word}$. The root + affix is a stem in this structure, but the embedded root alone is not. This complicates the analysis of Diyari because the closure effect is predicted to apply specifically to stems, but the root|affix juncture behaves exactly like suffix-suffix junctures. Furthermore, it cannot be said that PN languages do not distinguish roots from higher-level morphological categories, like morphological stem or word, because of the abundant evidence for this distinction, both in stress, as shown by Dyirbal and Warlpiri, and non-stress phonological properties (Baker and Harvey, 2003). The solution to this problem proposed in (Kager, 1997) is that, in addition to the constraint motivating closure of stems, an independent constraint, ALIGNRIGHT(ROOT, PRWD), motivates prosodic closure of roots specifically. This assumption effectively distinguishes the two morphological categories, but allows for their combined effect in Diyari where both alignment constraints are ranked high.

This move raises an interesting theoretical question, however: what is the relationship between the morphology-phonology interface constraints? Two possibilities come to mind given the notion of stringency defined in (Prince,

1997). The two interface constraints at work in the analysis may be non-stringent in that they work on different morphological structures, as shown by the last two columns below. Or they could be stringent, where a general alignment constraint requiring all morphemes to end in PrWds, ALIGNRIGHT(MORPH, PRWD), stands in a stringency relation with ALIGNRIGHT(ROOT, PRWD), as shown by the second and last constraint columns.

(6)   Stringent and non-stringent relations with interface constraints

/ooo|o–o/	NONRECUR	ALIGNRTMORPH	ALIGNRTSTEM	ALIGNRTROOT
a. {(ó o)(ò | o) – o}		**	*	*
b. {{(ó o) o} | o – o}	*	*	*	
c. {{(ó o) o | o } – o}	*	*		*
d. {{{(ó o) o} | o } – o}	**			

ALIGNRIGHTROOT is in a stringency relation with ALIGNRIGHTMORPH because it has a proper subset of the violations of ALIGNRIGHTMORPH. This is not true of ALIGNRIGHTROOT and ALIGNRIGHTSTEM. As for the nonrecursive theory discussed above, it is naturally stringent: the two constraints, TAUTOMORPHEMICFOOT and ALIGNLEFT(MORPHEME, FOOT), must stand in a stringency relation. It is impossible to violate the former without violating the latter, but satisfaction of TAUTOMORPHEMICFOOT does not guarantee satisfaction of ALIGNLEFT (MORPHEME, FOOT), because a morpheme could start without a foot.

The relation between the interface constraints is more than just an aesthetic question about logical relations among constraints. Stringency relations have been identified in recent research as an important source of implicational relations and an attractive alternative to fixed rankings. For example, (de Lacy, 2004) shows that a fixed ranking approach to sonority-driven stress has empirical problems that are solved by employing stringency relations. How does the PN system contribute to this issue? The next section examines this question, in tandem with the recursivity issue, by studying the factorial typologies that are predicted by both the stringent and non-stringent versions of the recursive analysis, as well as the stringent nonrecursive theory.

3   Theory testing I: Recursivity and stringency

The three basic theories examined here differ principally in the content of the morphology-phonology interface constraints, given in the columns below. Each row indicates the key constraints for the three basic theories ('±R' refers to the recursive/nonrecursive distinction, and '±S' to stringent/nonstringent). The lack of a -R/-S theory is a predicted gap, because the nonrecursive theory is naturally stringent, as explained in section 2.

(7)   Interface constraints in basic theories

	AlignRtRoot	AlignRtStem	AlignRtMor	TautoMorFt	AlignLtMor
–R +S				✓	✓
+R +S	✓		✓		
+R –S	✓	✓			

In addition to the interface constraints, all three theories include the metrical constraints PARSESYLLABLE, ALLFEETLEFT, and ALLFEETRIGHT. FOOTBINARITY is excluded from this comparison, however, because no language in the system admits unary feet, so it is irrelevant to the relative harmony of mappings in this typology. Also, it turns out that in order to successfully account for the Pama-Nyungan continuum, two additional constraints are necessary for all theories: a standard constraint requiring the main stress foot to appear at the left edge of the word, MAINLEFT, and a constraint prohibiting two adjacent unfooted syllables, PARSESYLL2. The inclusion of the latter is argued for in (Kenstowicz, 1997), which notes that Jingulu (non-Pama-Nyungan) requires a constraint against a stress lapse in three successive syllables (Kenstowicz's LAPSE). Since Jingulu is identical to Dyirbal in terms of the structures examined here (with the data correction made in section 2), this constraint is clearly necessary. PARSESYLL2 is used here to avoid confusion with a different definition of lapse constraints used in section 4, though it could be defined, with somewhat different effects, as a self-conjoined *LAPSE constraint.

The typologies below assume that all theories work on the same mappings, i.e., they have to contend with the same inputs and outputs. One might object that the nonrecursive theory does not require a recursive PrWd, so it should not evaluate them. This type of structure, however, seems to be necessary for the stress of compounds and PrWd-external affixation, as argued in, e.g., (Peperkamp, 1997). It is sensible therefore to include recursive PrWds as a viable parse for all theories, though clearly there is not the same motivation for recursion in the nonrecursive theory, which should be reflected in its factorial typology.

In order to explore the above theories with a consistent set of mappings, the linguistic system described below was developed to approximate the structures found in PN languages. The system of variables for input and output structures given below successfully accounts for the main observations covered in the literature. The system is somewhat simplified, however, for practical reasons. For example, trisyllabic suffixes are excluded because they would expand the system greatly, with no real benefit, since their behavior is matched for the most part by other forms in the system.

(8)   The Pama-Nyungan system

    a.   *Variables for inputs*: words may be mono- and poly-morphemic, roots either have two or three syllables, poly-morphemic words may have one or two suffixes, suffixes may be mono- or disyllabic

    b.   *Outputs*: all possible binary parses of given inputs; all words contain at least one foot, and the first foot is always the main stress foot; recursive PrWds are only possible as a means of satisfying the interface constraints

This system of variables generates 14 inputs and 250 outputs. The forms of the PN system and the constraint violations predicted by each theory have been input into Excel spreadsheet files and run on OTSoft (Hayes et al., 2003) to create a factorial typology for each theory. In order to facilitate the replication of results and further linguistic exploration, the input files for each system are available from a link associated with a pre-press version of this paper on the Rutgers Optimality Archive. The ensuing discussions sometimes refer only to the output patterns produced by OTSoft from these files (which can be easily reproduced with the provided files), because space limitations prevent full visualization of the systems and their associated rankings.

Finally, each theory is tested against a set of 'core languages', i.e., attested languages that any theory should account for. In this section, there are three core PN languages, Dyirbal, Diyari, and Warlpiri, and four logical variations on their patterns that are well-attested, i.e., non-iterative stress patterns for both left-to-right and right-to-left syllabic trochee systems (LRNI, RLNI), and left-to-right and right-to-left iterative syllabic trochee systems (LRI, RLI). It is useful to define a set of core languages, because a theory's performance can be assessed in terms of its success in accounting for the core. Furthermore, as illustrated in section 4, core languages help define the structure of large factorial typologies in that they constitute landmarks that create consistent partitions within a typology. The partition structure also aids in theory comparison.

The typologies of the three basic theories, rooted in the PN system, are summarized below.

(9)   Factorial typologies I: basic theories

	#Cs	Pred	Core	#Core	Noncore
−R +S	8	109	7	11	98
+R +S	8	107	7	13	94
+R −S	8	165	7	15	150

Explanation of columns: #Cs = number of constraints in theory (thus #Cs! is number of possible rankings), Pred = predicted structurally distinct output patterns, Core = number of core languages successfully accounted for (out of 7), #Core = number of output patterns that are consistent with the core languages (a language may be consistent with more than one set of structural descriptions), Noncore = Pred − #Core, i.e., all the output patterns that are not consistent with the core languages, or are not yet attested.[4]

Several points can be made about these typologies which feed into research questions below. First, each theory successfully accounts for all the seven core languages, though the resulting factorial typologies seem to be rather unrestricted. If restrictiveness is a measure of the difference between attested and predicted patterns, all of the basic theories appear to overgenerate, with +R−S leading the pack. As discussed below, this problem is due in part to an unintended interaction between ALLFEETRIGHT and the constraints allowing recursion. Second, all of the theories predict the existence of different output patterns, with distinct structural descriptions, for the same stress patterns. This prediction is indicated above by the fact that the number of core languages is not equal to #core in each row. As a concrete example, there are two distinct grammars that generate different metrical analyses of Warlpiri in the recursive/ stringent theory (namely output pattern #30 and #32 generated by OTSoft from the +R+S input file). This prediction turns out to be an unavoidable consequence of the recursive theories, but tied to the interaction of the interface constraints and ALLFEETRIGHT in the nonrecursive theory, as examined in some detail in section 4.

An important theoretical consequence revealed by the above typologies is that each theory is capable of accounting for the core data, without mixing models that have different theoretical assumptions about the interface constraints. For example, the complicated morphological influences in Warlpiri have led (Kager, 1997) to propose a mixed model in which recursive structures, motivated by ALIGNRIGHT constraints, are necessary, as well as a constraint requiring prosodic alignment of the *left* edge of morphemes, as in the nonrecursive theory. However, a homogeneous recursive analysis is still possible with the independently motivated PARSESYLL2, as shown below in a comparative tableau (Prince, 2003).

(10) Comparative tableau for Warlpiri in recursive/stringent model

Input	Winner	Loser	AlignRtMorph	AlignRtRoot	NonRecPWd	AllFtLeft	AllFtRight	ParseSyll	ParseSyll2
a. /ooo|o/	{(óo)(ò|o)}	{{(óo)o}|o}	L	L	W	L	e	W	W
b. /ooo|o/	{(óo)(ò|o)}	{(óo)o-o}	e	e	e	L	e	W	W
c. /ooo|o-oo/	{(óo)(ò|o)-(òo)}	{{(óo)o}|o-(òo)}	L	L	W	L	L	W	W
d. /ooo|o-oo/	{(óo)(ò|o)-(òo)}	{(óo)o|(ò-o)o}	e	e	e	L	L	W	e
e. /ooo|oo-o/	{{{(óo)o}|(òo)}-o}	{(óo)(ò|o)(ò-o)}	W	W	L	W	W	L	e

In comparative tableaux, each row records the violation profile of a single winner-loser pair, where the cell at the intersection of a given row and column indicates that the above constraint either favors the winner (W), or loser (L), or neither (e). The tableau above reveals that, given the six basic constraints of +R+S (first six constraint columns), no ranking of constraints is consistent with the data, or the data have inconsistent ranking requirements (Tesar, 2004). If any one of the constraints is inserted at the top of the hierarchy, it would prefer at least one loser, and thus fail to account for Warlpiri. However, PARSESYLL2 resolves the inconsistency: inserting it at the top enables the interface constraints to be ranked. Criticisms of Kager's mixed model therefore cannot be based in the use of recursive PrWds (cf., (Baker, 1999), (Pensalfini, 1999)). Warlpiri simply provides further motivation for PARSESYLL2, which has already been motivated by different facts in Dyirbal and Jingulu.

While on the subject of the recursive analysis, two further objections, raised in passing in (Berry, 1996: 43), need to be addressed. The first is that the prosodic closure of stems is not perfectly satisfied at the syllable level: suffixes that start with a nasal+consonant sequence cause the nasal to be parsed in the syllable containing the stem-final vowel, e.g., *pa.ʎa|ŋ.ku-ɳa-lu* 'with an adze we (did)'. However, the desired recursive parse, {{pa.ʎa|ŋ}.ku-ɳa-lu}, is still the predicted winner when compared with the nonrecursive alternative {pa.ʎa|ŋ.ku-ɳa-lu}, because it fares much better on a (gradient) ALIGNRIGHTROOT (or, alternatively, nongradient alignment could be assessed at a prosodic level higher than segments).

Second, (Berry, 1996) states that the domains for stress are inconsistent for the domains needed to adequately describe a pattern of progressive vowel harmony in Warlpiri, and, in particular, the internal PrWd structure needed for stress makes incorrect predictions for this vowel harmony pattern. Examination of the domains discussed in (Nash, 1986), summarized on pages 98–99, however, suggests that the domain for vowel harmony is bracketed by the left edge of a stem, which is not in fact implied by the proposed analysis. Indeed, the original analysis of Diyari in (McCarthy and Prince, 1994) proposed an ALIGNLEFT(STEM, PRWD) constraint that would posit a {$_{PrWd}$ at the left edge of a stem. If this constraint is applied in a similar way to Warlpiri, it would correctly predict the left edge of the harmony domain. It appears, thus, that harmony rules are sensitive to the largest PrWd (or higher prosodic category if needed), while stress must reckon with all PrWds, which, interestingly, is a natural consequence of the geometry of metrical feet.

Returning to the issue of restrictiveness, all of the basic theories have large numbers of noncore patterns. Some of these noncore patterns, to an expert on stress, may seem odd and like the kind of pattern a theory should rule out systematically. While further study may uncover that some noncore patterns are indeed attested, and therefore really belong with the core data, all the analyst can do with this kind of information is examine its properties and conjecture as to its inherent plausibility. There are several noncore output patterns predicted by each theory that are 'just off the mark' of an attested pattern, and so one can imagine that they might develop from, or be the ancestor of, some core language. An interpretation of one such noncore pattern is discussed in some detail in section 4. However, there are other patterns that are rather distant from the core languages and seem to arise from the unintended consequences of the proposed constraints. A case in point is a set of systems that otherwise have non-iterative stress, but the availability of the recursive PrWd in polymorphemic words enables iterative stress by positing an additional PrWd for a second foot to align to, as shown below.

(11) Unintended effect of AllFtRight (see OTSoft output #92 of +R+S)

Input	Output	AllFtRt	ParseSyll	NonRec	AlignRtMor
a. /ooo|o/ ☞ {o o (ó | o)}			**		*
*{(ó o) (ò | o)}		*!*			*
b. /ooo|oo/ ☞ {{o(ó o)} | (ò o)}			*	*	
*{o o o | (ò o)}			**!*		*
*{o (ó o) | (ò o)}		*!*	*		*

This kind of non-uniform pattern of iterativity is predicted by each of the basic theories, and its various instantiations account for many of the noncore patterns. +R+S, for example, has 23 output patterns with this property. While it seems clear that this pattern of non-uniformity is problematic, it is a direct consequence of recursivity and the constraints of these theories. It turns out, however, that it is less a problem with recursivity, and more a problem with AllFeetRight, whose existence has been argued against for independent reasons in recent work ((Alber, 2005), (Kager, 2005)). The next section shows that removing AllFeetRight from the constraint set *CON* does in fact increase the viability of these theories in terms of their restrictiveness, as well as reveal other important consequences of their core assumptions.

4   Theory testing II: Factoring in gradience

Cross-linguistic work on directionality of stress has led to the removal of AllFeetRight from *CON*. This adjustment is required to account for the apparent absence of right-to-left disyllabic iambic systems (though see (Everett, 2003) for a potential counterexample) and limitations on dactyls, namely that they always involve a main stress foot. (Alber, 2005) accounts for these typological gaps by proposing that AllFeetRight be replaced by *Lapse, a constraint against two adjacent unstressed syllables. With a similar aim, (Kager, 2005) also replaces AllFeetRight with *Lapse. In addition, AllFeetLeft is replaced by two more stringent lapse constraints, LapseAtPeak and LapseAtEnd. These last two constraints require lapses to appear in prominent positions, namely, adjacent to a stress peak (LapseAtPeak), or to the end of a word (LapseAtEnd).

There are important differences between the two approaches, on which see (Alber, 2005) for extensive discussion. An important theoretical difference between the two is that Kager's theory does not require gradient constraint evaluation in the analysis of directionality because it abolishes both AllFeetLeft and AllFeetRight, two constraints that typically assess degrees of violation. It is of some interest to probe the difference between Alber's and Kager's theories, because Alber's retains AllFeetLeft, and in doing so requires gradient constraint evaluation, a power ascribed to *EVAL* that has been argued against in recent work (McCarthy, 2003c).

Six more factorial typologies were constructed based on the differences between the basic theories and these new theories of directionality, which are summarized below. The key difference, reflected in the labels below, is the degree to which gradient constraints are required. The basic theories of section 3 are fully gradient (+G) in the sense that they employ two gradient constraints, AllFeetLeft and AllFeetRight. Alber's theory is more restricted in using only AllFeetLeft, hence +Gr, for 'gradient-restricted'. Kager's theory is fully nongradient (-G) because it does away with constraints that require gradient constraint evaluation.

(12) Constraints responsible for directionality effects

	AllFtLt	AllFtRt	*Lapse	LapseEdge	LapsePeak
-R+S+G, +R+S+G, +R-S+G	✓	✓			
-R+S+Gr, +R+S+Gr, +R-S+Gr	✓		✓		
-R+S-G, +R+S-G, +R-S-G			✓	✓	✓

These new theories are applied below to the same PN linguistic system. However, the characterization of the set of core languages needs to be changed because, by dropping AllFeetLeft and AllFeetRight, the constraints now lack the ability to directly model non-iterative stress, so it is unfair to evaluate the +G theories with the same set of core languages as the +Gr/-G theories. With the non-iterative systems removed, all the theories are tested against the remaining five core patterns. The six new factorial typologies are summarized below, together with the three gradient theories from section 3.

(13) Factorial typologies II: basic models with gradience as a variable

	#Cs	Pred	Core	#Core	Noncore	Problem cases
-R +S +G	8	109	5	9	96	
-R +S +Gr	8	27	5	5	22	
-R +S -G	9	51	4	4	47	Dyirbal
+R +S +G	8	107	5	15	92	
+R +S +Gr	8	54	5	10	44	
+R +S -G	9	100	5	10	90	
+R -S +G	8	165	5	10	155	
+R -S +Gr	8	79	4	9	70	Warlpiri
+R -S -G	9	177	4	11	166	Warlpiri

As predicted, removing ALLFEETRIGHT vastly reduces the noncore patterns. In all cases, the number of noncore patterns in the +Gr theory is less than half the number of noncore patterns in the corresponding +G theory, and a reduction of 77% of the noncore patterns predicted by -R+S+G. This reduction in noncore patterns also eliminates the unnatural patterns of non-uniform iterativity, as desired. However, certain empirical problems arise as well when ALLFEETRIGHT is removed: -R+S-G cannot account for Dyirbal, and both the +Gr and -G nonstringent theories fail to account for Warlpiri. That is, no ranking of the constraints that define these theories can account for these problem cases. Given the inherent lack of restrictiveness of the gradient +G theories, and the typological problems with ALLFEETRIGHT raised by (Alber, 2005) and (Kager, 2005), these findings lead to some interesting conclusions about the other features of the theories.

First, these findings support a rather strong argument for stringent constraint relations. The problem with the nonstringent (-S) theories is that they either fail to account for Warlpiri (+R-S+Gr, +R-S-G), or overgenerate by a very large margin. The +R-S+G theory predicts the existence of 85 more noncore languages than the related +R-S+Gr theory, and 63 more noncore languages than the corresponding stringent theory +R+S+G. These numbers are somewhat telling, but the important point is that +R-S+G predicts the existence of the non-uniform patterns of iterativity discussed in section 3. There are some 47 noncore output patterns that have this property (starting with #93 of the output file for this theory). Consistent with other research on stringency, therefore, the theories with nonstringent constraint relations are either descriptively inadequate or lead to significant loss of restrictiveness.

The second conclusion is that there seems to be an argument for the necessity of gradient ALLFEETLEFT, in support of (Alber, 2005), though this conclusion is preliminary because of a caveat mentioned below. The fully gradient theories are out: they have non-uniform iterative stress, and they produce unattested right-to-left iambs and dactyl patterns (see above). This leaves four stringent theories, but -R+S-G can also be excluded because it fails to account for Dyirbal. Two +Gr theories remain (-R+S+Gr and +R+S+Gr) and one -G theory (+R+S-G). Since all three successfully account for the core languages, the focus of a comparison is on the predicted noncore patterns. One method of examining these patterns is to section off the factorial typologies based on the order of the core language in the list of output patterns generated by OTSoft. Because of the design of the input files, the core languages appear in the same order for all theories. One finds a reasonable amount of consistency, descriptively at least, in the character and shape of the noncore patterns between the landmark core languages, which allows one to see important differences in their noncore patterns. In the summary chart below, core languages are prefixed by '#' in a row that indicates the specific output pattern in the associated OTSoft output file. The total number of noncore patterns in a given partition is shown in square brackets. The input files weblinked to this paper on ROA contain an index with this partition structure for all of the nine theories examined here.

(14) Noncore partitions for successful theories

	-R+S+Gr [*n* =22]	+R+S+Gr [*n* =44]	+R+S-G [*n* =90]
a.	[7]	[11]	[0]
b. LRI	#8	#12, 13, 16	#1, 2, 3
c.	[7]	[9]	[11]
d. Warlpiri	#16	#24	#15
e.	[0]	[0]	[0]
f. Dyirbal	#17	#25, 27	#16, 18
g.	[2]	[8]	[25]
h. Diyari	#20	#36	#43
i.	[4]	[8]	[29]
j. RLI	#25	#45, 47	#73, 77, 85
k.	[2]	[8]	[25]

The differences between +R+S+Gr and +R+S-G lie principally in (14a,g,i,k). In (14a), for example, +R+S+Gr predicts a host of stress systems with patterns of ternary stress in words with even numbered syllables (see its output patterns #4–11), because of the role of PARSESYLL2 in these constraint systems. +R+S-G also has patterns of ternary stress, in a different partition (14g), but they always also contain recursive PrWds. So this theory seems to lack the descriptive capacity of +R+S+Gr, which allows for ternary stress in nonrecursive words. Another interesting difference is observed in the partition defined by Diyari and RLI in (14i). In both +R+S+Gr and +R+S-G, there are several patterns with obligatory second syllable main stress, largely an effect of the lapse constraints and PARSESYLL2 again. But for +R+S-G, LAPSEATEND can have a combined effect with ALIGNRIGHTROOT to require this in all words with trisyllabic stems, as in #64. Because +R+S+Gr lacks LAPSEATEND, it does not predict this pattern. Perhaps these output patterns will be found in some language, in which case, one could argue for +R+S-G over +R+S+Gr. However, at the present time, +R+S-G appears to be both too unrestricted, predicting at least three times as many output patterns in (14g,i,k), and, at the same time, too restrictive in partition (14a). Though this conclusion is rather tentative, it seems to support Alber's contention to retain gradient ALLFEETLEFT.

One problem with this conclusion, however, is that its validity is limited to the Pama-Nyungan system, which has exclusively suffixing morphology. When it is extended to languages with prefixing morphology, many of the problems associated with ALLFEETRIGHT also rear their head for ALLFEETLEFT, because of other necessary interface constraints. Thus, (Kager, 1997) has shown that closure effects at the right edge of stems in PN languages are also found at the left edge between prefix and stem junctures in Sibutu Sama (Austronesian). Such an effect requires ALIGNLEFTSTEM, a constraint forcing alignment of the left edge of stem and PrWd, to prohibit a foot that straddles the prefix|stem juncture. However, inclusion of such a constraint in a theory which includes ALLFEETLEFT will invariably bring about the non-uniform patterns of iterativity that motivated exclusion of ALLFEETRIGHT. While there is still an important difference between the +Gr and -G theories in terms of right edge effects, it appears the ultimate argument for retaining ALLFEETLEFT may not rest on restrictiveness.

Finally, let's consider the necessity of PrWd recursion in the analysis of Pama-Nyungan stress. The differences between the two remaining +Gr theories, -R+S+Gr and +R+S+Gr, are: (i) the recursive theory predicts more than one grammar (and thus distinct structural descriptions) for some of the core languages, namely Dyirbal and the iterative stress systems (14b,f,j), and (ii) +R+S+Gr predicts a somewhat larger range of noncore languages; see the noncore partitions in (14). Since there is apparently no known non-stress evidence for the distinct structures implied by (i), the last section discusses the kinds of evidence that might require these structures, and thereby support the recursive analysis.

There is, however, one important empirical difference in the noncore data that clearly separates the nonrecursive and recursive theories. As it turns out, there is explicit evidence bearing on this issue in a related Australian language. The matter in question arises from so-called 'evanescent' stress patterns documented in (Baker, 1999) for Ngalakgan (non-Pama-Nyungan). Evanescent stress involves sporadic assignment of prominence (stress or pitch accent) to the third syllable in a [ooo|o] word, which Baker analyzes as optional footing of the third root syllable and monosyllabic suffix, as in the two variants, *(jáwaŋ) (ḍà|ŋgi)* ~ *(jáwaŋ)ḍa|ŋgi*, for 'your beard'. Apparently this variable pattern is rather typical. Baker (personal communication) has found the same pattern in Warlpiri, and this pattern may have been the source of confusion for prior research on Dyirbal discussed in section 2. Details of the analysis of free variation aside, any theory should be able to account for both patterns with some consistent system, though different rankings may be needed for different patterns. Furthermore, the fact that the unstressed pattern is highly plausible and could easily develop through regular historical processes in languages like Warlpiri and Dyirbal suggests that any theory should be able to account for it with a single constraint system.

As for our two remaining theories, +R+S+Gr predicts the existence of the two variations, both for Dyirbal and Warlpiri, while -R+S+Gr does not. In particular, Dyirbal with [(óo)(òo)] is described by two different grammars, #25 and #27, and Dyirbal with [(óo)o|o] is described by the rankings of #30, 32 (see the OTSoft output files for full rankings). Likewise, standard Warlpiri is #24, and Warlpiri with [(óo)o|o] is described by #35. In both cases, the fundamental difference is the relative order of ALIGNRIGHTROOT and PARSESYLL2, suggesting that the variation can be treated by flipping the order of these constraints somehow. Interestingly, however, -R+S+Gr is incapable of predicting a [(óo) o|o] parse in either Dyirbal or Warlpiri without non-iterative stress in [oooo]. The problem is illustrated below with a comparative tableau, to show the inherent inconsistency between these structures.

(15) Comparative tableau for Dyirbal with [(óo)o|o]

Input	Winner	Loser	ALIGNLTMORPH	TAUTOMORFT	ALLFTLEFT	ALLFTRIGHT	PARSESYLL	PARSESYLL2	*LAPSE
a. /oooo/	(óo)(òo)	(óo) oo	e	e	L	e	W	W	W
b. /ooo|o/	(óo)o|o	(óo)(ò|o)	e	W	W	e	L	L	L
c. /ooo|o-o/	(óo)o|(ò-o)	(óo)(ò|o)-o	W	e	L	W	e	e	e
d. /ooo|o-oo/	(óo)o|(ò-o)o	(óo)o|o-(òo)	e	L	W	L	e	W	e
e. /ooo|o-oo/	(óo)o|(ò-o)o	(óo)(ò|o)-(òo)	e	e	W	W	L	e	L

No ranking of the above constraints will account for all of the data. If (15c) is removed from the data set above, after ranking ALIGNLTMORPH, there are no more constraints that can be ranked because each one favors a loser. The problem is in reckoning the poly-morphemic words with mono-morphemic forms like (15a), where iterative stress requires either PARSESYLL2, PARSESYLL, or *LAPSE to dominate ALLFTLEFT, which is inconsistent with the ranking requirements required by poly-morphemic forms. In sum, the -R+S+Gr constraint set is incapable of describing this pattern, so it does not extend to evanescent stress.

5   Conclusion

The linguistic exploration above supports a number of conclusions about the analysis of morphological influences on stress, and the nature of constraints in OT in general. First, it shows that a stringency relation between two morphology-phonology interface constraints, namely ALIGNRIGHTMORPH and ALIGNRIGHTROOT, is superior to a theory with parallel constraints for roots and stems. The factorial typologies of both were compared in a controlled linguistic system and it was shown that the latter either fails descriptively or significantly overgenerates, without any benefits for the analysis of known data. A second conclusion is that, while certain constraints that require gradient evaluation must be dispensed with, ALLFEETLEFT should not be. These assumptions make the factorial typologies more natural in the sense that they do not predict implausible patterns, like the patterns of non-uniform iterative stress, and also seem to provide the right balance between theoretical restrictiveness and descriptive freedom, though this latter point is still somewhat tentative.

The third conclusion is that the Pama-Nyungan continuum of morphological stress seems to require recursive PrWds that wrap morphological constituents. When compared to the nonrecursive alternative, it successfully accounts for all of the core data, including evanescent stress in Australian languages. Furthermore, it achieves this empirical coverage with independently motivated constraints. The nonrecursive analysis, on the other hand, proposes two constraints that appear to have limited application to other areas of phonology, and it cannot account for evanescent stress.

The recursive analysis makes clear predictions, however, that have not yet been tested. One of the most obvious ones is that it predicts more than one structural analysis for some of the core languages. For example, there are three different analyses for left-to-right noniterative stress in +R+S+Gr, stemming from the availability of recursion once, at all possible morpheme boundaries, or not at all. What kinds of evidence might be used to distinguish and thereby motivate these different analyses? The focus of this chapter has been on stress, but certainly non-stress phenomena could be brought to bear on this question. For example, if it could be shown that certain sandhi rules applied internally at morpheme edges in one language, but only between words in another, this could be ascribed to the availability of PrWd boundaries inside the morphological word. Similar patterns could be found for inventory restrictions, like constraints on segments at morpheme edges as opposed to word edges. If such differences were found, they could be attributed to restrictions on prosodic structure, rather than morpho-syntactic structure, a principle which has been argued for independently in (Selkirk, 1986).

Perhaps clitic placement could also be brought to bear on the possibility of recursion. Clitics are defined in relation to prosodic edges rather than morphological structure, so one form of evidence for different recursion possibilities would be the availability of 'internal clitics' aligned with a word-internal PrWd edge. Such a pattern would be easiest to see (and distinguish from simple affixes) in the systems where stem size determines the availability of recursion. For example, output pattern #13 for +R+S+Gr differs from #12 in having recursive PrWds in two syllable stems only, which could determine clitic placement. Finally, the different recursion possibilities might be useful in the analysis of allomorph selection. Indeed, many patterns of suppletive allomorphy depend on the syllable count of the stem (Hargus, 1993), which interacts with the possibility of recursion.

Finally, the larger chapter constitutes an extended argument for factorial typologies as a research tool. A basic point is that it is sometimes the case that prior research does not correctly characterize its consequences. Factorial typologies, aided considerably by software packages like OTSoft, enable careful validation of these predictions. Furthermore, while there are many examples of 'mature typologies', where a goodness of fit has been found between the predicted patterns and attested languages (see especially (Baković, 2006a), (Gordon, 2002), and (Hyde, 2002)), there are still interesting observations to be made when one is just embarking on a problem. As shown by the present chapter, important conclusions can be made even when testing the predicted typologies against a relatively small set of attested languages. One should always approach unattested patterns with care, but the analyst can still make informed decisions based on the inherent plausibility of a predicted pattern, and also when a theory clearly overgenerates. The identification of core attested data is particularly important here, because it is a consistent dataset to test theories against, and it helps organize the noncore data, as shown in section 4 with noncore partition structure. Another related point is that factorial typologies enhance the pattern recognition abilities of the analyst by clarifying patterns to be sought in further empirical research, like the predictions made by the different recursion patterns discussed immediately above. Finally, factorial typologies also feed research in the sense that they clarify new theories to be tested and compared against known ones. It is only after having identified the rather artificial patterns of the basic theories in section 3 that it became clear that there was a problem with the alignment constraint responsible for right-to-left directionality, which led to the creation of new theories in section 4.

Appendix A. The constraints

Metrical constraints ((McCarthy and Prince, 1993), (Kager, 1999))
>   FOOTBINARITY (FTBIN): feet are binary at either the syllabic or moraic level.
>   PARSESYLLABLE (PARSESYLL): syllables are dominated by feet.
>   ALLFEETLEFT/RIGHT (ALLFTLT/RT): the left/right edge of all prosodic feet are properly aligned with the left/right edge of some prosodic word.
>   PARSESYLLABLE2 (PARSESYLL2): no two adjacent syllables are unfooted.
>   MAINLEFT: the left edge of the prosodic word is properly aligned with the left edge of the main stress foot.

Morphology-phonology interface constraints, nonrecursive ((Crowhurst, 1994), (Berry, 1996))
>   ALIGNLEFT(MORPHEME, FOOT) = ALIGNLT(MORPH, FT)
>   All morphemes begin with a foot (i.e., the left edge of every morpheme is properly aligned with the left edge of some foot).
>   TAUTOMORPHEMICFOOT (TAUTOMORPHFT)
>   Feet never straddle a morpheme boundary (i.e., the syllables of each foot must be contained in a single morpheme).

Morphology-phonology interface constraints, recursive ((McCarthy and Prince, 1994), (Kager, 1997))
>   NONRECURSIVITY(PRWD) = NONRECUR(PRWD) (Selkirk, 1995)
>   PrWds are not recursive (i.e., PrWds do not dominate PrWds)
>   ALIGN(STEM, R, PRWD, R) = ALIGNRT(STEM, PRWD)
>   The right edge of all stems is properly aligned with the right edge of some PrWd.
>   ALIGN(ROOT, R, PRWD, R) = ALIGNRT(ROOT, PRWD)
>   The right edge of all roots is properly aligned with the right edge of some PrWd.
>   ALIGN(MORPHEME, R, PRWD, R) = ALIGNRT(MORPH, PRWD)
>   The right edge of all morphemes is properly aligned with the right edge of some PrWd.

Lapse constraints ((Green and Kenstowicz, 1995), (Kager, 2005))
>   *LAPSE: No two adjacent unstressed syllables
>   LAPSEATEDGE: Lapse must be adjacent to the right edge
>   LAPSEATPEAK: Lapse must be adjacent to a peak

Appendix B. Exemplification of the Pama-Nyungan data

The transcription conventions and abbreviations[5] below follow the sources: (Austin, 1981) pp. 30–31 and (Poser, 1989) for Diyari, (Dixon, 1972) p. 274–75, 280, 284, (Dixon, p.c.), and (Crowhurst, 1994) for Dyirbal, and (Nash, 1986) p. 99 ff., (Nash, p.c.), and (Berry, 1996) p. 32 ff. for Warlpiri.

	Diyari	*Dyirbal*	*Warlpiri*
óo	(ó o) kána 'man'	(ó o) búndiɲ 'grasshopper'	(ó o) wáti 'man'
óoo	(ó o) o pínadu 'old man'	(ó o) o ḍúgumbil 'woman'	(ó o) o wátiya 'tree'
óoòo	(ó o)(ò o) ɳándawàlka 'to close'	(ó o)(ó o) múlumíyan 'whale'	(ó o)(ò o) mánangkàrra 'spinifex plain'
ooo|o	(ó o)o | o púḻuru|ɳi 'mud-LOC'	(ó o)(ó | o) búrguɽúm-bu 'jumping ant-ERG'	(ó o)(ò | o) wátiyà|rla 'tree-LOC'
ooo|oo	(ó o)o | (ò o) pínadu|wàṛa 'old man-PL'	(ó o)o | (ó o) búrbula|gára 'Burbula-1 of pair'	(ó o)o | (ò o) yáparla|ngùrlu 'FaMo-ELATIVE'
ooo|o–o	(ó o)o | o – o Not available	(ó o)o | (ó – o) -o bánagay|mbá-ri-ɲu 'return-COM-REFL-P/P'	(ó o)o | (ò – o) wátiya|rlà-rlu 'tree-LOC-ERG'
ooo|o–oo	(ó o)o | o – (ò o) púḻuru|ɳi-màṭa 'mud-LOC-IDENT'	(ó o)o | (ó – o) o mándalay|mbál-bila 'play-COM-LEST'	(ó o)(ò | o)–(ò o) wátiyà|rla-jùku 'tree-LOC-STILL'
ooo|oo–o	(ó o)o | (ò o) - o Not available	(ó o)o | (ó o) - o Not available	(ó o)o | (ò o) - o wátiya|kàri-rli 'tree-1 of pair-ERG'
ooo|oo–oo	(ó o)o | (ò o) - (ò o) Not available	(ó o)o | (ó o) - (ó o) Not available	(ó o)o | (ò o) - (ò o) Not available
oo|o	(ó o) | o kána|ɳi 'man-LOC'	(ó o) | o wáyɳḍi|ŋu 'motion uphill-REL'	(ó o) | o wáti|ngka 'man-LOC'
oo|oo	(ó o) | (ò o) kána|wàṛa 'man-PL'	(ó o) | (ó o) búnḍul|múɲa 'spank-PART'	(ó o) | (ò o) ngáti|nyànu 'mother-POSS'
oo|o–o	(ó o) | o – o máda|la-ntu 'hill-CHAR-PROP'	(ó o) | (ó – o) wáyɳḍi|ŋú-gu 'motion uphill-REL-DAT'	(ó o) | (ò – o) wáti|ngkà-rlu 'man-LOC-ERG'
oo|o–oo	(ó o) | o – (ò o) ɳánda|na-màṭa 'hit-PART-IDENT'	(ó o) | (ó – o) o ḍáŋga|ná-mbila 'eat-PRON-WITH'	(ó o) | o – (ò o) wángka|ja-jàna 'speak-PST-3pl/NS'
oo|oo–o	(ó o) | (ò o) – o kána|wàra-ɳu 'man-PL-LOC'	(ó o) | (ó o) – o Not available	(ó o) | (ò o) – o yápa|rlàngu-rlu 'person-EX-ERG'
oo|oo–oo	(ó o) | (ò o) – (ò o) kána|wàra-ɳùndu 'man-PL-ABL'	(ó o) | (ó o) – (ó o) Not available	(ó o) | (ò o) – (ò o) Not available

Notes

1   A special thanks to Brett Baker, Ellen Kaisse, Steve Parker, Bruce Tesar, and audiences at the University of Toronto, University of Victoria, and National Taiwan Normal University for their detailed comments and questions. Thanks also to R.M.W. Dixon, David Nash, and Rob Pensalfini for prompt and informative answers to factual questions about the languages discussed here. This chapter was supported in part by standard research grant SSHRC-410–2005–1135. Any errors that remain, despite this help, are the fault of the author.

2   Important primary and secondary references for these languages are: (Austin, 1981) and (Poser, 1989) for Diyari (South Australia), (Dixon, 1972) and (Crowhurst, 1994) for Dyirbal (Northeast Queensland), (Hansen and Hansen, 1969) for Pintupi (Northern Territory), and (Nash, 1986) and (Berry, 1996) for Warlpiri (Northern Territory).

3   The above languages are used to exemplify the core languages under analysis because they feature prominently in prior theoretical work. However, a number of other Australian languages further exemplify these patterns: Wambaya (non-Pama-Nyungan) patterns with Warlpiri (Nordlinger, 1993), Gooniyandi (Bunaban) with Pintupi (McGregor, 1990), Ngalakgan metrical stress (non-Pama-Nyungan) closely resembles Warlpiri (Baker, 1999), and Jingulu (non-Pama-Nyungan) behaves in many ways like Dyirbal (Pensalfini, 2003), as described in this chapter and in (Dixon, 1972), though there are some differences between these last two, including a lexical class of stems with main stress on the second syllable.

4   A somewhat technical point about these theories is that their constraints do not fully establish the relative harmony among all the mappings in the PN system. In all theories, here and in section 4, there are some ties. But each member of a pair of forms that tie is harmonically bounded by other output forms in their respective candidate sets, so they will always be losers. In other words, the constraints do not fully determine the relative harmony of all mappings, but they are sufficient to prohibit these harmonically bound ties from surfacing in any language.

5   The individual morphemes inside of Diyari words given here are abbreviated as follows: LOC (locative), PL (plural), IDENT (identified information), CHAR (characteristic), PART (participial), and ABL (ablative). For Dyirbal words, the abbreviations here are consistent with the descriptions given in (Dixon, 1972), which is indexed by his list of Dyirbal affixes: ERG (ergative), COM (instrumentative/comitative), REFL (reflexive), P/P (present-past tense), LEST (verbal inflection indicating that an event might take place with unpleasant consequences), REL (relative clause inflection), PART (participial), DAT (dative), PRON (pronominal object), WITH ('with X'). The abbreviations for Warlpiri morphemes are derived from both Nash's index of Warlpiri suffixes and enclitics and Berry's abbreviation list: LOC (locative), ERG (ergative), ELATIVE (elative), STILL ('still' or 'yet'), POSS (possessive), PST (past verb inflection), 3pl/ NS (3rd person plural, nonsubject), EX ('for example').

8 Acoustics of epenthetic vowels in Lebanese Arabic[1]

Maria Gouskova and Nancy Hall

We show that epenthetic and lexical vowels in Lebanese Arabic, which are often transcribed as identical, are acoustically distinct: epenthetic vowels are either shorter or backer or both. We argue that this incomplete neutralization is the result of phonetics optionally accessing an intermediate level of phonological derivation. This is formalized in Optimality Theory with Candidate Chains (OT-CC): epenthesis requires a multi-step candidate chain, and phonetics can access any step of the chain. Furthermore, we suggest that the acoustic distinction helps learners construct the correct candidate chains for words with epenthetic vs. lexical vowels.

1   Introduction

Phonological accounts of epenthesis normally assume that epenthetic vowels are phonetically identical to lexical vowels—that is, that epenthesis fully neutralizes the underlying distinction between the presence and the absence of a vowel. We present experimental evidence showing that the epenthetic vowel that Lebanese Arabic inserts into final CC clusters, which is usually transcribed [i], is backer and shorter in duration than Lebanese lexical [i] for some speakers. We propose a way to understand these phonetic findings within the version of Optimality Theory with Candidate Chains (McCarthy 2007). We suggest that phonetics can draw on the intermediate stages of derivation that these candidate chains represent. This view of the relationship between phonetics and phonology offers a new way to tackle the learning problem presented by stress-epenthesis interactions.

A long line of phonetic research shows that phonological processes which have traditionally been described as neutralizing contrasts actually leave phonetic traces of the underlying distinctions, a phenomenon sometimes called incomplete neutralization. Incomplete neutralization has been found for final devoicing in Polish, German, and Catalan (for a recent review, see Warner et al. 2004, 2006), vowel deletion in French (Fougeron and Steriade 1997), vowel epenthesis in English (Davidson 2006), and stop insertion in English (Fourakis and Port 1986). While near-neutralization effects are sometimes too slight to be perceptible (Jongman 2004), Port and O'Dell (1985) show that listeners are better than chance at distinguishing supposedly neutralized words. Whether incomplete neutralization reflects underlying morphophonemic distinctions or just orthography is still controversial.

The finding of incomplete neutralization in vowel epenthesis is particularly interesting because vowel epenthesis is often involved in opaque interactions with other processes, particularly stress. If listeners can make use of incomplete neutralization to tell which vowels are epenthetic and which are not, this simplifies the problem of learning the opaque interaction. We emphasize, however, that opaque stress-epenthesis interactions do not depend on the existence of a phonetic difference between epenthetic and underlying vowels; we found some speakers who completely neutralize the distinction yet still avoid stressing epenthetic vowels.

The paper is structured as follows. In §2, we review the grammar of epenthesis and stress in Lebanese. In §3, we present our experiment, which found acoustic differences between epenthetic and lexical [i]. In §4, we propose a way to model incomplete neutralization in Optimality Theory with Candidate Chains (McCarthy 2007), and we propose a modified learning strategy that can make use of the acoustic difference between epenthetic and lexical vowels to determine underlying representations.

2   Epenthesis and stress in Lebanese Arabic

The description of Lebanese phonology given here is based on Abdul-Karim (1980) and Haddad (1983, 1984). Lebanese has three short vowels, standardly transcribed [a, i, u] (although they are actually fairly centralized), and five long vowels [aː eː oː iː uː]. Syllable structure is restricted: onsets are obligatory; codas are permitted; complex codas are limited to two consonants and can only occur word-finally and only following short vowels. Coda clusters are also subject to further restrictions, especially sonority sequencing constraints, and these are often enforced through epenthesis.

Epenthesis applies in two circumstances. First, Lebanese breaks up three or four-consonant clusters (which only arise through morpheme concatenation). Epenthetic vowels are underlined.

(1)   Epenthesis in /CCC/ clusters

/katab-t-l-a/	ka.tá.bit.la	'she wrote to her'	cf. katábt	'I wrote'
/ʔalf-na/	ʔá.lif.na	'our thousand'	cf. ʔálf	'thousand'
/ʔibn-na/	ʔí.bin.na	'our son'	cf. ʔíb.n-i	'my son'

Second, Lebanese often breaks up two-consonant clusters word-finally. According to Haddad (1983:60), epenthesis is possible in any final CC cluster as long as neither consonant is a glide.[2] In some clusters, epenthesis is obligatory, in others optional. Haddad presents an exhaustive discussion covering every final CC cluster occurring in the language; our summary here omits some subpatterns involving cluster types that do not occur in our experimental data.

Epenthesis is obligatory in clusters consisting of an obstruent followed by a sonorant, as below.[3]

(2) Obstruent-sonorant final clusters: epenthesis required

/mitl/	mítil	'like' (preposition)	/ʒisr/	ʒísir	'bridge'
/nidr/	nídir	'low'	/ʔifl/	ʔífil	'lock'
/ʔibn/	ʔíbin	'son'	/ʔism/	ʔísim	'name'

The situation of two-obstruent or two-sonorant clusters is more complicated. Haddad reports that epenthesis is obligatory in a cluster of two coronal fricatives, and when a stop is followed by [f] or by a non-coronal stop. Examples of such clusters are given in (3a). In a cluster of a coronal fricative followed by [f], the realization without epenthesis is possible but 'questionable,' as shown in (3b). In other non-guttural obstruent-obstruent clusters, realizations without epenthesis are acceptable, as shown in (3c). Among sonorant-sonorant clusters, epenthesis is required in /mn/, /rl/, /rm/, /nl/, and /ml/ (see (3d)), but not in /mr/ or /lm/; /rn/ without epenthesis is questionable.

(3) Epenthesis required in some obstruent-obstruent and sonorant-sonorant clusters

(a)	/mazʒ/	máziʒ	'mixing'	(c)	/dist/	dísit ~ dist	'boiler/tub'
	/kitf/	kítif	'shoulders'		/rakdˤ/	rákidˤ ~ rakdˤ	'running'
	/rikb/	ríkib	'riding'		/nafs/	náfis ~ nafs	'self'

(b)	/nasf/	násif ~ nasf 'detonation'	(d)	/naml/	námil	'ants'

In clusters of a sonorant followed by an obstruent, like those in (4), epenthesis is optional but not required.

(4) Epenthesis optional in obstruent-sonorant clusters

/bint/	bínit ~ bint	'girl'	/fils/	fílis ~ fils	'1/1000 of a dinar'
/ramz/	rámiz ~ ramz	'symbol'	/kalb/	kálib ~ kalb	'dog'
/ʔird/	ʔírid ~ ʔird	'monkey'	/ʔalf/	ʔálif ~ ʔalf	'one thousand'

Epenthesis interacts opaquely with stress. Lebanese Arabic has the Latin Stress Rule (Mester 1994) with the added complication that superheavy syllables (CVVC, CVCC) attract stress in final position (see (5a)). A word that has no final superheavy syllables will be stressed on a penult if it is heavy and on the antepenult otherwise. In a disyllable with no final superheavy syllable, the first syllable is stressed.[4]

(5) (a) Stress a final superheavy syllable
    Ɂa.kált   'I ate'   bi.xal.líːk 'he lets you'
    naz.zált 'I brought down'   mak.ta.báːt 'libraries'

(b) Else a heavy penult
    náz.zal   'he brought down'   ma.ʕáː.rik 'battles'
    ma.lák.na 'our king'   mak.táb.ti 'my library'

(c) Else the antepenult (or penult in two-syllable word)
    Ɂá.ka.lit 'she ate'   Ɂá.kal   'he ate'
    sá.ħa.bit 'she withdrew'   sá.ħab   'he withdrew'

These patterns are disrupted if the penult or the antepenult contains an epenthetic vowel. In most such cases, stress is assigned as if the epenthetic vowel weren't there, which can result in unstressed closed penults as in (6a,b), or penultimate stress where antepenultimate stress might be expected as in (6c) (McCarthy 2007). There is one systematic exception, shown in (6d): a vowel inserted into an underlying four-consonant cluster does receive stress.

(6) Stress-epenthesis interactions

  (a) /Ɂibn-na/   Ɂí.b<u>i</u>n.na   'our son'

  (b) /katab-t-l-a/   ka.tá.b<u>i</u>t.la 'she wrote to her'

  (c) /katab-t/   ka.tá.b<u>i</u>t   'I wrote' (cf. /katab-it/ → ká.ta.bit 'she wrote')

  (d) /katab-t-l-ha/ ka.tab.t<u>í</u>l.ha 'I wrote to her'

Opaque stress-epenthesis interactions are interesting for a number of reasons. They have been brought to bear on rule-ordering (Broselow 1982), representational differences between epenthetic and lexical vowels (Piggott 1995), parallelism (Alderete 1999a, Broselow 2008), contrast preservation (Łubowicz 2003), and issues in learnability (Alderete and Tesar 2002), which we discuss in §4.2. Whatever the account of stress-epenthesis interactions, phonological treatments assume that epenthetic vowels are phonetically identical to lexical vowels in most dialects of Arabic. We set out to test this assumption for Lebanese.

3   Phonetic study

We aim to identify the phonetic characteristics of epenthetic vowels in Lebanese Arabic and to compare them to lexical vowels. Although there is plenty of descriptive work on Arabic by native speakers (Haddad 1983, 1984, Nasr 1959, 1960, Abdul-Karim 1980 for Lebanese alone), epenthetic vowels of Arabic have never been studied instrumentally (to our knowledge). The available descriptions of Levantine epenthesis give an impressionistic transcription of both vowels as [i], so our null hypothesis is that epenthetic and lexical [i] are acoustically identical. Haddad (1983) notes, however, that 'this representation is rather inadequate since an inserted vowel is more prone to suprasegmental features such as 'guttural' and 'emphatic' [pharyngealized] than an underlying vowel is' (p.61) and that 'a precise description of the quality of the epenthetic vowel. . . is too complicated to deal with here' (p.87) This suggests that some phonetic difference between the vowels might exist.

If any difference does exist, we would expect, based on results from other work on incomplete neutralization (Warner et al. 2004), that the difference would be in the direction of preserving the underlying vowel-zero constrast. Thus, we might expect the epenthetic vowel to be more 'slight' than lexical [i]: shorter duration, less peripheral/more centralized, and lower intensity.

3.1   Design

3.1.1 Materials

The experiment compared near-minimal pairs of words. One word in each pair had the underlying form /CVCC/, and would be pronounced CVCiC if epenthesis occurred. Its match was a word of the underlying form /CVCiC/, which would be pronounced CVCiC. The second vowel in each word is the one being measured.

In Arabic, word shape relates to morpho-syntactic class. /CVCC/ words are usually singular nouns, although our list also includes a preposition and two adjectives. The /CVCVC/ word was usually a /CiCiC/ verb, known as form I in the Arabic verbal morphology system, in the masculine singular past. Every item was a bare stem form, without prefixes or suffixes.

A few pairs were perfect minimal pairs (e.g. /libs/ 'clothing' vs. /libis/ 'he wore'), but most pairs were near matches, where every phoneme except the initial consonant was the same (e.g., /mitl/ 'like' vs. /ʔitil/ 'he got killed'). For three pairs, the voicing of the middle consonant was not matched (e.g., /kizb/ 'lies' vs. /kisib/ 'he earned'), but this was not expected to affect the following vowel's quality or duration.[5] The pairs were also matched for the quality of the first vowel in order to avoid any difference due to vowel-to-vowel coarticulation effects. Two pairs had /a/ in the initial syllable; the rest had /i/. Neither the middle nor the last consonant were pharyngealized in any of the target words, since it is well-known that pharyngealization lowers F2 (Herzallah 1990, Zawaydeh 1999). The first consonants in each pair were matched for pharyngealization: /ʕilm/ 'knowledge' could be compared to /ʕilim/ 'he knew' but not to /silim/ 'he was safe.' Stress was always initial, so the vowels being measured were in unstressed position.

We found in pilot work that speakers (even from the same city) vary in whether or how they produce certain words, for several reasons. First, epenthesis is optional in many of the /CVCC/ words, and some speakers epenthesize more often than others. Second, form I verbs fall into two arbitrary phonological classes, /CaCaC/ and /CiCiC/, and speakers vary as to which vowel pattern goes with which CCC root. For example, some people say [kifil] for 'he guaranteed,' some say [kafal] (and some people can say both). First syllable vowels in the nominal forms also sometimes varied (e.g., /rakb/ for /rikb/ 'riding'). Third, speakers sometimes simply rejected a word as a colloquial lexical item. For example, several speakers accepted [ʔitil] for 'he got killed,' but other speakers had no form I for this verb root, preferring to use form VII, [nʔatal]. Fourth, some speakers tended to drift into the classical register, which has different consonants: for example, [kiðib] rather than [kizib] for 'lies.' If speakers produced any of these variant forms of a test item, or failed to produce an item, the whole pair had to be excluded for that speaker. This variability was part of the reason that we decided to attempt to record as many pairs as possible, rather than recording many repetitions of a small number of pairs (as in Dinnsen and Charles-Luce 1984). It was impossible to be sure in advance that any given pair would work on all subjects. In fact, out of a maximum of 29 possible pairs, each speaker produced only 9 to 23 in usable form.

To minimize this problem, we also included rhyming 'backup' words in the list where available, to be analyzed only if a target word was produced in unusable form. For example, if a speaker failed to produce [ʔifil] 'lock' (perhaps by not epenthesizing, or by using classical [q] instead of colloquial [ʔ]), we substituted their token of [tifil] 'coffee grounds.' The full list of target items and backups is given in Table 1. Fillers were added to bring the word total up to 140.[6]

Table 1: Underlying forms of target items, including 'backups'

Epenthesis		Lexical [i]	
ʃibl, ʔibl	'cub,' 'doe'	ʔibil, dibil	'accepted,' 'withered'
mitl	'like' (preposition)	ʔitil	'got killed'
ʔifl, tifl	'lock,' 'coffee grounds'	kifil	'guaranteed'
mitr, sitr	'meter,' 'modesty'	kitir	'increased'
kibr	'size'	kibir	'grew'
fikr, zikr, bikr	'thought,' 'belly button,' 'firstborn'	sikir	'got drunk'
nidr	'low'	ʔidir	'was able to'
kifr, zifr	'blasphemy,' 'greasy food'	wifir	'became abundant'
ʒisr, nisr, kisr	'bridge,' 'eagle,' 'break'	xisir, ʒisir	'lost,' 'dared'
ʔidm	'the old (plural)'	ʔidim, nidim	'became antiquated,' 'regretted'
ʔism, ʒism	'name,' 'body'	lizim, disim	'was required,' 'was fattening'
ħiʒn	'sadness'	ħiʒin	'felt sad'
libs, dibs	'clothing,' 'syrup'	jibis, libis	'dried up,' 'wore'
wisx	'dirty'	bizix	'spent freely'
rikb	'riding'	rikib	'rode'
dibʔ	'glue'	dibiʔ	'stuck'
kizb	'lies'	kisib, risib	'earned,' 'failed'
naml	'ants'	xamil	'languid' (adjective)
nimr	'tiger'	ximir	'rose (bread)'
film	'film'	silim	'was safe'
ʕilm, ħilm	'knowledge,' 'dream'	ʕilim	'knew'
ʒild	'leather'	wilid	'was born'
ʔird	'monkey'	birid	'caught cold'
kils, fils	'whitewash,' 'fils (coin)'	ʒilis	'became straight'
ʔalf	'thousand'	ʔalif	'alif' (letter)

3.1.2   Orthographic issues

The list of words was presented in ordinary Arabic consonantal script. Short vowels are not normally written in Arabic, which is in one way convenient for our study: since the orthography gives speakers no clue to the vowel's underlying status, it less likely to affect production (but see §3.3.1 for qualification of this point). The lack of orthographic distinctions does, however, introduce a methodological problem. A vowelless written word is frequently ambiguous, out of context, between two or more words (لبس 'l-b-s' can be either /libis/ 'he wore' or /libs/ 'clothing'). This could lead speakers to produce the wrong words.

We took several steps to remove this ambiguity. We presented each word with an English translation (similarly, Dinnsen 1985 used Spanish glosses of Catalan homographs in his study of incomplete neutralization; see also Broselow et al. 1997 for use of English glosses of Arabic words). The speakers looked through the entire list before recording, to make sure they knew which words we meant. However, it was not clear whether speakers actually used the translations during recording; jumping between two languages (particularly with different alphabets) is difficult, and one speaker had limited English. So we also divided the words into alternating blocks of about 20 items, where the words in each block (both test items and fillers) were either all nouns (plus a few adjectives or prepositions, since a few /CVCC/ target items are of these classes), or all form I /CVCVC/ verbs. Forms within each block were pseudo-randomized; the first and the last item in each block was a filler. We explicitly pointed out to subjects that most of the words in each block were a single part of speech. This strategy was largely successful in preventing part of speech mixups.

3.1.3   Participants

The participants were eight speakers of Arabic from Lebanon, who currently live in the US (Washington, DC area) or UK (Essex). All speakers consider Lebanese Arabic their native language, although all speak English (and probably French, although we did not confirm this with all of them). All of the speakers are literate in Arabic and familiar with Modern Standard Arabic. While we did not systematically collect sociological information (for example, for several speakers we did not ask about their religion), the following gives an idea of their backgrounds. Women are identified as W, men as M. **W1** is a university student in her mid-20's, from a village in Southern Lebanon near Palestine, and has also lived briefly in Kuwait. **W2** is a university student in her early 20's, Muslim, from a village near Beirut. She has also lived in Norway and speaks Norwegian. **W3** is an administrative assistant in her 40's, from a village in Northern Lebanon. She formerly taught Standard Arabic and is a rather prescriptive speaker. **W4** is an administrative assistant in her late 20's, from Beirut, who has also lived in Palestine. **W5** is a graduate student in her late 20's, Christian, who grew up in Byblos and Beirut, only leaving Lebanon for graduate school. **M1** is a restaurant owner in his late 30's, Christian, from Beirut. **M2** is a restaurant owner in his mid 50's, from a village in Northern Lebanon, who has also lived in Beirut (he offered to 'speak Beiruti' for us but was asked to use his native variety). **M3** is a restaurant owner in his 60's, from Beirut, who also spent some time in Palestine. His knowledge of English is limited, so M1 sometimes translated for him during the recording session. A fourth man was also recorded, but had trouble speaking colloquially to the microphone and did not produce enough tokens with epenthesis for analysis.

The subject group is not completely linguistically homogeneous. Colloquial Arabic shows considerable microvariation, some of which correlates with region, urban/rural origin, religion, age and gender. In recruiting subjects abroad, we were not able to control for these factors. However, we do not see this as a problem, because our subjects are probably typical of the mix of people one might encounter in a city like Beirut, where most subjects had lived at some time. Linguistic heterogeneity is the reality in many Arabic-speaking cities (Holes 1995), and hence a study of a somewhat heterogeneous group is quite relevant for understanding dialect-wide features such as stress-epenthesis interaction.[7]

3.1.4 Procedure

Recordings were made in 2005 in Washington DC and Colchester, UK, in quiet rooms at the speakers' workplaces or universities. Subjects W2 and W5 were recorded directly into a laptop computer; the other subjects were recorded using a Sony cassette tape recorder and a Sehnheiser MD 511 microphone.

Each speaker looked through the word list to familiarize him/herself with all the words, crossing out or replacing any words that did not belong to his/her own colloquial dialect, and then read the word list once. Speakers were asked to use their own colloquial pronunciations (which some speakers referred to as 'slang' in English) rather than classical or standard forms, and we discussed the difference to make sure speakers understood what we intended. One speaker, W2, asked and was given permission to make notes on her list to remind herself to use colloquial pronunciations. Besides changing classical consonants to colloquial, she wrote in the epenthetic vowels. Several speakers neverthe-less tended to drift into the formal register during recording. If we noticed speakers producing non-Lebanese features such as interdental fricatives, we asked them to repeat the words in their colloquial dialect (cf. Broselow et al.

1997). Speakers read the list of words in a frame sentence. For speakers W1 and W2, the frame sentence was [ʔúːli____ʔawáːm] 'Say (feminine.singular. imperative) quickly.' The feminine imperative was imagined to be directed at the experimenter. The word [ʔawáːm] (which W2 pronounced [ʔaweːm]) is rather colloquial, and we hoped that its presence in the frame would help speakers remain in the colloquial register. However, W3 found [ʔawáːm] ungrammatical in this position, so she and W4, who was recorded in the same session, used the word [ʕamáhalak] 'slowly.' However, we decided later that the initial pharyngeal was undesirable, as it could conceivably affect the epenthetic vowel's F2 (even though pharyngealization spread across word boundaries is not reported). For the remaining speakers, the word 'twice' ([marratéːn], or [martéːn] with syncope) was used instead. While the change of frames is not ideal, it induced no noticeable changes in pronunciation of the target words. Nor did the frame sentence seem to affect speech rate; W2 spoke the slowest despite using the word 'quickly.'

To check the speakers' stress grammars, we elicited some test words, such as 'our son,' 'we understood,' and 'I wrote to her.' All speakers stressed them as in (6).

The recordings were digitized at 44,100 Hz in acoustic analysis software *Praat* (Boersma and Weenink 2005). Vowels were segmented manually by visually inspecting the spectrograms and waveforms. A vowel boundary was judged to coincide with a sharp change in energy and the onset or offset of clear formant structure. Formants were measured using Praat's Burg algorithm. We collected average measurements for the first three formants, since the vowels appeared in a variety of contexts, which undoubtedly affected their quality in different ways. We also measured the duration of the entire rhyme of the second syllable of the word, just in case vowel segmentation turned out to be difficult in different consonantal contexts (which it didn't).

3.2   Results

We performed separate factorial analyses of variance (ANOVA) for each measure as a dependent variable. The independent variables were underlying status (epenthetic vs. lexical) and subject. There was a significant main effect of underlying status for vowel duration and F2 ($p \leq .001$); underlying status was marginally significant for rhyme duration ($p = .070$), and not significant for F1 or F3. Table 2 gives the combined ANOVA results; Table 3 gives ANOVAs for the formants broken down by speaker gender.

Table 2: ANOVA main effects of underlying status: combined genders

	Epenthetic		Lexical			
	mean	s.d.	mean	s.d.	$F(1,240)$	p
F1 (Hz)	467	76	462	69	.78	.377
F2 (Hz)	1728	201	1809	222	21.12	*<.001
F3 (Hz)	2768	263	2770	250	.19	.667
Rhyme dur (ms)	252	72	264	83	3.31	.070
V duration (ms)	76	27	85	25	10.94	*.001

ep: N=128; lex: N=128. A star indicates that the differences are significant at α =.05

Table 3: ANOVA main effects of underlying status: formants by gender

	Epenthetic		Lexical			
	mean	s.d.	mean	s.d.		p
Men					$F(1,100)$	
F1 (Hz)	435	55	420	64	1.26	.264
F2 (Hz)	1606	155	1711	216	6.93	*.010
F3 (Hz)	2547	154	2554	138	.273	.603
Women					$F(1,140)$	
F1 (Hz)	489	82	492	56	.10	.757
F2 (Hz)	1813	185	1879	200	16.78	*<.001
F3 (Hz)	2924	207	2922	192	.03	.863

Men: ep: N=53, lex: N=53; Women: ep: N=75, lex: N=75

A Tukey HSD post-hoc test revealed a significant interaction between subject and underlying status for F2, and no interaction for any of the other measures. To explore this variation, we performed a two-tailed t-test for each subject to determine whether epenthetic and lexical vowels differ. Results are shown in Table 4, and individual performances on duration and F2 are graphed in Figures 1 and 2. (In both figures, error bars show standard error.)[8]

Table 4: Individual two-tailed paired t-tests for F2

	Epenthetic	Lexical	Difference				N
Subject	mean	mean	mean	s.d.	T	p	(pairs)
W1	1566	1559	7	137	0.173	.866	12
W2	1947	2124	**−177**	128	−4.165	***.003**	9
W3	1708	1979	**−271**	213	−4.588	***.001**	13
W4	1937	1939	−2	99	−0.093	.927	20
W5	1845	1838	8	83	0.422	.677	21
M1	1615	1718	**−103**	256	−1.919	**.068**	23
M2	1637	1804	**−167**	182	3.901	***.001**	18
M3	1545	1559	−14	106	−0.469	.648	12

A star indicates that the differences are significant at α = .05 ($p < .00625$, with Bonferroni adjustment).

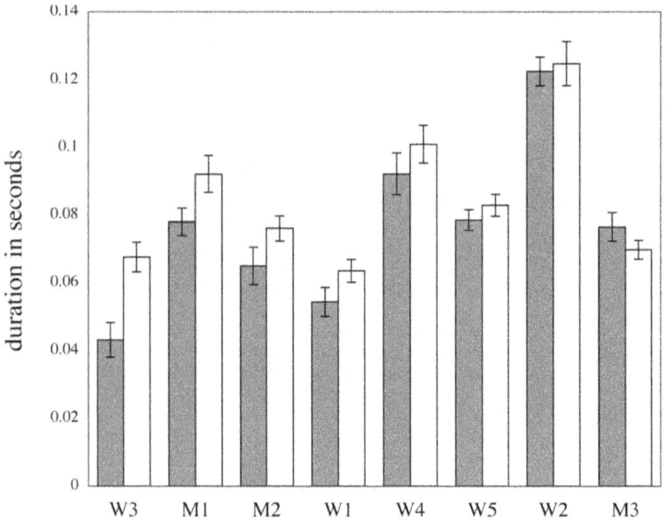

Figure 1: Individual results for duration

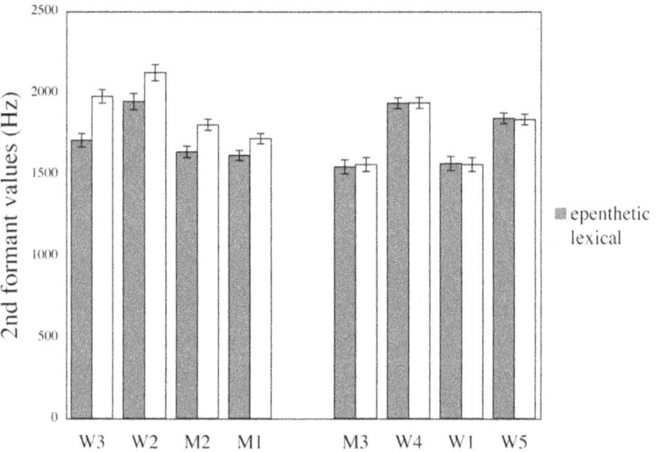

Figure 2: Individual results for F2

Subjects appear to fall into two groups as regards F2. Subjects W2, W3 and M2 each have a significant difference between epenthetic and lexical vowels. Subject M1 has a difference that does not reach significance, but is still strong. We can call this group, whose results are boldfaced in Table 4, the 'differentiators.' Subjects W1, W4, W5, and M3 are 'non-differentiators'; they have differences that are extremely small. The groups are not defined by any sociological factor such as religion, age, gender or region of origin; nor do they correlate with the choice of frame sentence. Thus, we cannot say what factors affect this variation in the epenthetic vowels' F2; only that some variation exists.[9]

With respect to vowel duration, the other measure that came up significant in the ANOVA, subjects range from having a very slight (but non-significant) trend towards longer epenthetic vowels to having a strong trend towards shorter epenthetic vowels. However, the subjects seem to vary along a continuum; there is no clear grouping into differentiators and non-differentiators as there is with F2. The subjects who differentiate F2 tend to also have fairly large differences in duration, except W2, who has only a very small difference in duration although her difference in F2 is significant.

3.3   Discussion

We have found that Lebanese speakers, as a group, produce epenthetic '[i]' with a shorter duration than lexical [i]. Furthermore, half of our speakers produced the epenthetic vowel with a significantly lower F2 than lexical [i], suggesting that it might be more appropriately transcribed [ɨ] for them. This finding is in keeping with other studies of incomplete neutralization, which have shown phonetic traces of underlying distinctions. The differences between lexical and epenthetic vowels go exactly in the expected direction. For speakers who differentiate, epenthesis introduces something *less than an [i]*: the vowel is backer and shorter, all properties that would make this vowel closer to [ɨ] or [ə]—and, arguably, to zero.

3.3.1   The role of orthography

Lebanese Arabic raises orthographic issues not seen in any of the incomplete neutralization studies on other languages. Whether incomplete neutralization is an artefact of orthography is a subject of ongoing debate; thus, some argue that when a contrast is not represented orthographically, neutralization is complete.

In Dutch, Warner et al. (2006) find complete neutralization for the underlying contrast between a singleton /t/, as in /heːt/, and a fake (morphological) geminate composed of a past tense morpheme /-t/ and a word-final /t/ as in /heːt-t/, a distinction that is not represented orthographically. Conversely, Warner et al. (2004) found that a purely orthographic difference between double and single consonants did trigger incomplete neutralization in Dutch, despite not corresponding to any underlying distinction. Kopkalli (1993) finds a complete neutralization of final voicing in Turkish, where the final devoicing is represented in the language's orthography, but Dinnsen and Charles-Luce (1984) find incomplete neutralization of final voicing in Catalan, whose orthography also represents final devoicing. Fourakis and Iverson (1984) find that neutralization of final voicing is complete in German when the experimental task does not involve reading; Jassem and Richter (1989) have similar results for Polish.

Arabic differs from all of these cases in that the everyday orthography represents neither neutralization nor non-neutralization of the short vowel–zero contrast: it doesn't represent short vowels at all. In this sense, our written stimuli should not bias the subjects either towards or against neutralization, and we believe this is the only study of incomplete neutralization where the orthography has this characteristic.

The situation in Arabic is complicated by the fact that there is an optional way to write vowels, using diacritics above or below the consonants. Lebanese schoolchildren learn to read and write fully voweled texts in the standard and classical registers, which differ considerably from the colloquial phonologically and in other ways. These texts represent underlying /i/ with the symbol *kasra*, a short line below the consonant (⸗). In the environments where colloquial Lebanese has epenthetic [i], standard texts have the symbol *sukuun*, a circle above the consonant (⸚), indicating absence of a vowel. If subjects mentally drew up these fully voweled standard forms when doing the study, the *kasra* vs. *sukuun* distinction could bias them towards non-neutralization. We cannot be sure whether this happened. We should note that fully voweled texts have a very limited place in the Lebanese written corpus, being confined to special genres such as religious scripture, poetry, and books for beginning readers. The vast majority of everyday written materials, such as newspapers, novels, and textbooks, do not include short vowels, which suggests that speakers are not likely to automatically visualize the vowel diacritics when looking at a consonantal text. On the other hand, since writing is associated with the standard register more than the colloquial register, the very use of written stimuli might be a factor biasing speakers towards formality and hence non-neutralization.

As mentioned above, one speaker, W2, made notes on her stimulus sheet to remind herself to use colloquial pronunciations. She went through the Arabic orthographic forms and systematically marked colloquial consonants, and also wrote in the epenthetic vowels using the symbol *kasra*. This speaker is one of the group who strongly differentiated epenthetic and underlying vowels in F2. Evidently, seeing the epenthetic vowels written like lexical /i/ in her word list did not cause her to produce them as [i].

In short, we cannot conclusively say how orthography may have affected our results, but would like to point out that expanding incomplete neutralization studies to languages with a different relation between orthography and phonology, including languages with non-Latin orthographic systems, may help elucidate the relation between orthography and phonetic realization.

3.3.2   Is Lebanese stress-epenthesis interaction opaque?

The standard view of stress-epenthesis interaction in Lebanese is that it is completely opaque: epenthetic [i] behaves differently than lexical [i] for stress, but there are no surface clues (in an isolated word, without morphological analysis) as to which vowel is the epenthetic one (Alderete and Tesar 2002 make this assumption explicit).

While this might describe the speech of some individuals considered in isolation, we believe that in the non-idealized setting of the Lebanese speech community, learners do have some clear clues available as to which vowels are epenthetic. The variability of epenthesis is one clue: the stressed lexical vowel in /fihimna/ [fhím.na] 'he understood us' always has a correspondent in the unsuffixed [fí.him] 'he understood,' but the unstressed vowel in /dist-na/ [dí.sit.na] 'our boiler' only has a correspondent in [dís(i)t] 'boiler' some of the time.

Moreover, we have shown that information about the epenthetic vowels being different is sometimes present in the acoustic signal. Whether listeners can take advantage of this information to identify lexical items is not known; the question needs to be answered in a perception study. We expect that listeners could tell the difference between lexical and epenthetic vowels in at least some people's speech (but recall that some speakers do appear to neutralize completely). The JND (just noticeable difference) for F2 in consonantal context is about 50 Hz (Kewley-Port 1995), and our differentiators produced an average difference of 166 Hz, far greater than the JND. A conservatively estimated JND for duration is about 20 ms (Klatt 1976), which some of our speakers approximate (W3 produced a difference of 25 ms). (Of course, the raw magnitude of durational differences depends on prosodic position, and we looked only at words in a clause-internal position. Charles-Luce (1985) found that incomplete neutralization effects for final devoicing were stronger for words in clause-final position. Hence, a different frame sentence might produce larger durational differences.) Durational differences found in incomplete neutralization studies are typically smaller than ours—in fact, they often barely reach 5 ms. Since some of these studies have found that speakers could use these subphonemic differences for word disambiguation (Port and O'Dell 1985, Port and Crawford 1989, Warner et al. 2004), we expect that our speakers could also do this with the relatively large differences found in some Lebanese speech.

4   Incomplete neutralization and phonology

Incomplete neutralization is a phonetic fact. The question is, is it a problem for phonology, and does phonology need to say anything about it? Some argue that it puts the very concept of neutralization in question (Dinnsen and Charles-Luce

1984), but we believe that it is a powerful argument for the reality of phonological processes and underlying representations (Blumstein 1991 articulates this argument very well). In order for a difference to exist, speakers have to think of lexical and epenthetic vowels as different, and they have to apply a (possibly gradient) process to reduce or eliminate the difference.

In the remainder of the paper, we discuss a way to relate incomplete neutralization to an OT grammar, and also the implications of incomplete neutralization for the problem of learning stress-epenthesis interactions.

4.1 Incomplete neutralization as accessing an intermediate representation

One way of thinking about incomplete neutralization is as access to an intermediate stage of a derivation. Instead of pronouncing the fully neutralizing surface phonological representation, the speaker is pronouncing something between the underlying and the surface representation. This may be a partially devoiced consonant, a partially nasalized vowel, or, in the case of epenthesis, something that is between zero and [i].

We will assume here that at the phonological level, all epenthesizing speakers share the same fully neutralized surface representation for the outputs, i.e., with an epenthetic [i]. At the level of phonetic implementation, however, speakers optionally access the intermediate stage (this notion will be made precise below). This assumption of phonological sameness and phonetic optionality allows us to explain why not all speakers differentiate the vowels phonetically. It is also consistent with the observation that incomplete neutralization is variable and highly sensitive to experimental design: pragmatics, orthography, and other non-phonological factors may increase or decrease the magnitude of the effects (sociolinguistic work on near-mergers is also relevant; see Labov (1994)). This might mean that the explanation for the 'why' of incomplete neutralization lies outside of phonology proper. Incomplete neutralization meshes with assumptions about phonological mappings, however, and ideally phonological theory should be able to model it.

Until recently, the notion of intermediate stages of derivation has been inimical to almost all versions of Optimality Theory. However, one way to formalize our intuition is offered by Optimality Theory with Candidate Chains (OT-CC, McCarthy 2007, Becker 2006a), a theory that has been proposed precisely to capture opaque interactions like that of Levantine stress and epenthesis.

In OT with Candidate Chains, a candidate consists of a derivational chain from the input to the output, which includes the starting point (the input) and the endpoint (the phonological surface form with all of the necessary structure fully assigned). The mapping from the input to the output is gradual: it proceeds in incremental steps rather than in a simple 'quantum leap' characteristic of classic, parallel OT (Prince and Smolensky 1993/2004, McCarthy and Prince 1995). Each derivational step corresponds to a single violation of a faithfulness constraint. It is impossible, for example, to map /tat/ to [tade] in one step, since it involves both the insertion of [e] and the voicing of /d/. Instead, /tat/ maps to *tate*, which then maps to *tade*. A chain starts with the fully faithful parse, and each successful step inherits all of the faithfulness violations of the previous one.

McCarthy (2007) analyzes Levantine stress similarly: the optimal mapping of /ʔibn-na/ to [ʔíbin̪.na] must involve intermediate stages. Stress is assigned first (ʔíbn.na), and the cluster is broken up by epenthesis afterwards. This chain <ʔíbn.na, (ʔíbn).na, (ʔí.bin̪)na> beats the transparent alternative chain <ʔibn. na, ʔi.bin.na, (ʔibín)na> because a special PRECEDENCE constraint requires that epenthesis precede insertion of stress. (See McCarthy 2007 for a detailed exposition.)

We propose a small refinement to this analysis. In the case of epenthesis, the shape of a chain depends on the theory of epenthesis. We believe, following a body of work on epenthesis, that zero would not map directly to [i]; rather, [ɨ] and [ə] have to be intermediate stages. Steriade 1995, Howe and Pulleyblank 2004, Gouskova 2003 and others have argued that epenthetic vowels are subject to faithfulness constraints that limit their prominence (sonority). An ideal epenthetic vowel is one that is least noticeable, i.e., one that is shortest and least sonorous. The more sonorous the epenthetic vowel, the greater the disparity between the input and the output. The sonority hierarchy for vowels (see Parker (2002) and the references therein) is the basis for the following faithfulness hierarchy of DEP constraints on vowel epenthesis:

(7)   DEP/ɨ >> DEP /ə >>DEP /i,u >>DEP /e,o >> DEP/a

If sonority is understood to be a cumulative property, where [a] has all of the sonority of schwa and then some (see de Lacy (2002) for one formalization), then a mapping from zero to [a] entails the most faithfulness violations, a mapping to [e]—somewhat fewer, to [i]—still fewer, and so on. Thus, we propose that in order to epenthesize [i], the candidate chain must contain a mapping from zero to [ɨ] to [ə] to [i], as in the following:

(8)　Candidate chain for epenthesis of [i]:

/CC/　<CC,　CɨC,　CəC,　CiC>

Dᴇᴘ/ɨ,　Dᴇᴘ/ə,　Dᴇᴘ/i,u

The winning candidate is not just the last link in the chain, CiC, but the entire chain. This chain contains considerably more information than just the surface representation CiC: it encodes what CiC came from (that is, CC) and the intermediate steps of this mapping.

Furthermore, we suggest that phonetics can access this entire chain rather than just the last link. This explains why the epenthetic vowel for some of our speakers is sometimes closer in quality to [ɨ] or even [ə]. Thus, the speakers are phonetically implementing an intermediate stage of the derivation:

(9)　Phonetic interpretation of /CC/:　phonological output: <CC,　CɨC,　　　CəC,　　　CiC>
　　　　　　　　　　　　　　　　　　phonetic realization:　　　　[CɨC] or　[CəC] or　[CiC]

　　　Phonetic interpretation of /CiC/:　phonological output: <CiC,　CiC>
　　　　　　　　　　　　　　　　　　phonetic realization:　　　　[CiC]

We leave open the possibility that perhaps even the first member of the chain, the fully faithful CC, can optionally surface. This is one way of looking at the fact that a single speaker may be inconsistent as to whether he or she pronounces an epenthetic vowel in a particular word.

Even though speakers varied in the phonetic quality of their epenthetic vowels and also in whether they epenthesized in the first place, they all shared the same opaque stress grammar. This is consistent with our theory: we claim that our speakers use different phonetic implementations of the same candidate chain. Since in this chain, stress is assigned before epenthesis, we may expect to see something less than a full epenthetic [i], but we do not expect to see differences in how stress is assigned.

Our theory of incomplete neutralization makes several predictions. First, it predicts that an incompletely neutralized variant should always be between the underlying and the surface representation. Lebanese phonology categorically rules out epenthesis of anything more prominent than [i] (i.e., CeC and CaC). Epenthesis of a more prominent vowel requires a longer candidate chain and therefore would not be expected to emerge in this grammar.

Our theory also predicts that incomplete neutralization should in principle be an option for any phonological processes that involve a truly synchronic derivation, but not for alternations that involve, for example, multiple listed allomorphs. In English *a/an* allomorphy, the allomorphs are not derived from a common underlying representation, so we would not expect speakers to produce anything in-between *a* and *an*. Incomplete neutralization is expected to exist only when the phonetic form is phonologically derived. The choice of which specific derivations give rise to incomplete neutralization lies outside of phonology proper, but our model can accommodate any gradual mapping.

This theory is not meant to be a complete account of near-neutralization, which often involves partial devoicing and other not-quite-phonemic distinctions. A phonological candidate chain for devoicing does not involve an intermediate 'half-voiced' stage, since 'half-voiced' has no status phonologically. We speculate that perhaps the phonetics may interpolate phonetic continua between members of a chain for mappings such as devoicing.

Candidate chains do two jobs. First, they are crucial to the analysis of opaque stress in Lebanese (see McCarthy 2007)—an account that works without relying on the phonetic distinction or indeed any representational distinction. The phonological analysis explains how stress is assigned both by speakers who do and who do not distinguish the vowels phonetically. Second, candidate chains provide information for the phonetics about the derivational history of the epenthetic form, so speakers have the option to neutralize partially as opposed to fully. Speakers have the same phonology but may differ as to which epenthetic vowel along the available continuum they access in the phonetic implementation.

4.2   Incomplete neutralization and learning

Our phonetic findings are also relevant to the question of how learners acquire correct underlying forms. Learning an OT grammar involves finding a constraint ranking that generates outputs that match those of the target grammar (Tesar and Smolensky 1998 et seq.). Learning starts with phonotactics and is complicated by tasks such as resolving structural ambiguity and deciding between several grammars of differing restrictiveness. Most relevant to our concerns is the assumption, shared by much of the work in learnability theory, that early non-morphological learning proceeds under the Identity Map Hypothesis (IM): every output is mapped to an identical input.

Alderete and Tesar (2002) note that opaque stress-epenthesis interactions present the learner with a type of subset problem (Prince and Tesar (2004) and others). The learner can account for all the surface forms of a stress-epenthesis grammar (such as Levantine) by positing a less restrictive grammar in which stress is lexical. In such a grammar, faith to stress is ranked above the markedness constraints that determine default stress placement. Stress is indicated in the underlying forms, so that 'our son' [ʔíbinna] is underlyingly /ʔíbin-na/, not /ʔibn-na/, and the presence of underlying stress would account for surface stress differences between [ʔíbinna] and regular words like [darábna]. This superset grammar can accommodate stress in just about any position—unlike its subset, the correct grammar in which only epenthetic vowels are unstressable but stress is otherwise predictable. If the learner settles on a superset grammar, there is a danger of producing ungrammatical forms. Alderete and Tesar suggest that at least part of the solution is to modify IM. To learn the correct subset grammar, the learner must first consider unfaithful origin as the explanation for deviant stress and move on to the lexical stress grammar only if that doesn't work. This modification is necessary if one adopts the view that the learner only ever encounters idealized, phonetically invariant data.

The finding that Lebanese learners are exposed to phonetic differences between epenthetic and underlying vowels (not necessarily from all speakers, but from some), opens the possibility of a different solution to this particular learning problem. We propose here that the learner can use phonetic variation of the kind we found as additional motivation to posit distinct underlying representations, and, crucially, correct candidate chains to go with these URs.[10] Learning Lebanese stress requires positing a vowel-zero contrast for [ʔíbɪnna] and [darábna] and selecting the correct candidate chain for each output. Recall that in the analysis of Levantine (McCarthy 2007), the correct candidate chain for the opaque [ʔíbɪnna] is <ʔibn.na, (ʔíbn)na, (ʔí.bɨn)na, (ʔí.bən)na, (ʔí.bin) na>. This chain and associated input must be distinguished from the wrong chain /ʔíbinna/, [ʔíbinna], which contains no interesting derivations at all. We have shown that in the Lebanese speech community, /ʔibn/ 'son' can be pronounced as either [ʔibɪn] or [ʔibɪn]; we conjecture that similar variability characterizes suffixed forms in which stress is opaque, as well. Under our theory that phonetic realizations can optionally represent different parts of the candidate chain, the existence of these variant outputs is consistent with the longer candidate chain and epenthesis but not with the lexical stress analysis, since under such an analysis, there would be no account for the variant pronunciation with the backer vowel. We propose that the learner can use such information from incomplete neutralization as an additional clue that there is a multi-step derivation. The Identity Map Hypothesis is modified as follows:

(10) Modified Identity Map Hypothesis (MIM): The phonological content of surface forms is mapped directly into candidate chain representations: every observed output must be identical to some member of the word's candidate chain.

We assume that the learner is able to distinguish ordinary, low-level phonetic variation (such as occurs in all vowels due to normal variability in the magnitude or overlap of articulatory gestures) from the type of exceptional phonetic variation that we found in epenthetic vowels only. When the learner realizes that a given word can be pronounced with an unusual degree of phonetic variation,

MIM requires him or her to construct a longer candidate chain that includes additional derivational steps accommodating the various observed forms. A longer candidate chain of this sort entails an unfaithful mapping: generally, a faithful mapping only requires the assignment of prosodic structure, which can be done in two steps (syllabification, footing). Therefore, the learner can use phonetic variability that is the product of incomplete neutralization to diagnose unfaithful input-output mappings and to construct a grammar that can account for opaque consequences of derivation.

Our proposal is not meant to be a complete theory of candidate chain construction. The learner cannot rely exclusively on phonetic variation for the purpose of constructing candidate chains; in some cases, as for some Lebanese speakers, it may be absent or barely discernible, so there needs to be a mechanism in place for generating candidate chains that is independent of variation. Furthermore, not all phonetic variation is due to incomplete neutralization—some results from optional low-level phonetic processes. This kind of variation is probably not problematic for our point. For example, the learner might encounter variable partial nasalization of vowels in syllables with nasal codas, i.e., both [ãn] and [an]. Under our proposal, the learner would automatically posit the chain /an/, [ãn] <an, ãn>. This is not necessarily problematic, though, because presumably, the variation in nasalization is general and does not correlate with underlying distinctions. If, on the other hand, only *derived* outputs are variable in the way we documented, the learner has additional evidence that the salient and robust surface differences produced by opacity are due to underlying distinctions.

5   Conclusion

Our phonetic study of epenthetic and lexical [i] in Lebanese Arabic falsifies the null hypothesis that these vowels are identical on the surface, which is assumed in most phonological work on Arabic stress-epenthesis interactions. The vowels are reliably different for some (though not all) speakers. We see this as a positive result for phonology rather than a challenge to it. First, the presence of phonetic differences between epenthetic and lexical vowels simplifies the task of learning opaque stress-epenthesis interactions, offering another line of attack on a thorny learnability problem. Second, the results support the existence of abstract underlying representations and processes that change them. Third, because the vowels are identical for some speakers but different for others, phonological accounts of stress-epenthesis interactions must work independently of phonetics, i.e., they must work even if no phonetic differences existed. At the same time, if phonology is to say anything about incomplete neutralization, it needs to provide certain information to phonetics. We discussed one possibility for implementing this in Optimality Theory with Candidate Chains. Because a candidate in this theory contains the entire derivational history of the phonological output, phonetics can optionally access forms other than the fully neutralizing one, which provides a way to model incomplete neutralization.

Notes

1   We would like to thank John McCarthy for suggesting that epenthetic vowels in Arabic merit phonetic study, and for teaching us phonology. For valuable feedback and advice, thanks to Ron Artstein, Ellen Broselow, Lisa Davidson, Diamandis Gafos, Greg Guy, Ghada Khattab, Ania Łubowicz, John Singler, Phil Scholfield, Jennifer Smith, and the audiences at NYU, Stony Brook, the London Phonology Seminar, and the 2006 Manchester Phonology Meeting. Special thanks to Lisa Zsiga for advice in the early stages of the project. Thanks to our experiment participants for their generosity and patience. For help in locating speakers, thanks to Graham Horwood, the Georgetown Center for Contemporary Arabic Studies, Our Lady of Lebanon Church, and Fettoosh Restaurant and the Lebanese Taverna in Washington, DC. The mistakes are all ours. Authors' names are in alphabetical order.

2   Glides vocalize in the environment c_#; glide-initial final clusters remain intact. We did not include such clusters in our experiment.

3   However, even where epenthesis is basically obligatory, another factor can interfere: educated Lebanese learn in school to speak Standard Arabic, which lacks epenthesis in final CC clusters. One speaker we consulted, a former teacher of Standard Arabic, occasionally lacked epenthesis in environments where Haddad describes it as obligatory. She was probably drifting into a non-colloquial register.

4   It is controversial whether Lebanese has secondary stress (Nasr 1959), but this is irrelevant to our study.

5   Mitleb (1984) shows that voicing does not affect vowel duration in another Levantine dialect, Jordanian.

6   Thanks to Ghada Khattab for extensive help in locating near-minimal pairs—a difficult task due to the lack of colloquial Lebanese dictionaries.

7   Even subjects recruited in Lebanon, from a small area, would likely be linguistically heterogeneous. We have conducted a similar study on Palestinian Arabic in Haifa, Israel, with speakers who live in a single neighborhood and are connected through bonds of family or friendship. Nevertheless, they showed considerable linguistic variation in terms of lexical items, consonant inventory, and quality of the epenthetic vowel. Haddad (1984) found similar microvariation in his study of Lebanese syncope, observing, 'no matter to what extent the variables (in a

sociolinguistic sense) have been restricted or narrowed down, such as interviewing male peers of the same dialectal area, or even brothers or sisters, no less variability has been observed.'

8   We performed t-tests for the other measures as well; W3 had a significant difference in vowel duration, but no other results were significant for any subject.

9   A reviewer commented that the F2 values are somewhat low for both lexical and epenthetic [i]; as noted above, the three short vowels of Lebanese are fairly centralized, particularly in unstressed position as here, so [i] should be understood as only a broad transcription. The fact that /i/ and /u/ are only marginally contrastive (Haddad 1984) may also contribute to /i/ being realized as rather back.

10   For additional discussion of learning underlying representations and candidate chains, see Tesar (2005), McCarthy (2007).

9 The onset of the prosodic word[1]

Junko Ito and Armin Mester

In one of the pioneering works of Optimality Theory (Prince and Smolensky 1993/2004), McCarthy (1993a) offers a comprehensive analysis of *r*-insertion in non-rhotic dialects of English, and suggests that the constraint driving the process is not an onset-related constraint, but rather a constraint requiring prosodic words to end in a consonant ('FINAL-C'). While morphological categories such as roots or stems are sometimes subject to templatic requirements involving an obligatory final consonant, independent evidence for a requirement of this kind on genuine prosodic constituents, such as surface prosodic words, is sparse. This paper shows that, while McCarthy's treatment remains, in its essentials, a model of optimality-theoretic analysis, it is unnecessary to take recourse to FINAL-C once the onset requirements for different levels of the prosodic hierarchy, together with their associated faithfulness properties, are better understood.

1 Introduction

This paper is a contribution to the study of a particular region of the prosodic hierarchy – the area falling between the prosodic word and the phonological phrase. The larger goal (see also Ito and Mester 2007a,b) is to explore the consequences of a framework with minimal assumptions about prosodic levels above the word-internal constituents, positing only the two layers of constituency below the intonational phrase that all researchers agree on: the prosodic word and the phonological phrase (1).

(1)

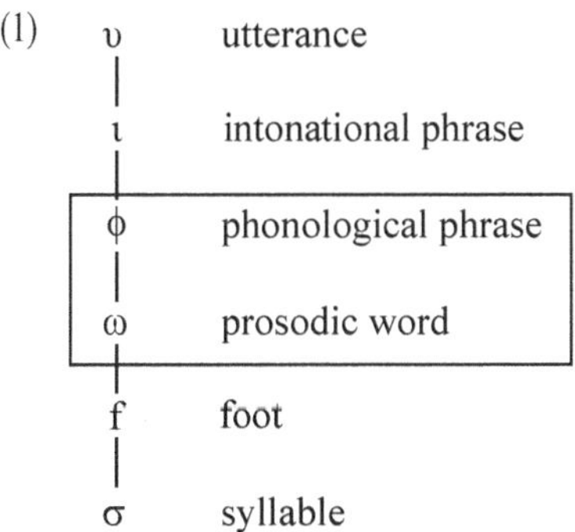

Note the absence of additional categories between ϕ and ω, such as the 'clitic group' (Nespor and Vogel 1986, Hayes 1989, Nespor 1999), and the distinction between 'major' and 'minor' phonological phrases (McCawley 1968, Selkirk and Tateishi 1988; renamed as 'intermediate' and 'accentual' phrases, respectively, in Pierrehumbert and Beckman 1988). The standard picture of the prosodic hierarchy, we argue, has too many categories, and at the same time, too little structure. We motivate a sparse hierarchy where prosodic adjunction plays a large role in parsing phonological strings, in the way indicated in (2) (for head-final structures).

(2) Prosodic word projections: Phonological phrase projections:

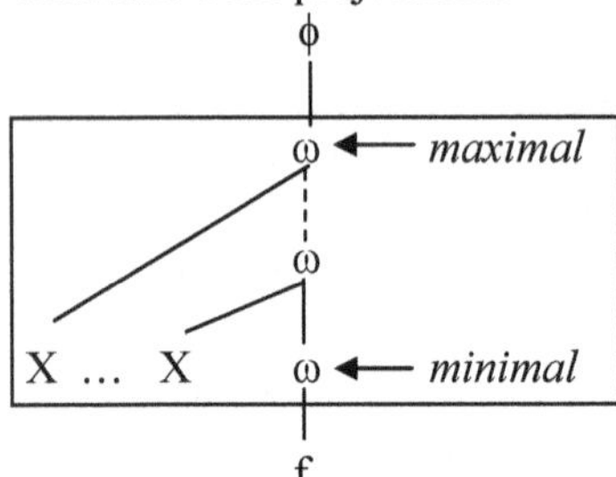

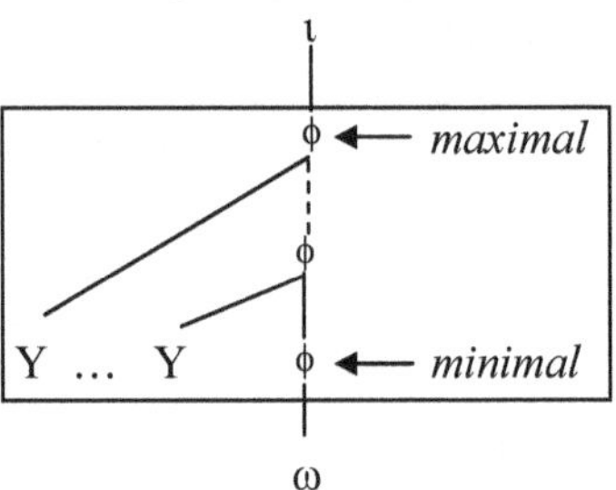

For a given prosodic category κ, we refer to the resulting larger structure as the maximal (projection of) κ, and its innermost subconstituent of type κ as the minimal (projection of) κ, along lines familiar from syntactic constituent structure (see in particular Grimshaw's (2005) work on extended projection). In the interest of notational convenience, we sometimes use κ' and κ_ι for the maximal and minimal κ, respectively, as indicated in (3).

(3) $\kappa' =_{\text{def}}$ the maximal (projection of) κ: κ not dominated by κ.
     $\kappa_\iota =_{\text{def}}$ the minimal (projection of) κ: κ not dominating κ.

Within a particular grammar, independent factors relating to syntax-phonology alignment, depth of projection, and length impose limits on the size of extended ω- and ϕ-structures. The important point here is the distinction between categories and their instantiations. By singling out maximal and minimal projections, our claim is that the theory maintains the right amount of flexibility to distinguish what needs to be distinguished while avoiding an over-abundance of descriptive categories. It is always tempting to add new levels in order to cope with the different domains that the empirical facts of individual languages seem to demand. The difficulty is to do so in a way that does not lose sight of the overall explanatory goal – minimally, a motivated identification of categories across languages, such that the 'xyz-phrase' of one language can be confidently equated with the 'XYZ-phrase' of another, in a way that is comparable to the security of such identifications in syntactic research.[2]

In a larger context, our proposal is situated in the Weak Layering theory of prosodic structure of Ito and Mester (1992), formulated in optimality-theoretic terms by Selkirk (1995), where a prosodic category κ may dominate the same category κ (in violation of Strict Layering) if compelled by higher-ranking constraints. In such cases the resulting structure violates a constraint against recursivity.

The empirical focus of this paper is the *r*-sandhi phenomenon in English, and an influential analysis developed in two important papers by John McCarthy (McCarthy 1991, 1993a), with subsequent discussion by various researchers, and many attempts at reanalysis. *R*-sandhi, which occurs in several non-rhotic varieties of English, refers to the appearance of both underlying and non-underlying *r* as hiatus breakers in forms like *moth*[ə r]*is* and *ide*[ə r]*is,* for speakers who otherwise have *moth*[ə] and *ide*[ə]. This paper revisits the prosodic conditions of this process. Our first step will be to get a clear view of the varying range of contexts where *r*-sandhi occurs in different non-rhotic varieties, including non-standard dialects spoken in the British Isles. Building on previous analyses – most importantly, Kahn (1976, 1980) and McCarthy (1993a) – our ultimate aim, within the overall approach sketched above in (2), is a better understanding of the prosodic structure of collocations formed by full lexical words with associated function words.

In the process, we will have occasion to revisit the Final-C constraint posited by McCarthy (1993a). We will argue that this constraint, often viewed as problematic, can indeed be dispensed with while preserving all the major insights of McCarthy's analysis. As we will show, progress in the area depends on a proper analysis of the phonology of word onsets, including both markedness and faithfulness properties. In a nutshell, and in terms of the theoretical assumptions laid out above, *r*-sandhi does not result from a Final-C requirement applying at the end of the prosodic word (which would amount to a kind of obligatory coda, unparalleled elsewhere in the study of syllabic form), but rather from an Initial-C requirement applying at the beginning of the maximal prosodic word (i.e., a member of the Onset family of constraints). Furthermore, the coda properties of linking and intrusive *r*, leading to its overall ambisyllabic status, are not due to the existence of some constraint demanding the presence of a coda, but are explained by the location of the source of the segment's featural content – viz., the vowel of the preceding syllable. In a similar way, we anticipate that other cases where Final-C has been invoked will yield to similar kinds of reanalysis once the prosodic structures involved have been correctly identified.

2   Syllable-based explanations: ambisyllabicity and flapping

The concept of the syllable is central to phonological constituent structure and has long been indispensable for serious phonological analysis. 'Closed syllable' vs. 'open syllable', 'heavy syllable' vs. 'light syllable' play a central role as environments for sounds changes and phonological processes in both neogrammarian and structuralist linguistics. In a curious contrast with generative syntax, early generative phonology was an attempt to break away from this tradition and to do phonology without phonological constituent structure. The non-viability of strict segmentalism was quickly recognized, and syllable structure was shown to be irreplaceable in providing the environments for many, if not most, phonological processes (see Hooper 1972 and Vennemann 1972, among others). These works viewed the role of the syllable mainly as adding another boundary to the set of boundary symbols available to phonology, thus continuing the essentially linear conception of phonological structure, i.e., as consisting of a string of segments and boundary symbols, inherited from Chomsky and Halle (1968).

Kahn (1976), in a detailed study of allophonic processes in English conditioned by syllable structure, took the crucial step from boundary markers to genuine constituency, marking the beginning of a formal and principled study of syllabic phonology. Together with other roughly simultaneous pioneering research in autosegmental and metrical phonology, it was this work that led to the modern theory of prosodic structure as a hierarchy of constituents standing in correspondence to grammatical structure, and providing the domains in which phonological processes take place.

Kahn's central argument has two parts: (i) The environments of segmental processes (aspiration, glottalization, and flapping in American English) make essential and irreducible reference to syllable structure, and (ii) these syllable structure specifications cannot be reduced to boundary symbols ordered within the linear string of segments, but require genuine prosodic constituent structure. The process of flapping (or more accurately, tapping) is of central importance in this context. Word-internally, the flapped segment belongs both to the coda of the first syllable and to the onset of the following syllable (through Kahn's (1980) rule of 'Medial Ambisyllabification'), as shown in (4).

(4)

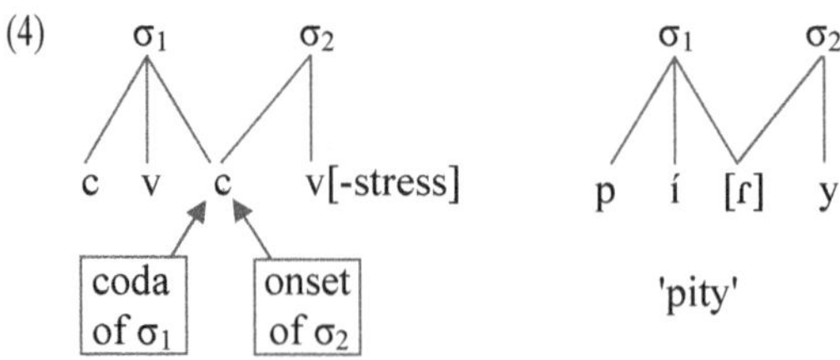

Prototypical word-internal examples appear in (5). Ambisyllabification applies to all consonants, but is most tangible for underlying /t/, which is ambisyllabically realized as a flap. Flapping is obligatory between stressed and stressless syllables, as in (5a). Between two stressless syllables, it is optional (5b).

(5)   Flapping in the onset of unstressed syllable
    a.   betting   →   bé[ɾ]ĭng
          water   →   wá[ɾ]ĕr
          pity   →   pí[ɾ]y̆

    b.   ability   →   abílĭ[t,ɾ]y̆
          affirmative →   affĭrmă[t,ɾ]ĭve

There is no flapping in the onset of word-internal syllables with primary or secondary stress; instead we find aspirated [tʰ] (6).

(6)   Aspiration in the onset of stressed syllables
       atone   →   ă[tʰ]óne
       fatigue   →   fă[tʰ]ígue
       latex   →   lá[tʰ]èx

While word-medial ambisyllabification is coda-creating and restricted to onsets of unstressed syllables (*a[ɾ]ŏm* vs. *a[tʰ]ómic*), ambisyllabification across a word boundary, illustrated in (7), is onset-creating and takes place before unstressed and stressed syllables alike.

(7)   σ₁   σ₂   →   σ₁   σ₂
      /\ | /\···|
      c v c # v   c v c # v

Illustrative examples for both cases appear in (8).

(8)   a.   Pre-unstress environment:
            go[ɾ] it, a[ɾ] Amánda's, isn't tha[ɾ] amázing?

      b.   Pre-stress environment:
            go[ɾ] émail, a[ɾ] Émily's, wasn't tha[ɾ] áwful?

The process involves a rule of 'Trans-Word-Boundary Ambisyllabification', which Kahn (1980: note 11) identifies as the reassertion of the universal preference for onsets (9) at word junctures.

(9)   σ   →   σ
       | /|
       c # v   c # v

The concept of ambisyllabicity that lies at the core of Kahn's analysis is not without its critics, and there have been several attempts, starting with Kiparsky (1979), to replace it with some other environment, mainly 'foot-internal' (see Jensen 2000 for a recent comprehensive discussion). It is no surprise that this kind of substitution is often possible – after all, foot-internally is where ambisyllabicity is most expected, and not at foot edges, where crisp prosodic edges are called for (see Ito and Mester 1999a:208 for a formal analysis). But the two are not co-extensive, as dramatically highlighted by pre-stress external sandhi cases of flapping such as *go[ɾ] email* (8b), etc. In Kiparsky's (1979) original reanalysis, such recalcitrant cases are captured by means of opaque rule application, where the cover feature 'lax' gets assigned cyclically in non-foot-initial position, and is then post-cyclically cashed in, after resyllabification, for different phonetic properties (flapping, glottalization) in different contexts (prevocalically vs. other environments). In this analysis, the *t* of *got* becomes [+lax] on its own cycle, which is then either spelled out as [+glottalized], or as [+voiced] after resyllabification has applied in *got email*.[3] Virtually every aspect of this analysis – cyclic rule ordering, opaque rule application, use of cover features – is at variance with current theoretical assumptions. For these reasons, even though what we have to say here could perhaps be restated in terms of a foot domain account, we follow McCarthy (1993a) and retain classical Kahnian ambisyllabicity, given that it unifies the pre-unstress and pre-stress environments of flapping in (5) and (8) in a natural way that is not easily available to a foot-domain account (see also Gussenhoven 1986 and Rubach 1996 for further arguments in favor of ambisyllabicity).

The fact that VC#V leads to ambisyllabicity calls for a comparison with underlying V#CV. The issue already attracted the attention of structuralist phonologists,[4] who noted, citing segmentally identical but prosodically contrasting minimal pairs like *an aim* (with ambisyllabic [n], in Kahn's terms) and *a name* (pure onset [n]), that the two remain distinct in all styles of speech. The post-Bloomfieldian principle of the separation of linguistic levels, with its concomitant rejection of all grammatical prerequisites for phonemic analysis, led to the postulation of juncture phonemes in this context, linearly ordered between segmental phonemes, an analytical tradition carried on in classical generative theory in the form of boundary symbols (see Pyle 1972 for a discussion of the problematic aspects of such reifications of the edges of phonological constituents). McCarthy and Prince (1993a) take up this well-known junctural contrast and illustrate it with the example in (10).

(10) a. /C#V/ juncture – ambisyllabicity: *sought Ed* = [sɔɾɛd]
    b. /V#C/ juncture – heterosyllabicity: *saw Ted*   = [sɔtʰɛd]

Departing from their analysis in some respects and closely following Kahnian ideas, we can rationalize these findings as arising out of a simple interaction of syllable wellformedness (cf. Kahn's (1980: note 11) characterization of (9) as a reassertion of the universal preference for onsets at word junctures) with syntax-prosody mapping constraints governing stems (or morphological words), as in (11) and (12).[5] The perfectly aligned candidate (11a) violates ONSET, and the resyllabifying candidate (11c) violates both ALIGN-RIGHT and ALIGN-LEFT, leading to the selection of the ambisyllabic (11b), which violates only the latter.[6]

(11)

sought Ed	ALIGN-RIGHT (stem, ω)	ONSET	ALIGN-LEFT (stem, ω)
a. $[_\omega\,\sigma_1\ ]\ [_\omega\,\sigma_2\ ]$ *s ough t*	*E d*		*!	
b. ☞ $[_\omega\,\sigma_1\ ]\ [_\omega\,\sigma_2\ ]$ *s ough*[ɾ]	*E d*			*
c. $[_\omega\,\sigma_1\ ]\ [_\omega\,\sigma_2\ ]$ *s ough t*	*E d*	*!		*

The contrasting example (12) shows no corresponding linking of onset-/t/ to coda position. The winning candidate (12c) violates none of the three constraints, reflecting Kahn's (1980: note 12) diagnosis that no ambisyllabicity is expected here since, as syllabified at the word level, 'the input string already has the preferred syllable shape'.

(12)

saw Ted	ALIGN-RIGHT (stem, ω)	ONSET	ALIGN-LEFT (stem, ω)
a. $[_\omega\,\sigma\ ]\ [_\omega\,\sigma\ ]$ *s aw*	*T e d*	*!	*	*
a. $[_\omega\,\sigma\ ]\ [_\omega\,\sigma\ ]$ *s aw*	[ɾ]*e d*	*!		
c. ☞ $[_\omega\,\sigma\ ]\ [_\omega\,\sigma\ ]$ *s aw*	*T e d*			

3　*R*-sandhi in non-rhotic English

Flapping is restricted to certain dialect areas, including North American, Australian, and Cockney, even though its deeper syllabic source, the ambisyllabic configuration, is arguably pan-dialectal. A second sandhi process, involving *r*, is found in a different and partially overlapping group of dialects, all of which share the loss of *r* in syllable codas. Most well-known as a feature of the *Received Pronunciation* ('RP') of British English, *r*-sandhi is also found in other non-rhotic variants of English, as spoken in New Zealand, Eastern Massachusetts, South Africa, and in the Deep South of the U.S. The process occurs after the non-high vowels [ə, ɔ:, ɑ:] and is found both at word junctures and word-internally at morpheme boundaries ('level II', in terms of level-ordered morphology (Siegel 1974)).

(13)　*r*-sandhi

	Linking *r* (underlying, etymologic)	Intrusive *r* (non-underlying, non-etymologic)
External sandhi:	bette⊬ / bette⌒r off	comma / comma⌒r̲ in
	sta⊬ / sta⌒r is	law　 / law⌒r̲ of
Internal sandhi:	soa⊬ / soa⌒r ing	withdraw / withdraw⌒r̲ al
	sta⊬ / sta⌒r y	Kafka / Kafka⌒r̲ esque

Since our focus is on phonological structure and not phonetic details of articulation, we render linking and intrusive [ɹ] as 'r' and 'r̲', respectively, for easy legibility. Kahn (1976) and McCarthy (1993a) have argued that the liaison element (the rhotic linking consonant, whether underlying or intrusive) is always ambisyllabic, as in (14), showing a mixture of onset and coda properties.

(14)　σ_1　σ_2　　　σ_1　σ_2

　　st a r　i s　　　law r̲　o f

R-sandhi is very productive, as shown by the intrusive *r* in loanwords like *the Stella⌒r̲Artois event* and in the interlanguage of non-rhotic English learners of foreign languages (French: *j'étais déjà⌒r̲ici*; German: *ich habe⌒r̲eine Reservierung*; Latin: *hosanna⌒r̲in excelsis*) (after Wells 1982 and McMahon 2000). Sandhi phenomena of this kind are widespread, and the English facts have close parallels in other languages. For example, Bavarian German has an *r*-sandhi process virtually identical to (13), with both linking and intrusive *r* (the latter underlined), as shown in (15), where Standard German glosses have been added for comparison.[7]

(15) *r*-sandhi in Bavarian German

a. Internal	zwoa	*zwei*	'two'
sandhi:	da zwoa͡ ra	*der Zweier*	'the two'
	owa	*ober*	'upper'
	Owa͡ rammagau	*Oberammergau*	(place name)
b. External	wia͡ ri gsɑgd hɑb	*wie ich gesagt habe*	'as I said'
sandhi:	ma͡ runs	*man/wir uns*	'one/we us'
	kema͡ ris	*gekommen ist*	'has come'
	Mia kena͡ rɑwa͡ raa͡ ran ɑndasmɔi kema.	*Wir können aber auch ein andermal kommen.* lit. 'We can however also another time come.'	'But we can also come another time.'

3.1   Hiatus avoidance and onset

Given the background of the flapping case (11), where the assignment of the consonant to the following syllable in utterances like *sough*[ɾ] *Ed* is clearly driven by the constraint ONSET, it is a natural expectation that linking and intrusive *r* in non-rhotic dialects of English should be another ONSET effect.[8] After all, the prosodic context and the resulting configuration of ambisyllabicity are entirely parallel for flapping and for *r*-sandhi. A starting point for such an onset-driven analysis is shown in (16) for a case of intrusive *r, saw͡* [ɾ]*Ed*, where the constraint against insertion (DEP) is ranked below ONSET (see Anttila and Cho 1998).

(16) ONSET » DEP

saw Ed	ONSET	DEP
a. [ω σ] [ω σ] s aw E d	*!	
b. [ω σ] [ω σ] ☞ s aw [r] E d		*

There are naturally many questions of detail, to be taken up in section 4,[9] but the broad outlines of such an onset-driven analysis seem straightforward.

3.2   FINAL-C and the function word gap

It comes as somewhat of a surprise, therefore, that this is by no means a universally accepted conclusion. In a groundbreaking early contribution to Optimality Theory (Prince and Smolensky 1993/2004), McCarthy (1993a) offers a comprehensive and theoretically insightful analysis of *r*-sandhi in one specific dialect, that of Eastern Massachusetts. He starts out (1993a:2) with the observation that 'it is generally agreed that *r* is inserted to resolve hiatus, by separating two adjacent hetero-syllabic vowels' (i.e., the effect of a hiatus-resolving ONSET constraint). His own analysis, however, does not involve ONSET, but rather makes crucial use of a different constraint, 'FINAL-C', which declares prosodic words ending in a vowel ill-formed.

(17) FINAL-C: *V]$_\omega$ (A prosodic word ends in a consonant.)

FINAL-C is a surprising assertion in that it bans one of the few uncontested desiderata of prosodic form, the open syllable, in a specific context. While the ends of words are known to be prosodically non-prominent, and prone to weakenings and deletions of all kinds, involving both vowels and consonants, it is a different matter altogether to conceptualize a subset of these phenomena as a direct preference for word-final consonants.

McCarthy's basic analysis is summarized in (18) – (20), where each tableau combines the evaluation of two separate inputs, with violation marks applying equally to each candidate in each cell. FINAL-C is dominated by a coda condition ruling out *r* exclusively occupying coda position.[10] Thus no intrusive or linking *r* appears when the form stands in isolation (18) and before C-initial words (19).

(18)	*Wanda* *Homer*	CODA-COND	FINAL-C
	[$_\omega$ σ σ] ☞ *Wanda* ☞ *Home⊦*		*
	[$_\omega$ σ σ] *Wandar* *Homer*	*!	

(19)	*Wanda left* *Homer left*	CODA-COND	FINAL-C
	[$_\omega$ σ σ] [$_\omega$ σ] ☞ *Wanda left* ☞ *Home⊦ left*		*
	[$_\omega$ σ σ] [$_\omega$ σ] *Wandar left* *Homer left*	*!	

When the second word is V-initial, however, *r* can be inserted in the coda and simultaneously occupy onset position, as an ambisyllabic consonant. CODA-COND is crucially not violated: As is usual for licensing conditions of this type (see Ito 1986, 1989, and Goldsmith 1989), *r* is allowed in the coda if the segment is also linked to the onset of the following syllable.

(20)	*Wanda arrived* *Homer arrived*	CODA-COND	FINAL-C
	[ω σ σ] [ωσ σ] *Wanda arrived* *Home≠ arrived*		*!
	[ω σ σ] [ωσ σ] ☞ *Wandar arrived* ☞ *Homer arrived*		

Substituting ONSET for FINAL-C in the tableaux above creates no problems: The winning candidates in (18) and (19) will have no violations, and in (20) the violation profile does not change. So why have recourse to the prima facie unmotivated FINAL-C, instead of the prosodically well-motivated hiatus-resolving ONSET constraint? After all, FINAL-C, which requires prosodic words to end in a consonant, is a strange prosodic wellformedness constraint and is more like an '*anti*-wellformedness' constraint requiring a consonant in a marked position, where it leads to perceptual and articulatory difficulties. Why not use ONSET?

This is where a crucial observation about *r*-sandhi becomes important. McCarthy (1993a) argues that recourse to FINAL-C makes sense of the fact (originally observed in Kahn 1976; see also McCarthy 1991) that *r*-insertion fails to take place after phrase-medial function words, which are taken to not constitute prosodic words on their own, following standard views. This is indeed an interesting restriction on *r*-sandhi in non-rhotic variants of American English, and we turn to the details below, including the somewhat divergent facts in dialects spoken outside the American continent. Besides its optimality-theoretical insights, McCarthy's paper is noteworthy for the systematic study of this important restriction on the process: *R*-insertion does not indiscriminately apply to break up hiatus, but leaves hiatus after function words unresolved, as shown in (21).

(21) No intrusive r after function words in non-rhotic American English
   a.   Didja eat   *didja‿reat
   b.   I wanna eat   *I wanna‿reat
   c.   He went to eat *he went to‿reat
   d.   The apples   *the‿rapples

The analysis is built on the uncontroversial assumption that function words do not constitute prosodic words in themselves (following the standard prosodic distinction between lexical and function words motivated in Selkirk 1984 and subsequent work), and in English show proclitic behavior, as a default. This results in a crucial difference in ω-parsing (McCarthy 1993a:7):

(22) a.   (Let) [Wanda$_\omega$] [eat$_\omega$]   →   (Let) [Wanda r̂$_\omega$][eat$_\omega$]
    b.   (I'm) [gonna eat$_\omega$]   →   (I'm) [gonna eat$_\omega$]   ([*gonna r̂ eat$_\omega$])

Focusing on this difference in parsing, McCarthy (1993a) argues that the constraint driving *r*-sandhi should not be Onset, but rather a constraint requiring prosodic words to end in a consonant – i.e., Final-C (17) – the consonant of choice in the case of English being *r*. With Final-C, so the reasoning goes, the issue in (22a) is no longer whether the syllable *eat* begins with an onset, but whether the preceding prosodic word *Wanda* ends in a consonantal coda, and *r*-sandhi is the way the grammar chooses to supply the required consonant. But in (22b), Final-C does not demand a coda at the end of a function word like *gonna*, so *gonna eat* is optimally realized without *r*. Onset, on the other hand, which simply requires an onset in all syllables, wrongly predicts *r*-insertion in **gonna r̂eat* (and in all examples in (21)).

The function word gap constitutes a strong argument in favor of Final-C, and against an onset-driven approach. In fact, it might be too strong – as we will see in the next section, the very success in deriving the function word gap from first principles turns into a liability in dialects where intrusive *r* appears precisely in the position whose exclusion motivated the move away from Onset to Final-C in the first place, namely, after function words.

3.3   *R*-insertion after function words in Cockney English

It is well known that Cockney English and some other dialects spoken in the British Isles show a more extensive process of *r*-insertion because more vowels are reduced to schwa, the main sponsor of the inserted segment. For example, Wells (1991) points out that 'the broad Cockney vowel corresponding to RP /aʊ/ in *mouth* is phonetically [æə], leading to intrusive *r* in phrases such as *how*[r] *it happened*. (Socially intermediate London speech has [æʊ], with no *r*-intrusion; the types of intrusive *r* mentioned […] are all absent from RP.)' This leads to insertions as in (23) (examples in this section are taken from McMahon 2000, Sivertsen 1960, Trudgill 1974, and Wells 1982).[11]

(23) a.   Cockney

        tomato and   tomat[ə r]and cucumber production
        window up   pull the wind[ə r]up
        you how   I'll tell y[ə ræː]
        you a   give [jə rə] job

   b.   Norwich[12]

        to it   t[ə r]it
        by a   run over b[ə rə] bus
        of old   lot [ə r]old
        to eat   out t[ə r]eat
        to eight quarter t[ə r]eight

These accents with more pervasive *r*-insertion differ from RP and from non-rhotic North American in terms of the degree of vowel reduction (*window* [wɪndə], etc.), but this alone does not account for *r*-sandhi cases like *give you* [jə r]*a job* – after all, non-rhotic North American accents also reduce *you* to [jə], but still do not allow such post-function-word contractions (*didja eat, *didja reat*). Crucially, the British dialects shown in (23) show intrusive *r* not only after a lexical word but also after a function word – i.e., precisely in the context where the constraint FINAL-C, which demands a C only ω-finally, is designed to remain silent.

An interesting question is what happens in these dialects to the prototypical clitics of English – the indefinite and definite articles *a* and *the*, both of them function words in proclisis to following nouns and adjectives. In both cases, the usual outcome, as in other dialects of English, involves the special lexical allomorphs [ən] and [ði:] which are selected prevocalically, preempting any *r*-sandhi. Sivertsen's (1960:136) Cockney materials, however, also include the following transcription:

(24) Indefinite *a* with intrusive *r*:
    not a hope   not [ə rəʊp]

This is the kind of intrusion one might have deemed impossible, on the basis of the American English facts alone.[13]

A first idea might be that what is different about the grammar of post-function-word *r*-inserters is simply the prosody of function words themselves. Are they perhaps parsed as full prosodic words (25a) in Cockney and Norwich English, so that FINAL-C would still be responsible for *r*-insertion?

(25) A non-solution: a dialect difference in function word parsing
    a.   Post-function-word *r*-inserters: (quarter) [to $_\omega$][eight $_\omega$] → t[ə͡r]eight
    b.   *r*-inserters with function word gap: (quarter) [to eight $_\omega$] → t[ə] eight

However, this is not a promising route to take. The relevant forms (*of, to, you, a*, and *by* in (23)) are all pronounced with an unstressed [ə] and fail to meet the standard phonological criteria for parsability as independent prosodic words (Selkirk 1984). They can only be analyzed as proclitic (25b) – a characteristic shared by most, if not all, dialects of English.[14]

Looking at these dialect data, there is clearly no sense in which *r*-insertion is barred from applying after function words in their normal parse – i.e., as proclitics. What we have here, then, is insertion in all the prosodic contexts that give rise to intrusive *r*, including after a genuine function word. Thus, different from the variety of English that McCarthy (1993a) was analyzing, *r*-sandhi in these dialects seems to be triggered by Onset, not by Final-C. We will return to a formal analysis of these facts in section 4.5.

3.4   Final-C in Universal Phonology

We are faced with a situation, then, where Final-C seems to provide a better explanation for some dialects, and Onset for other dialects. This is at least a partial vindication of the onset-account of *r*-sandhi, the traditional approach to the phenomenon adopted by virtually all analyses apart from McCarthy's (1993a) Final-C account. Having two entirely different explanations of *r*-sandhi for two very similar dialects of the same language is not very satisfying. An appeal to constraint reranking is certainly thinkable, with Onset and Final-C acting as the decisive constraints in different grammars, but a unified approach that manages to reduce the variation to a single factor would certainly be more principled, all else being equal. In addition, without an interesting factorial typology emerging, simply moving specific constraints around in the ranking amounts to a facile stipulation to 'account for the facts' – a practice perhaps too easily resorted to in OT analyses.

In a more general vein, Final-C has remained controversial as a universal constraint, and independent evidence for a requirement of this kind on surface prosodic words is sparse (but see Bonet and Lloret 2005) – as opposed to morphological templates, where a final consonant is often part of the defining shape (see Wiese 2001). Thus all Proto-Indo-European roots have the form CVC (according to Benveniste's (1935) theory), i.e., they end in an obligatory final consonant (including laryngeals), and similar generalizations are familiar from many languages and language families, such as Bantu or Mayan. Similarly, Arabic stems are required to end in a consonant (McCarthy and Prince 1990b). But these 'Final-C' requirements are part of the canonical forms of morphological categories such as roots or stems, not conditions on output prosody.

Prima facie counterevidence to FINAL-C as a constraint on prosodic words is found in languages like Maori (Hale 1973) that ban any kind of consonant cluster and have only open syllables – (C)V, (C)VV – with the additional option of allowing a word-final consonant, only to undergo a subsequent sound change deleting all word-final consonants, destroying precisely the configuration called for by FINAL-C.

Optimality theorists are quick to point out, quite accurately, that such evidence is not lethal as long as FINAL-C is a violable constraint. True enough, the Maori change could be described as a shift from the ranking [FINAL-C » NoCODA » MAX-C] to [NoCODA » FINAL-C » MAX-C]. Since final consonants are only admitted, not required, at the earlier stage, DEP-C needs to be high-ranking in order to prevent epenthesis from inserting final C's across the board. This points to a persistent problem with 'anti-wellformedness' constraints like FINAL-C: As a reviewer reminds us, pathological rankings arise very easily, such as [FINAL-C » NoCODA » F], where F is shorthand for MAX, DEP, and other relevant faithfulness constraints. This predicts the existence of the implausible language (CV)* CVC, where all final syllables are closed but all other syllables open.

Whatever the status of FINAL-C in Universal Phonology, however, we are here concerned with a different point: The dialectal evidence shows that a full explanation of *r*-sandhi in English cannot lie in this constraint; an appeal to ONSET therefore remains essential. As we will show in the next section, once ONSET is part of the game, it is a straightforward matter to extend the account to also cover the dialects with the 'function word gap' which seemed to require an appeal to FINAL-C. In fact, the presumed shortcomings of the onset approach disappear once the markedness and faithfulness properties of word onsets in an extended word projection are properly understood.

4 Extended word structures and ONSET

What we need, then, is a refined version of the ONSET-based approach. To recapitulate, the FINAL-C approach accounts for *r*-sandhi and the function word gap by the conjunction of the three assumptions in (26).

(26) a. Both intrusive *r* and linking *r* are ambisyllabic, and therefore do not violate the Coda Condition against *r* exclusively linked to the syllable coda.
　　 b. Full lexical words are prosodic words (ω); function words are not.
　　 c. The constraint responsible for intrusive *r* and linking *r* is FINAL-C: $*V]_\omega$.

We agree with the ambisyllabicity analysis (26a) and the non-ω-hood of function words (26b), but replace FINAL-C (26c) with a specific version of the ONSET constraint – namely a version specific to the beginning of ω', the *maximal prosodic word*. We will now show that it is unnecessary to take recourse to the problematic FINAL-C constraint once the onset requirements for prosodic words and their associated faithfulness properties are taken into account.

4.1   Proposal

Our proposal involves the three main ingredients in (27), which we will subsequently take up one by one.

(27) Main ingredients of the analysis
    a.   Adjunction to ω, up to a prosodic word constituent of maximal size.
    b.   Strict onset requirement in maximally prominent positions.
    c.   Positional faithfulness (anti-epenthesis) at the beginning of prosodic words.

As discussed in section 1, we assume the prosodic hierarchy in (28) (repeated from (1) above), with the option of recursivity at every level, and with a distinction between maximal and minimal instantiations of categories.

(28) υ   utterance

      ι   intonational phrase

      φ   phonological phrase

      ω   prosodic word

      f   foot

      σ   syllable

In agreement with earlier researchers, including Selkirk (1995), among others, we assume that function words in English form adjunction structures with following lexical words. Our specific proposal appears in (29).

(29)

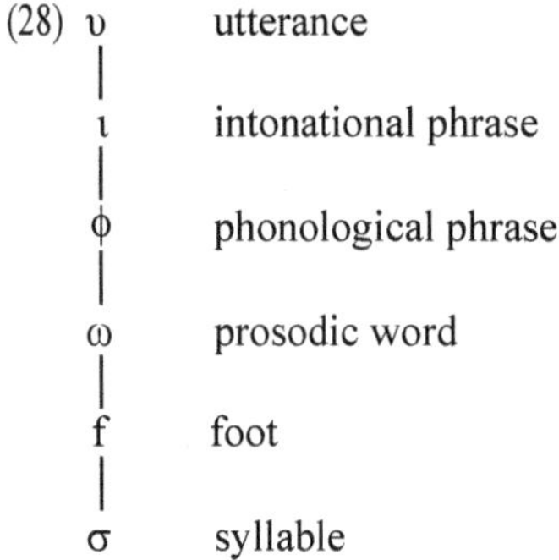

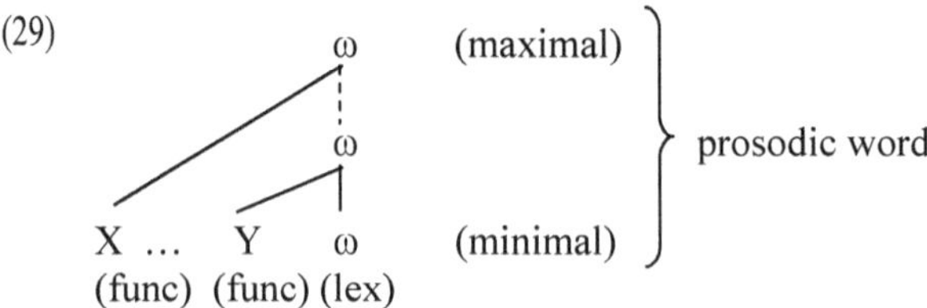

The resulting larger structure is referred to as ω' ('maximal prosodic word') and its innermost subconstituent of type ω as ω_1 ('minimal prosodic word'), in the way shown in (30) (following the general scheme given in (3) in section 1).

(30) ω' = maximal (projection of) ω: ω not dominated by ω.

   ω_1 = minimal (projection of) ω: ω not dominating ω.

Maximal prosodic words roughly correspond to the 'clitic groups' of other theories; we leave the question open whether the minor (or 'intermediate') phrase needs to be distinguished from the maximal prosodic word – in terms of (2) (see section 1), it could be identified as the minimal phonological phrase. What interests us here is that maximal words are subject to a specific instance of the onset requirement, stated in (31):

(31) ONSET(ω'): *$[_{\omega'}$ V (Maximal projections of ω cannot begin with a vowel.)

The constraint in (31) is violated by vowel-initial maximal prosodic words, but not elsewhere – non-maximal prosodic words (i.e., those dominated by another prosodic word) are only subject to the normal ONSET requirement. ONSET(ω') is part of a group of onset constraints that also includes the requirement for stressed syllables to have an onset, resulting in derived contrasts in Dutch and German involving glottal stop epenthesis in cases like *The*[ʔ] *áter* vs. *thèatrálisch* 'theater, theatrical'. Another related requirement is the foot-initial onset requirement seen, for example, in the Australian language Aranda (Goedemans 1994). It appears, then, that (31) is just another piece of the well-established family of constraints (see also Smith 2002, Flack 2006, 2007a and section 4.5 below).

   The last ingredient in our analysis (27c) is simply an instance of positional faithfulness (Beckman 1997) – a constraint against epenthesis at the beginning of prosodic words. The relevant constraint, which we refer to as DEP(ω-init), is formulated in (32).

(32) DEP(ω-init): Any element of the output in ω-initial position has an input
   correspondent.

DEP(ω-init) governs the left edge of any prosodic word constituent, whatever its size. It is violated by intrusive *r*, but not by linking *r*. We return to this constraint in some more detail in section 4.3.

   In (33) and (34) we illustrate the kind of prosodic parsing we are arguing for here. The relevant syntax-phonology mapping constraint is the LEX≈PR constraint of Prince and Smolensky (1993/2004:45) – the familiar requirement on lexical words (*saw, Ann, eat, add,* etc.) to be left-/right-aligned with prosodic words (see Selkirk 1995 for relevant discussion and motivation). No such requirement exists for function words (*gonna, to,* etc.), which are themselves simply dominated by the lower prosodic categories (*gonna* by f, *to* by σ), and are adjoined to the following lexical word (maximal projections of ω are circled for perspicuity).

(33) *r*-inserting candidates

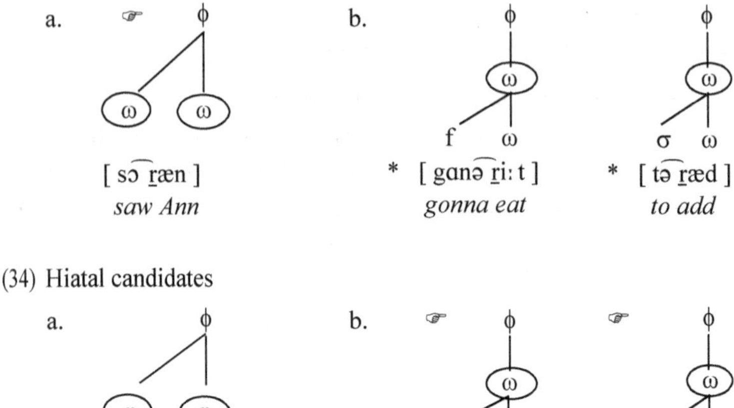

The *r*-inserting candidates in (33) are in competition with the hiatal candidates in (34). For a phrase φ consisting of two maximal prosodic words, such as *saw Ann*, the preference for the *r*-inserting (33a) follows from the fact that ONSET(ω') – the requirement for maximal prosodic words to have an onset – dominates DEP(ω-init) – the constraint against epenthesis in prosodic word-initial positions:

(35) ONSET(ω') » DEP(ω-init)

On the other hand, a prosodic word that is in construction with a preceding function word, such as *eat* in *gonna eat*, is not maximal, but forms a subpart of an extended ω-structure. Therefore ONSET(ω') is silent in this case, and since general ONSET ranks lower than DEP(ω-init) (36), no intrusive *r* is found in this context, and the hiatus structure (34b) wins over (33b).

(36) DEP(ω-init) » ONSET

The overall prosodic constructions involving functions words (such as *gonna eat* and *to add*) are themselves maximal prosodic words, and are hence subject to the higher-ranking ONSET(ω') constraint. This is why *r*-insertion is found on procliticized V-initial function words, as illustrated in (37) where the relevant maximal prosodic words are circled.[15]

(37)

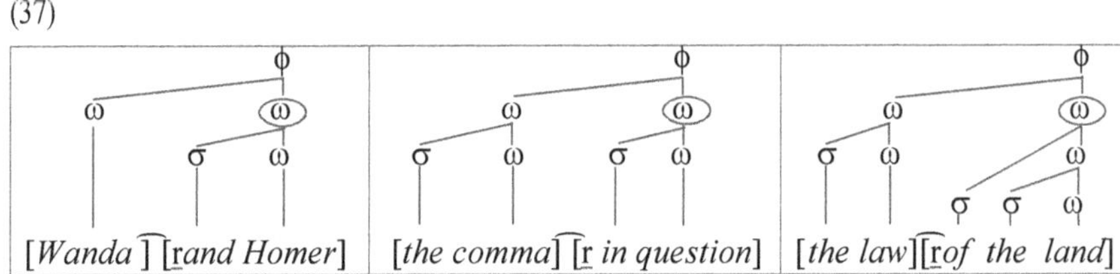

Assembling all of these findings, we arrive at the overall ranking in (38), where ONSET(ω') dominates DEP(ω-init), followed by their more general versions, ONSET and DEP, ranked in the same order.

(38) ONSET(ω') » DEP(ω-init) » ONSET » DEP

We return below to the consequences of the fact that general ONSET dominates general DEP. For the two pairs of related constraints in (38) we assume, with Beckman (1997:37–38), that the ranking [*position-specific » general*] can be taken as fixed without loss of generality. We will consider the factorial typology produced by this set of constraints in section 5.

4.2   Illustration and ranking

We now illustrate this analysis in more detail. As already pointed out, the requirement for maximal prosodic words to have a firm consonantal beginning dominates the constraint against non-input material in prominent prosodic word-initial position, as shown in bold in (39). This allows intrusive *r* to fill the onset of a maximal ω.

(39) ONSET(ω') » DEP(ω-init)

saw Ann	ONSET(ω')	DEP(ω-init)	ONSET	DEP
☞ [$_\omega$ˈ*saw*][$_\omega$ˈ*rAnn*]		*		*
[$_\omega$ˈ*saw*][$_\omega$ˈ*Ann*]	*!		*	

When the onset of a maximal prosodic word is not involved, as in the case of words that are in prosodic construction with preceding functional material, DEP(ω-init) prevents intrusive *r*. It is thus the dominance relation [DEP(ω-init) » ONSET] (40) that explains why there is no *r*-insertion after function words in dialects adopting this kind of ranking.

(40) Dep(ω-init) » Onset

gonna eat	Onset(ω¹)	Dep(ω-init)	Onset	Dep
$[_{\omega'}(_f gonna)\,\overline{[_\omega\underline{\textrm{r}}eat]}]$		*!		*
☞ $[_{\omega'}(_f gonna)\,[_\omega eat]]$			*	

to add	Onset(ω¹)	Dep(ω-init)	Onset	Dep
$[_{\omega'}(_\sigma to)\,\overline{[_\omega\underline{\textrm{r}}add]}]$		*!		*
☞ $[_{\omega'}(_\sigma to)\,[_\omega add]]$			*	

It also follows straightforwardly (see (41)) that V-initial function words at the left edge of a maximal prosodic word are still regulated by Onset(ω¹).

(41) Onset(ω¹) » Dep(ω-init)

Wanda and Homer	Onset(ω¹)	Dep(ω-init)	Onset	Dep
☞ $[_{\omega'}Wanda][_{\omega'}\underline{\textrm{r}}and\,[_\omega Homer]]$		*		*
$[_{\omega'}Wanda][_{\omega'}and\,[_\omega Homer]]$	*!		*	

This brings us to a small and rather obvious issue that needs to be resolved. As McCarthy (1993a) points out, while it is true that in non-rhotic American accents function words reject intrusive *r* (**gonna ͡reat*), they do not reject linking *r*, and in fact require it: (*for eating* [fə ͡riːɾɪŋ], **fo' eating* [fə iːɾɪŋ]). It is therefore only the epenthetic nature of intrusive *r* that excludes it after function words in the onset of a non-maximal ω. The other variant of *r*-sandhi, linking (i.e., underlying) *r*, is not ruled out here, and is in fact obligatory as an onset filler. This set of facts follows straightforwardly in our analysis. As (42) shows, when a function word ends in an underlying *r*, connecting this segment to the onset of the following ω (that the function word is in construction with) does not violate Dep(ω-init). We have here a case of the emergence of the unmarked (McCarthy and Prince 1994).

(42) Emergence of Onset:

for eating	Onset(ω¹)	Dep(ω-init)	Onset	Dep
☞ $[_{\omega'}(_\sigma\overline{for})\,[_\omega eating]]$				
$[_{\omega'}(_\sigma fo')\,[_\omega eating]]$			*!	

Here the *r* is underlying material, even though originating in a different morpheme. The contrast between (42) and (40) testifies to the continued synchronic relevance of the distinction between linking *r* and intrusive *r*.

4.3 Why insert *r*?

We have so far treated intrusive *r* simply as an epenthetic segment, without addressing any of the issues concerning the nature of the segment that have been debated in the literature. In this section, we will briefly lay out our assumptions insofar as they are immediately relevant for our analysis: Why insert *r*, of all segments?

Viewing intrusive *r* as simply triggering a DEP violation (as in (40) above, e.g.) makes the implausible claim that the [ɹ] of English, a segment that has struck few observers as a model of unmarkedness, is in fact the default consonant of the language. Noting this fact, McCarthy (1993a) adopts a (later much criticized) rule of *r*-insertion (Ø→r), which stands outside of the OT constraint system and serves to expand the candidate set without accruing faithfulness violations.[16]

More recently, turning away from the view that inserted *r* is only the synchronically arbitrary and unnatural remnant of the historical development (*r*-deletion followed by rule inversion, see McMahon 2000 for a thorough exposition), other approaches have emerged which look at *r*-insertion not in isolation, but in the context of the other hiatus processes in English. Relevant work includes Baković (1999) and Uffmann (2005), building on previous research including Kahn (1976:69–70), Broadbent (1991), and Gnanadesikan (1997:159–162), and we here follow their lead. The basic idea is that *r*-insertion is a kind of diphthongization, parallel to the transitional glide found after high vowels in similar contexts. Some examples of the latter appear in (43) (from Gimson and Cruttenden 2001:288–290).

(43)	*my arms* [maɪ ʲɑːmz]	*may ask* [meɪ ʲɑːsk]	*he ought* [hiː ʲɔːt]
	annoy Arthur [ənɔɪ ʲɑːθə]	*beauty and* [bjuːtɪ ʲənd]	
	window open [wɪndəʊ ʷəʊpən]	*now and then* [naʊ ʷənd ðen]	*you aren't* [juː ʷɑːnt]

The same authors also note that this transitional [ʲ] remains distinct from phonemic [j], citing contrasts as in (44).

(44) a. *my ears* [maɪ ʲɪəz] b. *my years* [maɪ jɪəz]

In the case of the (tense and diphthongized) front vowels [iː, eɪ], the back vowels [uː, oʊ], and the diphthongs [aɪ], [oɪ], and [aʊ], the glide elements [ʲ] and [ʷ] serve to smooth the hiatus (*see Ann* [siː ʲæn], *know Ann* [noʊ ʷæn], etc.). The remaining vowels that occur word-finally, [ɑː, ɔː, ə], lack a corresponding glide element, and the segment [ɹ] appears as their closest consonantal counterpart (45), parallel to the glide in (43) and (44a). This account is most appealing for low vowels and schwa, whose production is known to be often accompanied by pharyngeal constriction (Gnanadesikan 1997, Gick 2003). As Uffmann (2005) observes, there is indeed a dialect where intrusive *r* only occurs after these vowels, not after [ɔː] (see also Wells 1991). Many questions in this area still remain to be answered (see the works cited above for further details), but all in all an approach that sees intrusive *r* as sponsored by the preceding vowel seems well motivated.

(45) *Shah of Persia*   *spa and music*
     [ʃɑː ɹəf pəːʒə]   [spɑː ɹænd mjuːzɪk]

     vanilla ice cream   *saw Ann*
     [vənɪlə ɹajskɹijm]   [sɔː ɹæn]

Seen in this light, *r*-insertion has two parts: (i) insertion of a bare segmental root node, and (ii) place features of the preceding vowel are recruited to fill in the empty root node. The regular interface constraint aligning the right edge of a stem (or a morphological word) to a prosodic constituent, minimally a syllable, then anchors these place features to the coda, creating ambisyllabicity, the source of the 'Final-C' syndrome.

DEP(ω-init) and DEP in the analysis presented above should therefore be replaced by DEP-ROOT(ω-init) and DEP-ROOT, respectively – constraints against insertion of a bare segmental root node (and not of a whole segment with all its place features). This is shown in (46), where the winning candidate (46b), with a one-to-many correspondence relation, violates lower-ranking INTEGRITY.

(46) *Wanda ate*

	/wandə eɪt/	ONSET(ω')	DEP-ROOT(ω-init)
a.	[ω'wandə] [ω'eɪt]	*!	
b. ☞	[ω'wandə] [ω'ɹeɪt] [place]		*

Candidates such as *[wandə] [jeɪt] or *[wandə] [weɪt] violate higher-ranking DEP-place, as does post-pausal /ɛd/→*[rɛd] in (47).[17]

(47) *Ed*

	/ɛd/	DEP-PLACE	ONSET(ω')	DEP-ROOT(ω-init)
☞	[ω'ɛd]		*!	
	[ω'rɛd]	*!		*

The analysis of the intrusive *r* in *saw rEd* thus parallels that of the trans-word flapping situation in *sought Ed* discussed in section 2 above. The final [t] in *sought* is made ambisyllabic because of the ONSET requirement (now identified as ONSET(ω^1)). Here too, the onset-filling material comes from the previous word. In both cases, what appears to be a requirement that there be a final consonant in a prosodic word is, rather, the enforcement of the alignment constraint matching the right edge of every stem or morphological word with the right edge of a syllable. Together with ONSET(ω^1), the result is a linked structure (either at the level of the root node, as in the ambisyllabic case, or at the level of the place node in the intrusive *r* case).

Nowhere in this analysis is there a need for an appeal to FINAL-C, or to some other constraint imposing special closure properties on prosodic words. Rather, the analysis simply asserts that every syllable needs an onset, and that this is even more urgent at the beginning of a maximal ω-complex, with a positional faithfulness constraint against ω-initial epenthesis ranked in between. Non-insertion after a function word is just a consequence of the parochial ranking in (48) (repeated from (36)), and not excluded for some fundamental reason, as in the FINAL-C analysis.

(48) ONSET(ω^1) » DEP-ROOT(ω-init) » ONSET » DEP-ROOT

4.4   Other *r*-sandhi locations

So far we have shown how the overall ranking in (48) accounts for the *r*-sandhi between two maximal prosodic words (49a) and in extended prosodic word structures (49b).

(49) a.

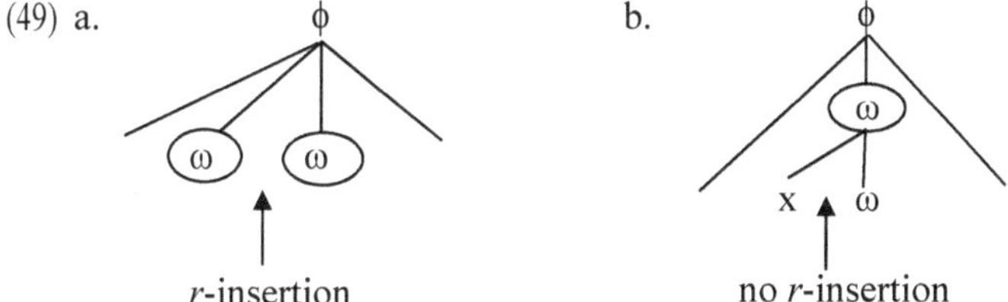

b.

r-insertion   no *r*-insertion

It remains to make sure that the present analysis can account for all other *r*-sandhi locations. We identify three such cases discussed in McCarthy (1993a).

(50) a.   Phrase-finally after function words
(e.g., [*If you hafta*$_\phi$][*ɾAnne might help*$_\phi$]; [*Are ya gonna*$_\phi$][*ɾor aren't ya*$_\phi$]?)

   b.   Enclitics in construction with a preceding prosodic word
(e.g., *draw ɾit; saw ɾ(h)im*)

   c.   Word-medial cases of *r*-insertion at level II morpheme boundaries
(e.g., *draw ring; withdraw ɾal*)

In phrase-final position, *r*-insertion occurs even after function words, as in (50a), where the phrasal parse is marked by [... $_\phi$]. Given the layering principles

of the prosodic hierarchy, the left/right edges of higher prosodic units correspond to left/right edges of lower prosodic units (Hayes 1989b). As illustrated
schematically in (51), phrase-final function words such as *hafta* and *gonna*
must in this position be parsed as prosodic words – the explanation given for
the FINAL-C account – but it also means that the following phrase must begin
with a prosodic word, and because of its position, it can only be a maximal one.

(51)

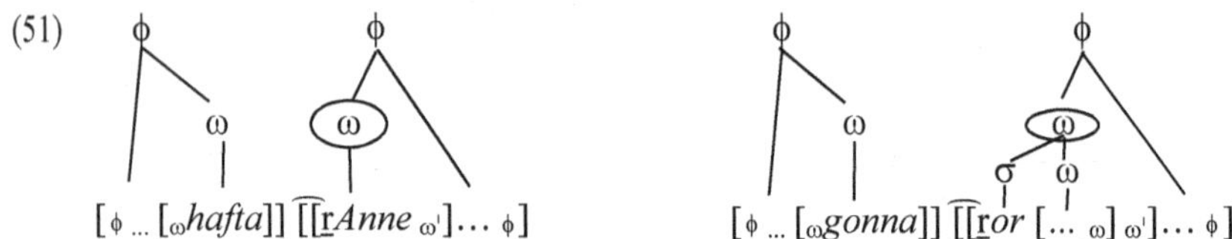

Phrase juncture *r*-sandhi is therefore a straightforward consequence of high-
ranking ONSET(ω').

   Turning to enclitic cases (50b) (*draw ̄ rit,* etc.), these are prosodified as
extended word structures, where the extension is found to the right.

(52)

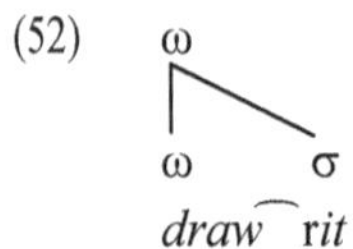

For the enclitic *it*, an adjoined syllable, neither ONSET(ω') nor DEP-ROOT(ω-init)
are relevant. Instead, we see here the effects of the ranking of the general
constraints [ONSET » DEP-ROOT], which results in intrusive *r* (53).

(53) Encliticization

draw it	ONSET(ω')	DEP-ROOT(ω-init)	ONSET	DEP-ROOT
☞ [[*draw* ₍ω₎]*rit* ₍ω₎]				*
[[*draw* ₍ω₎] *it* ₍ω₎]			*!	

There is a clear difference in phrasing between such word+enclitic collocations
and stem+level II suffix combinations. The latter are involved in the third case
listed in (50), word-medial *r*-insertion at level II morpheme boundaries, such
as *draw ̄ ring* or *withdraw ̄ ral* (50c). As shown by Hayes (1989b:207) for *visit it*
vs. *visited*, the /t/ may be slightly aspirated in *visited*, but not in *visit it*. In our
terms, *visit it* and *draw it* are extended prosodic word structures (53), whereas
visited and *drawing* are prosodified as single (nonextended) prosodic words. In
ω-medial position, the two high-ranking constraints are irrelevant, and ONSET
» DEP-ROOT again explains the *r*-sandhi, as (54) shows.

(54) Affixation

draw+ing	Onset(ω')	Dep-root(ω-init)	Onset	Dep-root
☞ [*draw͡.ring*$_\omega$]				*
[*draw.ing*$_\omega$]			*!	

Here we find an advantage of the present Onset-driven analysis over that of the Final-C analysis. The Final-C constraint correctly controls the phrase junctures (50a) and encliticized forms (50b), since the appropriate junctures also coincide with ω-final positions. However, for the word-medial cases of *r*-insertion, it becomes necessary to require a recursive ω-structure as in (55), so that *r* can be inserted prosodic word-finally.

(55) [[*draw*$_\omega$]*ing*$_\omega$] → [[*draw* r$_\omega$]*ing*$_\omega$]

This kind of replication of morphological structure as prosodic structure for level II phonology was standard practice in early OT (see McCarthy and Prince 1993b), following the lead of the version of Lexical Phonology developed in Inkelas (1989). With Correspondence Theory (McCarthy and Prince 1995, Benua 1997, among others), however, output-output (OO-) correspondence constraints have in many cases made such recursive prosodic structure mimicking recursive grammatical structure unnecessary. To take a standard example for illustrative purposes, consider *condem<n>*, where the output of the base form has deleted the stem-final *n*, resolving the illicit final cluster. With level I suffixation, *condemnation*, the stem-final *n* is simply resyllabified as the onset of the vowel-initial suffix. However, with level II suffixation, *condem<n>ing*, higher-ranked (level II) OO-correspondence enforces deletion of the stem-final *n* in correspondence to the base output.

Interestingly, standard OO-correspondence constraints do not provide a solution for *r*-sandhi since here the unaffixed base form ([*draw*$_\omega$] for intrusive *r*, [*sta#*$_\omega$] for linking *r*) lacks *r* – precisely the property to be copied over to the derived forms [*draw͡.ring*$_\omega$] and [*star͡.ring*$_\omega$].

Attempts to pursue an analogy-based analysis would need recourse to more powerful, and therefore more problematic, versions of OO-correspondence where phrasal forms like *draw͡ rEmily* or *draw͡ rit* figure directly in the computation of the lexical form [*draw͡.ring*$_\omega$] (see also note 3 above). Besides questions of power, this also raises issues of redundancy, since we would have ended up with a theory having both OO-relations and extra prosodic complexity replicating morphological structure. In our Onset-driven analysis, no such recursive prosodic structure mimicking morphological constituency is required; hence there is no redundancy with respect to OO-correspondence constraints.[18]

4.5   An empirical argument for the onset-driven analysis

A major empirical argument showing that what drives *r*-insertion is an ONSET-constraint and not FINAL-C is the fact that the function word gap – the non-appearance of intrusive *r* after phrase-medial function words in non-rhotic American English – is only one half of the story. In the very same context, several British dialects show intrusive *r* (e.g., *to eat* as [$_\omega$ ($_\sigma$*tə*) [$_\omega$ *reat*]] in the dialect of Norwich, etc., see (23) above). This is no anomaly in the ONSET-driven analysis, but a consequence of a slight difference in constraint ranking: Instead of dominating ONSET, DEP-ROOT(ω-init) is dominated by it, as in (56).

(56)

to eat	ONSET(ω')	ONSET	DEP-ROOT(ω-init)	DEP-ROOT
☞ [$_\omega$ ($_\sigma$*tə*) [*reat*$_\omega$]]			*	*
[$_\omega$ ($_\sigma$*tə*) [*eat*$_\omega$]]		*!		

A FINAL-C analysis cannot account for this dialect with a simple reranking of the relevant constraints since the constraint driving *r*-insertion, FINAL-C, holds only for prosodic words and has nothing to say about function words like *to*, neither in American nor in British dialects.

If our goal is a unified analysis of the overall system of English accents, where different modes of *r*-sandhi emerge out of different rankings of the same constraints, this means that we cannot use, as the main driving force for *r*-sandhi, a constraint that has the function word gap already built into it. In other words, for this reason alone we cannot rely on FINAL-C, even if the other problems connected with this constraint (see the discussion in section 3.4) did not exist.

Looking at the other side of things, are there reasons to worry about the soundness of a theory with specific versions of syllable structure constraints like ONSET for prominent positions, such as beginnings of maximal prosodic words? A reviewer raises the question whether there are any languages which consistently ban onsetless syllables only word-initially while permitting them word-internally, noting that the opposite pattern (onsetless syllables *permitted* word-initially, but *banned* word-internally) is well-attested.

Fortunately, these worries have been laid to rest in recent work by Flack (2006, 2007a), a detailed typological survey showing that the phonotactic restrictions holding at different prosodic levels stand in a systematic pattern of upward inheritance ('any restriction which can hold on syllable onsets can also hold word-initially, phrase-initially, and utterance-initially, and any coda restriction can also hold word-finally, phrase-finally, and utterance-finally'

(Flack 2006:1)). Flack develops a constraint format that captures this kind of patterning in an elegant way. Regarding the question at hand, word onsets vs. syllable onsets, she provides an illustrative list of more than twenty languages, from Babungo (Niger-Congo, Cameroon) to Yagua (Peba-Yaguan, Peru), where onsets are required in all and only word-initial syllables.

A fundamental insight of OT relates to the fact that wellformedness is a multi-faceted affair. There are many different, and often conflicting, dimensions of markedness and of faithfulness in terms of which structures need to be compared. A structure scoring high on one scale can score low on another one, and since different grammars rank the constraints differently, no single grand cross-linguistic chain of wellformedness can exist, where structures would be lined up from good to bad to ugly. For the case at hand, just as there are positional markedness constraints such as $\text{ONSET}(\omega')$ ruling out marked structures in prominent positions, there are also positional faithfulness constraints (such as $\text{IDENT}(\sigma_1)$ (Beckman 1997) or $\text{DEP}(\omega\text{-init})$ (this paper)) and other constraints (such as $\text{ALIGN}(\text{MWd}, \text{Left}, \omega, \text{Left})$, see McCarthy and Prince 1993a) demanding specific faithfulness to input structures (including marked structures) in a similar set of prominent environments. Consequently, the existence of languages banning onsetless syllables only word-initially does not preclude the existence of languages banning them only word-internally (Axininca Campa (McCarthy and Prince 1993b) is a familiar example). The upshot is that word-initial onsetless syllables are not in a general way more marked or less marked than word-internal ones.

5   Dialect variation and factorial typology

In order to probe the soundness of the constraint system we have developed, we conclude by studying the factorial typology of the four central constraints that are involved. They can be ranked in $4! = 4{\times}3{\times}2{\times}1{=}24$ ways. $[\text{ONSET}(\omega') \gg \text{ONSET}]$ is a fixed ranking, leaving only 12 of these 24 rankings, and the other fixed ranking $[\text{DEP-ROOT}(\omega\text{-INIT}) \gg \text{DEP-ROOT}]$ reduces this number to the 6 rankings shown below in (57)–(62). A more detailed investigation across the English-speaking world would be needed to reach a firm conclusion, but this factorial typology seems to closely approximate the actual range of variation found in terms of *r*-insertion, with the usual caveat that not every dialect predicted to exist is guaranteed to actually be spoken (or be spoken by enough speakers to gain it an entry on a dialect map). Ranking I (57) captures non-rhotic dialects with the function word gap, and ranking II (58) non-rhotic dialects without the function word gap, as discussed earlier.

254   *Phonological Argumentation*

(57) Ranking I: *r*-insertion between words (but not after function words) and word-internally

Input	Output candidates	ONSET(ω')	DEP-ROOT(ω-init)	ONSET	DEP-ROOT
saw Ann	☞ $[_{\omega'}$ *saw*$][\underline{\text{ɾ}}Ann\,_{\omega'}]$		*		*
	$[_{\omega'}$ *saw*$][$ *Ann*$\,_{\omega'}]$	*!		*	
gonna eat	$[_{\omega'}(_f$ *gonna*$)[\underline{\text{ɾ}}eat\,_{\omega}]]$		*!		*
	☞ $[_{\omega'}(_f$ *gonna*$)[$ *eat*$\,_{\omega}]]$			*	
for eating	☞ $[_{\omega'}(_\sigma$ *for*$)[eating\,_{\omega}]]$				
	$[_{\omega'}(_\sigma$ *fo'*$)\,[eating\,_{\omega}]]$			*!	
draw+ing	☞ $[draw.\underline{\text{ɾ}}ing\,_{\omega}]$				*
	$[draw\,.ing\,_{\omega}]$			*!	

(58) Ranking II: *r*-insertion between words (including after function words) and word-internally

Input	Output candidates	ONSET(ω')	ONSET	DEP-ROOT(ω-init)	DEP-ROOT
saw Ann	☞ $[_{\omega'}$ *saw*$][\underline{\text{ɾ}}Ann\,_{\omega'}]$			*	*
	$[_{\omega'}$ *saw*$][$ *Ann*$\,_{\omega'}]$	*!	*		
gonna eat	☞ $[_{\omega'}(_f$ *gonna*$)[\underline{\text{ɾ}}eat\,_{\omega}]]$			*	*
	$[_{\omega'}(_f$ *gonna*$)[$ *eat*$\,_{\omega}]]$		*!		
for eating	☞ $[_{\omega'}(_\sigma$ *for*$)[eating\,_{\omega}]]$				
	$[_{\omega'}(_\sigma$ *fo'*$)[eating\,_{\omega}]]$		*!		
draw+ing	☞ $[draw.\underline{\text{ɾ}}ing\,_{\omega}]$				*
	$[draw\,.ing\,_{\omega}]$		*!		

Ranking III results in a kind of *r*-insertion, reported as one variant of RP, which allows the process between words but avoids it word-internally.

(59) Ranking III: *r*-insertion between words (but not after function words), but not word-internally

Input	Output candidates	ONSET(ω')	DEP-ROOT(ω-init)	DEP-ROOT	ONSET
saw Ann	☞ $[_{\omega'}$ *saw*$][\underline{\text{ɾ}}Ann\,_{\omega'}]$		*	*	
	$[_{\omega'}$ *saw*$][Ann\,_{\omega'}]$	*!			*
gonna eat	$[_{\omega'}(_f$ *gonna*$)[\underline{\text{ɾ}}eat\,_{\omega}]]$		*!	*	
	☞ $[_{\omega'}(_f$ *gonna*$)[$ *eat*$\,_{\omega}]]$				*
for eating	☞ $[_{\omega'}(_\sigma$ *for*$)[eating\,_{\omega}]]$				
	$[_{\omega'}(_\sigma$ *fo'*$)\,[eating\,_{\omega}]]$				*!
draw+ing	$[draw.\underline{\text{ɾ}}ing\,_{\omega}]$			*!	
	☞ $[draw.\,ing\,_{\omega}]$				*

Ranking IV is interesting since it has the opposite distribution of *r*-insertion (word-internally, but not between words). We have met speakers claiming to speak this kind of variety, but further investigation is clearly called for. Generally speaking, as a reviewer reminds us, there seem to be many languages (for example, in Niger-Congo) that freely tolerate V-syllables in word-initial position but do not tolerate word-internal hiatus.

(60) Ranking IV: *r*-insertion word-internally, but not between words

Input	*Output candidates*	Dep-root(ω-init)	Onset(ω')	Onset	Dep-root
saw Ann	$[_{\omega'}$ *saw*$][ɾAnn_{\omega'}]$	*!			*
	☞ $[_{\omega'}$ *saw*$][$ *Ann*$_{\omega'}]$		*	*	
gonna eat	$[_{\omega'}(_f$ *gonna*$)[ɾeat_{\omega}]]$	*!			*
	☞ $[_{\omega'}(_f$ *gonna*$)[$ *eat*$_{\omega}]]$			*	
for eating	☞ $[_{\omega'}(_\sigma$ *for*$)[eating_{\omega}]]$				
	$[_{\omega'}(_\sigma$ *fo'*$) [eating_{\omega}]]$			*!	
draw+ing	☞ $[draw.ɾing_{\omega}]$				*
	$[draw .ing_{\omega}]$			*!	

Finally, ranking V (which produces the same results as ranking VI) holds for varieties of English without *r*-insertion.

(61) Ranking V: No *r*-insertion anywhere (same result as ranking VI)

Input	*Output candidates*	Dep-root(ω-init)	Onset(ω')	Dep-root	Onset
saw Ann	$[_{\omega'}$ *saw*$][ɾAnn_{\omega'}]$	*!		*	
	☞ $[_{\omega'}$ *saw*$][$ *Ann*$_{\omega'}]$		*		*
gonna eat	$[_{\omega'}(_f$ *gonna*$)[ɾeat_{\omega}]]$	*!		*	
	☞ $[_{\omega'}(_f$ *gonna*$)[$ *eat*$_{\omega}]]$				*
for eating	☞ $[_{\omega'}(_\sigma$ *for*$)[eating_{\omega}]]$				
	$[_{\omega'}(_\sigma$ *fo'*$) [eating_{\omega}]]$				*!
draw+ing	$[draw.ɾing_{\omega}]$			*	
	☞ $[draw .ing_{\omega}]$				*!

(62) Ranking VI: No *r*-insertion anywhere (same result as ranking V)

Input	Output candidates	Dep-root(ω-init)	Dep-root	Onset(ω')	Onset
saw Ann	$[_{\omega'}$ saw$][\underline{r}$Ann $_{\omega'}]$	*!	*		
	☞ $[_{\omega'}$ saw$][$ Ann $_{\omega'}]$			*	*
gonna eat	$[_{\omega'}(_f$ gonna$)[\underline{r}eat$ $_{\omega}]]$	*!	*		
	☞ $[_{\omega'}(_f$ gonna$)[$ eat $_{\omega}]]$				*
for eating	☞ $[_{\omega'}(_\sigma$ for$)[$eating $_{\omega}]]$				
	$[_{\omega'}(_\sigma$ fo'$)$ $[$eating $_{\omega}]]$				*!
draw+ing	$[draw.\underline{r}ing$ $_{\omega}]$		*		
	☞ $[draw$ .ing $_{\omega}]$				*!

6   Conclusion

The final ranking of the constraints responsible for *r*-sandhi in the non-rhotic dialects of English with the function word gap is given in (63).

(63) Dep-place

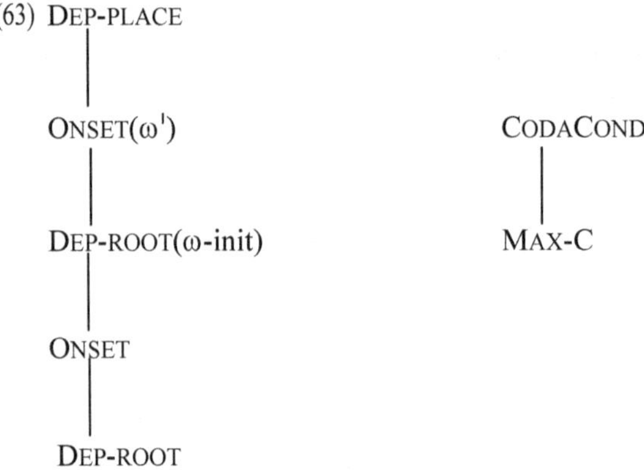

A proper understanding of the larger prosodic collocations formed by prosodic words and function words, as well as the constraints and faithfulness properties of word onsets, allows us to avoid appealing to a problematic 'anti-wellformedness' constraint like Final-C.

Empirically, our analysis not only accounts for the complex distribution of the linking *r*-consonant in RP and the Eastern Massachusetts dialect, but also extends straightforwardly to the different distributions in other dialects. While preserving the central insights of McCarthy (1993a), which remains not just a classic but also a model of optimality-theoretic analysis, the present proposal is theoretically grounded in correspondence theory (positional faithfulness), and is a natural outgrowth of a conception of prosodic structure that views function words as occupying positions within extended word structures (maximal prosodic words). From a broader perspective, this is made possible by an approach to the prosodic hierarchy that radically reduces the number of universal prosodic categories while enriching the set of structural relations that they enter into.

Notes

1   For helpful questions and comments about earlier versions of this paper, we are grateful to Adam Albright, Ryan Bennett, Eulàlia Bonet, Ricardo Bermúdez-Otero, Bruce Hayes, Daniel Kaufman, Shigeto Kawahara, Ania Łubowicz, Joan Mascaró, Bruce Morén, Jeremy O'Brien, Marc van Oostendorp, Jaye Padgett, Steve Parker, Anthi Revithiadou, Curt Rice, Christian Uffmann, Jean-Roger Vergnaud, Michael Wagner, Rachel Walker, Colin Wilson, Moira Yip, and an anonymous reviewer. We are also grateful to audiences at the 2005 Phonology Forum (Fukuoka, Japan), at a 2005 USC Linguistics colloquium, at the 2007 OCP 4 (Rhodes, Greece), and to our students in seminars at UC Santa Cruz and at the 2005 Linguistic Institute at MIT and Harvard, whose questions and challenges led to many improvements. A special note of thanks to Kyle Rawlins and David Teeple, whose unpublished seminar papers on *r*-sandhi had a significant influence on our thinking about the issues.

2   The problem is made harder by the strategy sometimes encountered of literally defining prosodic categories that should be part of Universal Phonology in terms of language-specific processes and phonetic properties (cf. terms like 'accent phrase', 'tone group', etc.); see Truckenbrodt (2007) for discussion.

3   Bermúdez-Otero (2007) revives Kiparsky's analysis, including this use of the feature [lax], in the context of a stratal OT-account, with important new evidence involving *l*-darkening and pre-fortis clipping (as in *látèx*), showing that it is not possible to account for all of the phenomena involved just by appealing to the ambisyllabic context. As long as OT-grammar continues to distinguish lexical and postlexical levels, however, it is unclear what the evidence implies for ambisyllabicity itself. For example, *l*-darkening might be word-level, but flapping (and ambisyllabicity) phrase-level. For pre-fortis clipping, neither ambisyllabicity nor the foot-medial position provides the right environment, and either approach is free to adopt another kind of analysis, such as Bermúdez-Otero's ω-domain account. An additional issue arises with *r*-sandhi: Since the *r* shows a mixture of onset and coda properties (McCarthy 1999a describes it as 'lenited relative to the unambiguous onset *r*', with supporting spectrograms), an analysis without ambisyllabicity might have to resort to considerable abstractness and claim, in a recapitulation of history, that non-rhotic dialects permit coda *r* at the word level, only to rule it out at the phrase level. In this view, the linking *r* of *hea*[r] *Ann* inherits its coda properties from an abstract earlier stratum where *hear* actually has a coda *r* (a transderivational account seems impossible since

the isolation form is *r*-less), and a form like *saw*[r] needs to receive an intrusive *r* at the word level, only to lose it again, Duke-of-York style, at the phrase level unless a vowel-initial word follows (*saw*[r] *Ann*).

4 See Bloomfield (1933:113), Hockett (1958:54–61), and Harris (1951:79–89). The latter presents an especially detailed and lucid treatment of the issues.

5 Here 'ω' indicates 'prosodic word', '|' the morphological word boundary, '☞' the winning candidate, and '!' a fatal violation. Following McCarthy (2002), we do not use the redundant shading of candidate cells, for typographical clarity.

6 The question of whether all gradient OT-constraints can be reinterpreted as categorical (McCarthy 2003c) is not relevant here. We assess alignment violations as in the version of alignment theory in Ito and Mester (1999a:201–210): Noncrisp linkage is not disaligning (e.g., [ɾ] in (11b) fulfills ALIGN-RIGHT), but violates a separate CRISPEDGE constraint. In languages with full resyllabification across words, such as Spanish, ONSET and CRISPEDGE are ranked higher than ALIGN-RIGHT.

7 The examples in (15) are from our own field notes (Deggendorf, Lower Bavaria, Dec. 2005) and from Merkle (1975:30–33). Besides insertion of *r*, there is also insertion of *n*, as in *won i* 'where I'. As Christian Uffmann (personal communication) has pointed out to us, there are even sporadic appearances of *r*-sandhi in Standard German – for example, in the denominal adjectives *Jena-r-er* and *Fulda-r-er* based on the place names *Jena* and *Fulda*.

8 This is one reason why a direct appeal to a hiatus constraint is less attractive in this case, even if such as constraint is part of the constraint set (as argued in Borroff 2003, among others). It is clear that not all instances of hiatus resolution are driven by ONSET; see Ola Orie and Pulleyblank (1998) for a case where the crucial factor is word and foot minimality.

9 In particular, the constraint DEP against simple segment insertion will be replaced by a constraint involving the insertion of a segmental root node, with place features spreading from the preceding vowel (Baković 1999 and Uffmann 2003, 2005). This means *r*-insertion is a kind of diphthongization, and cannot occur utterance initially where there is no preceding vocalic content (see section 4.3).

10 As a reviewer reminds us, the highly sonorous *r* is not a dispreferred coda in itself – rather, it is precisely its high sonority and similarity to vowels that predestines it to vocalize and become part of the syllable nucleus. CODA-COND should here be understood as an abbreviation for this much more complex interaction.

11 Thanks to Daniel Kaufman for first bringing these dialect facts, and their relevance, to our attention.

12 Trudgill (1974:162) also notes an interesting OCP-type restriction in Norwich speech: '[I]ntrusive *r* does not occur in contexts like *extra eggs*, where an /r/ precedes an unstressed /ə/ in the same syllable.'

13 Sivertsen (1960) comments that '[t]his is not the usual way of bridging the hiatus after the unstressed indefinite article: it is more common to use the form /an/: /fájn+anə́wm+fòh+ðəm/ *find a home for them*. Curiously enough, in the few cases where /ər/ has been recorded for the indefinite article it has only been where the next word starts with /h/ in RP.' Our proposal is that the influence of *h*-ful RP speech – i.e., the style of speech that does not drop the *h* in a word like *hope* – is powerful enough in this case to prevent the selection of the appropriate pre-V allomorph [ən] before *hope* [oʊp] (the phonology is reminiscent to that of *h-aspiré* words in French), and in just this case *r*-insertion takes over.

14 A related empirical finding concerns linking *r*, not intrusive *r*: Cockney English shows examples of linking *r* where it is exclusively an onset and not at all connected to coda position, i.e., where its appearance cannot be motivated by FINAL-C. Sivertsen (1960:137) points out that '[l]inking /r/ may also occur when a potential preceding /ə/ is missing, so that there is no hiatus to bridge', citing the forms below (reproduced here in the original phonemic transcriptions).

after them	/áhftrəm/
alter it	/ówltrit/
remember it	/rimémbrit/
over it	/ə́wvrit/
good for himself	/gúd+frisélf/

A full analysis of these forms would require a better understanding of their syllabification, and their relation to the corresponding forms with vowels, than we possess at the moment. What seems clear, however, is that the linking *r* in these output forms is not associated to some ω-final coda position, making it difficult to motivate it by a constraint demanding ω-final codas. On the other hand, the forms do not seem to present obstacles for an onset-based analysis.

15 The occurrence of intrusive *r* in compounds (*schwa-r-epenthesis, spa-r-experience,* etc.) shows that the second member must be a maximal word, i.e., the whole compound is prosodically some kind of phrase.

16 In fact, a rule with a full-fledged environment such as Ø→r/__# is necessary (McCarthy 1993a:18, note 12) in order to avoid initial epenthesis (*Alan* → **Ralan*), and is still not sufficient to cover word-internal intrusive *r* at level II junctures. As Uffmann (2005) observes, an analysis assimilating intrusive *r* to linking *r* by positing a floating *r* lexically at the end of all lexical items subject to *r*-intrusion in a prevocalic context is not viable because of the productivity of the process, as seen in loanwords and even in interlanguage productions (see section 3 above), where a lexical solution is out of the question. The process must be able to deal with input material that lacks *r*.

17 David Teeple (personal communication) points out that there is a crosslinguistic tendency, seen also in English (/ɛd/ → **[jɛd]), for features of the nucleus not to spread leftwards to fill the onset.

18 It is worth pointing out that our analysis does not depend on very specific assumptions about the prosodic structures involved. Even though the contrast

between the extended word structure $[[draw_\omega] \mathrm{rit}\ _\omega]$ and the simplex word structure $[draw.ring_\omega]$ is well motivated (see the discussion in the text), the *r*-insertion facts themselves would be correctly predicted even without this kind of difference in prosodification.

10 Infixation as morpheme absorption[1]

Ania Łubowicz

This article examines data from the languages Palauan and Akkadian where identical infixes and prefixes respond differently to feature cooccurrence restrictions (OCP). In both languages, OCP is enforced on the root domain. While prefixes are not subject to OCP, identical infixes need to conform to OCP restrictions. To explain the asymmetry between identical infixes and prefixes, I propose that infixes are part of the root morpheme in the output while prefixes are outside of the root domain. Infixes become part of the output root morpheme via a process of what I will call morpheme absorption. Empirical consequences of this proposal are explored.

1 Introduction

The interaction of phonology and morphology is fundamental to the study of sound patterns and morphological processes (Kiparsky 1982, Mohanan 1982, McCarthy and Prince 1996, Yip 1989, among others). It has been observed that phonological processes are often affected by morphological structure and vice versa. In this article, I will investigate the relation between infixation and feature cooccurrence restrictions in Palauan and Akkadian, and present phonological evidence for the morphological structure of an infix.

The study of infixation has received a lot of attention in recent phonological theory (Blevins 1999, Buckley 2000, Crowhurst 1998, 2001, Downing 1998, Klein 2005, McCarthy 2000a, McCarthy and Prince 1993a,b, Majors 1997, Nelson 2003, Prince and Smolensky 1993/2004, Yu 2003, 2004a,b). The standard view of infixation in Optimality Theory (Prince and Smolensky 1993/2004) is that an infix is a separate affix in the input and retains its affixal status in the output, known as 'Consistency of Exponence'. Most infixes are regarded as prefixes or suffixes displaced from their edgemost position for prosodic or phonotactic reasons (Buckley 2000, Crowhurst 1998, 2001, Downing 1998, McCarthy 1982, McCarthy and Prince 1996, 1993a,b, Prince and Smolensky 1993/2004).

In this article I will examine root cooccurrence restrictions (OCP_{ROOT})[2], which will provide evidence for the resulting root morpheme in the output. I will show that infixes in Palauan (Finer 1985, Flora 1974a,b, Josephs 1975, 1990, Wilson 1972, Zuraw 2002) and Akkadian (Barthélemy 1998, Beesley and Karttunen 2000, Caldwell et al. 1977, Huehnergard 1997, McCarthy 1979a, 1981, 1986, 1993, Reiner 1966, Streck 2003, Von Soden 1952) are subject to root-domain OCP while segmentally identical prefixes are not. To explain the asymmetry between identical infixes and prefixes, I will propose that infixes are part of the resulting root morpheme rather than a separate morpheme. They become part of the root morpheme in the output via a process of morpheme absorption. Prefixes, on the other hand, are separate from the root. This solves the problem of different responses to feature coocurrence restrictions by one and the same affix in different positions in a word. I will also show that feature coocurrence restrictions and morpheme absorption explain why the [-ta-] affix in Akkadian alternates between an infix and a prefix. It becomes a prefix to avoid morpheme absorption and consequential violation of feature cooccurrence restrictions.

In addition, I will present an OT analysis of infix absorption. Constraints on morpheme locality and morpheme faithfulness will be examined to explain this process. This article continues the line of research begun by others, whereby morphological structure can be altered in the output (see Section 3).

The organization of this article is as follows. Section 2 presents Palauan data. Section 3 describes the proposal. Section 4 applies the proposal to Palauan. Section 5 discusses another case of morpheme absorption – metathesis in Akkadian. Section 6 concludes the article with an overview of the results.

2   Palauan verb marker affix

In Palauan (Finer 1985, Flora 1974a,b, Josephs 1975, 1990, Wilson 1972, Zuraw 2002), an Austronesian language spoken in the Palauan Islands of western Micronesia, there is a verb marker [-m-] which alternates between an infix and a prefix. When infixed, it is located after the first consonant of the stem. In this case, the choice between prefixing and infixing is determined by the morphosyntactic features of the verb, and is not predictable on phonological grounds. This is shown in (1). (The code following each item marks the source and page number where the item was found: F for Flora, FN for Finer, and J for Josephs.)[3]

(1)   Palauan verb marker (Finer 1985, Flora 1974b, Josephs 1975, 1990)

    a.   Prefixation

dakt	'fear'	**mə**-dákt	'be/get fearful' F212
rur	'shame'	**mə**-rúr	'be/get ashamed' F212
ʔúu	'shadow'	**mə**-ʔúw	'be/get shady' F212
latk	'remembrance'	**mə**-látk	'been/gotten remembered, recalled' F218
dasaʔ-	'carve'	**mə**-dásəʔ	'been/gotten carved' F215
loʔad-	'break cord'	**mə**-lóʔəd	'been/gotten broken (cord) by pulling' F218

    b.   Infixation

láŋəl	'crying'	ḷ-**m**-áŋəl	'cry' F222
lúut	'return'	ḷ-**m**-úwt	'return' F221
rurt	'running'	rə-**m**-úrt	'run' J456 (1990)
latk	'remembrance'	l-**m**-átk	'remembered (pl. 3rd non-hum)' F218
loʔad-	'break cord'	l-**m**-óʔəd	'broken cord (pl. 3rd non-hum)' F218
dakul-	'bury'	θ-**m**-ákl	'buried (pl. 3rd non-hum)' F218

As shown in (2), the verb marker undergoes a process of labial dissimilation
when immediately adjacent to a labial consonant (Finer 1985, Josephs 1975).
The verb marker dissimilates to a rounded vowel [o] or [u]. Adjacent labials
trigger dissimilation of both the infixed and prefixed verb marker.[4]

(2)   Local dissimilation

    a.   Prefixation

búrək	'swelling'	o-**b**úrək	'be/get swollen' J30 (1990)
bóes	'gun'	o-**b**óes	'be/get shot' FN100
báil	'article of clothing'	o-**b**áil	'be/get clothed' FN100
bəkáll	'action of driving'	o-**b**əkáll	'be/get driven' FN100
baloʔ-	'shoot'	o-**b**áləʔ	'been/gotten shoot' F216
basaʔ-	'count'	o-**b**ásəʔ	'been/gotten counted' F216
buŋut-	'curl'	o-**b**únt	'been/gotten curled' F216

    b.   Infixation

tábək	'patch'	t-**o**-bəkíy	'patched (3rd sg.)' F219
sebok-	'kick'	s-**o**-bəkíy	'kicked (3rd sg.)' F219
dobaʔ-	'halve'	d-**o**-bəʔíy	'halved (3rd sg.)' F219

As shown in (3), non-adjacent labials trigger dissimilation only of the infixed
verb marker. The prefixed verb marker stays the same.[5]

(3)   Non-local dissimilation

    a.   Prefixation

kekədéb	'short'	**mə-(ke)kədéb**	'be/get short' J116 (1975)
dub	'poison'	**mə-dúb**	'be/get poisoned/bombed' Jxxxi (1990)
sésəb	'fire'	**mə-sésəb**	'been/gotten burnt' F215
tábək	'patch'	**mə-tábək**	'been/gotten patched' F215
kimud-	'cut hair'	**mə-kímd**	'been cut (hair)' F215
ʔarom-	'taste'	**mə-ʔárəm**	'been tasted' F215

    b.   Infixation

rébət	'action of falling'	**r-u-ébət**	'fall (from)' F221
ʔárm	'suffering'	**ʔ-u-árəm**	'suffer' F221
sisəbáll	'entrance'	**s-ó-isəb**	'go into' FN101
sebok-	'kick'	**s-u-ébək**	'kicked (pl. 3rd person non-human)' F219
teʔib-	'pull out'	**t-u-éʔəb**	'pulled out (pl. 3rd person non-human)' F219
dalom-	'plant'	**d-u-áləm**	'planted (pl. 3rd person non-human)' F219

As shown in (4), only affixes dissimilate. There is no dissimilation in simple
roots.

(4)   No dissimilation in simple roots

máməd	'bedding given to visitors' FN102
máməs	'type of fish (silvery in color and larger than sardine)' J140 (1990)
báb	'area or space above' J4 (1990)
beáb	'rat' J7 (1990), FN102
mətáb	'dead fish in trap' J200 (1990)

In the examples above, there exists an asymmetry in dissimilation between
segmentally identical infixes and prefixes in cases of non-adjacent labial consonants in the root morpheme. Infixes dissimilate but identical prefixes do not. We
need to provide an explanation of why nonadjacent labials trigger dissimilation
only of the infixed verb marker. Under the standard view of infixation (Prince
and Smolensky 1993/2004), there should be no difference in the way identical
prefixes and infixes respond to OCP violations since neither is associated with
the root morpheme in the output. They should either both dissimilate or neither
should undergo dissimilation.[6]

One attempt to account for this asymmetry (Finer 1985) gives two separate
rules of dissimilation for prefixes and infixes. But since they are one and the
same affix it does not provide a uniform account.

I propose that this asymmetry between identical prefixes and infixes gives
evidence for their different morphological affiliation in the output. Specifically,

I propose that infixes are part of the output root morpheme and thus respond to root cooccurrence restrictions while prefixes are outside of the root domain and thus not subject to OCP_{ROOT}. Infixes become part of the root morpheme via a process of morpheme absorption, whereby the affix is incorporated into the root morpheme.[7]

3   The proposal: Morpheme absorption in Optimality Theory

In this section I show that feature cooccurrence restrictions provide evidence for the morphological structure of an infix and define morpheme absorption.

3.1   The argument

Palauan contributes to the body of evidence for similarity avoidance on place of articulation for labial consonants. Cross-linguistically, there are restrictions on place of articulation cooccurring within a certain domain (McCarthy 1986, Yip 1988, 1989). Some researchers argue for a cognitive basis for feature cooccurrence restrictions (Pierrehumbert 1993). The standard term is Obligatory Contour Principle or OCP.[8]

As shown in Section 2, adjacent labials trigger dissimilation of the infixed and prefixed verb marker. Non-adjacent labials trigger dissimilation only of the infixed verb marker. I propose that there exists a constraint against more than one labial consonant within the root domain, formulated as follows:

(5) $\text{OCP}_{\text{ROOT}}(\text{C-lab})$
      Avoid more than one labial consonant within the root domain.[9]

The importance of domain for OCP evaluation has been discussed in great detail in the works of McCarthy (1986, 1989), Mester and Ito (1986), and Yip (1988, 1989). In this article, the relevant domain is the root morpheme.

The asymmetry in the way infixes and prefixes respond to OCP_{ROOT} restrictions provides evidence for the content of the root morpheme in the output. I propose that infixes are part of the output root morpheme and thus respond to OCP restrictions while prefixes are not. Infixes become part of the output root morpheme via a process of morpheme absorption, illustrated below. In this paper, I will follow Horwood (2002, 2004) and assume that the affix is already infixed in the input by the morphosyntax.[10]

(6)   Morpheme absorption
      a. Absorption of infixes   b. No absorption of prefixes

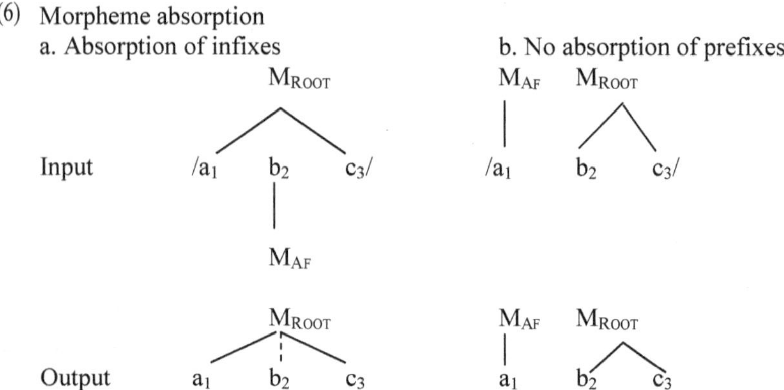

In the representation of infixes (6a), the input affix is incorporated into the root morpheme in the output. No such incorporation takes place for prefixes (6b).[11]

This interpretation is parallel to other proposals where morphological structure may be altered in the output, including tier conflation in autosegmental phonology and root-and-pattern morphology (McCarthy 1986, 1989, Yip 1989), bracket erasure in lexical phonology (Kiparsky 1982, Mohanan 1982), work on prefixes in Athabaskan and Bantu languages (Hargus 1987, Marlo 2004, Speas 1984), and morphological haplology (McCarthy and Prince 1995, de Lacy 1999). The idea that morphological or syntactic structure is retrievable from phonological evidence is also found in Selkirk (1984, 1995).

3.2   Morpheme absorption in OT

This section defines morpheme absorption in Optimality Theory (Prince and Smolensky 1993/2004, McCarthy and Prince 1993b). In OT the morphological structure of the input cannot be altered in the output, called 'Consistency of Exponence'. However, morpheme absorption argues that an input affix can be absorbed by the root morpheme in the output. In effect, the input morphological structure is reassigned in the output. See Walker and Feng (2004), McCarthy and Wolf (2005), Horwood (2002), and Legendre et al. (1998) for related proposals.

In the remainder of this section, I define the markedness constraint that compels morpheme absorption and the faithfulness constraint that militates against it.

3.2.1 Morpheme locality

Palauan gives phonological evidence that morpheme absorption is a property of the grammar. In Palauan, an input affix becomes part of the root morpheme in the output. Formally, there must be a constraint that compels morpheme absorption. I propose that it is a markedness constraint against discontinuous morphemes, called MORPHEME LOCALITY.

(7) MORPHEME LOCALITY (M-LOC)
  Let M_i be a morpheme and xyz be segments, where xyz∈Output,
  If xyz are adjacent and x & z∈M_i,
  then y∈M_i.
  Informally: No discontinuous morphemes.

This constraint rules out any segment that intervenes between segments of a morpheme and that is not itself part of the same morpheme. In terms of evaluation, a star is assigned for any segment that intervenes between segments of a morpheme that is not itself part of the same morpheme.

This constraint is similar to MORPHEME-OUTPUT-CONTIGUITY (Landman 2003) which requires that 'the portions of the output standing in correspondence and belonging to the same morpheme (in the output) form contiguous strings'. One difference is that MORPHEME-OUTPUT-CONTIGUITY is a faithfulness constraint (see Landman 2003) and defines contiguity with reference to the input. MORPHEME LOCALITY (see (7)), on the other hand, is a markedness constraint and defines contiguity with no reference to the input.[12]

It has been shown in the literature that contiguous domains play an essential role in a number of phonological and morphological processes. Contiguity has been used to account for morphologically-derived environment effects involving epenthesis and deletion (Landman 2003), morpheme structure conditions (Kenstowicz 1994, Spencer 1993), the relation between epenthesis, deletion, and syllabification (Alber 2001, Alber and Plag 2001, Lamontagne 1996), blocking of a phonological process (Baković 1994), base-reduplicant identity effects (McCarthy and Prince 1995), and the locality of reduplication (Hendricks 1999, Riggle 2004). This article extends contiguous domains to morpheme absorption.

3.2.2 Morpheme faithfulness

In addition to a constraint on morpheme locality, a constraint is needed to prevent morpheme absorption. If morpheme absorption were freely allowed, there would be no reference to morphological boundaries in the output (see Kiparsky 1982, McCarthy 1982). There would be no concept of distinct output morphemes, which is contrary to the evidence. As has been shown there exist processes that are restricted to apply only in morphologically derived environments. If morpheme boundaries were erased in the output, no such restrictions would be enforced in an output-oriented model of phonology.

I propose a faithfulness constraint on morpheme dependency which guarantees that input and output morpheme affiliation does not change. A segment cannot belong to different morphemes in the input and output (cf. McCarthy 2000a).[13]

(8) MORPHEME DEPENDENCY (M-DEP)
Let M_i be a morpheme and S_j be a phonological element in two related morpho-phonological representations,
M_1 and $S_1 \in$ Input,
M_2 and $S_2 \in$ Output,
$M_1 \, \Re \, M_2$, and
$S_1 \, \Re \, S_2$,
If $S_2 \in M_2$, then $S_1 \in M_1$.
Informally: Only a segment whose input correspondent belongs to the morpheme M_i belongs to the morpheme M_i in the output.

This constraint bans morpheme absorption. It is a faithfulness constraint that preserves morphological affiliation of non-epenthetic input and output segments. One star is assigned for any phonological element in the output morpheme whose input correspondent belongs to a different morpheme. MORPHEME DEPENDENCY is a violable constraint, which means that new morphological affiliation may be acquired. This is a significant departure from the assumption that morpheme information available in the input does not change in the output.

Constraints on morpheme faithfulness have already been proposed in the literature in the form of morpheme contiguity (see references in the previous section), morpheme identity (Walker and Feng 2004), M-PARSE constraints (McCarthy and Wolf 2005), constraints on morpheme linear order (Horwood 2002), and constraints on morpheme realization (Kurisu 2001, among others). See especially Walker and Feng (2004) on a model of morpho-phonological correspondence.

3.2.3 The typology

In Palauan infixes are absorbed by the root morpheme in the output but prefixes are not. This is when morpheme markedness (M-LOC) outranks morpheme faithfulness (M-DEP). Under this ranking, an infix becomes part of the root morpheme in the output. I will illustrate it with the word [lmátk] 'remembered, pl. 3rd non-hum' (shown in (1b)).

In the representation of the candidates, I will indicate separate morphemes by separate bracketing. For instance, a candidate with a single bracket [lmatk] indicates that there is a single morpheme in the output. A candidate with a nested structure [l[**m**]atk] indicates that there are two separate morphemes and one of them is contained within the other. A candidate with two sequential brackets indicates that there are two morphemes in a sequential order, [**mə**][dákt]. The original affix morpheme, including the epenthetic schwa, is in bold font.

(9)   Morpheme absorption for infixes: M-Loc >> M-Dep

/l-**m**-atk/	M-Loc	M-Dep
☞ a. [l**m**atk]		*
b. [l[**m**]atk]	*!	

Candidate (a) wins since it satisfies the markedness constraint on morpheme locality. The candidates in (9) are phonetically homophonous. Let us recall that the argument for positing different morphological structures comes from OCP-violations (see Section 3.1).

There is no absorption for prefixes since prefixes are outside of the root domain and vacuously satisfy Morpheme Locality.

(10)   No morpheme absorption for prefixes: M-Loc >> M-Dep

/**m**-dakt/	M-Loc	M-Dep
☞ a. [**mə**][dakt]		
b. [**mə**dakt]		*!

Candidate (b) loses since it incurs an unnecessary violation of faithfulness. There are no discontinuous morphemes and thus no reason to violate morpheme faithfulness.

There are various ways to satisfy Morpheme Locality. Two alternatives will be discussed in this article: morpheme absorption (Section 4) and morpheme reordering (Section 5). I will propose that reordering violates a constraint on precedence relations, called Linearity (see Section 5 for definition, also McCarthy and Prince 1995, Horwood 2002). There are also cases where infixes are not absorbed. This is when faithfulness constraints outrank the constraint against discontinuous morphemes. The following table shows the typology of alternations induced by Morpheme Locality. The constraint $\mathbb{C}$ in (11c–d) blocks the unmarked repair.

(11) M-Loc-driven alternations

Ranking	Result
a. M-Loc, Linearity >> M-Dep	Morpheme absorption
b. M-Loc, M-Dep >> Linearity	Morpheme reordering
c. C, M-Loc >> Linearity >> M-Dep d. C, M-Loc >> M-Dep >> Linearity	Two repairs: absorption unless blocked by C Two repairs: reordering unless blocked by C
e. M-Dep, Linearity >> M-Loc	Faithful: no morpheme absorption or reordering

As will be shown in the next section, Palauan follows the constraint ranking in (a). In Palauan, due to morpheme absorption, infixes dissimilate when there is another labial in the root domain. Prefixes resist dissimilation. In Akkadian, as will be shown in Section 5, the ranking in (c) holds. An infix becomes a prefix to avoid morpheme absorption and consequential OCP violation.[14]

4   Application to Palauan

In this section I show how the proposal works for Palauan.

4.1   Overview of the analysis

As we saw in Section 2, in Palauan, the verb marker [-m-] is either infixed or prefixed to the verb stem depending on the class of verbs. The verb marker alternates between [mə], [m], [o] and [u]. Following Flora (1974b), I assume that the schwa vowel is epenthetic (cf. Finer 1985). The vowel alternants of the verb marker are a result of labial dissimilation (Flora 1974b). Both prefixes and infixes dissimilate when the labial is adjacent to the verb marker. But when there is a non-adjacent labial consonant anywhere in the stem, the infixed verb marker dissimilates but the prefixed verb marker does not undergo dissimilation. Below, I repeat the data on non-local dissimilation.[15]

(12) Non-adjacent labial dissimilation in infixes (cf. (3b))

rébət	'action of falling'	r-**u**-ébət	'fall (from)' F221
ʔárm	'suffering'	ʔ-**u**-árəm	'suffer' F221
sebok-	'kick'	s-**u**-ébək	'kicked (pl. 3rd person non-human)' F219
dalom-	'plant'	d-**u**-áləm	'planted (pl. 3rd person non-human)' F219

(13) No non-adjacent labial dissimilation in prefixes (cf. (3a))

dub	'poison'	**mə**-dúb	'be/get poisoned/bombed' Jxxxi (1990)
sésəb	'fire'	**mə**-sésəb	'been/gotten burnt' F215
tábək	'patch'	**mə**-tábək	'been/gotten patched' F215
kimud-	'cut hair'	**mə**-kímd	'been cut (hair)' F215

The infixed verb marker in (12) dissimilates to a rounded vowel. The prefixed verb marker resists dissimilation. In the rest of this section I will account for this asymmetry.

Following Finer (1985), I propose that dissimilation in this case is the result of avoidance of more than one labial consonant in the root domain.

(14) OCP_{ROOT}(C-lab)
Avoid more than one labial consonant within the root domain.

The argument for OCP to be (C-lab) rather than (labial) is because dissimilation is not triggered by rounded vowels. When there is a rounded vowel in the word, the infix remains a bilabial nasal.[16] Dissimilation is a repair for OCP violations. Due to dissimilation, the infix loses its consonantal place of articulation and becomes a rounded vowel.

Furthermore, I propose that OCP_{ROOT}(C-lab) is satisfied vacuously when [mə] is a prefix, since the prefix is a separate morpheme from the root morpheme in the output. Identical infixes, on the other hand, are subject to OCP_{ROOT}(C-lab) since they are part of the root morpheme in the output. They become part of the output root morpheme via a process of morpheme absorption.

(15) The proposal
   a. Infixation

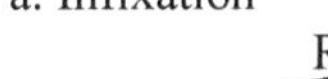
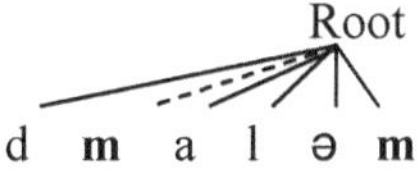

   b. Prefixation

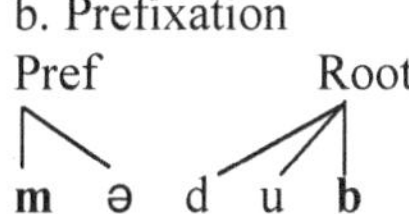

For dissimilation to occur, OCP outranks faithfulness to consonantal place of articulation.

(16) Dissimilation takes place

OCP_{ROOT}(C-lab) >> IDENT(place)

4.2   Root and affix faithfulness

There is one more fact we need to take into account before showing the full analysis. As was shown in Section 2, dissimilation in Palauan takes place only under affixation. Underlying root segments do not dissimilate. This is reviewed below.

(17) No dissimilation of underlying root segments (cf. (5))

máməs   'type of fish (silvery in color and larger than sardine)' J140 (1990)
beáb   'rat' J7 (1990), FN102
mətáb   'dead fish in trap' J200 (1990)

The difference between (12) and (17) is in the morphological affiliation of the relevant segment in the input. The absorbed infix, as in (12), is an input affix whereas the root segments, as in (17), belong to the root in the input. Following McCarthy and Prince (1995), Beckman (1998), and Smith (1997), I propose there are separate faithfulness constraints for roots versus affixes and root faithfulness outranks affix faithfulness. Unlike McCarthy and Prince (1995), I define the domain of the constraints in the input rather than the output. I will refer to them as I-IDENT.[17]

(18) I-IDENT$_{ROOT}$(F)

An input segment in a root morpheme and its output correspondent must have identical feature specifications.

(19) I-IDENT$_{AFFIX}$(F)

An input segment in an affix morpheme and its output correspondent must have identical feature specifications.

The following ranking accounts for the difference between affix and root segments in their response to OCP restrictions.

(20) ROOT over AFFIX faith (McCarthy and Prince 1995)

I-IDENT$_{ROOT}$(place) >> OCP$_{ROOT}$(C-labial) >> I-IDENT$_{AFFIX}$(place)

Given this ranking, it is more important to retain the identity of input root segments than it is to satisfy OCP. The opposite is true of input affix identity. This analysis not only explains why roots can violate OCP but also determines which segment is affected in dissimilation.[18]

4.3   The analysis

The formal analysis is represented in the following tableaux. Let us first consider dissimilation of the infix. The following tableau shows three candidates, two with dissimilation and one with no dissimilation.

(21) Dissimilation of the infix

/d-m-alom/	I-IDENT$_{ROOT}$(place)	OCP$_{ROOT}$(C-labial)	I-IDENT$_{AFFIX}$(place)
☞ a. [duáləm]			*
b. [dmáləm]		*!	
c. [dmáləu]	*!		

In all candidates the infix is absorbed by the root morpheme in the output. The candidate where the infix dissimilates, candidate (a), wins. It satisfies OCP at the cost of affix identity. The competing candidate, candidate (b), incurs a fatal violation of OCP. Candidate (c), where the root labial dissimilates is ruled out by I-IDENT$_{ROOT}$(place).

Let us now consider prefixes. The tableau below shows two candidates, one with dissimilation, and the other remaining faithful to the input. Neither undergoes absorption.

(22) No dissimilation of the prefix

/m-dub/	I-IDENT$_{ROOT}$(place)	OCP$_{ROOT}$(C-labial)	I-IDENT$_{AFFIX}$(place)
a.　[o][dúb]			*!
☞　b.　[mə][dúb]			

The candidate with no dissimilation, candidate (b), wins. The competing candidate, candidate (a), incurs an unmotivated violation of faithfulness.

Finally, underlying root segments are allowed to violate OCP. This is explained by high-ranking root faithfulness. The following tableau shows a candidate with dissimilation, candidate (a), and one without dissimilation, candidate (b).

(23) No dissimilation of the root

/mames/	I-IDENT$_{ROOT}$(place)	OCP$_{ROOT}$(C-labial)	I-IDENT$_{AFFIX}$(place)
a.　[mauəs]	*!		
☞　b.　[maməs]		*	

The candidate with dissimilation, candidate (a), violates I-IDENT$_{ROOT}$ and thus is eliminated.

Another obvious alternative to dissimilation would be to re-order the morphemes in the output so that the infix becomes a prefix and is outside the root domain. This alternative and its analysis are discussed in detail in the next section. As shown in the next section, morpheme re-ordering incurs a violation of LINEARITY. In Palauan, I propose that LINEARITY is ranked above affix identity (I-IDENT$_{AFFIX}$(place)), and thus re-ordering does not take place.

In addition, the infix could resist absorption, satisfy OCP and thus avoid dissimilation. To rule this out, I assume that the constraint against discontinuous morphemes, M-LOC, outranks I-IDENT$_{AFFIX}$(place), so that it is more important to avoid discontinuous morphemes than to avoid dissimilation. It is also crucial that the faithfulness constraint against absorption, M-DEP, be ranked below M-LOC and LINEARITY so that discontinuous morphemes are avoided through absorption (see Section 3).

The following constraint ranking has been established in this section. This is followed by summary tableaux.

(24) Constraint ranking

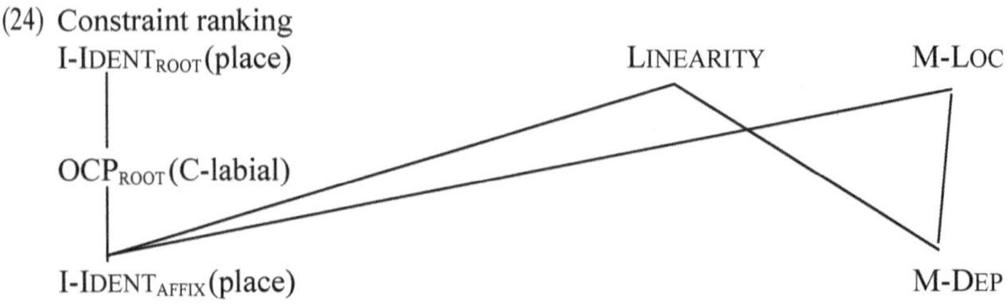

(25) Summary tableaux[19]

I: /[d-m-alom]/	I-Id$_{Rt}$(pl)	OCP$_{Rt}$(C-lab)	Linearity	MLoc	I-Id$_{Af}$(pl)	MDep
☞ a. [duáləm]					*	*
b. [dmáləm]		*!				*
c. [mə][daləm]			*!			
d. [d[m]áləm]				*!		
II: /m-dub/	I-Id$_{Rt}$(pl)	OCP$_{Rt}$(C-lab)	Linearity	MLoc	I-Id$_{Af}$(pl)	MDep
a. [o][dúb]					*!	
☞ b. [mə][dúb]						
c. [mədúb]						*!
III: /mames/	I-Id$_{Rt}$(pl)	OCP$_{Rt}$(C-lab)	Linearity	MLoc	I-Id$_{Af}$(pl)	MDep
a. [mauəs]	*!					
☞ b. [maməs]		*				
IV: /l-m-atk/	I-Id$_{Rt}$(pl)	OCP$_{Rt}$(C-lab)	Linearity	MLoc	I-Id$_{Af}$(pl)	MDep
☞ a. [lmatk]						*
b. [l[m]atk]				*!		
c. [mə][lakt]			*!			

As shown in the above tableaux, infixes are absorbed by the root morpheme in the output (tableaux I and IV) but prefixes are not absorbed (tableau II). When there is an OCP violation as a result of absorption, the infix dissimilates (tableau I). Underlying roots do not dissimilate (tableau III). This explains why infixes in Palauan undergo dissimilation but identical prefixes do not. The infix is part of the output root morpheme and thus needs to dissimilate to satisfy OCP. The prefix is outside of the root domain and thus not subject to OCP. This also accounts for the fact that underlying root segments do not dissimilate.

5   Metathesis in Akkadian

In this section I argue that morpheme absorption and feature cooccurrence restrictions explain why the [-ta-] infix in Akkadian sometimes becomes a prefix.

5.1   The data

Akkadian is a northeastern Semitic language spoken in the area of modern Iraq from 2500 B.C. until 1 A.D. In Akkadian, there is a process of [-ta-] infixation (Barthélemy 1998, Beesley and Karttunen 2000, Caldwell et al. 1977, Huehnergard 1997, McCarthy 1979a, 1981, 1986, 1993, Reiner 1966, Streck 2003, Von Soden 1952). The [-ta-] infix marks (i) perfect tense (see (26a)), and verb stem modifications (see (26b) and (26c)). In each case, I give the infinitive followed by the verb form with the [-ta-] infix. The [-ta-] infix is often realized as [-t-] due to vowel deletion (see McCarthy 1986). For the ease of presentation, I will underline the stem.[20]

(26) Infixation (Caldwell et al. 1977, Huehnergard 1997, Von Soden 1952)

a. Perfect tense

Infinitive		Infixed Form	
<u>šakān</u>-um	'to settle'	i-<u>š-**ta**-kan</u>	'he has settled' H155
<u>kanāš</u>-um	'to subject'	i-<u>k-**ta**-nuš</u>	'he has subjected' C78
<u>šarāq</u>-um	'to steal'	i-<u>š-**ta**-riq</u>	'he has stolen' H155
<u>maqāt</u>-um	'to fall'	i-<u>m-**ta**-qut</u>	'he has fallen' H155
<u>qerēb</u>-um	'to draw near'	i-<u>q-**te**-rib</u>	'he has drawn near' C78

b. Gt-stem

<u>magār</u>-um	'to agree'	<u>mi-**t**-gur</u>-um	'to agree with one another' H393
<u>mahār</u>-um	'to face'	<u>mi-**t**-ḫur</u>-um	'to face one another' H393
<u>maḫāS</u>-um	'to strike/hit'	<u>mi-**t**-ḫūS</u>-um	'to fight with one another' C117
<u>rakāb</u>-um	'to mate'	<u>ri-**t**-kub</u>-um	'to lie upon one another' H393
<u>akāl</u>-um	'to eat'	<u>a-**t**-kul</u>-um	'to devour one another' C116
<u>alāk</u>-um	'to go'	<u>a-**t**-luk</u>-um	'to go forever' C116

c. Gtn-stem

<u>apāl</u>-um	'to answer'	<u>a-**ta**-ppul</u>-um	'to answer, pay repeatedly' H412
<u>babāl</u>-um	'to carry'	<u>i-**ta**-bbul</u>-um	'to carry repeatedly' H412
<u>maqāt</u>-um	'to fall'	<u>mi-**ta**-qqut</u>-um	'to fall again and again' H411
<u>alāk</u>-um	'to walk about'	<u>a-**ta**-lluk</u>-um	'to be in motion, walk about' H411
<u>palāḫ</u>-um	'to fear'	i-<u>p-**ta**-llaḫ</u>	'he lived in constant fear' C138

As shown in (27), when the root initial consonant (first radical) is a coronal obstruent (d, T, s, S, z, but not š), [-ta-] surfaces as a prefix rather than an infix. Prefixation in Akkadian is considered to involve metathesis (McCarthy 1979a). The process of metathesis takes place in non-prefixed forms of Gt, Dt, Gtn, and Dtn stems, which are infinitive, imperative and verbal adjectives.[21]

(27) Metathesis

Infinitive		*Actual*	*Expected*	
Sabāt-um	'to quarrel'	t-iSbut-um	*Si-t-but-um	'to touch one another' C118
saqār-um	'to speak'	t-isqar-ī	*si-t-qar-ī	'pronounce forever!' V124
zakār-um	'to speak'	t-izkur-um	*zi-t-kur-um	'to speak' H530
dakāš-um	'to swell'	t-idkuš-at	*di-t-kuš-at	'is swollen' C118

As shown in (28), when [-ta-] and the root initial coronal consonant (d, T, s, S, z) are strictly adjacent, [-ta-] remains an infix and the consonant of the infix assimilates to the first root consonant. This takes place in prefixed forms of Gt, Dt, Gtn and Dtn stems which include durative, perfect, preterite, and participle, as well as in perfect tense of the G stem.[22]

(28) Total assimilation

Infinitive		*Actual*	*Expected*	
damāq-um	'to improve'	i-d-**da**-miq	*i-d-**ta**-miq	'he has improved' H155
Tarād-um	'to send'	i-T-**Ta**-rad	*i-T-**ta**-rad	'he has sent' H155
sahāp-um	'to cover'	i-s-**sa**-hap	*i-s-**ta**-hap	'he has covered' H155
Sabāt-um	'to seize'	i-S-**Sa**-bat	*i-S-**ta**-bat	'he has seized' H155
zak-ûm	'to be clean'	i-z-**za**-k-um	*i-z-**ta**-k-um	'he has cleared' H155

The infix [-ta-] is located after the first CV of the innermost stem. The stem includes derivational but not inflectional prefixes. Multiple infixation is possible. Affixation in Akkadian is analyzed in McCarthy (1993) as negative prosodic circumscription of the initial mora. Similar to Palauan, I will assume the [-ta-] affix is already infixed in the input in the actual position by the morphosyntax of the language.

In the rest of this section, I will show that metathesis in Akkadian is a result of dissimilation. An infix becomes a prefix to avoid morpheme absorption and consequential OCP violation. The argument is parallel to the Palauan case presented in the previous section. I will also explain why total assimilation takes place.

5.2   The analysis

Semitic roots avoid adjacent homorganic consonants (Greenberg 1950, Frisch et al. 2004, Frisch and Zawaydeh 2001, McCarthy 1986, 1988, 1994). One class of such consonants are coronal obstruents. I formulate this restriction as an OCP constraint against adjacent coronal obstruents in the root domain.

(29) OCP_{ROOT}(cor-obs)
       Avoid adjacent coronal obstruents within the root domain.[23]

The proposal here is that infixes are absorbed by the root morpheme in the output, so infixes and roots form one domain for OCP evaluation. Prefixes, on the other hand, are outside of the root domain so prefixes and roots form two separate domains for OCP evaluation. OCP is violated when [-ta-] is an infix but satisfied when [-ta-] is a prefix. I propose that, in order to satisfy OCP within the root domain, prefixation takes place. This is shown below. The relevant affix and the coronal obstruent in the root are in bold font.[24]

(30) The proposal
       a. Infixation

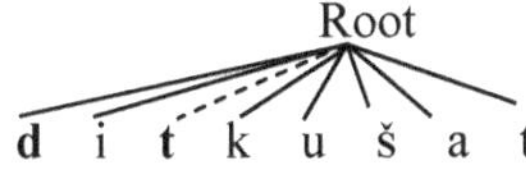

       b. Prefixation

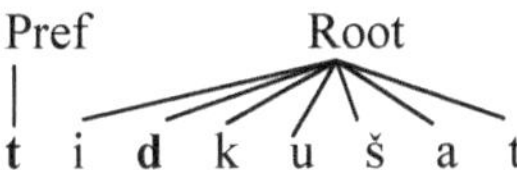

Since infixes are contained in the root domain, infixed [-ta-], as in di-t-kušat (30a) violates OCP. Prefixed [ta-], as in t-idkušat (30b), satisfies OCP because prefixes are outside of the root domain. As in the section on Palauan, I will represent separate morphemes with separate bracketing.

For prefixation to occur, OCP must outrank a faithfulness constraint that militates against metathesis, called LINEARITY (McCarthy and Prince 1995, Horwood 2002). I assume that morphemes have linear relations in the input and, when the input infix becomes a prefix in the output, it incurs a violation of LINEARITY.[25]

(31) LINEARITY ('No Metathesis')
       S_1 is consistent with the precedence structure of S_2, and vice versa.
       If x, y ∈ S_1; x', y' ∈ S_2; x𝕽x' and y𝕽y'; then x < y iff x' < y'.

The ranking is given below followed by the relevant tableau.

(32) OCP_{ROOT}(cor-obs) >> LINEARITY

(33) Prefixation takes place

/Si-**ta**-butum]/	OCP_{ROOT}(cor-obs)	LINEARITY
a. [Sitbutum]	*!	
☞ b. [t][iSbutum]		*

Candidate (a) violates OCP since the infix is absorbed by the root morpheme and there is another coronal obstruent in the root domain. Candidate (b) wins since it satisfies OCP. The prefix is outside of the root domain.

Similar cases are discussed in Yip (1998). Yip argues that extraposition in Classical Greek and Hindi takes place to avoid OCP violation. A constituent moves out of its original domain. Other similar cases include resolution of stress clash (Hayes 1995) and tone flop (Clements and Ford 1979).

5.3   Assimilation

There is another way in which OCP violations are repaired in Akkadian. When the [ta-] infix and the coronal obstruent are adjacent, total assimilation takes place. The consonant in the infix assimilates in voicing, emphasis and stridency to the adjacent root obstruent. I will assume that total assimilation violates a faithfulness constraint against coalescence, called UNIFORMITY (McCarthy and Prince 1995).

(34) UNIFORMITY ('No Coalescence')
      No element of S_2 has multiple correspondents in S_1.

Since Akkadian shows both metathesis and total assimilation as repairs of OCP, we need to account for how the choice is made between them. I propose that it is better to assimilate than to metathesize, but assimilation is not always an option, and that is when metathesis takes place. To capture this idea I propose the following ranking:

(35) LINEARITY >> UNIFORMITY

This is illustrated in the following tableau.

(36) Total assimilation is favored over prefixation

/i-z_1-t_2a-kum/	LINEARITY	UNIFORMITY
☞ a. [iz$_{12}$ akum]		*
b. [t$_2$][iz$_1$akum]	*!	

Candidate (b) loses since it violates Linearity, the constraint against metathesis.

But total assimilation is not always an option. Here, I follow Gafos (1998, 1999) and assume that articulatory locality is a necessary condition for phonological assimilation. In CVC sequences the two consonantal gestures are not contiguous and thus, no Consonant-to-Consonant spreading takes place over a vowel. I call this constraint Articulatory Locality, A-Loc.[26]

(37) Articulatory Locality (A-Loc)
   No C-to-C spreading across a vowel.

A-Loc compels violation of Linearity. That is, when assimilation is not an option, metathesis takes place.

(38) A-Loc >> Linearity

(39) Prefixation takes place when total assimilation is not an option

/S_1i-t_2a-butum/	A-Loc	Linearity
☞ a. [t_2][iS_1butum]		*
b. [S_1iS_2butum]	*!	

Candidate (b) loses since it violates locality.

Unlike in Palauan, in Akkadian the infix does not dissimilate to avoid OCP violation (/Si-ta-but/→*Sinbut). In terms of constraints, I propose that feature identity, Ident(sonorant), outranks Linearity so that it is more harmonic to re-order the morphemes than it is to dissimilate.

Finally, the infix could simply resist absorption, satisfy OCP and thus, avoid movement. To rule this out, I propose that the constraint against discontinuous morphemes, M-Loc, outranks Linearity. According to this ranking, it is more important to avoid a discontinuous morpheme than to avoid movement. Since not all infixes undergo metathesis, Linearity must outrank M-Dep. It is better to absorb the morpheme than to metathesize. But absorption is not an option when it would necessitate dissimilation.

The following constraint ranking has been established in this section. This is followed by summary tableaux.

(40) Constraint ranking

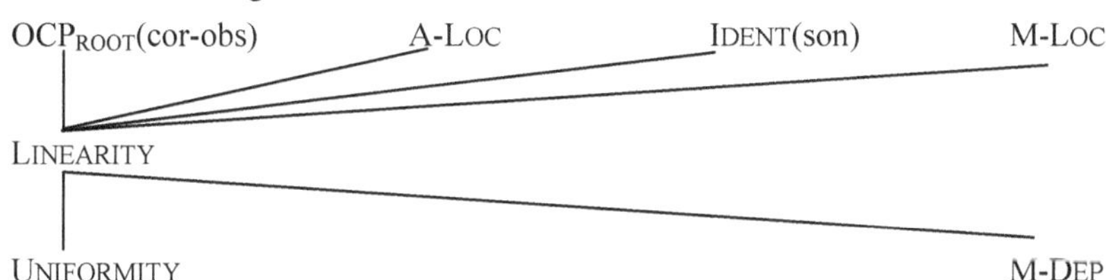

(41) Summary tableaux

I: /Si-ta-butum/	OCP$_{RT}$	ALOC	ID(son)	MLOC	LINEARITY	UNIFORMITY	MDEP
a. [Sitbutum]	*!						*
☞ b. [t][iSbutum]					*		
c. [SiSbutum]		*!				*	*
d. [Sinbutum]			*!				*
e. [Si[t]butum]				*!			
II: /i-z-ta-kum/	OCP$_{RT}$	ALOC	ID(son)	MLOC	LINEARITY	UNIFORMITY	MDEP
a. [iztakum]	*!						*
b. [t][izakum]					*!		
☞ c. [izzakum]						*	*
d. [iznakum]			*!				*
e. [iz[ta]kum]				*!			
III: /i-š-ta-kan/	OCP$_{RT}$	ALOC	ID(son)	MLOC	LINEARITY	UNIFORMITY	MDEP
a. [iš[ta]kan]				*!			
b. [t][išakan]					*!		
☞ c. [ištakan]							*

As shown in the above tableaux, infixes metathesize in order to avoid morpheme absorption and consequential OCP violation (tableau I). When the infix and the coronal obstruent are adjacent, the consonant in the infix assimilates to the obstruent (tableau II). When OCP is satisfied, infixes are absorbed by the root morpheme in the output (tableau III). In summary, to avoid adjacent coronal obstruents within the root domain, either total assimilation takes place, or [-ta-] becomes a prefix. Prefixation takes place when total assimilation is not an option. This analysis gives further evidence for the different morphological affiliation of identical prefixes and infixes.

6   Conclusion

In this article, I have analyzed data from Palauan and Akkadian where identical infixes and prefixes respond differently to feature cooccurrence restrictions on the root domain. In Palauan, infixes dissimilate while identical prefixes do not. In Akkadian, an infix becomes a prefix. From this analysis the following typology has emerged:

(42) OCP-driven alternations
Palauan: OCP-ROOT, LINEARITY >> IDENT   Dissimilation   Section 4
Akkadian: OCP-ROOT, IDENT >> LINEARITY   Metathesis   Section 5

To explain the asymmetry between identical infixes and prefixes, I have argued that infixes are part of the output root morpheme and thus respond to OCP while prefixes are outside of the root domain and thus not subject to OCP. In this proposal, infixes become part of the resulting root morpheme via a process of morpheme absorption.

I have also developed an OT analysis of morpheme absorption. A markedness constraint against discontinuous morphemes, MORPHEME LOCALITY, interacts with a morphological faithfulness constraint, MORPHEME DEPENDENCY. Morpheme absorption takes place when the markedness constraint outranks the faithfulness constraint, thus compelling a single morphological affiliation of contiguous segments in the output.

This work builds on research begun by others, where a certain amount of information about morphology is retrievable from the phonology (see references in Section 3). In this article, similarity avoidance gives evidence for the morphological structure of an infix. It also contributes to the line of research whereby morphological structure can be altered in the output.

Notes

1   I am grateful to John McCarthy for bringing this topic to my attention. Thanks also to Brett Borchardt, Maria Gouskova, Shigeto Kawahara, Nicole Nelson, Steve Parker, and Rachel Walker for insightful comments. I would also like to thank the participants of GLOW 29 and of a colloquium at UC Santa Cruz, especially Junko Ito, Joan Mascaró, Armin Mester, Jaye Padgett, and Marc van Oostendorp.

2   Alderete (1997), Baković (2006b), Boersma (2000), Frisch (1996), Frisch et al. (2004), Fukazawa (1999), Goldsmith (1976), Gouskova (2004), Hayes (1995), Hewitt and Prince (1989), Ito and Mester (1998), Keer (1999), Leben (1973), MacEachern (1999), McCarthy (1981, 1986, 1988, 1989), Myers (1987, 1997), Odden (1988, 1994), Pierrehumbert (1993), Rose (2000), Rose and Walker (2004), Suzuki (1998), Yip (1988, 1989, 1995a, 1998).

3   The verb marker is a prefix in stative intransitive verbs and in active transitive verbs in the imperfective and middle aspects. It is an infix in active transitive verbs in the perfective aspect and in a class of active intransitive verbs. As reported by Flora (1974b), similar affixes are found across other Polynesian languages, such as Timugon Murut, Yami and Tagalog (see McCarthy and Prince 1995, Crowhurst 1998, 2001).

4   See Flora (1974a) for the generalization.

5   Flora (1974a,b) adopts the practice of marking the dissimilated [u] verb marker
    as a glide [w].

6   When the infix follows a stem initial labial, in many cases the infix becomes
    a prefix (e.g., báis→o-máis 'wander, walk around' J5, bákəs→o-mákəs 'walk,
    take a step' J5), or coalesces with the stem initial consonant (e.g., bíkəl→ míkəl
    'raise' J258, bitəkíll→ mítəʔ 'capsize' J259). There are also a small number of
    words where the verb marker is realized as [o] but the initial consonant is other
    than a labial, which I will treat as exceptions (Finer 1985).

7   The asymmetry between infixes and prefixes is not a function of distance from
    the labial consonant (see (3)). Thus, I argue it is a function of the content of
    the root morpheme. Additional evidence for the infix+root unit comes from
    Ce- reduplication where the verb marker infix remains in the base under redu-
    plication rather than surfacing as a prefix. In comparison, a verb marker prefix
    appears external to reduplication (see Finer 1985, pp. 115–16, 129).

8   See Section 1 for references. Alderete (1997), Ito and Mester (1998), and
    MacEachern (1999) formulate OCP as self-conjunction of markedness con-
    straints. Pierrehumbert (1993) replaces OCP with *REPEAT.

9   Labial cooccurrence restrictions are also found in Cantonese language games
    (Yip 1989), Akkadian affixes (McCarthy 1986), and Tagalog (McCarthy 2003c).

10 An alternative is to propose alignment constraints that refer to specific mor-
    phemes and via ranking result in the infixed output pattern (see McCarthy and
    Prince 1993a). See Horwood (2002) for arguments in favor of morpheme order-
    ing by the morphosyntax over parochial alignment.

11 Though the input affix morpheme is not realized as such in the output, its con-
    tent is realized as part of the output root morpheme. I follow Kurisu (2001) and
    assume that this does not violate MORPHEME REALIZATION.

12 For the purposes of the argument in this paper, either constraint would work.
    The differences emerge when we allow epenthetic segments to be absorbed by
    the output morpheme. While MORPHEME LOCALITY prohibits any discontinuous
    morphemes, MORPHEME-OUTPUT-CONTIGUITY only limits contiguity of segments
    standing in correspondence. MORPHEME-OUTPUT-CONTIGUITY also disallows
    internal epenthesis even if epenthetic segments are absorbed by the output
    morpheme, while MORPHEME LOCALITY allows such structures. This study opens
    avenues for future research, including the study of the morphological affiliation
    of epenthetic segments, the results of morpheme alternations other than absorp-
    tion (i.e., splitting or coalescence), among others. Thanks to Maria Gouskova for
    a discussion of this point.

13 This constraint is vacuously satisfied by epenthetic segments. Further research
    may require this constraint to be extended to epenthetic segments. If this would
    be the case, the constraint would be formulated as: $\forall y$ such that $y \in$ Output, $y \in M_i$
    only when $\exists x$ s.t. $x \in$ Input, $x \Re y$ and $x \in M_i$.

14   The relevance of prosodic, morphological and syntactic structure on similarity avoidance has been discussed by Frisch et al. (2004), Yip (1989, 1998), McCarthy (1986). Yip (1998) shows that in Hindi OCP is only active in the same phonological phrase. McCarthy (1986) shows that OCP(labial) in Akkadian affects prefixes but not suffixes.

15   It is common for dissimilation to be stronger or more necessary, the closer together two segments are to each other in a phonological string. See Frisch et al. (2004), Hyman and Mchombo (1992), Odden (1994), Pierrehumbert (1993), and Suzuki (1998).

16   The same distinction between rounded consonants and vowels exists in Akkadian labial dissimilation (McCarthy 1986) (but see Cantonese, Yip 1989).

17   It is only possible to define the domain for a constraint in the input when the domain is contrastive in the input. McCarthy (2000a) uses this type of formulation when proposing symmetric Anchoring constraints from input to output and from output to input to account for prosodic circumscription. Gouskova (2004) uses root faithfulness in a similar way to account for syllable contact phenomena.

18   Another way to account for this is to use comparative markedness (McCarthy 2003a) by distinguishing old and new OCP_{ROOT} constraints. The idea would be that only new OCP_{ROOT} violations are resolved but old OCP_{ROOT} violations are not changed ($OCP_{ROOT\text{-}NEW}$>>IDENT(place)>>$OCP_{ROOT\text{-}OLD}$). This requires defining old and new OCP violations and their domains. I do not pursue this alternative here. The comparative markedness analysis would not be able to determine without additional constraints why it is the affix that dissimilates.

19   The optimal candidate in (25 (II)) also incurs a violation of DEP-V since it involves schwa insertion. I assume that schwa insertion takes place for phonotactic reasons.

20   There are four basic stems in Akkadian (G, D, Š, and N). Each can be modified with the [-ta-] infix. The modified stems are referred to as Gt, Dt, and Št stems (commonly, Xt-stems). If a further modification occurs, we obtain Gtn, Dtn, Ntn and Štn stems (commonly, Xtn-stems). The meaning of Xt-stems is passive, reciprocal, reflexive, causative, and separative (see (26b)), and of Xtn-stems iterative, distributive and augmentative (see (26c)). In the presentation of the data, vowels with a diacritic indicate a long vowel, symbols T and S stand for emphatic consonants, ḫ with a hook is compared to the pronunciation of *ch* in German 'ach' or Scottish 'loch' (H2). In addition to the [-ta-] affix, we can distinguish three additional morphemes: [-um] case ending suffix, [i-] third person singular prefix, and [-ī] feminine singular ending in the imperative.

21   Recent work on metathesis includes Blevins and Garrett (2004), Hume (2001, 2004b), McCarthy (2000b).

22   Other assimilations involving the [-ta-] infix include (i) regressive total assimilation when the infix is immediately followed by {d, T, s, S, z, š} (ḫi-s-sas instead

of *ḥ̬i-*t*-sas 'consider! (ms)' H391), (ii) voicing assimilation after the first radical g (i-g-**da**-mar instead of *i-g-**ta**-mar 'he has finished' H156), and (iii) nasal and glide assimilation where the initial radical n and w assimilate to [t] (i-**t-ta**-din instead of *i-**n-ta**-din 'he has delivered' C79, i-**t-ta**-bal instead of *i-**w-ta**-bal 'he has carried away' C79). The nasal and glide delete in word-initial position.

23   The definition of OCP here is similar to Rose (2000) and McCarthy (1986) – intervening vowels do not count for the purposes of the OCP, but consonants do. Other OCP(coronal) restrictions are attested in Berber, Chumash, and English, among others (Baković 2006b, Yip 1989).

24   For representation of Semitic roots, see Gafos (1998), Graf (2004), Ussishkin (1999) or McCarthy (1986), Prunet et al. (2000) for an alternate view.

25   See Horwood (2002), McCarthy (1989), and McCarthy (2003c) on the linear order of morphemes. In the following tableaux, I will assign a single violation to Linearity whenever an infix becomes a prefix. See Horwood (2002) on how to count violations of Linearity.

26   See also Gafos and Lombardi (1999), Ní Chiosáin and Padgett (2001), and Walker (2000b). Gafos and Lombardi (1999) show that some consonantal gestures can propagate over a vowel, as long as they do not conflict with the articulation of the intervening vowel. See also Walker (2000a,c), and Rose and Walker (2004) for non local C-to-C assimilation as copying.

11 Vowel length in Arabic verb stems[1]

Sam Rosenthall

The long vowels in Classical Arabic verb stems that are concomitant with glide deletion can be characterized as cases of compensatory lengthening. Glide deletion, however, does not always result in a long vowel. This paper proposes that cases of short vowels resulting from glide deletion are the consequence of constraint conflict defined by Optimality Theory. The distribution of long vowels in verb stems involves constraints on the verb stem conflicting with syllable markedness and faithfulness constraints. This paper argues for a triconsonantal analysis of all verb roots containing glides, contra Gafos (2003). This paper also argues for a prosodic analysis of verb stems, in accordance with the Prosodic Morphology Hypothesis. The prosodic organization, however, is obscured by conflict with higher ranking constraints.

1   Introduction

The phonology of Arabic weak verbs, i.e., those containing a glide as one of the radicals, includes deletion of the glide and lengthening of the vowel.[2] The combination of glide deletion and vowel lengthening is a typical example of compensatory lengthening (see Hayes 1989a) evident in a rule-based, derivational approach to Arabic phonology where the intermediate stage of the derivation of the stem is equal to the CVCVC shape of the strong verb (see Brame (1970), Angoujard (1990), Bohas (1980, 1997), and Thiry (1989)). This is exemplified with deletion of the medial and final glides of perfective stems in (1). The strong verb √ktb is included for comparison.[3] All data are from Mahadin (1982).

(1) a.   √zyd → zayada → za:da   'increase 3masc. sing.'
           √qwl → qawala → qa:la   'say 3masc. sing.'

      b.   √rmy → ramaya → rama: 'throw 3masc. sing.'
           √dʕw → daʕawa → daʕa: 'call 3masc. sing.'

      cf. √ktb → kataba → kataba 'write 3masc. sing.'

The long surface vowels in (1) are the result of preserving the mora count of the intermediate stage, as expected by compensatory lengthening.

Compensatory lengthening, however, is not a consistent outcome of glide deletion in Arabic. Blind stems, i.e., stems with a glide as the initial radical, have various forms. For these stems, the glide deletes without concomitant vowel lengthening, (2a), or the glide surfaces as part of a diphthong, (2b). This alternation occurs in active imperfective stems, exemplified with subjunctive forms. The absence of a long surface vowel in the active stem is even more puzzling when compared to the passive stem, which contains a long vowel.

(2)   active   passive

a. √wjd yajida   yu:jada 'find 3masc. sing. subj.'

b. √wjl yawjala   n/a   'be afraid 3masc. sing. subj.'

The presence of the long vowel in [yu:jada] is expected from an intermediate form that would contain the glide, *yuwjada*. The glide, as part of a diphthong, would be moraic and its mora would be preserved after deletion of the glide. Following the same derivational steps, the short vowel in the active is not an expected outcome of glide deletion.

More cases of deviation from the compensatory lengthening pattern are found with other weak verb stems. Hollow verbs, those with a glide as the medial radical, surface with short vowels in the jussive, but with long vowels in other imperfective forms. Similarly, lame verbs, those with a glide as the final radical, also have short vowels in the jussive, shown in (3).

(3)   subjunctive jussive

a. √qwl yaqu:la   yaqul   'say 3masc. sing.'
    √xwf yaxa:fa   yaxaf   'fear 3masc. sing.'

b. √rmy yarmiya   yarmi   'throw 3masc. sing.'
    √bgy yabga: yabga   'stay 3masc. sing.'

cf. √ktb yaktuba   yaktub 'write 3masc. sing.'

The absence of a long vowel in the jussives of hollow stems in (3a) appears to follow from McCarthy's (1979a, 1981) observation that Arabic verb templates must end with a CVC sequence. McCarthy's generalization is based on strong verb stems, and as McCarthy (2005) notes, it is not intended to account for weak verbs, although it can apply to hollow verbs in the jussive. This condition does not apply uniformly to the subjunctive stems of weak verbs or lame verbs in the jussive where there is glide deletion, (3b).

This paper proposes that the distribution of surface long vowels in weak verb stems is a consequence of constraint interaction as defined by Optimality Theory (Prince and Smolensky 1993/2004). Long vowels in stems are the result of compensatory lengthening except when lengthening conflicts with higher ranking constraints. In the jussive, for example, a constraint prohibiting heavy syllables and a constraint prohibiting non-moraic glides interact to ensure short vowels and glide deletion in both hollow and lame stems. Long vowel distribution from glide deletion in blind stems requires an interaction involving another constraint that prohibits a specific vowel distribution in active stems. The distribution of vowel length is also influenced by a prosodic constraint on the shape of the verb stem. It is proposed here that Arabic verb stems must be equal to an iambic foot, in accordance with the Prosodic Morphology Hypothesis (McCarthy and Prince 1990a). The actual expansion of the iambic foot is determined by constraint interaction. In most cases, the stem is aprosodic; hence, the role of the prosodic template is obscured.

This paper is in three sections. The first section introduces the relevant constraints and compensatory lengthening in Optimality Theory and the prosodic template for verb stems. The second section discusses vowel length in blind and hollow stems. The third section discusses the constraint on the jussive stem and its interaction with other constraints to account for the various stem shapes.

2   Vowel length in weak verb stems

2.1   Overview of constraints

The distribution of high vowels and glides, following Rosenthall (1997), is due to a markedness constraint called {I/U}=μ, which ensures that vocalic elements {I} and {U} are parsed moraically.[4] Glides in onsets (which are featurally identical to high vowels) are a consequence of harmonic violations of {I/U}=μ, for example, an input like /CViV/ or /CVyV/ surfaces as [CV.yV.] due to ONSET conflicting with and dominating {I/U}=μ. The requirement for a syllable to have an onset compels a non-moraic parse of the glide in violation of {I/U}=μ. Both ONSET and {I/U}=μ can be satisfied in other configurations at the expense of violating some other constraint. One parse that satisfies both constraints is a diphthong, e.g., [au], where the high vowel is moraic, satisfying {I/U}=μ, but at the expense of a bimoraic nucleus which violates NODIPHTHONG (Rosenthall 1997).

Glides in Arabic verbs delete in numerous contexts, not all of which are relevant here. Of particular importance is the glide deletion shown in (1), e.g., [qa:la] and [rama:]. Deletion in these cases follows from the satisfaction of {I/U}=μ at the expense of violating MAX-IO, which ensures input/output faithfulness.[5] The deletion of the glide means that no parse of the glide (moraic or not) is optimal so the glide cannot surface as a component of a diphthong. Hence the constraint NODIPHTHONG also dominates MAX-IO. The constraint interaction compelling deletion is shown in (4), putting aside vowel length and the interaction between the higher ranking constraints.

(4)

/a+√qwal+a/	{I/U}=μ	NoDiph	Max-IO
a.　　qa.wa.la.	*!		
b.　☞　qa:.la.			*
c.　　qaw.la.		*!	

Diphthongs occur in Arabic verb stems, but with a limited distribution. Hollow verb stems never contain a diphthong, but lame verb stems do so only when the following suffix is consonant-initial; otherwise the glide deletes.

(5)　root　　/+a/ 3masc. sing.　/+ta/ 2masc. sing.
　　　√rmay　rama:　　　　　ramayta
　　　√dʕaw　daʕa:　　　　　daʕawta

The glide surfaces as the second component of the diphthong due to a constraint interaction that includes FINAL-C (McCarthy 1993a) that ensures the stem is consonant-final. Diphthongs, therefore, only occur under the duress of satisfying a condition on the stem (see Rosenthall 2006 for a full analysis). The diphthongs in blind stems occur as a consequence of ANCHOR (McCarthy and Prince 1995), which ensures a segment at a designated periphery in the input has a correspondent at the designated periphery in the output. The relevant periphery here is the left edge of the root and ANCHOR-L conflicts with and dominates NoDiph.

An important phonotactic constraint in Arabic prohibits two adjacent high vocoids in the same syllable, that is, onset plus vowel sequences *[wi], *[yu], vowel plus coda sequences *[uy], *[iw], and vowel sequences [ui], [iu]. These sequences are marked because adjacent syllable positions have a sonority plateau. This restriction extends beyond tautosyllabic sequences to include any sequence of high vocoids. This more general constraint is called *ADJACENTHIGHVOCOIDS (*ADJHIVOC) which prohibits sequences of high vocoids. The constraints used throughout this paper are summarized in (6). Other constraints are introduced during the discussion of specific phenomena.

(6)　{I/U}=μ: vocalic elements {I} and {U} are moraic.
　　　NoDiph: no bi-vocalic nuclei.
　　　ANCHOR-L: The left edge of the root of the input has a correspondent at the left
　　　　edge of the root in the output.
　　　*ADJHIVOC: No sequences of high vocoids.

Glide distribution partially depends on the syllable structure of Arabic. The syllable canon of Classical Arabic includes CV, CVV, CVC, CVG and final superheavy syllables in a specific context (McCarthy 1979a). The absence of onset clusters is due to *COMPLEX (Prince and Smolensky 1993/2004), which is undominated. Superheavy (CVVC and CVCC) syllables, according to McCarthy (1979), occur word-finally before a pause. Arabic syllables, therefore, are limited to a bimoraic maximum, that is, two elements in the rime. This is characterized by a constraint called SYLLABLEMAXIMUM (McCarthy and Prince 1986), which is satisfied differently word-medially and word-finally. In Arabic, a word-medial peripheral coda (adjoined to a CVC or CVV syllable) is not optimal, but a word-final peripheral coda is optimal in certain conditions.

The inputs to the constraint ranking used here follow Gafos' (2003) representations, which, for perfective stems, include the consonantal root and a bivocalic vocalism. Including both vowels in the input is justified because the second vowel of the measure I perfective stem must be part of the root since it is idiosyncratic, e.g., |katab| 'write', |rakib| 'ride' ('|' is used to indicate stem boundaries). Gafos (2003) proposes that the first vowel of the active perfective stem is a prefix. Hence, the input is /a+√ktab/ and the prefix vowel and the root form the stem by a constraint interaction not discussed here. The Arabic roots are represented here as √CCVC, where the vowel is different in different morphological classes.[6] For the verb 'write' the assumed inputs are as follows: the active perfective is /a+√ktab/, the passive perfective is /u+√ktib/, the active imperfective is /√ktub/ and the passive imperfective is /√ktab/. The passive perfective (not discussed by Gafos) is assumed to have the same input form as other inputs even though both vowels are predictable.

2.2   Vowel length

The Optimality-theoretic analysis of vowel length distribution resulting from glide deletion presented here resembles analyses of similar phenomena in other languages. Following Kager (1999), compensatory lengthening is understood using McCarthy's (1999b) Sympathy Theory. The optimal candidate is determined by best-satisfaction of the constraints with respect to the input and a designated failed candidate, called the sympathetic candidate. In this case, the sympathetic candidate is the faithful parse of the input. Compensatory lengthening is the result of faithful mora correspondence with respect to the sympathetic candidate.

The constraint ranking is illustrated with [qa:la] from /a+√qwal+a/. From this input the faithful candidate is [qawala] with a glide surfacing non-moraically as an onset. This candidate, however, violates {I/U}=μ, which is not harmonic.

The sympathetic candidate is determined by the selector constraint, which in this case is MAX-IO, that is, input/output faithfulness of all consonants, including glides. The relevant intercandidate faithfulness constraint is MAX-❀O-μ, which ensures every mora of the sympathetic candidate has a correspondent in the output. The constraints interact as shown in (7).

(7)

/a+√qwal+a/	{I/U}=μ	MAX-❀O-μ	MAX-IO
a. ❀ qa.wa.la.	*!		✓
b. ☞ qa:.la.			*
c. qa.la.		*!	*

(7a) is the only candidate that has a faithful parse of the input consonants; hence, it is the only candidate that can serve as the sympathetic candidate. The optimal candidate must preserve the mora count of this candidate. The sympathetic candidate is not optimal for reasons mentioned above. The absence of a long vowel in (7c) violates intercandidate mora correspondence because the initial syllable is monomoraic. The long vowel in (7b), on the other hand, satisfies mora correspondence and, therefore, it is the optimal candidate.

Intercandidate faithfulness conflicts with {I/U}=μ, although this is not apparent in (7). Their interaction is visible in verbs with consonant-initial suffixes, e.g., [qulta] (</√a+qwal+ta/) 'say 2masc. sing.'. The faithful parse of this input is [qawalta] with four moras, three from the vowels and one from the moraic coda consonant. The surface form has only two vowels and a moraic coda; hence, there must be a surface violation of MAX-❀O-μ under the duress of satisfying {I/U}=μ. This is shown in (8), ignoring the vowel change in the stem.

(8)

/a+√qwal+ta/	{I/U}=μ	MAX-❀O-μ	MAX-IO
❀ qa.wal.ta.	*!		✓
☞ qul.ta.		*	**

Another potential candidate that would satisfy both {I/U}=μ and MAX-❀O-μ is [qa:lta], but this candidate violates the undominated SYLLABLEMAXIMUM constraint.

Mora faithfulness in the hollow stem does not necessitate Sympathy because the number of input moras is equivalent (or less than) the number of output moras. Hence, MAX-IO-μ is sufficient. Sympathy becomes relevant in cases where the number of output moras is influenced by coda consonants in the sympathetic candidate. The long vowel in a lame stem with a consonant-initial suffix, e.g., [duʕi:ta] (<u+√dwiʕ+ta) 'call 2masc. sing. pass.' is accounted for by assigning a mora to the stem-final consonant, which is deleted.

(9)

/u+√dʕiw+ta/	*ADJHIVOC	MAX-❀O-μ	MAX-IO
a. ❀ du.ʕiw.ta.	*!		✓
b. ☞ du.ʕi:.ta.			*
c. du.ʕi.ta.		*!	*

Sympathy is necessary here because the coda is assigned a mora by GEN, not the input. The surface long vowel, therefore, must be due to best-satisfaction with respect to the sympathetic candidate.

Mora preservation from the sympathetic candidate can be satisfied in more than one way since more than one vowel can potentially surface as long. The output of the 3masc. sing. of √rmy is [rama:] with [ramaya] as the sympathetic candidate. The candidate [ra:ma], however, also satisfies intercandidate mora faithfulness. Similarly, [qala:] is a candidate parse of /a+√qwal+a/. The non-optimality of these candidates is attributed to the faithfulness violation evident when comparing the precedence relation of the moras and the segments in the two candidates. Only the relevant segments are given subscripts.

(10) Sympathetic candidate

$$
\begin{array}{lll}
\mu_1 \qquad \mu_3 \qquad \mu_5 & \text{a.}\quad \mu_1\,\mu_3 \qquad \mu_5 & \text{b.}\quad \mu_1 \qquad \mu_3\,\mu_5 \\
|\quad\ \ |\quad\ \ | & \qquad \vee \qquad | & \qquad\ | \qquad \vee \\
r\,a_1\,m_2\,a_3\,y_4\,a_5 & r\,a{:}_1\,m_2\ a_3 & r\,a_1\,m_2\ a_3{:}
\end{array}
$$

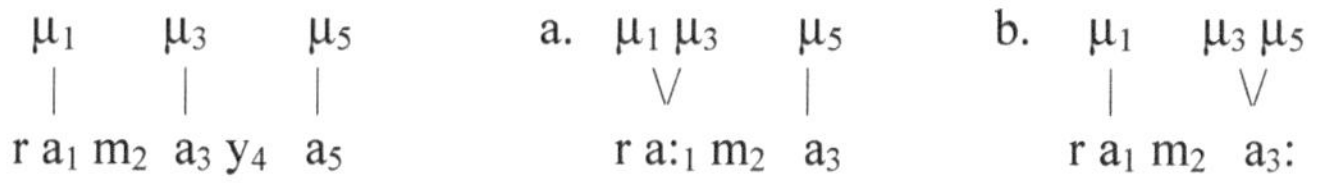

The problem with [ra:ma] is that the long vowel occurs away from where deletion occurs. The distribution of long vowels is constrained to occur in the vicinity of deletion. When the long vowel is not constrained in this way, there is a marked precedence relation among the segments and moras. The mora μ_3 precedes the segment [m$_2$] in violation of LINEARITY (McCarthy and Prince 1995). When the long vowel surfaces where deletion has occurred, as in (10b), there is no LINEARITY violation since μ_3 follows [m$_2$]. LINEARITY, therefore, is used to ensure that moras are associated locally when there is consonant deletion.

2.3   Paradigm uniformity in Arabic verb stems

The shape of Arabic strong verb stems lends itself to an analysis using paradigm uniformity because the stem shape is invariant throughout the paradigm. The imperfective stem is CVCCVC, e.g., |yaktab|, and CVCVC in the perfective, e.g., |katab|. The invariant shape of the imperfective is intriguing because prosodically it consists of a heavy syllable followed by a light syllable, |yak. tab.| (with a non-moraic final consonant (McCarthy and Prince 1990a,b)), which is aprosodic. This stem violates McCarthy and Prince's (1995) STEM=PRWD constraint and is counterintuitive given the role of iambic templates in Arabic (McCarthy and Prince 1990a,b).

The aprosodic template, as McCarthy (2005a) argues, is a consequence of optimal paradigms (cf. Kenstowicz's (1997) paradigm uniformity). McCarthy argues that the imperfective stem is CVCCVC (heavy-light) because this is the only stem that is compatible with the phonotactic constraints of the language. This is illustrated in (11) where paradigm uniformity (Kenstowicz 1997) ensures that the stem shape is consistent throughout the verb paradigm. A stem that is equal to a prosodic constituent (the light-heavy iamb in (11b)) is compatible with a vowel-initial suffix, but it is not compatible with a consonant-initial suffix because the output would contain a superheavy syllable in violation of SYLLMAX. Verb paradigms are represented by one form with a consonant-initial and one with a vowel-initial suffix unless other forms are relevant.

(11)

/ya+√ktub+a/ /ya+√ktub+na/	SYLLMAX	PARADIGM UNIFORMITY	STEMSHAPE
a. ☞ yak.tu.ba. yak.tub.na.			H L
b. ya.kut.ba. ya.kutb.na.	*!		L H
c. ya.kut.ba yak.tub.na		*!	L H H H

Even though conflict between stem shape and syllable size occurs only when there is a consonant-initial suffix, the demands of uniformity compel all stems to have an aprosodic (heavy-light) shape. Surface violations of PARADIGMUNIFORMITY occur with geminated verbs, e.g., [jarra], [jararta] 'pull' (not discussed here), and in lame verbs in the jussive discussed in section 4.

Weak verb stems, with the various deletion phenomena associated with them, also exhibit uniform stem shapes. This uniformity is argued here to be partially responsible for the distribution of vowel length. The various stem shapes of strong and weak verbs can be organized as a preference hierarchy based on different expansions of the iambic foot, following Prince's (1990) IAMBICQUANTITY constraint for harmonic parsing of iambic feet: LH is more harmonic than LL and H, which in turn are more harmonic than the aprosodic HL. The verb stems are evaluated by a constraint called STEMSHAPE.

All stem types (except subminimal words) are observed. Since Optimality Theory only considers output candidates, the prosodic shape of the stem changes depending on whether the following suffix is vowel- or consonant-initial. The final consonant of the stem is assigned a mora because it is in a coda when followed by a consonant-initial suffix. Segmentally, the stems are invariant, but prosodically there is this alternation. However, the stems are prosodically invariant, modulo moraic codas. This is denoted here as 'L⁺', which means that the syllable is light before a vowel-initial suffix and heavy before a consonant-initial one. Examples of all stem shapes are shown in (12a) and the hierarchy is given in (12b).

(12) a.   LH: √xwf   LL⁺: √wjl   H: √qwl   HL⁺: √ktb
         ya.xa:.fa.   ya.ji.da.   qa:.la.   yak.tu.ba.   '3masc. sing.'
         ya.xaf.na.   ya.jid.na.   qul.na.   yak.tub.na.   '3fem. pl.'
         'fear, subj.'   'find, subj.'   'say, perf.' 'write, subj.'

   b.   STEMSHAPE
        LH > LL⁺, H > HL⁺ > L⁺

Less preferred stem shapes are optimal as a result of constraint conflict; for example, a LH stem is never harmonic for strong verbs. Hence, HL⁺ (e.g., |yaktab|) is harmonic in the imperfective and LL⁺ (e.g., |katab|) is harmonic in the perfective. High ranking DEP-μ ensures moras are not added to increase harmony of the stem. An H stem is never harmonic for strong verbs since consonants do not delete.

Hollow verb stems in the perfective have an H stem, as shown in (7) and (8). This stem shape is lower on the preference hierarchy, but the more harmonic LH disyllabic stem incurs a violation of {I/U}=μ. Therefore, {I/U}=μ conflicts with and dominates STEMSHAPE. The ranking of STEMSHAPE and MAX-❀O-μ is established in section 3.

(13)

/a+√qwal+a/ /a+√qwal+ta/	{I/U}=μ	STEMSHAPE	MAX-❀O-μ	MAX-IO
a. ❀ qa.wa.la. qa.wal.ta.	*!	L L⁺		✓
b. ☞ qa:.la. qul.ta.		H	*	*
c. qa.la. qul.ta.		L⁺!	* *	*

(13a) remains the sympathetic candidate (or the sympathetic paradigm). Candidate paradigms (13b) and (13c) both have violations of MAX-❀O-μ with consonant-initial suffixes. (13c) fatally violates STEMSHAPE because the L⁺ stem is less preferred.

3 Blind stems

Blind verb stems, as mentioned, show an alternation between a glide surfacing as part of a diphthong and glide deletion. In cases where there is glide deletion, there is a length alternation.

(14)　　active　　passive
　　a.　√wjd　　yajida　　yu:jada　　'find 3masc. sing. subj.'
　　b.　√wjl　　yawjala　　n/a　　'be afraid 3masc. sing. subj.'

The optimality-theoretic analysis of compensatory lengthening applies straight-forwardly to passive imperfectives of blind stems, as shown in (15).

(15)

/yu+√wjad+a/	*ADJHIVOC	MAX-⊛O-μ	MAX-IO
a. ⊛ yuwjada	*!		✓
b. ☞ yu:jada			*
c. yujada		*!	*

(15a) is the only candidate that satisfies MAX-IO so it is the sympathetic candidate. It is not the optimal candidate because the vocoid sequence [uw] violates the high ranking constraint against this sequence. All candidates have an additional violation of this constraint incurred by the prefix.

Active imperfective forms of blind stems differ from the passive forms insofar as the former have either glide deletion or the glide surfaces as part of a diphthong, as seen in (16). Glide deletion, in this case, does not result in a long vowel.

(16) a.　deletion　　　　　　b.　diphthong
　　　　|yajid|　'find'　　　　　　|yawjal|　'be afraid'
　　　　|yasil|　'arrive'　　　　　|yawjuz|　'be brief'
　　　　|yabig|　'perish'　　　　　|yaysar|　'become easy'
　　　　|yaʕir|　'be rough'　　　　|yayʕas|　'renounce'

The discussion of these stems begins with the diphthongs in (16b), which are a consequence of the constraint interaction determining glide distribution discussed in section 1. Glides must be moraic, as they are as the second component of a diphthong. Given the established constraint ranking in (4), there is no way for the glide to surface. The crucial constraint however is ANCHOR-L; deletion is not optimal because it compels a violation of this higher ranking constraint.

(17)

/ya+√wjal+a/	Anchor-L	NoDiph	Max-IO
a. ❀ ☞ yaw.jala		*	✓
b. ya:.jala	*!		*
c. ya.jala	*!		*

(17a), with a diphthong, is the optimal candidate because both (17b and c) violate Anchor-L. Blind verbs with a palatal glide always surface with diphthongs, e.g., |yaysur| (<√ysur) 'insignificant' and |yayʔas| (<√yʔas) 'renounce', satisfying Anchor-L.

Surface violations of Anchor-L are optimal in some cases, as must be the case in (16a) where there is glide deletion. Glide deletion in these stems is peculiar for two reasons: (1) deletion, as mentioned, is accompanied by a short vowel in contrast to deletion in other contexts and (2) it is particular to blind stems with bilabial glides followed by high front vowels. To account for deletion, Brame (1970) posits the following rule: w → ø / __Ci. Brame's rule serves as the basis for a constraint that leads to optimal short vowels. What is not permitted in Arabic is a moraic high back rounded vocoid followed by a high front vowel in measure I active stems. This is captured in the following constraint.

(18) $*U_\mu Ci_{Active/I}$: A measure I active verb stem cannot contain a moraic high back vocoid followed by a high front vowel.

The high back vocoid referenced in the constraint can be a vowel or a moraic glide, since these segments are indistinguishable, so neither [...uCi...] nor [...wCi...] is permitted. At this point there is no attempt to reduce this constraint to more fundamental constraints or other aspects of Arabic phonology.[7] The constraint crucially refers to a moraic vocoid; a non-moraic one, that is, a glide, does not violate it.

The fact that a non-moraic glide does not violate $*U_\mu Ci$ has repercussions for the selection of the sympathetic candidate (and ultimately the output) during the evaluation of constraint satisfaction for blind verb stems. The candidate with a moraic glide (shown in bold in (19b)) and the candidate with a non-moraic glide, (19a), are simultaneously evaluated with the latter emerging as the sympathetic candidate.[8]

(19)

/ya+√wjida/	DEP-❀O-μ	*U$_μ$Ci	{I/U}=μ	ANCHOR-L	MAX-❀O-μ	MAX-IO
a. ❀ yaw.ji.da.			*!			✓
b. yaw.ji.da.		*!				✓
c. ☞ ya.ji.da.				*		*
d. ya:.ji.da.	*!			*		*

Since the sympathetic candidate, (19a), has a non-moraic glide the optimal candidate cannot have a long vowel. A long vowel candidate, (19d), would require adding a mora in violation of a high ranking constraint, DEP-μ, that prohibits mora insertion. Therefore, the vowel surfaces as short satisfying mora faithfulness with respect to the sympathetic candidate.

Deletion of the glide from a blind root crucially depends upon *U$_μ$Ci since the glide surfaces as part of a diphthong, (16b), when the root vowel is any other vowel. There are, however, some blind verb stems with low vowels and glide deletion, but without vowel lengthening.

(20) perfective   imperfective
   |wadaʕ| |yadaʕ| *|yawdaʕ| 'put'
   |watiʔ| |yataʔ| *|yawtaʔ| 'set foot'
   |wasiʕ| |yasaʕ| *|yawsaʕ| 'be wide'
   |wagaʕ| |yagaʕ| *|yawgaʕ| 'fall'

These stems are unique, as Brame notes, insofar as the third radical is [ʕ] or [ʔ]. Brame proposes that the underlying roots in (20) contain a high front vowel, e.g., √wdiʕ, and the low vowel in the stem is due to assimilation to the lowness of the laryngeal consonant. A complete analysis of these stems is complicated by the specific nature of the assimilation process; it only occurs with the third radical of imperfective verbs. An optimality-theoretic analysis of these verbs requires that the faithful candidate be the sympathetic candidate for mora distribution (vowel length) and some other interaction is required to determine vowel quality.

The difference between the imperfective stems |yajid| and |yawjal| is the deletion of the glide in the former as a consequence of satisfying *U$_μ$Ci. In the perfective, both verbs have stems with the CVCVC shape of strong verbs, that is, |wajad| and |wajil|, based on the triliteral verb roots √wjd and √wjl, respectively. Gafos (2003) presents an alternative analysis to account for the difference seen in the imperfective stems. Gafos claims that |yajid| is based on a biliteral root, √jd, whereas |yawjal| is based on a triliteral root. The similar stem shape in the perfective is due to a glide insertion process to ensure template satisfaction.

Assigning a biliteral root to |yajid | is not feasible when more data are considered, namely √wjid in the passive imperfective where there is a long vowel, |yu:jad|, which can only be the result of compensatory lengthening. Therefore, the glide must be part of the verb root. Additional support for triliteral roots for all blind verbs is seen in verbs with two stems (Mahadin 1982). In the imperfective, the glide surfaces when the stem vowel is [u] or [a], but deletes when it is [i]. This is predicted by the established constraint ranking and is not compatible with a biliteral analysis of these roots.

(21) root   perfective   imperfective
     √wbg |wabag|~|wabig| |yabig|~|yawbag| 'perish'
     √wjz |wajaz|~|wajuz| |yajiz|~|yawjuz| 'concise'

4   Hollow stems

The long vowel of the perfective stem of a hollow verb, e.g., |qa:l| (</a+√qwal/), is due to the constraint interaction in (7), which serves as the basis for determining vowel length in all verb stems. Glide deletion and concomitant long vowels occur in imperfective stems as well, as shown in (22).

(22)   √qwul 'say' √xwaf 'fear' √zyid 'increase'
     a.   yaqu:la   yaxa:fa   yazi:da   '3masc. sing. subj.'
     b.   taqulna   taxafna   tazidna   '2fem. pl. subj.'

The long vowels in (22a) appear to follow in an obvious way from the established constraint ranking, but there are some peculiarities due to the selection of the sympathetic candidate. From the surface forms in (22) the sympathetic candidate should be a faithful parse that includes a moraic glide (which is deleted in the optimal candidate) and the mora is preserved by intercandidate faithfulness. A problem arises because this potential sympathetic candidate for /ya+√xwaf/, for example, is |ya.xwaf.|, which contains a rising diphthong.[9] The constraint prohibiting these diphthongs (where the glide precedes the low vowel), called NoRise (Rosenthall 1994), is undominated in Arabic; therefore, the sympathetic candidate must include a non-moraic glide and a moraic coda in the initial syllable. The selection of the sympathetic candidate is shown in the partial tableau (23).

(23)

/ya+√xwaf/	NoRise	{I/U}=μ	Max-IO
a. ✿ |yax.waf.|		*	✓
b. |ya.xwaf.|	*!		✓

The sympathetic candidate has the same stem shape as a strong verb in the imperfective.

Turning to the optimal candidate, the glide in the optimal candidate deletes under the duress of satisfying {I/U}=μ. The problem is determining the distribution of the moras. The mora assigned to the coda consonant of the sympathetic candidate cannot be parsed with that consonant due to a high ranking constraint against geminates at the left edge of the verb stem. This means that intercandidate faithfulness can be satisfied two ways: either the first syllable contains a long vowel, e.g., |ya:xaf|, or the second syllable does, e.g., |yaxa:f|, since neither candidate violates Linearity discussed in section 1.2.

(24) Sympathetic candidate

$$\mu_1 \quad \mu_2 \quad \mu_4$$
$$\mid \quad \mid \quad \mid$$
$$y\,a_1\ x_2\ w_3\ a_4\ \ f$$

a.
$$\mu_1\ \mu_2 \quad \mu_4$$
$$\vee \quad \mid$$
$$y\,a{:}_1\ x_2\ a_4\ \ f$$

b.
$$\mu_1 \quad \mu_2\ \mu_4$$
$$\mid \quad \vee$$
$$y\,a_1\ x_2\ a_4{:}\ f$$

The non-optimality of the stem |ya:xaf| is somewhat surprising since it is HL, like the strong verb stems, and satisfies intercandidate faithfulness. Furthermore, this potential stem would avoid the vowel length alternation in the paradigm. The fact that that the optimal stem has a long vowel in the second syllable, [yaxa:fa], or mora deletion, [taxafna], is a consequence of the preference for a LH iambic stem. A hollow verb in the imperfective is the only case where the most preferred stem surfaces.

(25)

/ya+√xwaf+a/ /ta+√xwaf+na/	{I/U}=μ	StemShape	Max-✿O-μ	Max-IO
a. ✿ yax.wa.fa. tax.waf.na.	*!	H L⁺		✓
b. ya:.xa.fa. ta:.xaf.na.		H L⁺!		*
c. ☞ ya.xa:.fa. ta.xaf.na.		L H	*	*
d. ya.xa.fa. ta.xaf.na.		L L⁺!	* *	*

The preference for a LH iambic stem compels mora deletion before consonant-initial suffixes, thus establishing that StemShape conflicts with and dominates

Max-❀O-μ. Mora deletion throughout the paradigm, as in (25d), results in the less preferred LL stem.

The blind stems discussed in section 2 must now be reconsidered in light of the interaction between StemShape and intercandidate faithfulness. The LL stem of [yajida]/[tajidna] is optimal because there is no way for a long vowel to surface, as demonstrated in (19). The long vowel in the passive ([yu:jada]/ [tu:jadna]) is problematic because satisfaction of higher ranking StemShape should compel an optimal LL stem, which is preferred to the HL stem.

McCarthy (2005a) observes that LL stems are actually disfavored as a consequence of stress assignment in Classical Arabic. According to McCarthy, stressing a light syllable rather than a heavy syllable violates the Stress-to-Weight Principle (SWP), which states 'if stressed, then heavy'.[10] As a consequence of SWP, a candidate paradigm with stress on heavy syllables is preferred to a candidate paradigm with stress on light syllables; therefore, a LL stem will be less harmonic than a HL stem. The constraint SWP conflicts with and dominates StemShape and intercandidate faithfulness. Therefore, there is no mora deletion to improve harmony of the stem. A LH heavy stem, not shown in (26), violates Linearity.

(26)

/yu+√wjad+a/ /yu+√wjad+na/	*AdjHiVoc	SWP	StemShape	Max-❀O-μ	Max-IO
a. ❀ yuw.ja.da. yuw.jad.na.	*!		H L⁺		✓
b. ☞ yu:.ja.da. yu:.jad.na.			H L⁺		*
c. yu.ja.da. yu.jad.na.		*!	L L⁺	* *	*

The distribution of vowel length in the imperfective stems of hollow verbs is accounted for by an iambic template. It is only in this context that the maximal iamb is preferred. Other expansions of the iamb occur with other weak stems, but for many stems (including all strong verbs) the prosodic character of the template is obscured by conflict with higher ranking constraints.

5   Jussive stems

Jussive stems display a variety of surface alternations for both hollow and lame stems. A unified account of these stem shapes is possible by positing a prosodic constraint on the shape of the jussive stem.

Hollow verbs in the jussive have a length alternation not unlike that found in other imperfective stems. A long vowel occurs only when there is a vowel-initial suffix, (27c); otherwise the stem vowel is short, (27a). The subjunctive is included for comparison.

(27)   *jussive*   *subjunctive*

   a. yaqul   b. yaqu:la   'say 3masc. sing.'
        yahab   yaha:ba   'fear 3masc. sing.'
  cf. yaktub   yaktaba   'write 3masc. sing.'

   c. taqu:li: d. taqu:li: 'say 2fem. sing.'
        taha:bi: taha:bi: 'fear 2fem. sing.'
  cf. taktubi: taktuba   'write 2fem. sing.'

The long vowels in the subjunctive stems (27b and d) and in the jussives in (27c) are accounted for by the constraint ranking in (25). Problems emerge accounting for the short vowels found in the jussive forms in (27a). A reasonable generalization is that the jussive verb has some restriction on long vowels, but long vowels are permitted as seen in (27c). Looking at the jussives in (27a), it appears that long vowels are not permitted in the final syllable (putting aside the long vowel suffix in (27c)). A potential explanation might be that a long vowel in the jussives in (27a) would create a superheavy syllable, e.g., [yaqu:l], violating SYLLMAX, which dominates intercandidate faithfulness.

The absence of superheavy syllables is an attractive explanation for the short vowels, but it cannot be extended to other phenomena found in the jussive. The alternative pursued here is that the short vowel in the jussive is a consequence of a constraint that ensures that the final syllable of the jussive is a light syllable. This means that the final consonant of a strong verb in the jussive is non-moraic. The constraint and the representation of a strong verb are given below.

(28) a.   *H]$_{jussive}$: The final syllable of a jussive verb cannot be a heavy syllable.

    b.

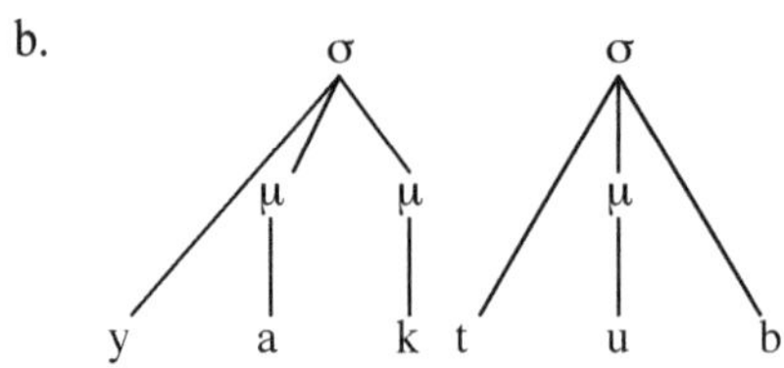

The non-moraicity of the final consonant is consistent with McCarthy and Prince's (1990a) claim that the final consonant of Arabic templates is extrasyllabic.

The evidence that supports the non-moraicity of word-final consonants in jussives comes from glide deletion (without vowel lengthening) in lame stems. Compare this to the long vowels that are a consequence of deletion in the subjunctive.

(29)   root   jussive   subjunctive
        √gbay   yabga   yabga: 'stay 3masc. sing.'
        √rdaw   yarda   yarda: 'approve 3masc. sing.'
   cf. √ktub   yaktub   yaktubu   'write 3masc. sing.'

The prohibition against heavy syllables at the right edge means that a bimoraic diphthong (or a long vowel) is not harmonic. A lame stem with the CVCCVC shape of a strong verb would have a non-moraic glide in violation of {I/U}=μ. Therefore, the glide deletes, as shown in (30). The ranking between {I/U}=μ and *H]$_{\text{jussive}}$ is discussed presently.

(30)

/ya+√bgay/	{I/U}=μ	*H]$_{\text{jussive}}$	Max-⊛O-μ	Max-IO
a. yab.gay.	*!		*	✓
b. ⊛ yab.gay.		*!		✓
c. yab.ga:.		*!		*
d. ☞ yab.ga.			*	*

The sympathetic candidate is (30b), with a bimoraic diphthong, but this candidate is not optimal due to the fatal violation of the constraint on the jussive. (30c), with a long vowel, also violates *H]$_{\text{jussive}}$. (30d), with a short vowel and glide deletion, best-satisfies the constraint ranking. Notice that this candidate is optimal irrespective of Sympathy.

Accounting for the alternations in the jussive is complicated by apparent cases of diphthongs found in lame stems.

(31)   root   3masc. sing.   2fem. sing.
        √bgay   yabga   tabgay   'stay'
   cf. √ktub   yaktub   taktubi: 'write'

The occurrence of the final glide in the feminine singular is a consequence of an alternation affecting suffixes. The 2fem. jussive suffix is /i:/ which violates the prohibition against final heavy syllables in the jussive. The suffix, therefore, is predicted to delete. However, since the long vowel is part of a suffix, its preservation in the output is conceivably related to affix faithfulness (Alderete 1999b), that is, the suffix vowel must be parsed. Positing a high ranking affix faithfulness constraint is problematic for two reasons: (1) suffix vowels delete at the expense of parsing the root vowel and (2) suffix vowels undergo length alternations in the jussive and elsewhere.

(32) a. long → short: /u:/   √rmy → ramau   cf. katabu: '3masc. pl. perf.'

                  /u:na/   √bgy → yabgauna   cf. yaktubu:na '3masc. pl. ind.'

   b. short → ø: /u/   √rmy → yarmi: cf. yaktubu   '3masc. sing. ind.'

                         √bgy → yabga:

The vowel length alternations found in suffix vowels are best characterized as a chain shift (Rosenthall 2006) where long vowels can shorten (but not delete) and short vowels can delete.

The different surface forms of underlying long vowels are captured by a constraint that prohibits long vowels from becoming short (or non-moraic in the case of high vowels) and another that prohibits deletion (see Kirchner (1996), Łubowicz (2003) for optimality-theoretic analyses of chain shifts). For the purposes of the analysis here, shortening underlying long vowels violates the constraint *Long→Short, and deleting long vowels violates a higher ranking constraint *Long→ø. The 2nd feminine singular form is accounted for by shortening as shown in (33). The glide that surfaces in 2nd feminine forms appears to be the glide of the root, but it is not. The final glide is the surface correspondent of the suffix.

(33)

/ta+√bgay+i:/	*AdjHiVoc	*Long→Short	{I/U}=μ	*H]$_{jussive}$	Max-IO
a. ☞ tab.ga.yi:.	*!				✓
b. tab.ga.yi.	*!	*			✓
c. tab.gay.		*	*!		*
d. ☞ tab.gay.		*		*	*

A bimoraic diphthong surfaces because any parse of the underlying glide and suffix violates the constraint prohibiting adjacent high vocoids. This compels deletion of the underlying glide. The suffix vowel has a surface correspondent to satisfy *Long→ ø and this compels a violation of the prosodic restriction on the jussive.

One candidate not mentioned above is [tabgi:] with deletion of both vocoids from the root but having a parse of the long vowel suffix. This candidate appears to be optimal because it satisfies both *AdjHiVoc and *Long→ Short at the expense of lower ranking *H]$_{juss}$. Here, as elsewhere, paradigm uniformity is relevant. The candidate stem in this case, |tagb|, is not compatible with the complete paradigm, which includes [yab.ga.] and [tab.gay.] (in (31)), and [yab. gay.na.] '3fem. pl.'. The only stem that is compatible with all suffixes is |CVb. ga(y)|, which is HL⁺.

Diphthongs in the jussive only occur when the vowel of the root is low. A lame verb with a high vowel surfaces with the long vowel suffix and deletion of both the glide and the root vowel.

(34)

	3masc. pl.	2fem. sing.
√rmiy	yarmu:	tarmi:
√dʕuw	yadʕu:	tadʕi:
cf. √ktub	yaktubu:	taktubi:

The preservation of the long vowel suffix is a consequence of the constraint ranking, particularly the constraint against sequences of high vocoids. Since this constraint is high ranking and any combination of stem plus suffix violates it, the stem vocoids must delete because the long vowel suffix must have a surface correspondent.

(35)

/ta+√dʕuw+i:/	*ADJHIVOC	*LONG→ SHORT	*H]$_{jussive}$	MAX-IO
a. ❀ tad.ʕu.wi:.	*!		*	✓
b. tad.ʕu.wi.	*!	*		✓
c. tad.ʕuy.	*!	*		*
d. ☞ tad.ʕi:.			*	*
e. tad.ʕi.		*!		*

(35c), which is segmentally equivalent in shape to the optimal candidate in (33), is not harmonic here because it violates *ADJHIVOC. The candidates that satisfy *ADJHIVOC are (35d and e), which differ only in vowel length. The short vowel candidate violates *LONG→ SHORT so the long vowel in (35d) is harmonic with an inconsequential violation of the jussive constraint. The stem in this case is |tadʕ|, the H expansion of the iamb. Any disyllabic parse violates *ADJHIVOC.

Lame stems with high vowels lead to violations of paradigm uniformity, e.g., √rmiy → [yar.mu:.] '3masc. pl. juss.' and [yar.mi:.na.] '3fem. pl. juss.' (cf. [yaktubu:] and [yaktubna]), where there is a H stem and a HL⁺ stem in the paradigm. The candidate disyllabic stem of the 3masc. pl. [yar.mi.yu:.] contains adjacent high vocoids and so it is not optimal. The stem alternation is conditioned by satisfaction of *ADJHIVOC so paradigm uniformity, therefore, is dominated by *ADJHIVOC.

The established constraint ranking appears to apply straightforwardly to hollow stems, as shown in (36).

304   *Phonological Argumentation*

(36)

/ya+√hyab/	NoRise	{I/U}=μ	*H]$_{\text{jussive}}$	Max-✿O-μ	Max-IO
a. ✿ yah.yab.		*!			✓
b. ya.hyab.	*!		*		✓
c. ya.ha:b.			*!		*
d. ☞ ya.hab.				*	*

However, a problem emerges because the surface form violates high ranking SWP since a light syllable is stressed. The established ranking actually predicts that the stem [ya:hab] is optimal because it satisfies *H]$_{\text{jussive}}$ and Max-✿O-μ, as well as SWP. Another problem presented by hollow verbs is that paradigm uniformity is violated. The 3masc. form [yahab] is LL due to the constraint on the jussive, but other stems, e.g., [yaha:bi:], are LH.

Starting with the latter problem, the apparent violation of paradigm uniformity is avoided by providing an invariant stem for the hollow verb. The hollow verb paradigm is uniformly LH if the final consonant of the jussive is moraic, that is, the coda weight in the jussive is variable as a result of constraint interaction (see Rosenthall and van der Hulst 1999). The final syllable of the jussive is light except in lame stems when it is heavy under the duress of satisfying StemShape. Assigning a mora to word-final codas in the jussive does not interfere with stress assignment. All final syllables (except superheavy syllables) are extrametrical; therefore, the moraicity of the final consonant is not relevant. A heavy final syllable (shown in bold) is the result of conflict between StemShape and *H]$_{\text{jussive}}$, illustrated in (37). Alternatively, [yahab] is LL and StemShape is satisfied by allowing LL and LH (a LL$^+$ iamb, which includes closed syllables and long vowels) stems in the same paradigm to satisfy ParadigmUniformity.

The problem posed by the SWP violation in [yahab] remains problematic in the analysis presented here. There does not appear to be a higher ranking constraint that is fatally violated by |ya:hab|. One way to incorporate the fact that |ya:hab| is aprosodic is to use a weaker version of SWP, which states that stems must contain a heavy syllable (Stem ⊃ H) regardless of stress. The constraints for stress placement would be lower ranking. The ranking for a hollow stem in the jussive is shown in (37).

(37)

/ya+√hyab/ /ta+√hyab+i:/ /ya+√hyab+na/	Stem⊃H	{I/U}=μ	StemShape	*H]ⱼᵤₛₛ	Max-IO
a. ❀ yah.yab. tah.ya.bi:. yah.yab.na.		*!	H L⁺		✓
b. ☞ ya.hab. ta.ha:.bi:. ya.hab.na.			L H	*	*
c. ya.hab. ta.ha.bi:. ya.hab.na.	*!		L L⁺		*
d. ya:hab. ta:.ha.bi:. ya:.hab.na.			H L⁺!		*

The LL⁺ stem in (37c) violates Stem⊃H so it cannot be optimal. (37b) has a moraic coda so this candidate paradigm satisfies Stem⊃H with a LH iambic stem. Only the LH stem in (37b) and the HL⁺ stem in (37d) satisfy the two highest ranking constraints, but the latter fatally violates StemShape.

Vowel length distribution in the jussive is similar to the distribution in other imperfective stems. The jussive, however, requires a specific constraint to account for alternations occurring in forms without a suffix, for example, 3masc. sing. forms. The hollow verb stem in the jussive (as in other imperfective forms) is the only case where the prosodic template of the stem emerges. The hollow stem is optimally an invariant LH iambic template, thus ensuring that long vowels never occur stem-initially.

6 Conclusion

Vowel length in weak verb stems is due to compensatory lengthening stemming from glide deletion. However, short vowels surface in some contexts in which long vowels are predicted. These short vowels are the result of constraints conflicting with the constraint interaction that leads to long vowels. The vowel length alternation in blind stems is due to a constraint prohibiting a specific sequence of moraic vocoids. This allows for a triliteral analysis of all blind verb roots, which is necessary to account for long vowels in other contexts. In the jussive, the length alternation is due to a violable constraint prohibiting word-final heavy syllables. Furthermore, the distribution of vowel length provides evidence for a prosodic analysis of verb stems based on an iambic foot. Verb stems are prosodic when possible, given interaction with other constraints. The maximal iamb template is only visible in imperfective forms of hollow verbs. In all other cases, the prosodic template is obscured by higher ranking constraints.

Notes

1   I would like to thank Steve Parker for many comments and suggestions on an earlier draft of the paper and I would also like to thank Stuart Davis for his comments. The paper has also benefited from comments from the audience at the Mid-Continental Workshop on Phonology in Iowa City (October 2006).

2   The weak roots will be referred to by the names used by Brame (1970). These names and the traditional names are given below

	Brame	*traditional*
glide-initial verb:	blind	assimilated
glide-medial verb:	hollow	hollow
glide-final verb:	lame	defective

3   The following abbreviations are used throughout the paper:

1 = First person	masc = masculine	subj = subjunctive	sing = singular
2 = Second person	fem = feminine	ind = indicative	pl = plural
3 = Third person	perf = perfective	juss = jussive	pass= passive

4   The vocalic features assumed here are {I}, {U}, and {A} (cf. Schane 1984, Kaye 1989). Mid vowels and front round vowels are derived by combinations of these features: {I}=[i], {U}=[u], {A}=[a], {I,A}=[e], {U,A}=[o], and {I,U}=[ü]. Classical Arabic does not have mid or front round vowels.

5   The MAX constraints must be partitioned to refer to different classes of consonants since non-approximants are not deleted in verb stems (except for glottal stops, not discussed here) whereas glides delete. Glide deletion is due to a low ranking MAX-IO and non-approximant parsing is a consequence of an undominated MAX-[-approx] constraint. The use of MAX-IO is a simplification; the distribution of glides and all vocoids actually involves MAX-FEATURE constraints that are not germane to the discussion here (see Rosenthall 2006).

6   The second vowel of the perfective active can be determined by the imperfective vowel by ablaut rules (Brame (1970), Chekayri and Scheer (1996)), but this is not pursued here.

7   The *uCi* sequence replicates the passive vocalism. Its absence in active forms is conceivably related to a more general aversion to the passive vocalism pattern occurring in active stems. The constraint *$U_\mu Ci$ is limited to measure I verbs because this sequence does occur in other measures, namely, measure IV verbs,

such as |yu:jid| (</wjd/) and |yuqi:l| (</qwl/). The measure IV passives for these stems are |yu:jad| and |yuqa:l|, respectively (cf. |yuktib| 'active', |yuktab| 'passive').

8   There is no direct conflict between *U$_\mu$Ci and {I/U}=µ. The interaction of these constraints is a 'latent' interaction (McCarthy 1999b) since the former is undominated and {I/U}=µ is dominated, e.g., [ramaya:] 'throw 3masc. dual'. Also the ranking of {I/U}=µ above ANCHOR-L appears problematic for perfective stems because the glide surfaces non-moraically and satisfies ANCHOR-L. The word-initial glide in perfectives requires other constraint interactions that determine the distribution of vowel features in stems (Rosenthall 2006).

9   Another potential candidate is |ya.xwaf| with the glide as part of the onset. This would violate {I/U}=µ as well as the undominated *COMPLEX.

10   McCarthy (1979) reconstructs Classical Arabic stress assignment as follows: stress the rightmost non-final heavy syllable; otherwise stress the initial syllable.

References

Abdul-Karim, Kamal (1980) *Aspects of the Phonology of Lebanese Arabic*. PhD dissertation, University of Illinois at Urbana-Champaign.

Abramson, A. (1971) The coarticulation of tones: an acoustic study of Thai. In T. L. Thongkum, V. Panupong, P. Kullavanijaya and M. R. K. Tingsabadh (eds) *Studies in Tai and Mon Khmer Phonetics and Phonology, in Honour of Eugénie J. A. Henderson* 1–9. Bangkok: Chulalongkorn University Press.

Adler, A. N. (2006) Faithfulness and perception in loanword adaptation: a case study from Hawaiian. *Lingua* 116: 1024–45.

Alber, Birgit (2001) Regional variation at edges: glottal stop epenthesis and dissimilation in Standard and Southern varieties of German. *Zeitschrift fur Sprachwissenschaft* 20: 3–41.

Alber, Birgit (2005) Clash, lapse, and directionality. *Natural Language and Linguistic Theory* 23: 485–542.

Alber, Birgit and I. Plag (2001) Epenthesis, deletion, and the emergence of the optimal syllable in creole: the case of Sranan. *Lingua* 111: 811–40.

Albright, A. (2002) A restricted model of UR discovery: evidence from Lakhota. Unpublished ms, University of California, Santa Cruz.

Albright, A. (2004) The emergence of the marked: root-domain markedness in Lakhota. Handout from the meeting of the Linguistic Society of America.

Albright, A. (2006) Gradient phonotactic effects: lexical? grammatical? both? neither? Handout from the meeting of the Linguistic Society of America.

Alderete, John (1997) Dissimilation as local conjunction. In K. Kusumoto (ed.) *Proceedings of the Twenty-Seventh North East Linguistic Society* 17–32. Amherst, MA: Graduate Linguistic Student Association.

Alderete, John (1999a) Head dependence in stress-epenthesis interaction. In Ben Hermans and Marc van Oostendorp (eds) *The Derivational Residue in Phonological Optimality Theory* 29–50. Amsterdam: Benjamins.

Alderete, John (1999b) *Morphologically Governed Accent in Optimality Theory*. PhD dissertation, University of Massachusetts Amherst.

Alderete, John (2001) Dominance effects as transderivational anti-faithfulness. *Phonology* 18: 201–53.

Alderete, John and Bruce Tesar (2002) Learning covert phonological interaction: an analysis of the problem posed by the interaction of stress and epenthesis. RuCCS Technical Report TR-72, Rutgers University. Rutgers Optimality Archive 543.

Ali, L., R. Daniloff and R. Hammarberg (1979) Intrusive stops in nasal-fricative clusters: an aerodynamic and acoustic investigation. *Phonetica* 36: 85–97.

Allen, Sidney (1975) *Accent and Rhythm*. Cambridge Studies in Linguistics 12. Cambridge: Cambridge University Press.

Altshuler, Daniel (2006) Osage fills the gap: the quantity insensitive iamb and the typology of feet. Unpublished ms, Rutgers Optimality Archive 870.

Angoujard, Jean-Pierre (1990) *Metrical Structure of Arabic.* Dordrecht: Foris Publications.

Ansre, G. (1961) *The Tonal Structure of Ewe.* MA thesis, Kennedy School of Missions of the Hartford Seminary Foundation. Hartford Studies in Linguistics, Number 1.

Anttila, Arto (1995) Deriving variation from grammar: a study of Finnish genitives. Unpublished ms, Rutgers Optimality Archive 63.

Anttila, Arto (1997) Deriving variation from grammar. In F. Hinskens, R. van Hout and W. L. Wetzels (eds) *Variation, Change and Phonological Theory* 35–68. Amsterdam: John Benjamins.

Anttila, Arto (2002) Morphologically conditioned phonological alternations. *Natural Language and Linguistic Theory* 20: 1–42.

Anttila, Arto (2007) Variation and optionality. In Paul de Lacy (ed.) *The Cambridge Handbook of Phonology* 519–36. Cambridge: Cambridge University Press.

Anttila, Arto and Young-Mee Cho (1998) Variation and change in optimality theory. *Lingua* 104: 31–56.

Anttila, Arto and Young-Mee Cho (2004) Variation and change in optimality theory. In John J. McCarthy (ed.) *Optimality Theory in Phonology* 569–80. Malden: Blackwell.

Arakawa, S. (1977) *Gairaigo jiten* (second edition). Tokyo: Kadokawa.

Archangeli, Diana and Douglas Pulleyblank (1994) *Grounded Phonology.* Cambridge: The MIT Press.

Archangeli, Diana and Douglas Pulleyblank (2007) Harmony. In Paul de Lacy (ed.) *The Cambridge Handbook of Phonology* 353–78. Cambridge: Cambridge University Press.

Austin, Peter (1981) *A Grammar of Diyari, South Australia.* Cambridge: Cambridge University Press.

Baayen, R., R. Piepenbrock and L. Gulikers (1995) *The CELEX Lexical Database* (CD-ROM). Philadelphia: Linguistic Data Consortium.

Baertsch, Karen and Stuart Davis (2003) The split margin approach to syllable structure. In T. A. Hall and S. Hamann (eds) *ZAS Papers in Linguistics* 32: 1–14. Berlin: Zentrum für Allgemeine Sprachwissenschaft, Typologie und Universalienforschung.

Bailey, Todd M. and Ulrike Hahn (1998) Determinants of wordlikeness. In Morton Ann Gernsbacher and Sharon J. Derry (eds) *Proceedings of the 20th Annual Conference of the Cognitive Science Society* 90–95. London: Lawrence Erlbaum.

Baker, Brett (1999) *Word Structure in Ngalakgan.* PhD dissertation, University of Sydney.

Baker, Brett and Mark Harvey (2003) Word structure in Australian languages. *Australian Journal of Linguistics* 23: 3–34.

Baković, Eric (1994) Strong onsets and Spanish fortition. In C. Giordano and D. Ardron (eds) *MIT Working Papers in Linguistics* 23: 21–39.

Baković, Eric (1999) Deletion, insertion, and symmetrical identity. *Harvard Working Papers in Linguistics* 7.

Baković, Eric (2000) *Harmony, Dominance and Control*. PhD dissertation, Rutgers University.

Baković, Eric (2006a) Antigemination, assimilation, and the determination of identity. *Phonology* 22: 279–315.

Baković, Eric (2006b) Partial identity avoidance as cooperative interaction. In Michal Temkin Martínez, Asier Alcázar and Roberto Mayoral Hernández (eds) *Proceedings of the Thirty-third Western Conference on Linguistics* 13–25. Fresno: Department of Linguistics, California State University, Fresno.

Barnes, J. (2002) *Positional Neutralization: A Phonologization Approach to Typological Patterns*. PhD dissertation, University of California, Berkeley.

Barry, William J. (1989) Perception and production of English vowels by German learners: instrumental phonetic support in language teaching. *Phonetica* 46: 155–68.

Barthélemy, F. (1998) A morphological analyzer for Akkadian verbal forms with a model of phonetic transformations. In M. Rosner (ed.) *Computational Approaches to Semitic Languages* 73–81. Montreal, Quebec: Université de Montréal.

Bat-El, Outi (1994) Stem modification and cluster transfer in Modern Hebrew. *Natural Language and Linguistic Theory* 12: 571–96.

Bat-El, Outi (1996) Selecting the best of the worst: the grammar of Hebrew blends. *Phonology* 13: 283–328.

Bateman, J. (1990) Iau segmental and tone phonology. *Nusa* 32: 29–42.

Battistella, Edwin L. (1990) *Markedness: the Evaluative Superstructure of Language*. Albany, NY: State University of New York Press.

Bauer, Winifred (1993) *Māori*. New York and London: Routledge.

Baumbach, E. J. M. (1987) *Analytical Tsonga Grammar*. Pretoria: University of South Africa.

Beaumont, Clive H. (1979) *The Tigak Language of New Ireland*. Pacific Linguistics Series B, No. 58. Canberra, Department of Linguistics, Research School of Pacific Studies: The Australian National University.

Becker, Michael (2004) Lexical exceptions: putting the grammar to work. Handout of a talk presented at HUMDRUM, Rutgers University.

Becker, Michael (2006a) Ccamelot – an implementation of OT-CC's GEN and EVAL in Perl. Handout of talk presented at the 80th meeting of the Linguistic Society of America, Albuquerque, NM.

Becker, Michael (2006b) Learning the lexicon through the grammar – evidence from Turkish. Unpublished ms, University of Massachusetts Amherst.

Beckman, Jill (1997) Positional faithfulness, positional neutralisation, and Shona vowel harmony. *Phonology* 14: 1–46.

Beckman, Jill (1998) *Positional Faithfulness*. PhD dissertation, University of Massachusetts Amherst.

Beechey, T. (2005) A non-representational theory of geminate inalterability and integrity. Unpublished ms, University of Massachusetts Amherst.

Beesley, K. and L. Karttunen (2000) Finite-state non-concatenative morphotactics. *Proceedings of the Fifth Workshop of the ACL Special Interest Group in Computational Phonology* 1–12.

Bendor-Samuel, J. T. (1960) Some problems of segmentation in the phonological analysis of Terena. *Word* 16: 348–55.

Benua, L. (1997/2000) *Transderivational Identity: Phonological Relations between Words*. PhD dissertation, University of Massachusetts Amherst. Published 2000, New York: Garland.

Benveniste, Émile (1935) *Origines de la Formation des Noms en Indo-Européen*. Paris: Adrien Maisonneuve.

Berent, Iris, Daniel L. Everett and Joseph Shimron (2001) Do phonological representations specify variables? Evidence from the Obligatory Contour Principle. *Cognitive Psychology* 42: 1–60.

Berent, Iris and Joseph Shimron (1997) The representation of Hebrew words: evidence from the Obligatory Contour Principle. *Cognition* 64: 39–72.

Berent, Iris, Joseph Shimron and Vered Vaknin (2001) Phonological constraints on reading: evidence from the Obligatory Contour Principle. *Journal of Memory and Language* 44: 644–65.

Berkley, Deborah Milam (1994) The OCP and gradient data. *Studies in the Linguistic Sciences* 24: 59–72.

Berkley, Deborah Milam (2000) *Gradient Obligatory Contour Principle Effects*. PhD dissertation, Northwestern University, Chicago.

Bermúdez-Otero, Ricardo (2007) Word-final prevocalic consonants in English: representation vs. derivation. Revised handout, Old World Conference in Phonology 4, Rhodes, 20 January 2007. http://myweb.tiscali.co.uk/bermudez/OCP4.pdf.

Bernhardt, B. H. and J. P. Stemberger (1998) *Handbook of Phonological Development*. San Diego: Academic Press.

Berry, Lynn (1996) *Alignment and Adjacency in Optimality Theory: Evidence from Warlpiri and Arrente*. PhD dissertation, University of Sydney.

Best, Catherine T. (1994) The emergence of native-language phonological influences in infants: a perceptual assimilation model. In H. C. Nusbaum and J. Goodman (eds) *The Development of Speech Perception: the Transition from Speech Sounds to Spoken Words*. 167–224. Cambridge, MA: The MIT Press.

Blevins, Juliette (1994) A phonological and morphological reanalysis of the Māori passive. *Te Reo* 37: 29–53.

Blevins, Juliette (1999) Untangling Leti infixation. *Oceanic Linguistics* 38: 383–403.

Blevins, Juliette (2001) *Nhanda: an Aboriginal Language of Western Australia.* Oceanic Linguistics Special Publication 30. Honolulu: University of Hawai'i Press.

Blevins, Juliette (2004) *Evolutionary Phonology.* Cambridge: Cambridge University Press.

Blevins, Juliette (2006) A theoretical synopsis of Evolutionary Phonology. *Theoretical Linguistics* 32: 117–66.

Blevins, J. and A. Garrett (2004) The evolution of metathesis. In B. Hayes, R. Kirchner and D. Steriade (eds) *Phonetically Based Phonology* 117–56. Cambridge: Cambridge University Press.

Bloomfield, Leonard (1933) *Language.* London: George Allen and Unwin LTD.

Blumstein, Sheila (1991) The relation between phonetics and phonology. *Phonetica* 48: 108–19.

Boersma, Paul (1998) *Functional Phonology: Formalizing the Interactions between Articulatory and Perceptual Drives.* PhD dissertation, University of Amsterdam. Published The Hague: Holland Academic Graphics.

Boersma, Paul (2000) The OCP in the perception grammar. Unpublished ms, Rutgers Optimality Archive 435.

Boersma, Paul and Bruce Hayes (2001) Empirical tests of the Gradual Learning Algorithm. *Linguistic Inquiry* 32: 45–86.

Boersma, Paul and David Weenink (2005) *Praat: doing phonetics by computer* (computer program, version 4.3.19). Retrieved July 20, 2005 from http://www.praat.org/.

Bohas, Georges (1980) Glides medians et finaux en arabe. *Analyses, theorie* 1: 83–100.

Bohas, Georges (1997) *Matrices, Étymons, Racines: Éléments d'une théorie lexicologique du vocabulaire arabe.* Leeuven: Peeters.

Bonet, Eulàlia and Maria-Rosa Lloret (2005) More on alignment as an alternative to domains: the syllabification of Catalan clitics. *Probus* 17: 37–78.

Borroff, Marianne (2003) Against an ONSET analysis of hiatus resolution. Unpublished ms, Rutgers Optimality Archive 586.

Bradley, Travis G. (2001) *The Phonetics and Phonology of Rhotic Duration Contrast and Neutralization.* PhD dissertation, Pennsylvania State University.

Bradley, Travis G. and Ann Marie Delforge (2006) Systemic contrast and the diachrony of Spanish sibilant voicing. In Randall Gess and Deborah Arteaga (eds) *Historical Romance Linguistics: Retrospectives and Perspectives* 19–52. Amsterdam: John Benjamins.

Bradshaw, M. M. (1999) *A Crosslinguistic Study of Consonant-Tone Interaction.* PhD dissertation, Ohio State University.

Brame, Michael (1970) *Arabic Phonology.* PhD dissertation, MIT.

Broadbent, Judith (1991) Linking and intrusive r in English. *UCLA Working Papers in Linguistics* 3: 281–302.

Broselow, Ellen (1982) On predicting the interaction of stress and epenthesis. *Glossa* 16: 115–32.

Broselow, Ellen (1991) The structure of fricative-stop onsets. Unpublished ms, State University of New York, Stony Brook.

Broselow, Ellen (2000) Stress, epenthesis, and segment transformation in Selayarese loans. In S. S. Chang, L. Liaw and J. Ruppenhofer (eds) *Proceedings of BLS 25* 211–25. Berkeley: Berkeley Linguistics Society.

Broselow, Ellen (2004) Language contact phonology: richness of the stimulus, poverty of the base. In K. Moulton and M. Wolf (eds) *Proceedings of NELS 34* 1–21. Amherst, MA: Graduate Linguistic Student Association.

Broselow, Ellen (2006) Stress adaptation in loanword phonology: perception and learnability. Unpublished ms, State University of New York, Stony Brook.

Broselow, Ellen (2008) Stress-epenthesis interactions. In Bert Vaux and Andrew Nevins (eds) *Rules, Constraints and Phonological Phenomena* 121–49. Oxford: Oxford University Press.

Broselow, Ellen, Su-I Chen and Marie Huffman (1997) Syllable weight: convergence of phonology and phonetics. *Phonology* 14: 47–82.

Browman, C. P. and L. M. Goldstein (1995) Dynamics and articulatory phonology. In R. F. Port and T. van Gelder (eds) *Mind as Motion: Explorations in the Dynamics of Cognition* 175–93. Cambridge, MA: The MIT Press.

Brown, Dee (1970) *Bury my Heart at Wounded Knee: an Indian History of the American West*. New York: Henry Holt and Company.

Browne, Wayles (1981) Slavic -ba and English *slil: two persistent constraints. *Folia Slavica* 4: 219–25.

Buckley, E. (2000) Explaining Kashaya infixation. *Proceedings of BLS 23* 14–25.

Bye, Patrik and Paul de Lacy (2008) Metrical influences on fortition and lenition. In Joaquim Brandão de Carvalho, Tobias Scheer and Philippe Ségéral (eds) *Lenition and Fortition*. Studies in Generative Grammar 99. 173–206. Berlin: Mouton de Gruyter.

Caballero Hernández, G. (2005) The stress system of Central Raramuri: root privilege, prosodic faithfulness and markedness reversals. Unpublished ms, University of California, Berkeley. Rutgers Optimality Archive 706.

Caldwell, T., J. Oswalt and J. Sheehan (1977) *An Akkadian Grammar*. Milwaukee, Wisconsin: Marquette University Press.

Campbell, L. (1998) *Historical Linguistics: an Introduction*. Cambridge, MA: The MIT Press.

Casali, Roderic F. (1996) *Resolving Hiatus*. PhD dissertation, UCLA. Published 1998, New York: Garland.

Casali, Roderic F. (1997) Vowel elision in hiatus contexts: which vowel goes? *Language* 73: 493–533.

Chafe, W. L. (1976) *The Caddoan, Iroquoian, and Siouan languages*. The Hague: Mouton.

Chang, Y.-C. (1988) Sandhi tonal des syntagmes dissyllabiques du Min-Nan parlé à Taiwan. *Cahier de Linguistique Asie Orientale* 17: 193–234.

Charles-Luce, Jan (1985) Word-final devoicing in German: effects of phonetic and sentential contexts. *Journal of Phonetics* 13: 309–24.

Chekayri, Abdellah and Tobias Scheer (1996) The apophonic origin of glides in the verbal system of Classical Arabic. In J. Lecarme, Jean Lowenstamm and Ur Shlonsky (eds) *Studies in Afroasiatic Grammar* 62–76. The Hague: Holland Academic Graphics.

Chen, M. (2000) *Tone Sandhi: Patterns across Chinese Dialects*. Cambridge: Cambridge University Press.

Chinneck, J. W. and E. W. Dravnieks (1991) Locating minimal infeasible constraint sets in linear programs. *ORSA Journal on Computing* 3: 157–68.

Cho, Taehong and Patricia Keating (2001) Articulatory strengthening at the onset of prosodic domains in Korean. *Journal of Phonetics* 28: 115–90.

Chomsky, Noam and Morris Halle (1965) Some controversial questions in phonological theory. *Journal of Linguistics* 1: 97–138.

Chomsky, Noam and Morris Halle (1968) *The Sound Pattern of English*. New York: Harper & Row.

Clark, Ross (1976) *Aspects of Proto-Polynesian Syntax*. Te Reo monograph. Auckland, New Zealand: Linguistic Society of New Zealand.

Clements, G. N. and K. Ford (1979) Kikuyu tone shift and its synchronic consequences. *Linguistic Inquiry* 10: 179–210.

Clements, G. N. and E. V. Hume (1995) The internal organization of speech sounds. In John A. Goldsmith (ed.) *The Handbook of Phonological Theory* 245–306. Cambridge: Blackwell.

Clements, George N. and Samuel Jay Keyser (1983) *CV Phonology: a Generative Theory of the Syllable*. Cambridge: The MIT Press.

Coetzee, Andries (2002) Between-language frequency effects in phonological theory. Unpublished ms, University of Massachusetts Amherst.

Coetzee, Andries (2004) *What it Means to be a Loser: Non-Optimal Candidates in Optimality Theory*. PhD dissertation, University of Massachusetts Amherst.

Coetzee, Andries (2005) The OCP in the perception of English. In Sonia Frota, Marina Vigario and Maria Joao Freitas (eds) *Prosodies* 223–45. New York: Mouton de Gruyter.

Coetzee, Andries (2006) Variation as accessing 'non-optimal candidates' – a rank-ordering model of EVAL. Unpublished ms, University of Michigan. http://www-personal.umich.edu/~coetzee/publications.html.

Coetzee, Andries (2008) Grammaticality and ungrammaticality in phonology. *Language* 84: 218–57.

Coetzee, Andries and Joe Pater (2008) Weighted constraints and gradient phonotactics in Muna and Arabic. *Natural Language and Linguistic Theory* 26: 289–337.

Coleman, John and Janet Pierrehumbert (1997) Stochastic phonological grammars and acceptability. In *Computational Phonology: Third Meeting of the ACL Special Interest Group in Computational Phonology* 49–56. Somerset: Association for Computational Linguistics.

Creel, S. C., E. L. Newport and R. N. Aslin (2004) Distant melodies: statistical learning of non-adjacent dependencies in tone sequences. *Journal of Experimental Psychology: Learning, Memory, and Cognition* 30: 1119–30.

Crowhurst, Megan (1994) Prosodic alignment and misalignment in Diyari, Dyirbal, and Gooniyandi: an optimizing approach. In R. Aranovich et al. (eds) *Proceedings of the West Coast Conference on Formal Linguistics 13* 16–31. Stanford: Stanford Linguistics Association.

Crowhurst, Megan (1996) An optimal alternative to conflation. *Phonology* 13: 409–24.

Crowhurst, Megan (1998) Um-infixation and prefixation in Toba Batak. *Language* 74: 590–604.

Crowhurst, Megan (2001) Coda conditions and Um-infixation in Toba Batak. *Lingua* 111: 561–90.

Crowley, T. (1997) *An Introduction to Historical Linguistics.* Oxford: Oxford University Press.

Davidson, Lisa (2006) Phonology, phonetics, or frequency: influences on the production of non-native sequences. *Journal of Phonetics* 34: 104–37.

Davidson, L. and R. Noyer (1997) Loan phonology in Huave: nativization and the ranking of faithfulness constraints. In B. Agbayani and S.-W. Tang (eds) *Proceedings of the West Coast Conference on Formal Linguistics 15* 65–79. Stanford: CSLI.

Davis, Stuart (1984) Some implications of onset-coda constraints for syllable phonology. *Proceedings of the Chicago Linguistic Society 20* 46–51. Chicago: Chicago Linguistics Society.

Davis, Stuart (1991) Coronals and the phonotactics of nonadjacent consonants in English. In C. Paradis and J. F. Prunet (eds) *The Special Status of Coronals: Internal and External Evidence* 49–60. San Diego: Academic Press.

de Boer, Bart (2001) *The origins of vowel systems.* Studies in the evolution of language. Oxford: Oxford University Press.

de Lacy, Paul (1998) Sympathetic stress. Unpublished ms, University of Massachusetts Amherst. Rutgers Optimality Archive 294.

de Lacy, Paul (1999) Haplology and correspondence. In Paul de Lacy and Anita Nowak (eds) *University of Massachusetts Occasional Papers 24* 51–88. Amherst, MA: Graduate Linguistic Student Association.

de Lacy, Paul (2002) *The Formal Expression of Markedness.* PhD dissertation, University of Massachusetts Amherst. Rutgers Optimality Archive 542.

de Lacy, Paul (2003) Maximal words and the Māori passive. In John McCarthy (ed.) *Optimality Theory in Phonology: a Reader* 495–512. Oxford, UK: Blackwell.

de Lacy, Paul (2004) Markedness conflation in optimality theory. *Phonology* 21: 145–99.

de Lacy, Paul (2006a) *Markedness: Reduction and Preservation in Phonology.* Cambridge: Cambridge University Press.

de Lacy, Paul (2006b) The roles of transmissibility and the phonological component. *Theoretical Linguistics* 32: 185–96.

de Lacy, Paul (this volume) Phonological evidence.

de Lacy, Paul (to appear) Glossolalia as a targetless L2. Unpublished ms, Rutgers University.

de Lacy, Paul and John Kingston (2006) Synchronic explanation. Unpublished ms, Rutgers University and University of Massachusetts Amherst.

Dempwolff, O. (1939/2005) *Grammar of the Jabêm Language in New Guinea* (translated by Joel Bradshaw and Francisc Czobor). Oceanic Linguistics Special Publication No. 32. Honolulu: University of Hawai'i Press.

Denwood, Philip (1999) *Tibetan.* Amsterdam: John Benjamins Publishing Company.

Dinnsen, Daniel (1985) A re-examination of phonological neutralization. *Journal of Linguistics* 21: 265–79.

Dinnsen, Daniel and Jan Charles-Luce (1984) Phonological neutralization, phonetic implementation, and individual differences. *Journal of Phonetics* 12: 49–60.

Dixon, Robert M. W. (1972) *The Dyirbal Language of North Queensland.* Cambridge: Cambridge University Press.

Dixon, Robert M. W. (1980) *The Languages of Australia.* Cambridge: Cambridge University Press.

Dohlus, K. (2005) Phonetics or phonology: asymmetries in loanword adaptations—French and German mid front rounded vowels in Japanese. *ZAS Papers in Linguistics* 42: 117--35.

Donohue, M. (2003) The tonal system of Skou, New Guinea. In Shigeki Kaji (ed.) *Proceedings of the Symposium Cross-linguistic Studies of Tonal Phenomena: Historical Development, Phonetics of Tone, and Descriptive Studies* 329–65. Tokyo: Tokyo University of Foreign Studies, Research Institute for Language and Cultures of Asia and Africa.

Downer, G. (1961) Phonology of the word in Highland Yao. *Bulletin of the School of Oriental and African Studies* 24: 531–41.

Downer, G. (1967) Tone-change and tone-shift in White Miao. *Bulletin of the School of Oriental and African Studies* 30: 589–99.

Downing, L. (1998) On the prosodic misalignment of onsetless syllables. *Natural Language and Linguistic Theory* 16: 1–52.

Dupoux, E., K. Kakehi, Y. Hirose, C. Pallier and J. Mehler (1999) Epenthetic vowels in Japanese: a perceptual illusion? *Journal of Experimental Psychology: Human Perception and Performance* 25: 1568–78.

Edmondson, J. and K. J. Gregerson (1996) Bolyu tone in a Vietic perspective. *Mon-Khmer Studies* 26: 117–33.

Egerod, S. (1956) *The Lungtu Dialect: a Descriptive and Historical Study of a South Chinese Idiom*. Copenhagen: Ejnar Munksgaard.

Everett, Daniel L. (2003) Iambic feet in Paumari and the theory of foot structure. *Linguistic Discovery* 2: 22–44.

Fallon, Paul (2002) *The Synchronic and Diachronic Phonology of Ejectives*. PhD dissertation, Ohio State University. Published New York: Routledge.

Ferguson, Charles A. (1975) Sound patterns in language acquisition. In Daniel P. Dato (ed.) *Developmental Psycholinguistics: Theory and Applications* 1–16 Washington, DC: Georgetown University Press.

Finer, D. (1985) Reduplication and verbal morphology in Palauan. *Linguistic Review* 6: 99–130.

Finley, S. (2006) Exceptions in vowel harmony are local. Unpublished ms, Johns Hopkins University, Baltimore, Maryland.

Fischer-Jørgensen, E. (1972) PTK et BDG français en position intervocalique accentuée. In Albert Valdman (ed.) *Papers in Linguistics and Phonetics to the Memory of Pierre Delattre* 143–200. The Hague: Mouton.

Flack, Kathryn (2006) Restrictions on the edges of prosodic domains. Unpublished ms, University of Massachusetts Amherst.

Flack, Kathryn (2007a) Phonotactic restrictions across prosodic domains. Handout of talk presented at the Annual Meeting of the Linguistic Society of America, Anaheim, CA. http://people.umass.edu/flack/ papers/.

Flack, Kathryn (2007b) Templatic morphology and indexed markedness constraints. *Linguistic Inquiry* 38: 749–58.

Flemming, Edward (1995/2002) *Auditory Representations in Phonology*. PhD dissertation, UCLA. Published 2002, New York: Routledge.

Flemming, Edward (1999) How to formalize constraints on perceptual distinctiveness. Handout of paper presented at 'The role of speech perception phenomena in phonology,' a satellite workshop to ICPhS, San Francisco.

Flemming, Edward (2001) Scalar and categorical phenomena in a unified model of phonetics and phonology. *Phonology* 18: 7–44.

Flemming, Edward (2004) Contrast and perceptual distinctiveness. In Bruce Hayes, Robert Kirchner and Donca Steriade (eds) *Phonetically-based Phonology* 232–76. Cambridge: Cambridge University Press.

Flora, Marie JoAnn (1974a) *Palauan Phonology and Morphology*. PhD dissertation, University of California, San Diego.

Flora, JoAnn (1974b) The Palauan /m/ affix. *Oceanic Linguistics* 13: 213–27.

Fougeron, Cecile and Donce Steriade (1997) Does deletion of French schwa lead to neutralization of lexical distinctions? *EUROSPEECH*: 943–46.

Fourakis, Marios and Gregory Iverson (1984) On the 'incomplete neutralization' of German final obstruents. *Phonetica* 41: 140–49.

Fourakis, Marios and Robert Port (1986) Stop epenthesis in English. *Journal of Phonetics* 14: 197–221.

Franklin, Karl J. (1971) *A Grammar of Kewa, New Guinea*. Pacific Linguistics Series C, No. 16. Canberra: Australian National University.

Frisch, Stefan (1996) *Similarity and Frequency in Phonology*. PhD dissertation, Northwestern University. Rutgers Optimality Archive 198.

Frisch, Stefan A., Janet B. Pierrehumbert and Michael B. Broe (2004) Similarity avoidance and the OCP. *Natural Language and Linguistic Theory* 22: 179–228.

Frisch, Stefan A. and Bushra Adnan Zawaydeh (2001) The psychological reality of OCP-place in Arabic. *Language* 77: 91–106.

Fudge, E. C. (1969) Syllables. *Journal of Linguistics* 5: 253–86.

Fujimura, Osamu (1979) An analysis of English syllables as cores and affixes. *Zeitschrift für Phonetik, Sprachwissenschaft und Kommunicationsforschung* 32: 471–76.

Fukazawa, H. (1999) *Theoretical Implications of OCP Effects on Features in Optimality Theory*. PhD dissertation, University of Maryland, College Park. Rutgers Optimality Archive 307.

Fukazawa, H., M. Kitahara and M. Ota (1998) Lexical stratification and ranking invariance in constraint-based grammars. In M. Gruber, D. Higgins, K. Olson and T. Wysocki (eds) *Chicago Linguistics Society 34*, vol. 2, 47–62. Chicago: Chicago Linguistic Society.

Gafos, Adamantios I. (1998) Eliminating long distance consonantal spreading. *Natural Language and Linguistic Theory* 16: 223–78.

Gafos, Adamantios I. (1999) *The Articulatory Basis of Locality in Phonology*. New York: Garland.

Gafos, Adamantios I. (2003) Greenberg's asymmetry in Arabic: a consequence of stems in paradigms. *Language* 79: 317–55.

Gafos, Adamantios and Linda Lombardi (1999) Consonant transparency and vowel echo. In Pius Tamanji, Masako Hirotani and Nancy Hall (eds) *Proceedings of the Twenty-Ninth Meeting of the North Eastern Linguistics Society* 81–96. Amherst, MA: Graduate Linguistic Student Association.

Gandour, J. (1974) Consonant types and tone in Siamese. *Journal of Phonetics* 2: 337–50.

Gandour, J., S. Potisuk and S. Dechongkit (1994) Tonal coarticulation in Thai. *Journal of Phonetics* 22: 477–92.

Gelbart, B. (2005) *The Role of Foreignness in Phonology and Speech Perception*. PhD dissertation, University of Massachusetts Amherst.

Gessner, S. (2003) *The Prosodic System of the Dakelh (Carrier) Language*. PhD dissertation, University of British Columbia.

Ghini, Mirco (2001) *Asymmetries in the Phonology of Miogliola*. New York: Mouton de Gruyter.

Gick, Bryan W. (2003) An X-Ray investigation of pharyngeal constriction in American English schwa. *Phonetica* 59: 38–48.

Gimson, A. C. and Alan Cruttenden (2001) *Gimson's Pronunciation of English*. London: Arnold.

Gnanadesikan, Amalia (1995) Markedness and faithfulness constraints in child phonology. Unpublished ms, University of Massachusetts Amherst.

Gnanadesikan, Amalia (1997) *Phonology with Ternary Scales*. PhD dissertation, University of Massachusetts at Amherst. Rutgers Optimality Archive 195.

Goedemans, Rob (1994) An optimality account of onset sensitivity in QI languages. Unpublished ms, Rutgers Optimality Archive 26.

Goldsmith, John (1976) *Autosegmental Phonology*. PhD dissertation, MIT. Published 1979, New York: Garland.

Goldsmith, John (1989) Autosegmental licensing, inalterability, and harmonic application. In C. Wiltshire, R. Graczyk and B. Music (eds) *Papers from CLS 25* 145–56. Chicago: Chicago Linguistic Society.

Goldsmith, John (1990) *Autosegmental and Metrical Phonology*. Oxford and Cambridge, MA: Blackwell.

Golston, C. (1996) Direct OT: representation as pure markedness. *Language* 72: 713–48.

Golston, C. and P. Yang (2001) Hmong loanword phonology. In C. Féry, A. Dubach Green and R. van de Vijver (eds) *Proceedings of HILP 5*: 40–57. Potsdam: University of Potsdam.

Gomez-Imbert, E. and M. Kenstowicz (2000) Barasana tone and accent. *International Journal of American Linguistics* 66: 4–19.

Gordon, Matthew (2002) A factorial typology of quantity insensitive stress. *Natural Language and Linguistic Theory* 20: 491–552.

Gordon, Matthew (2007) Functionalism. In Paul de Lacy (ed.) *The Cambridge Handbook of Phonology* 61–78. Cambridge: Cambridge University Press.

Gordon, R. G., Jr. (ed.) (2005) *Ethnologue: Languages of the World* (15th edition). Dallas: SIL International.

Gouskova, Maria (2001) Falling-sonority onsets, loanwords, and syllable contact. In M. Andronis, C. Ball, H. Elston and S. Neuvel (eds) *Chicago Linguistics Society 37*, vol. 1, 175–85. Chicago: Chicago Linguistics Society.

Gouskova, Maria (2003) *Deriving Economy: Syncope in Optimality Theory*. PhD dissertation, University of Massachusetts Amherst.

Gouskova, Maria (2004) Relational hierarchies in Optimality Theory: the case of syllable contact. *Phonology* 21: 201–50.

Gouskova, Maria (2006) A templatic constraint in Tonkawa. Unpublished ms, New York University.

Gouskova, Maria and Nancy Hall (this volume) Acoustics of epenthetic vowels in Lebanese Arabic.

Graf, D. (2004) Alignment properties of affixes and their role in Hebrew morphology. Handout of a talk given at WECOL, Los Angeles, November 2004.

Green, A. Dubach (2005) Phonology limited. Unpublished ms, Centre for General Linguistics, Typology and Universals Research (ZAS), Berlin. Rutgers Optimality Archive 745.

Green, Thomas and Michael Kenstowicz (1995) The lapse constraint. In *Proceedings of the Formal Linguistics Society of Midamerica 6*, 1–14. Bloomington: Indiana University Linguistics Club.

Greenberg, Joseph H. (1950) The patterning of root morphemes in Semitic. *Word* 6: 162–81.

Greenberg, Joseph H. (1966) *Language Universals, with Special Reference to Feature Hierarchies*. Janua Linguarum, Series Minor 59. The Hague: Mouton.

Grimshaw, Jane (2005) *Words and Structure*. CSLI Lecture Notes. Stanford, CA: CSLI/University of Chicago Press.

Gussenhoven, Carlos (1986) English plosive allophones and ambisyllabicity. *Gramma* 10: 119–41.

Gussenhoven, Carlos (2004) *The Phonology of Tone and Intonation*. Cambridge: Cambridge University Press.

Gussenhoven, Carlos (2007) The phonology of intonation. In Paul de Lacy (ed.) *The Cambridge Handbook of Phonology* 253–80. Cambridge: Cambridge University Press.

Haddad, Ghassan (1983) Epenthesis and sonority in Lebanese Arabic. *Studies in the Linguistic Sciences* 14: 57–88.

Haddad, Ghassan (1984) *Problems and Issues in the Phonology of Lebanese Arabic*. PhD dissertation, University of Illinois at Urbana-Champaign.

Hakulinen, L. (1961) *The Structure and Development of the Finnish Language* (J. Atkinson, translator). Uralic and Altaic Series 3. The Hague: Mouton.

Hale, K. (1968) Review of Hohepa (1967) – 'A Profile Generative Grammar of Māori'. *Journal of the Polynesian Society* 77: 83–99.

Hale, Kenneth (1973) Deep-surface canonical disparities in relation to analysis and change: an Australian example. In T. Sebeok (ed.) *Current Trends in Linguistics* 401–58. The Hague: Mouton.

Hale, M. and Reiss, C. (2000) 'Substance abuse' and 'dysfunctionalism': current trends in phonology. *Linguistic Inquiry* 31: 157–69.

Halle, Morris and Michael Kenstowicz (1991) The Free Element Condition and cyclic versus noncyclic stress. *Linguistic Inquiry* 22: 457–501.

Ham, W. H. (1999) Tone sandhi in Saramaccan: a case of substrate transfer? *Journal of Pidgin and Creole Languages* 14: 45–91.

Hammond, M. (1995) There is no lexicon! Unpublished ms, University of Arizona. Rutgers Optimality Archive 45.

Han, M. S. and K.-O. Kim (1974) Phonetic variation of Vietnamese tones in disyllabic utterances. *Journal of Phonetics* 2: 223–32.

Han, M. S. and R. S. Weitzman (1970) Acoustic features of Korean /P T K/, /p t k/, and /ph th kh/. *Phonetica* 22: 112–28.

Hansen, K. C. and L. E. Hansen (1969) Pintupi phonology. *Oceanic Linguistics* 8: 153–70.

Haraguchi, Shosuke (1984) Some tonal and segmental effects of vowel height in Japanese. In Mark Aronoff and R. T. Oehrle (eds) *Language Sound Structure: Studies in Phonology Presented to Morris Halle by his Teacher and Students* 145–56. Cambridge, MA: The MIT Press.

Hargus, Sharon (1987) Infixation and bracketing erasure in Sekani. *Working Papers in Linguistics* 9: 83–117. University of Washington.

Hargus, Sharon (1993) Modeling the phonology-morphology interface. In Sharon Hargus and Ellen Kaisse (eds) *Phonetics and Phonology, Volume 4: Studies in Lexical Phonology* 45–74. San Diego: Academic Press.

Harris, Zellig (1951) *Methods in Structural Linguistics*. Chicago: University of Chicago Press.

Harris, John (2007) Representation. In Paul de Lacy (ed.) *The Cambridge Handbook of Phonology* 119–37. Cambridge: Cambridge University Press.

Haugen, E. (1950) The analysis of linguistic borrowing. *Language* 26: 210–31.

Hay, Jennifer, Janet Pierrehumbert and Mary Beckman (2004) Speech perception, well-formedness and the statistics of the lexicon. In J. Local, R. Ogden and R. Temple (eds) *Phonetic Interpretation: Papers in Laboratory Phonology VI* 58–74. Cambridge: Cambridge University Press.

Hayes, Bruce P. (1985) *A Metrical Theory of Stress Rules*. New York: Garland.

Hayes, Bruce (1989a) Compensatory lengthening in moraic phonology. *Linguistic Inquiry* 20: 253–305.

Hayes, Bruce (1989b) The prosodic hierarchy in meter. In Paul Kiparsky and Gilbert Youmans (eds) *Rhythm and Meter* 201–60. Orlando: Academic Press.

Hayes, Bruce (1995) *Metrical Stress Theory: Principles and Case Studies*. Chicago: University of Chicago Press.

Hayes, Bruce (1999) Phonetically driven phonology: the role of Optimality Theory and inductive grounding. In M. Darnell, E. A. Moravcsik, F. Newmeyer, M. Noonan and K. M. Wheatley (eds) *Formalism and Functionalism in Linguistics, Volume I*, 243–85. Amsterdam: Benjamins.

Hayes, Bruce (2004) Phonological acquisition in Optimality Theory: the early stages. In René Kager, Joe Pater and Wim Zonneveld (eds) *Constraints in Phonological Acquisition*. Cambridge: Cambridge University Press.

Hayes, Bruce, Robert Kirchner and Donca Steriade (eds) (2004) *Phonetically-Based Phonology*. Cambridge: Cambridge University Press.

Hayes, B. and Londe, Z. (2006) Stochastic phonological knowledge: the case of Hungarian vowel harmony. *Phonology* 23: 59–104.

Hayes, Bruce, Bruce Tesar and Kie Zuraw (2003) OTSoft 2.1, software package. UCLA and Rutgers University.

Hayes, Bruce and Colin Wilson (2008) A maximum entropy model of phonotactics and phonotactic learning. *Linguistic Inquiry* 39: 379–440.

Healey, A. (1964) *Telefol phonology*. Linguistic Circle of Canberra Publications, Series B, No. 3. Canberra: Australian National University.

Hendricks, S. (1999) *Reduplication without Templates: a Study of Bare-Consonant Reduplication*. PhD dissertation, University of Arizona, Tucson.

Herzallah, R. (1990) *Aspects of Palestinian Arabic Phonology: a Nonlinear Approach*. PhD dissertation, Cornell University. Distributed as *Working Papers of the Cornell Phonetics Laboratory No. 4*.

Hewitt, M. and A. Prince (1989) OCP, locality and linking: the N. Karanga verb. In E. Fee and K. Hunt (eds) *Proceedings of the West Coast Conference on Formal Linguistics 8*, 176–91. Stanford: Stanford Linguistics Association.

Hockett, Charles F. (1958) *A Course in Modern Linguistics.* New York: Macmillan.

Holes, Clive (1995) Community, dialect, and urbanization in the Arabic-speaking Middle East. *Bulletin of the School of Oriental and African Studies, University of London* 58: 270–87.

Hombert, J.-M., J. J. Ohala and W. G. Ewan (1979) Phonetic explanations for the development of tones. *Language* 55: 37–58.

Hooper, Joan B. (1972) The syllable in phonological theory. *Language* 48: 525–40.

Horwood, G. (1999) Anti-faithfulness and subtractive morphology. Unpublished ms, Rutgers University, New Brunswick, NJ. Rutgers Optimality Archive 466.

Horwood, G. (2002) Precedence faithfulness governs morpheme position. In L. Mikkelsen and C. Potts (eds) *Proceedings of the West Coast Conference on Formal Linguistics 21*, 166–79. Somerville, MA: Cascadilla Press.

Horwood, G. (2004) *Order without Chaos: Relational Faithfulness and Position of Exponence in Optimality Theory.* PhD dissertation, Rutgers University.

Howe, Darin (2004) Vocalic dorsality in revised articulator theory. Unpublished ms, University of Calgary.

Howe, Darin and Douglas Pulleyblank (2004) Harmonic scales as faithfulness. *Canadian Journal of Linguistics* 49: 1–49.

Hsieh, Feng-fan, Michael Kenstowicz and Xiaomin Mou (2006) Mandarin adaptations of coda nasals in English loanwords. Unpublished ms, MIT.

Huang, Tsan (2004) *Language-specificity in Auditory Perception of Chinese Tones.* PhD dissertation, The Ohio State University.

Hudak, T. J. (1996) *William J. Gedney's The Lue Language: Glossary, Texts, and Translations.* Michigan Papers in South and Southeast Asia 44. Center for South and Southeast Asian Studies, University of Michigan.

Huehnergard, J. (1997) *A Grammar of Akkadian.* Atlanta, Georgia: Scholars Press.

Hume, Elizabeth (2001) Metathesis: formal and functional considerations. In E. Hume, N. Smith and J. van de Weijer (eds) *Surface Syllable Structure and Segment Sequencing* 1–25. Leiden: HIL.

Hume, Elizabeth (2003) Language specific markedness: the case of place of articulation. *Studies in Phonetics, Phonology and Morphology* 9: 295–310.

Hume, Elizabeth (2004a) Deconstructing markedness: a predictability-based approach. Unpublished ms, Ohio State University. http://www.ling.ohio-state.edu/~ehume/.

Hume, Elizabeth (2004b) The indeterminacy/attestation model of metathesis. *Language* 80: 203–37.

Hume, Elizabeth (2006) Language-specific and universal markedness: an information-theoretic approach. Handout from the Annual Meeting of the Linguistic Society of America. http://www.ling.ohio-state.edu/~ehume/.

Hume, E. and K. Johnson (2001) A model of the interplay of speech perception and phonology. In E. Hume and K. Johnson (eds) *The Role of Speech Perception in Phonology* 3–26. San Diego: Academic Press.

Hume, Elizabeth and Georgios Tserdanelis (2002) Labial unmarkedness in Sri Lankan Portuguese Creole. *Phonology* 19: 441–58.

Huziwara, K. (2003) Tone sandhi in Chakma and Cak. Handout, 36th International Conference on Sino-Tibetan Languages and Linguistics, La Trobe University, Melbourne, November 30, 2003.

Hyde, Brett (2002) A restrictive theory of metrical stress. *Phonology* 19: 313–59.

Hyman, Larry (1970) The role of borrowing in the justification of phonological grammars. *Studies in African Linguistics* 1: 1–48.

Hyman, Larry M. (1976) Phonologization. In Alphonse Juilland (ed.) *Linguistic Studies Offered to Joseph Greenberg: Second Volume: Phonology*. Studia Linguistica et Philologica 4. Saratoga, California: Anma Libri.

Hyman, Larry M. (2001) The limits of phonetic determinism in phonology: *NC revisited. In E. Hume and K. Johnson (eds) *The Role of Speech Perception in Phonology* 141–86. San Diego: Academic Press.

Hyman, L. and S. Mchombo (1992) Morphotactic constraints in the Chichewa verb stem. *Proceedings of BLS 18*, 350–64. Berkeley: Berkeley Linguistics Society.

Ichikawa, S. (1929) *Foreign Influences on the Japanese Language.* Western Influences in Modern Japan Series, vol. 8. Tokyo: Japanese Council Institute of Pacific Relations.

Inkelas, Sharon (1989) *Prosodic Constituency in the Lexicon.* PhD dissertation, Stanford University. Published 1990, New York: Garland.

Inkelas, Sharon (1994) The consequences of optimization for underspecification. In Jill Beckman (ed.) *Proceedings of NELS 25*, 287–302. Amherst, MA: Graduate Linguistic Student Association.

Inkelas, Sharon (1999) Exceptional stress-attracting suffixes in Turkish: representations vs. the grammar. In Harry van der Hulst, René Kager and Wim Zonneveld (eds) *The Prosody-Morphology Interface* 134–87. Cambridge: Cambridge University Press.

Inkelas, Sharon (2000) Phonotactic blocking through structural immunity. In B. Stiebels and D. Wunderlich (eds) *Lexicon in Focus. Studia Grammatica 45*, 7–40. Berlin: Akademie Verlag.

Inkelas, S., O. Orgun and C. Zoll (1997) The implications of lexical exceptions for the nature of grammar. In I. Roca (ed.) *Derivations and Constraints in Phonology* 393–418. New York: Oxford University Press.

Inkelas, Sharon and Cheryl Zoll (2003) Is grammar dependence real? Unpublished ms, UC Berkeley and MIT. Rutgers Optimality Archive 587.

Inkelas, Sharon and Cheryl Zoll (2005) *Reduplication: Doubling in Morphology*. Cambridge: Cambridge University Press.

Ito, Chiyuki, Yoonjung Kang and Michael Kenstowicz (2006) The adaptation of Japanese loanwords into Korean. In Feng-fan Hseih and Michael Kenstowicz (eds) *Studies in Loanword Phonology (MIT Working Papers in Linguistics 52)* 65–104. Cambridge, MA: MITWPL.

Ito, Junko (1986) *Syllable Theory in Prosodic Phonology*. PhD dissertation, University of Massachusetts Amherst. Published 1988, New York: Garland.

Ito, Junko (1989) A prosodic theory of epenthesis. *Natural Language and Linguistic Theory* 7: 217–59.

Ito, Junko and Armin Mester (1992/2003) Weak layering and word binarity. In Takeru Honma, Masao Okazaki, Toshiyuki Tabata and Shin-ichi Tanaka (eds) *A New Century of Phonology and Phonological Theory. A Festschrift for Professor Shosuke Haraguchi on the Occasion of His Sixtieth Birthday* 26–65. Tokyo: Kaitakusha.

Ito, Junko and Armin Mester (1995a) Japanese phonology. In J. Goldsmith (ed.) *The Handbook of Phonological Theory*, 817–38. Oxford: Blackwell.

Ito, Junko and Armin Mester (1995b) The core-periphery structure in the lexicon and constraints on re-ranking. In Jill Beckman, Suzanne Urbanczyk and Laura Walsh Dickey (eds) *Papers in Optimality Theory* (University of Massachusetts Occasional Papers in Linguistics 18) 181–210. Amherst, MA: Graduate Linguistic Student Association.

Ito, Junko and Armin Mester (1998) Markedness and word structure: OCP effects in Japanese. Unpublished ms, University of California, Santa Cruz. Rutgers Optimality Archive 255.

Ito, Junko and Armin Mester (1999a) Realignment. In René Kager, Harry van der Hulst and W. Zonneveld (eds) *Proceedings of the Utrecht Workshop on Prosodic Morphology* 188–217. Cambridge: Cambridge University Press.

Ito, Junko and Armin Mester (1999b) The structure of the phonological lexicon. In Natsuko Tsujimura (ed.) *The Handbook of Japanese Linguistics* 62–100. Malden, MA and Oxford: Blackwell.

Ito, Junko and Armin Mester (2001) Covert generalizations in Optimality Theory: the role of stratal faithfulness constraints. *Studies in Phonetics, Phonology, and Morphology* 7: 273–99.

Ito, Junko and Armin Mester (2003) *Japanese Morphophonemics: Markedness and Word Structure*. Cambridge: The MIT Press.

Ito, Junko and Armin Mester (2007a) Categories and projections in prosodic structure. Handout of paper delivered at OCP 4 (Old World Conference in Phonology), January 2007, Rhodes, Greece.

Ito, Junko and Armin Mester (2007b) Prosodic adjunction in Japanese compounds. In *Formal Approaches to Japanese Linguistics: Proceedings of FAJL 4 (MIT Working Papers in Linguistics 55)* 97–111. Cambridge, Massachusetts.

Ito, Junko and Armin Mester (2007c) Systemic markedness and faithfulness. In J. Cihlar, A. Franklin, D. Kaiser and I. Kimbara (eds) *CLS 39:1 The Main Session. Papers from the 39*[th] *Annual Meeting of the Chicago Linguistic Society* 665–89. Chicago: Chicago Linguistic Society.

Ito, Junko, Armin Mester and Jaye Padgett (1995) Licensing and redundancy: underspecification in Optimality Theory. *Linguistic Inquiry* 26:571–614.

Jacobs, H. and C. Gussenhoven (2000) Loan phonology: perception, salience, the lexicon, and OT. In J. Dekkers, F. van der Leeuw and J. van de Weijer (eds) *Optimality Theory: Phonology, Syntax, and Acquisition* 193–209. Oxford: Oxford University Press.

Jakobson, Roman (1941) *Kindersprache, Aphasie, und Allgemeine Lautgesetze*. Uppsala: Almqvist and Wiksell.

Jakobson, Roman (1949) The sound laws of child language. In Roman Jakobson (ed.) *Studies on Child Language and Aphasia*. The Hague: Mouton

Jansen, W. (2004) *Laryngeal Contrast and Phonetic Voicing: a Laboratory Phonology Approach to English, Hungarian, and Dutch*. PhD dissertation, Rijksuniversiteit Groningen.

Jassem, Lutoslawa and Wiktor Richter (1989) Neutralization of voicing in Polish obstruents. *Journal of Phonetics* 17: 317–25.

Jeel, V. (1975) An investigation of the fundamental frequency of vowels after various Danish consonants, in particular stop consonants. *Annual Report of the Institute of Phonetics of the University of Copenhagen* 9: 191–211.

Jensen, John T. (2000) Against ambisyllabicity. *Phonology* 17: 187–235.

Johnson, Keith (2004) Cross-linguistic perceptual differences emerge from the lexicon. In Augustine Agwuele, Willis Warren and Sang-Hoon Park (eds) *Proceedings of the 2003 Texas Linguistics Society Conference: Coarticulation in Speech Production and Perception* 26–41. Somerville, MA: Cascadilla Press.

Jongman, Allard (2004) Phonological and phonetic representations: the case of neutralization. In Augustine Agwuele, Willis Warren and Sang-Hoon Park (eds) *Proceedings of the 2003 Texas Linguistics Society Conference: Coarticulation in Speech Production and Perception* 9–16. Somerville, MA: Cascadilla Press.

Josephs, L. (1975) *Palauan Reference Grammar*. Honolulu: University of Hawaii Press.

Josephs, L. (1990) *New Palauan-English Dictionary*. Honolulu: University of Hawaii Press.

Jun, Jongho (1995) *Perceptual and Articulatory Factors in Place Assimilation: an Optimality Theoretic Approach*. PhD dissertation, University of California, Los Angeles.

Kabak, B. (2003) *The Perceptual Processing of Second Language Consonant Clusters*. PhD dissertation, University of Delaware.

Kagaya, R. (1974) A fiberscopic and acoustic study of the Korean stops, affricates, and fricatives. *Journal of Phonetics* 2: 161–80.

Kagaya, R. and H. Hirose (1975) Fiberoptic electromyographic and acoustic analyses of Hindi stop consonants. *Annual Bulletin of the Research Institute for Logopedics and Phoniatrics* 9: 27–46.

Kager, René (1997) Generalized alignment and morphological parsing. *Rivista di Linguistica* 9: 245–82.

Kager, René (1999) *Optimality Theory*. Cambridge: Cambridge University Press.

Kager, René (2005) Rhythmic licensing theory: An extended typology. In *Proceedings of the Third International Conference on Phonology* 5–31. Seoul: The Phonology-Morphology Circle of Korea.

Kager, René (2008) Lexical irregularity and the typology of contrast. In K. Hanson and S. Inkelas (eds) *The Nature of the Word: Studies in Honor of Paul Kiparsky* 397–432. Cambridge, MA: The MIT Press.

Kahn, Daniel (1976) *Syllable-based Generalizations in English Phonology*. PhD dissertation, MIT. Published 1980, New York: Garland.

Kahn, Daniel (1980) Syllable-structure specifications in phonological rules. In Mark Aronoff and Mary-Louise Kean (eds) *Juncture* 91–105. Saratoga, CA: Amma Libri.

Kaisse, E. and P. Shaw (1985) On the theory of Lexical Phonology. *Phonology Yearbook* 2: 10–30.

Kang, Y. (2003) Perceptual similarity in loanword adaptation: English postvocalic word-final stops in Korean. *Phonology* 20: 219–73.

Karlsson, F. (1982) *Suomen kielen äänne- ja muotoraknne* [The Phonological and Morphological Structure of Finnish]. Helsinki: Werner Söderström Osakeyhtiö.

Karlsson, F. (1983) *Finnish Grammar* (A. Chesterman, translator). Juva: Werner Söderström Osakeyhtiö.

Karvonen, D. (1998) Finnish loanword phonology and the core-periphery structure of the lexicon. Unpublished ms, University of California, Santa Cruz.

Kavitskaya, D. (2002) *Compensatory Lengthening: Phonetics, Phonology, Diachrony*. New York: Routledge.

Kawahara, Shigeto (2005) Voicing and geminacy in Japanese: an acoustic and perceptual study. In K. Flack and S. Kawahara (eds) *University of Massachusetts Occasional Papers in Linguistics 31*, 87–120. Amherst, MA: Graduate Linguistic Student Association.

Kawahara, Shigeto (2006) A faithfulness ranking projected from a perceptibility scale: the case of [+voice] in Japanese. *Language* 82: 536–74.

Kawahara, Shigeto, Ono Hajime and Kiyoshi Sudo (2006) Consonant co-occurrence restrictions in Yamato Japanese. *Japanese/Korean Linguistics* 14: 27–38.

Kawahara, S., K. Nishimura and H. Ono (2003) Unveiling the unmarkedness of Sino-Japanese. In W. McClure (ed.) *Japanese/Korean Linguistics, Volume 12* 140–51. Stanford: CSLI.

Kawu, A. N. (1999) Faithfulness and markedness in loan vocabulary. Paper presented at Rutgers-UMass OT workshop [RumJClam] IV, Rutgers University, March 28.

Kaye, Jonathan (1989) *Phonology: a Cognitive View*. Hillsdale: LEA Publishers.

Keating, Patricia A. (1988) The phonology-phonetics interface. In Frederick J. Newmeyer (ed.) *Linguistics: the Cambridge Survey, vol. 1* 281–302. Cambridge: Cambridge University Press.

Keating, Patricia A. (1990) Phonetic representations in a generative grammar. *Journal of Phonetics* 18: 321–34.

Keating, Patricia A. (1996) The phonology-phonetics interface. In U. Kleinhenz (ed.) *Interfaces in Phonology* 262–78. Studia grammatical 41. Berlin: Akademie Verlag.

Keer, E. (1999) *Geminates, the OCP and the Nature of Con*. PhD dissertation, Rutgers University. Rutgers Optimality Archive 350.

Kenstowicz, Michael (1994) Syllabification in Chuckchee: a constraint-based analysis. In A. Davudsib, N. Maier, G. Silva and Wan Su Yan (eds) *Papers from the Fourth Annual Meeting of the Formal Linguistics Society of Midamerica* 160–81. University of Iowa.

Kenstowicz, Michael (1997) Uniform exponence: exemplification and extension. In Viola Miglio and Bruce Morén (eds) *University of Maryland Working Papers in Linguistics 5. Selected papers from Hopkins Optimality Theory Workshop/University of Maryland Mayfest 1997* 139–55.

Kenstowicz, Michael (2003) Salience and similarity in loanword adaptation: a case study of Fijian. Unpublished ms, MIT.

Kenstowicz, M. and A. Suchato (2006) Issues in loanword adaptation: a case study from Thai. *Lingua* 116: 921–49.

Kewley-Port, Diane (1995) Thresholds for formant-frequency discrimination of vowels in consonantal context. *Journal of the Acoustical Society of America* 97: 3139–46.

Kim, C.-W. (1982) Epenthesis and elision in metrical phonology. In I.-S. Yang (ed.) *Linguistics in the Morning Calm* 439–52. Hanshin, Seoul: Linguistics Society of Korea.

Kimball, Geoffrey D. (1991) *Koasati grammar*. Lincoln: University of Nebraska Press.

Kingston, John (2007) The phonetics-phonology interface. In Paul de Lacy (ed.) *The Cambridge Handbook of Phonology* 401–34. Cambridge: Cambridge University Press.

Kingston, John and Randy Diehl (1994) Phonetic knowledge. *Language* 70: 419–54.

Kiparsky, Paul (1979) Metrical structure assignment is cyclic. *Linguistic Inquiry* 10: 421–41.

Kiparsky, Paul (1982) Lexical phonology and morphology. In I.-S. Yang (ed.) *Linguistics in the Morning Calm* 1: 3–91. Hanshin, Seoul: Linguistics Society of Korea.

Kiparsky, Paul (1993) Blocking in nonderived environments. In S. Hargus and E. M. Kaisse (eds) *Phonetics and Phonology volume 4: Studies in Lexical Phonology* 277–313. San Diego: Academic Press.

Kiparsky, Paul (2003) Finnish noun inflection. In D. Nelson and S. Manninen (eds) *Generative Approaches to Finnic and Saami Linguistics* 109–61. Stanford, CA: CSLI.

Kiparsky, Paul (2006) The Amphichronic Program vs. Evolutionary Phonology. *Theoretical Linguistics* 32: 217–36.

Kiparsky, Paul (2008) Universals constrain change: change results in typological generalizations. In Jeff Good (ed.) *Language Universals and Language Change* 23–53. Oxford: Oxford University Press.

Kirchner, Robert (1993) Turkish vowel harmony and disharmony: an Optimality Theoretic account. Unpublished ms, UCLA. Rutgers Optimality Archive 4.

Kirchner, Robert (1996) Synchronic chain shifts in Optimality Theory. *Linguistic Inquiry* 27: 341–50.

Kirchner, Robert (1998) *An Effort-based Approach to Consonant Lenition*. PhD dissertation, UCLA.

Kirk, Cecilia (2001) *Phonological Constraints on the Segmentation of Continuous Speech*. PhD dissertation, University of Massachusetts Amherst.

Kisseberth, C. (1970) The treatment of exceptions. *Papers in Linguistics* 2: 44–58.

Kjellin, O. (1977) Observations on consonant types and 'tone' in Tibetan. *Journal of Phonetics* 5: 317–38.

Klatt, H. (1976) Linguistic uses of segmental duration in English: acoustic and perceptual evidence. *Journal of the Acoustical Society of America* 59: 1208–21.

Klein, T. (2005) Infixation and segmental constraint effects: UM and IN in Tagalog, Chamorro and Toba Batak. *Lingua* 115: 959–95.

Kochetov, Alexei (2002) *Production, Perception, and Emergent Phonotactic Patterns*. New York: Routledge.

Kohler, K. J. (1982) F0 in the production of lenis and fortis plosives. *Phonetica* 39: 199–218.

Kolehmainen, J. I. (1937) The Finnicisation of English in America. *American Sociological Review* 2: 62–66.

Kopkalli, H. (1993) *A Phonetic and Phonological Analysis of Final Devoicing in Turkish*. PhD dissertation, University of Michigan.

Kortlandt, F. H. H. (1975) Tones in Wakashan. *Linguistics* 143: 31–34.

Kraska-Szlenk, I. (1997) Exceptions in phonological theory. *Proceedings of the 16th International Congress of Linguists*. Oxford: Pergamon.

Kraska-Szlenk, I. (1999) Syllable structure constraints in exceptions. In J. R. Rennison and K. Kühnhammer (eds) *Phonologica 1996: Syllables!?* 113–31. The Hague: Thesus.

Kroeker, Barbara (1972) Morphophonemics of Nambiquara. *Anthropological Linguistics* 14: 19–22.

Kuhl, Patricia K. (1991) Human adults and human infants show a 'perceptual magnet effect' for the prototypes of speech categories, monkeys do not. *Perception and Psychophysics* 50: 93–107.

Kurisu, K. (2001) *The Phonology of Morpheme Realization*. PhD dissertation, University of California Santa Cruz.

Kurisu, K. (2006) Weak Derived Environment effect. Handout from NELS 37.

Labov, William (1994) *Principles of Linguistic Change*. Malden: Blackwell.

LaCharité, Darlene and Carole Paradis (2005) Category preservation and proximity versus phonetic approximation in loanword adaptation. *Linguistic Inquiry* 36: 223–58.

Ladd, D. Robert (1996) *Intonational Phonology*. Cambridge: Cambridge University Press.

Ladefoged, Peter and Ian Maddieson (1996) *The Sounds of the World's Languages*. Oxford: Blackwell.

Lamontagne, Greg (1993) *Syllabification and Consonant Cooccurrence Conditions*. PhD dissertation, University of Massachusetts Amherst.

Lamontagne, Greg (1996) Relativized contiguity. Unpublished ms, University of British Columbia.

Landaburu, J. (1979) *La langue des andoke (Amazonie colombienne): grammaire*. Langues et civilisations à tradition orale 36. Centre National de la Recherche Scientifique.

Landman, Meredith (2003) Morphological contiguity. In Angela Carpenter, Andries Coetzee and Paul de Lacy (eds) *Papers in Optimality Theory II* (University of Massachusetts Amherst Occasional Papers in Linguistics 26). Amherst, MA: Graduate Linguistic Student Association.

Laycock, D. C. (1965) *The Ndu Language Family*. Pacific Linguistics Series C No. 1, Linguistic Circle of Canberra. Canberra: The Australian National University.

Leben, W. (1973) *Suprasegmental Phonology*. PhD dissertation, MIT.

Legendre, G., P. Smolensky and C. Wilson (1998) When is less more? Faithfulness and minimal links in wh-chains. In P. Barbosa, D. Fox, P. Hagstrom, M. McGinnis and D. Pesetsky (eds) *Is the Best Good Enough? Optimality and Competition in Syntax* 249–89. Cambridge, MA: The MIT Press.

Li, J. (1996) Bugan, a new Mon-Khmer language of Yunnan Province, China. *Mon-Khmer Studies* 26: 135–60.

Lin, H.-B. (1988) *Contextual Stability of Taiwanese Tones*. PhD dissertation, University of Connecticut.

Lin, Y.-H. (1997) Syllabic and moraic structures in Piro. *Phonology* 14: 403–36.

Lindblom, Björn (1986) Phonetic universals in vowel systems. In John J. Ohala and Jeri J. Jaeger (eds) *Experimental Phonology* 13–44. Orlando: Academic Press.

Lindblom, Björn (1990) Explaining phonetic variation: a sketch of the H&H theory. In William J. Hardcastle and Alain Marchal (eds) *Speech Production and Speech Modelling* 403–39. Dordrecht: Kluwer.

Lombardi, Linda (1999) Positional faithfulness and voicing assimilation in Optimality Theory. *Natural Language and Linguistic Theory* 17: 267–302.

Lombardi, Linda (2003) Markedness and the typology of epenthetic vowels. In B. Palek, O. Fujimora and S. Haraguchi (eds) *Proceedings of LP2002*. Prague: Charles University Press and Meikai University Press.

Lovins, J. B. (1975) *Loanwords and the Phonological Structure of Japanese.* Bloomington: Indiana University Linguistics Club.

Löfqvist, A. (1975) Intrinsic and extrinsic F0 variations in Swedish tonal accents. *Phonetica* 31: 228–47.

Łubowicz, Anna (2002) Derived environment effects in Optimality Theory. *Lingua* 112: 243–80.

Łubowicz, Anna (2003) *Contrast Preservation in Phonological Mappings.* PhD dissertation, University of Massachusetts Amherst.

Luthy, M. J. (1973) *Phonological and Lexical Aspects of Colloquial Finnish.* Uralic and Altaic Series 119. Bloomington: Indiana University Publications.

MacEachern, M. (1999) *Laryngeal Cooccurrence Restrictions.* New York: Garland.

MacKay, D. J. C. (2003) *Information Theory, Inference, and Learning Algorithms.* Cambridge: Cambridge University Press.

Macken, M. A. (1995) Phonological acquisition. In J. A. Goldsmith (ed.) *The Handbook of Phonological Theory* 671–96. Cambridge: Blackwell.

Maddieson, Ian (1976) A further note on tone and consonants. *UCLA Working Papers in Phonetics* 33: 131–59.

Maddieson, Ian (1992) *UCLA Phonological Segment Inventory Database.* Los Angeles: UCLA.

Mahadin, Radwan Salim (1982) *The Morphophonemics of the Standard Arabic Tri-consonantal Verbs.* PhD dissertation, University of Pennsylvania.

Mahanta, S. (2007) *Directionality and Locality in Vowel Harmony.* PhD dissertation, Utrecht University, the Netherlands.

Majors, T. (1997) The interaction of infixation and reduplication in Tagalog. Handout from Linguistic Society of America Student Phonology Workshop, July 26, 1997.

Malone, T. (2006) Tone and syllable structure in Chimila. *International Journal of American Linguistics* 72: 1–58.

Manuel, S. Y. (1990) The role of contrast in limiting vowel-to-vowel coarticulation in different languages. *Journal of the Acoustical Society of America* 88: 1286–98.

Marlo, M. (2004) Phonologically conditioned exceptions in Bantu morphosyntax. Talk presented at NaPhC3, Concordia University, May 21–23, 2004.

Marslen-Wilson, W. (1984) Function and process in spoken-word recognition: a tutorial review. In H. Bouma and D. G. Bowhuis (eds) *Attention and*

Performance X: Control of Language Processes 125–50. Hillsdale, NJ: Erlbaum.

Mascaró, Joan (1996) External allomorphy as emergence of the unmarked. In Jacques Durand and Bernard Laks (eds) *Current Trends in Phonology: Models and Methods* 473–83. Salford, Manchester: European Studies Research Institute.

Mascaró, Joan (2003) Comparative markedness and derived environments. *Theoretical Linguistics* 29: 113–22.

Massaro, Dominic W. and Michael M. Cohen (1983) Phonological context in speech perception. *Perception and Psychophysics* 34: 338–48.

Matteson, E. (1965) *The Piro (Arawakan) Language*. Berkeley: University of California Press.

McCarthy, John J. (1979a) *Formal Problems in Semitic Phonology and Morphology*. PhD dissertation, MIT. Published 1985, New York: Garland.

McCarthy, John J. (1979b) On stress and syllabification. *Linguistic Inquiry* 10: 443–65.

McCarthy, John J. (1981) A prosodic theory of nonconcatenative morphology. *Linguistic Inquiry* 12: 373–418.

McCarthy, John J. (1982) Prosodic structure and expletive infixation. *Language* 58: 574–590.

McCarthy, John J. (1986) OCP effects: gemination and antigemination. *Linguistic Inquiry* 17: 207–63.

McCarthy, John J. (1988) Feature geometry and dependency: a review. *Phonetica* 45: 84–188.

McCarthy, John J. (1989) Linear order in phonological representation. *Linguistic Inquiry* 20: 71–99.

McCarthy, John J. (1991) Synchronic rule inversion. In L. Sutton, C. Johnson and R. Shields (eds) *Proceedings of the Annual Meeting of the Berkeley Linguistics Society* 192–207. Berkeley: Berkeley Linguistics Society.

McCarthy, John J. (1993a) A case of surface constraint violation. *Canadian Journal of Linguistics* 38: 127–53.

McCarthy, John J. (1993b) Template form in prosodic morphology. In L. Smith Stvan et al. (eds) *FLSM III: Papers from the Third Annual Meeting of the Formal Linguistics Society of Midamerica, Northwestern University, May 1992* 187–218. Bloomington: Indiana University Linguistics Club.

McCarthy, John J. (1994) The phonetics and phonology of Semitic pharyngeals. In Patricia Keating (ed.) *Papers in Laboratory Phonology III: Phonological Structure and Phonetic Form* 191–233. Cambridge: Cambridge University Press.

McCarthy, John J. (1999a) Appendix: a note on Boston r and the Elsewhere Condition. Unpublished ms, University of Massachusetts Amherst. http://wwwunix.oit.umass.edu/ ~jjmccart/appendix.pdf.

McCarthy, John J. (1999b) Sympathy and phonological opacity. *Phonology* 16: 331–99.

McCarthy, John J. (2000a) Faithfulness and prosodic circumscription. In J. Dekkers, F. van der Leeuw and J. van de Weijer (eds) *Optimality Theory: Syntax, Phonology, and Acquisition* 151–89. Oxford: Oxford University Press.

McCarthy, John J. (2000b) The prosody of phrase in Rotuman. *Natural Language and Linguistic Theory* 18: 147–97.

McCarthy, John J. (2002) *A Thematic Guide to Optimality Theory*. Research Surveys in Linguistics. Cambridge: Cambridge University Press.

McCarthy, John J. (2003a) Comparative markedness. *Theoretical Linguistics* 29: 1–51.

McCarthy, John J. (2003b) Comparative markedness. In Angela Carpenter, Andries Coetzee and Paul de Lacy (eds) *Papers in Optimality Theory II* (University of Massachusetts Occasional Papers in Linguistics 26) 147–246. Amherst, MA: Graduate Linguistic Student Association.

McCarthy, John J. (2003c) OT constraints are categorical. *Phonology* 20: 75–138.

McCarthy, John J. (2005a) Optimal paradigms. In T. Alan Hall, Renate Raffelstein and Laura Downing (eds) *Paradigms in Phonological Theory* 170–210. Oxford: Oxford University Press.

McCarthy, John J. (2005b) Taking a free ride in morphophonemic learning. *Catalan Journal of Linguistics* 4: 19–56.

McCarthy, John J. (2007) *Hidden Generalizations: Phonological Opacity in Optimality Theory*. Advances in Optimality Theory. London: Equinox.

McCarthy, John J. and Alan Prince (1986) Prosodic morphology. Unpublished ms, University of Massachusetts Amherst and Brandeis University.

McCarthy, John J. and Alan Prince (1990a) Foot and word in prosodic morphology: the Arabic broken plural. *Natural Language and Linguistic Theory* 8: 177–208.

McCarthy, John J. and Alan Prince (1990b) Prosodic morphology and templatic morphology. In Mushira Eid and John J. McCarthy (eds) *Perspectives on Arabic Linguistics II: Papers From the Second Annual Symposium on Arabic Linguistics* 1–54. Amsterdam: John Benjamins.

McCarthy, John J. and Alan Prince (1993a) Generalized alignment. In Geert Booij and Jaap van Marle (eds) *Yearbook of Morphology* 79–153. Dordrecht: Kluwer.

McCarthy, John J. and Alan Prince (1993b) Prosodic morphology I: constraint interaction and satisfaction. Technical Report #3, Rutgers University Center for Cognitive Science.

McCarthy, John J. and Alan Prince (1994a) The emergence of the unmarked: optimality in prosodic morphology. In Mercè Gonzàlez (ed.) *Proceedings of NELS 24* 333–79. Amherst, MA: Graduate Linguistic Student Association.

McCarthy, John J. and Alan Prince (1994b) Two lectures on prosodic morphology. Unpublished ms, University of Massachusetts Amherst and Rutgers University. Rutgers Optimality Archive 59.

McCarthy John J. and Alan Prince (1995) Faithfulness and reduplicative identity. In Jill Beckman, Suzanne Urbanczyk and Laura Walsh Dickey (eds) *Papers in Optimality Theory* (University of Massachusetts Occasional Papers in Linguistics 18) 249–384. Amherst, MA: Graduate Linguistic Student Association.

McCarthy, John J. and Alan Prince (1996) Prosodic morphology 1986. Technical Report #32, Rutgers University Center for Cognitive Science.

McCarthy, John J. and Alan Prince (1999) Faithfulness and identity in prosodic morphology. In Harry van der Hulst, René Kager and Wim Zonneveld (eds) *The Prosody-Morphology Interface* 218–309. Cambridge: Cambridge University Press.

McCarthy, John J. and Matthew Wolf (2005) Less than zero: correspondence and the null output. Unpublished ms, University of Massachusetts Amherst. Rutgers Optimality Archive 722.

McCawley, James D. (1968) *The Phonological Component of a Grammar of Japanese.* The Hague: Mouton.

McGregor, William (1990) *A Functional Grammar of Gooniyandi.* Amsterdam: John Benjamins.

McMahon, April M. S. (2000) *Change, Chance, and Optimality.* Oxford and New York: Oxford University Press.

Melnar, L. R. (2004) *Caddo Verb Morphology.* Lincoln: University of Nebraska Press.

Merkle, Ludwig (1975) *Bairische Grammatik.* München: Hugendubel.

Mester, Armin (1994) The quantitative trochee in Latin. *Natural Language and Linguistic Theory* 12: 1–61.

Mester, Armin and Junko Ito (1986) The phonology of voicing in Japanese: theoretical consequences for morphological accessibility. *Linguistic Inquiry* 17: 49–73.

Miller, G. A. and P. E. Nicely (1955) Analysis of perceptual confusions among some English consonants. *Journal of the Acoustical Society of America* 27: 338–52.

Mitleb, Fares M. (1984) Voicing effect on vowel duration is not an absolute universal. *Journal of Phonetics* 12: 23–27.

Miura, A. (1993) *English in Japanese.* New York: Weatherhill.

Mohanan, K. P. (1982) *Lexical Phonology.* PhD dissertation, MIT.

Mohanan, K. P. (1993) Fields of attraction in phonology. In John Goldsmith (ed.) *The Last Phonological Rule: Reflections on Constraints and Derivations* 61–116. Chicago, University of Chicago Press.

Morelli, Frida (1999) *The Phonotactics and Phonology of Obstruent Clusters in Optimality Theory.* PhD dissertation, University of Maryland.

Moreton, Elliott (2000) *Phonological Grammar in Speech Perception.* PhD dissertation, University of Massachusetts Amherst.

Moreton, Elliott (2002) Structural constraints in the perception of English stop-sonorant clusters. *Cognition* 84: 55–71.

Moreton, Elliott (2007) Phonotactic learning and phonological typology. Unpublished ms, University of North Carolina, Chapel Hill.

Moreton, Elliott (this volume) Underphonologization and modularity bias.

Moreton, Elliott and S. Amano (1999) Phonotactics in the perception of Japanese vowel length: evidence for long-distance dependencies. *Proceedings of the 6th European Conference on Speech Communication and Technology*, Budapest.

Moreton, Elliott and Erik R. Thomas (2007) Origins of Canadian Raising in voiceless-coda effects: a case study in phonologization. In Jennifer S. Cole and José Ignacio Hualde (eds) *Papers in Laboratory Phonology IX* 37–64. Berlin: Mouton.

Mosel, Ulrike (2004) Borrowing in Samoan. In J. Tent and P. Geraghty (eds) *Borrowing: a Pacific Perspective* 215–32. Pacific Linguistics. Canberra: The Australian National University.

Mosel, Ulrike and Even Hovdhaugen (1993) *Samoan Reference Grammar.* Scandinavian University Press.

Myers, Scott (1987) *Tone and the Structure of Words in Shona.* PhD dissertation, University of Massachusetts Amherst. Published 1991, New York: Garland.

Myers, Scott (1997) OCP effects in Optimality Theory. *Natural Language and Linguistic Theory* 15: 847–92.

Myers, Scott (1999) Tone association and f0 timing in Chichewa. *Studies in African Linguistics* 28: 215–39.

Myers, Scott (2002) Gaps in factorial typology: the case of voicing in consonant clusters. Unpublished ms, University of Texas at Austin. http://uts.cc.utexas.edu/~smyers/voicing.pdf.

Nagy, Naomi and William Reynolds (1997) Optimality Theory and variable word-final deletion in Faetar. *Language Variation and Change* 9: 37–56.

Nash, David (1986) *Topics in Warlpiri grammar.* New York: Garland.

Nasr, Raja T. (1959) The predictability of stress in Lebanese Arabic. *Phonetica* 4: 89–94.

Nasr, Raja T. (1960) Phonemic length in Lebanese Arabic. *Phonetica* 5: 209–11.

Nelson, N. (2003) *Asymmetric Anchoring.* PhD dissertation, Rutgers University.

Nespor, Marina (1999) The phonology of clitic groups. In Henk van Riemsdijk (ed.) *Clitics in the Languages of Europe* 865–87. Berlin: Mouton de Gruyter.

Nespor, Marina and Irene Vogel (1986) *Prosodic Phonology.* Dordrecht: Foris.

Newman, Rochelle S., James R. Sawusch and Paul A. Luce (1997) Lexical neighborhood effects in phonetic processing. *Journal of Experimental Psychology* 23: 873–89.

Newmeyer, Frederick (1998) *Language Form and Language Function.* Cambridge, MA: The MIT Press.

Newmeyer, Frederick (2003) Grammar is grammar and usage is usage. *Language* 78: 682–707.

Newport, E. L. and R. N. Aslin (2004) Learning at a distance: I. Statistical learning of non-adjacent dependencies. *Cognitive Psychology* 48: 127–62.

Ngata, H. M. (1993) *English-Māori Dictionary*. Wellington: Learning Media.

Ní Chasaide, A. (1999) Irish. *Handbook of the International Phonetics Association* 111–16. Cambridge: Cambridge University Press.

Ní Chiosáin, Máire and Jaye Padgett (2001) Markedness, segment realization, and locality in spreading. In Linda Lombardi (ed.) *Segmental Phonology in Optimality Theory: Constraints and Representations* 118–56. Cambridge: Cambridge University Press.

Ní Chiosáin, Máire and Jaye Padgett (2007) A perceptual study of Irish palatalization. Paper presented at the Annual Meeting of the Linguistic Society of America, Anaheim, CA.

Nordlinger, Rachel (1993) *A Grammar of Wambaya*. MA thesis, University of Melbourne.

Nouveau, D. (1994) *Language Acquisition, Metrical Theory, and Optimality: a Study of Dutch Word Stress*. PhD dissertation, Utrecht University.

Noyer, R. (1991) Tone and stress in the San Mateo dialect of Huave. *Proceedings of the Eastern States Conference on Linguistics (ESCOL)* 277–88.

Odden, David (1988) Anti antigemination and the OCP. *Linguistic Inquiry* 19: 451–75.

Odden, David (1994) Adjacency parameters in phonology. *Language* 70: 289–330.

Odden, David (1995) Tone: African languages. In John A. Goldsmith (ed.) *The Handbook of Phonological Theory* 444–75. Cambridge: Blackwell.

Odden, D. and M. Odden (1985) Ordered reduplication in KRhehe. *Linguistic Inquiry* 16: 497–503.

Odé, C. (2002) *Mpur Prosody: an Experimental-Phonetic Analysis with Examples from Two Versions of the Fenora Myth*. Osaka: ELPR [Endangered Languages of the Pacific Rim] Publications, Series A1–003.

Ohala, John J. (1983) The origin of sound patterns in vocal tract constraints. In Peter F. MacNeilage (ed.) *The Production of Speech* 189–216. New York: Springer.

Ohala, John J. (1990) The phonetics and phonology of aspects of assimilation. In J. Kingston and M. E. Beckman (eds) *Papers in Laboratory Phonology I: Between the Grammar and Physics of Speech* 258–75. Cambridge: Cambridge University Press.

Ohala, John J. (1994) Hierarchies of environments for sound variation; plus implications for 'neutral' vowels in vowel harmony. *Acta Linguistica Hafniensia* 27: 371–82.

Ohala, John J. (2005) Phonetic explanations for sound patterns: implications for grammars of competence. In W. J. Hardcastle and J. M. Beck (eds) *A Figure of Speech: a Festschrift for John Laver* 23–38. London: Erlbaum.

Ohala, John J. and James Lorentz (1977) The story of [w]: an exercise in the phonetic explanation for sound patterns. In Kenneth Whistler, Robert van Valin, Chris Chiarello, Jeri J. Jaeger, Miriam Petruck, Henry Thompson, Ronya Javkin and Anthony Woodbury (eds) *Proceedings of the 3rd Annual Meeting of the Berkeley Linguistics Society* 577–99. Berkeley: Berkeley Linguistics Society.

Ohde, R. N. (1984) Fundamental frequency as an acoustic correlate of stop-consonant voicing. *Journal of the Acoustical Society of America* 75: 224–230.

Ola Orie, Olanike and Douglas Pulleyblank (1998) Vowel elision is not always onset-driven. Unpublished ms, Rutgers Optimality Archive 290.

Orgun, C. O. (1996) *Sign-based Morphology and Phonology: with Special Attention to Optimality Theory*. PhD dissertation, University of California, Berkeley. Rutgers Optimality Archive 171.

Ota, M. (2004) The learnability of the stratified phonological lexicon. *Journal of Japanese Linguistics* 20: 19–40.

Padgett, Jaye (1995) *Stricture in Feature Geometry*. Stanford: Center for the Study of Language and Information.

Padgett, Jaye (1997) Perceptual distance of contrast: vowel height and nasality. In Rachel Walker, Motoko Katayama and Daniel Karvonen (eds) *Phonology at Santa Cruz Vol. 5* 63–78. Santa Cruz, CA: Linguistics Research Center, UC Santa Cruz.

Padgett, Jaye (2001) Contrast dispersion and Russian palatalization. In Elizabeth Hume and Keith Johnson (eds) *The Role of Speech Perception in Phonology* 187–218. San Diego, CA: Academic Press.

Padgett, Jaye (2003a) Contrast and post-velar fronting in Russian. *Natural Language and Linguistic Theory* 21: 39–87.

Padgett, Jaye (2003b) The emergence of contrastive palatalization in Russian. In D. Eric Holt (ed.) *Optimality Theory and Language Change* 307–35. Dordrecht: Kluwer Academic Press.

Padgett, Jaye (to appear a) Systemic contrast and Catalan rhotics. *Linguistic Review*.

Padgett, Jaye (to appear b) Russian voicing assimilation, final devoicing, and the problem of [v]. *Natural Language and Linguistic Theory*.

Padgett, Jaye and Marzena Zygis (2007) The evolution of sibilants in Polish and Russian. *Journal of Slavic Linguistics* 15: 291–324.

Pankratz, Leo and Eunice V. Pike (1967) Phonology and morphotonemics of Ayutla Mixtec. *International Journal of American Linguistics* 33:287–99.

Paradis, Carole and Darlene LaCharité (1997) Preservation and minimality in loanword adaptation. *Journal of Linguistics* 33: 379–430.

Paradis, Carole and Darlene LaCharité (2001) Guttural deletion in loanwords. *Phonology* 18: 255–300.

Paradis, Carole and J.-F. Prunet (1991) Introduction: asymmetry and visibility in consonant articulations. In Carole Paradis and J.-F. Prunet (eds) *The Special*

Status of Coronals: Internal and External Evidence 1–28. Phonetics and Phonology 2. San Diego: Academic Press.

Paradis, Carole and J.-F. Prunet (2000) Nasal vowels as two segments: evidence from borrowings. *Language* 76: 324–57.

Parker, Steve (1994) Laryngeal codas in Chamicuro. *International Journal of American Linguistics* 60: 261–71.

Parker, Stephen G. (2002) *Quantifying the Sonority Hierarchy*. PhD dissertation, University of Massachusetts Amherst. Amherst: Graduate Linguistic Student Association.

Pater, Joe (2000) Nonuniformity in English stress: the role of ranked and lexically specific constraints. *Phonology* 17: 237–74.

Pater, Joe (2004) Exceptions in Optimality Theory: typology and learnability. Handout from the Conference on Redefining Elicitation: Novel Data in Phonological Theory, New York University. http://people.umass.edu/pater/exceptions.pdf

Pater, Joe (2005) Learning a stratified grammar. In Alejna Brugos, Manuella R. Clark-Cotton and Seungwan Ha (eds) *Proceedings of the 29th Boston University Conference on Language Development* 482–92. Somerville, MA: Cascadilla Press.

Pater, Joe (2006) The locus of exceptionality: morpheme-specific phonology as constraint indexation. In L. Bateman, M. O'Keefe, E. Reilly and A. Werle (eds) *Papers in Optimality Theory III* (University of Massachusetts Occasional Papers in Linguistics 32), Amherst: Graduate Linguistic Student Association.

Pater, Joe and Andries W. Coetzee (2005) Lexically specific constraints: gradience, learnability, and perception. In *Proceedings of the 3rd Seoul International Conference on Phonology* 85–119. Seoul: The Phonology-Morphology Circle of Korea.

Payne, David L. (1990) Accent in Aguaruna. In Doris L. Payne (ed.) *Amazonian Linguistics: Studies in Lowland South American Languages* 161–84. Austin: University of Texas Press.

Peng, S.-H. (1997) Production and perception of Taiwanese tones in different tonal and prosodic contexts. *Journal of Phonetics* 25: 371–400.

Pensalfini, Robert (1999) Suffix coherence and stress in Australian languages. In John Henderson (ed.) *Proceedings of the 1999 Conference of the Australian Linguistic Society* 1–15. Crawley: The University of Western Australia.

Pensalfini, Robert (2003) *A Grammar of Jingulu, an Aboriginal Language of the Northern Territory*. Pacific Linguistics. Canberra: The Australian National University.

Peperkamp, Sharon (1997) *Prosodic Words*. PhD dissertation, University of Amsterdam.

Peperkamp, Sharon (2004) A psycholinguistic theory of loanword adaptations. In M. Ettlinger, N. Fleisher and M. Park-Doob (eds) *Proceedings of BLS 30* 341–52. Berkeley: Berkeley Linguistics Society.

Peperkamp, Sharon and Emmanuel Dupoux (2003) Reinterpreting loanword adaptations: the role of perception. In *Proceedings of the 15th International Congress of Phonetic Sciences*, 367–70.

Pierrehumbert, Janet (1993) Dissimilarity in the Arabic verbal roots. In A. Schafer (ed.) *NELS 23: Proceedings of the North East Linguistic Society 23* 367–81. Amherst: Graduate Linguistic Student Association.

Pierrehumbert, Janet and Mary Beckman (1988) *Japanese Tone Structure*. Linguistic Inquiry Monograph Series No. 15. Cambridge, MA: The MIT Press.

Piggott, Glyne L. (1995) Epenthesis and syllable weight. *Natural Language and Linguistic Theory* 13: 283–326.

Pike, E. V. (1948) Problems in Zapotec tone analysis. *International Journal of American Linguistics* 14: 161–70.

Poppe, Nicholas N. (1960) *Buriat Grammar*. Uralic and Altaic Series Vol. 2. Bloomington: Indiana University Press.

Port, Robert and Penny Crawford (1989) Incomplete neutralization and pragmatics in German. *Journal of Phonetics* 17: 257–82.

Port, Robert and Michael O'Dell (1985) Neutralization of syllable-final voicing in German. *Journal of Phonetics* 13: 455–71.

Poser, William (1989) The metrical foot in Diyari. *Phonology* 6: 117–48.

Potts, Christopher, Joe Pater, Rajesh Bhatt and Michael Becker (2009) Harmonic grammar with linear programming: From linear systems to linguistic typology. Unpublished ms, University of Massachusetts Amherst. Rutgers Optimality Archive 984.

Prince, Alan (1990) Quantitative consequences of rhythmic organization. In M. Ziolkowski, M. Noske and K. Deaton (eds) *Proceedings of the Chicago Linguistic Society 23: Parasession on the Syllable in Phonetics and Phonology* 355–98. Chicago: Chicago Linguistics Society.

Prince, Alan (1997) Endogenous constraints on Optimality Theory. Handout from a course of the Linguistics Society of America Summer Institute, Cornell University, Ithaca, NY.

Prince, Alan (2003) Arguing optimality. In Angela Carpenter, Andries Coetzee and Paul de Lacy (eds) *Papers in Optimality Theory II* (University of Massachusetts Occasional Papers in Linguistics 26) 269–304. Amherst, MA: Graduate Linguistic Student Association.

Prince, Alan (2007) In pursuit of theory. In Paul de Lacy (ed.) *The Cambridge Handbook of Phonology* 33–60. Cambridge: Cambridge University Press.

Prince, Alan and Paul Smolensky (1993/2004) *Optimality Theory: Constraint Interaction in Generative Grammar.* Technical Report CU-CS-696-93, Department of Computer Science, University of Colorado at Boulder, and Technical Report TR-2, Rutgers Center for Cognitive Science, Rutgers University, New Brunswick, NJ, April 1993. Revised version published 2004, Malden, MA and Oxford: Blackwell.

Prince, Alan and Bruce Tesar (2004) Learning phonotactic distributions. In René Kager, Joe Pater and Wim Zonneveld (eds) *Constraints in Phonological Acquisition* 245–91. Cambridge: Cambridge University Press.

Prunet, Jean-François, Renée Béland and Ali Idrissi (2000) The mental representation of Semitic words. *Linguistic Inquiry* 31: 609–48.

Pukui, Mary Kawena and Samuel H. Elbert (1979) *Hawaiian grammar*. Honolulu: University of Hawaii Press.

Pulleyblank, Douglas (2004) Harmony drivers: no disagreement allowed. In *Proceedings of the 28th Meeting of the Berkeley Linguistics Society* 249–67. Berkeley: Berkeley Linguistic Society.

Pyle, Charles (1972) On eliminating BMs. In Paul M. Peranteau, Judith N. Levi and Gloria C. Phares (eds) *Papers from the Eighth Regional Meeting, Chicago Linguistic Society* 516–32. Chicago: Chicago Linguistic Society.

Quick, Phil (2004) Creaky voice as a phonetic manifestation of the glottal stop in Pendau. In Andrea Rakowski and Norvin Richards (eds) *Proceedings of AFLA VIII: the Eighth Meeting of the Austronesian Formal Linguistics Association*. MIT Working Papers in Linguistics 44.

Quiggin, E. (1906) *A Dialect of Donegal*. Cambridge: Cambridge University Press.

Quintero, Carolyn (2005) *Osage Grammar*. Studies in the Anthropology of North American Indians. Lincoln: University of Nebraska Press.

R Development Core Team (2005) *R: a language and environment for statistical computing*. Vienna, Austria: R Foundation for Statistical Computing. http://www.R-project.org.

Rand, E. (1968) The structural phonology of Alabaman, a Muskogean language. *International Journal of American Linguistics* 34: 94–103.

Reiner, E. (1966) *A Linguistic Analysis of Akkadian*. The Hague: Mouton.

Rice, C. (2006) Norwegian stress and quantity: implications of loanwords. *Lingua* 116: 1171–94.

Rice, Keren (1999) Featural markedness in phonology: variation. *GLOT* 4: 3–6.

Rice, Keren (2007) Markedness in phonology. In Paul de Lacy (ed.) *The Cambridge Handbook of Phonology* 79–97. Cambridge: Cambridge University Press.

Riggle, J. (2004) Nonlocal reduplication. In Keir Moulton and Matthew Wolf (eds) *Proceedings of NELS 34*. Amherst: Graduate Linguistic Student Association. Rutgers Optimality Archive 693.

Rodrigues, Aryon D. (1999a) Macro-Jê. In R. M. W. Dixon and Alexandra Aikhenvald (eds) *The Amazonian Languages* 165–201. Cambridge: Cambridge University Press.

Rodrigues, Aryon D. (1999b) Tupi. In R. M. W. Dixon and Alexandra Aikhenvald (eds) *The Amazonian Languages* 107–22. Cambridge: Cambridge University Press.

Rose, Sharon (2000) Rethinking geminates, long-distance geminates, and the OCP. *Linguistic Inquiry* 31: 85–122.

Rose, Sharon and Rachel Walker (2004) A typology of consonant agreement as correspondence. *Language* 80: 475–531.

Rose, Y. and K. Demuth (2006) Vowel epenthesis in loanword adaptation: representational and phonetic considerations. *Lingua* 116: 1112–39.

Rosenthall, Sam (1994) *Vowel/Glide Alternations in a Theory of Constraint Interaction.* PhD dissertation, University of Massachusetts Amherst.

Rosenthall, Sam (1997) The distribution of prevocalic vowels. *Natural Language and Linguistic Theory* 15: 139–80.

Rosenthall, Sam (2006) Glide distribution in Classical Arabic verb stems. *Linguistic Inquiry* 37: 405–40.

Rosenthall, Sam and Harry van der Hulst (1999) Weight-by-position by position. *Natural Language and Linguistic Theory* 17: 499–540.

Rubach, Jerzy (1996) Shortening and ambisyllabicity in English. *Phonology* 13: 197–237.

Russell, K. (1995) Morphemes and candidates in Optimality Theory. Unpublished ms, University of Manitoba. Rutgers Optimality Archive 44.

Rutgers, Roland (1998) *Yamphu: Grammar, Texts, and Lexicon.* Leiden: Research School CNWS.

Sadeniemi, M. (ed.) (1973) *Nyksuomen Sanakirja* [Dictionary of Modern Finnish]. Porvoo, Finland: Werner Söderström Osakeyhtiö.

Salisbury, Mary (1993) *A Grammar of Pukapukan.* PhD dissertation, University of Auckland, New Zealand.

Sanders, Nathan (2003) *Opacity and Sound Change in the Polish Lexicon.* PhD dissertation, University of California, Santa Cruz.

Schane, Sanford A. (1984) The fundamentals of particle phonology. *Phonology Yearbook* 1: 129–55.

Schuh, R. G. (2002) Class handout for Linguistics 252, Bade/Ngizim Phonology and Morphology. Unpublished ms, Department of Linguistics, UCLA. Retrieved 25 August 2005 from http://www.humnet.ucla.edu/humnet/linguistics/people/schuh/Bade_Ngizim/ Handout_04.pdf.

Scobbie, James, John Coleman and Steven Bird (1996) Key aspects of Declarative Phonology. In J. Durand and B. Laks (eds) *Current Trends in Phonology: Models and Methods* 685–709. Manchester, England: European Studies Research Institute, University of Salford.

Sekiyama, K. and Y. Tohkura (1991) McGurk effect in non-English listeners: few visual effects for Japanese subjects hearing Japanese syllables of high auditory intelligibility. *Journal of the Acoustical Society of America* 90: 1797–1805.

Selkirk, Elisabeth O. (1982) The syllable. In Harry van der Hulst and Norval Smith (eds) *The Structure of Phonological Representations (Part II)* 337–83. Dordrecht: Foris.

Selkirk, Elisabeth O. (1984) *Phonology and Syntax: the Relation between Sound and Structure.* Cambridge, MA: The MIT Press.

Selkirk, Elisabeth (1986) On derived domains in sentence phonology. *Phonology* 3: 371–405.

Selkirk, Elisabeth (1995) The prosodic structure of function words. In Jill Beckman, Suzanne Urbanczyk and Laura Walsh Dickey (eds) *Papers in Optimality Theory* (University of Massachusetts Occasional Papers in Linguistics 18) 439–70. Amherst, MA: Graduate Linguistic Student Association.

Selkirk, Elisabeth and Koichi Tateishi (1988) Constraints on minor phrase formation in Japanese. In *Papers from the 24th Annual Regional Meeting of the Chicago Linguistic Society* 316–36. Chicago: Chicago Linguistic Society.

Serniclaes, W. (1992) *Etude Expérimentale de la Perception du Trait de Voisement des Occlusives du Français*. PhD dissertation, Universite Libre de Bruxelles, Institut de Phonétique.

Shaw, Patricia A. (1980) *Theoretical Issues in Dakota Phonology and Morphology*. New York: Garland Publishing.

Shen, X. S. (1990) Tonal coarticulation in Mandarin. *Journal of Phonetics* 18: 281–95.

Sherer, T. D. (1994) *Prosodic Phonotactics*. PhD dissertation, University of Massachusetts Amherst.

Shinohara, S. (2000) Default accentuation and foot structure in Japanese: evidence from adaptations of French words. *Journal of East Asian Linguistics* 9: 55–96.

Shinohara, S. (2006) Perceptual effects in final cluster reduction patterns. *Lingua* 116: 1046–78.

Siegel, Dorothy (1974) *Topics in English Morphology*. PhD dissertation, MIT.

Silverman, Daniel (1992) Multiple scansions in loanword phonology: evidence from Cantonese. *Phonology* 9: 289–328.

Sivertsen, Eva (1960) *Cockney Phonology*. Oslo Studies in English, No. 8. Oslo: Oslo University Press.

Smith, Jennifer (1997) Noun faithfulness: on the privileged behavior of nouns in phonology. Unpublished ms, University of Massachusetts Amherst. Rutgers Optimality Archive 242.

Smith, Jennifer L. (2002) *Phonological Augmentation in Prominent Positions*. PhD dissertation, University of Massachusetts Amherst. Published 2005, New York: Routledge.

Smith, Jennifer L. (2004) Making constraints positional: towards a compositional model of Con. *Lingua* 114: 1433–64.

Smith, Jennifer L. (2006a) Correspondence Theory vs. cyclic OT: beyond morphological derivation. In C. Davis, A. R. Deal and Y. Zabbal (eds) *Proceedings of NELS 36* 531–45. Amherst, MA: Graduate Linguistic Student Association.

Smith, Jennifer L. (2006b) Loan phonology is not all perception: evidence from Japanese loan doublets. In Timothy J. Vance and K. A. Jones (eds) *Japanese/Korean Linguistics, Volume 14* 63–74. Stanford: CSLI.

Smolensky, Paul (1995) On the internal structure of the constraint component Con of UG. Talk presented at UCLA, April 7, 1995.

Smolensky, Paul (1996) The initial state and 'richness of the base' in Optimality Theory. Technical Report JHU-CogSci-96-4, Cognitive Science Department, Johns Hopkins University. Rutgers Optimality Archive 154.

Snyder, W. C. and T. Lu (1997) Wuming Zhuang tone sandhi: a phonological, syntactic, and lexical investigation. In Jerold A. Edmondson and David B. Solnit (eds) *Comparative Kadai: the Tai Branch* 107–39. Summer Institute of Linguistics and the University of Texas at Arlington Publications in Linguistics, 124. Dallas: Summer Institute of Linguistics and the University of Texas at Arlington.

Sorace, Antonella and Frank Keller (2005) Gradience in linguistic data. *Lingua* 115: 1497–524.

Speas, P. (1984) Navajo prefixes and word structure typology. In M. Speas and R. Sproat (eds) *MIT Working Papers in Linguistics* 7: 86–109.

Spencer, A. (1993) The optimal way to syllabify Chukchee. Talk presented at Rutgers Optimality Workshop I, Rutgers University, New Brunswick, NJ.

Stairs Kreger, Glenn A. and Emily F. Scharfe de Stairs (1981) *Diccionario Huave de San Mateo del Mar*. Serie de Vocabularios y Diccionarios Indígenas 'Mariano Silva y Aceres,' Num. 24. Mexico City: Instituto Lingüístico de Verano.

Steriade, Donca (1995) Positional neutralization. In *Proceedings of NELS 24*. Amherst: Graduate Linguistic Student Association.

Steriade, Donca (1997) Phonetics in phonology: the case of laryngeal neutralization. Unpublished ms, UCLA.

Steriade, Donca (2001a) Directional asymmetries in place assimilation: a perceptual account. In Elizabeth Hume and Keith Johnson (eds) *The Role of Speech Perception in Phonology* 219–50. New York: Academic Press.

Steriade, Donca (2001b) The phonology of perceptibility effects: the P-map and its consequences for constraint organization. Unpublished ms, MIT.

Steriade, Donca (2002) Emergent properties of phonological competence. Handout from a presentation given at the 8th Conference on Laboratory Phonology, Yale University, New Haven, Connecticut, 29 June 2002.

Steriade, Donca (2004) Knowledge of similarity and narrow lexical override. In P. M. Nowak, C. Yoquelet and D. Mortensen (eds) *Proceedings of BLS 29* 583–98. Berkeley: Berkeley Linguistics Society.

Steriade, Donca (2008) The phonology of perceptibility effects: the P-map and its consequences for constraint organization. In K. Hanson and S. Inkelas (eds) *The Nature of the Word: Studies in Honor of Paul Kiparsky* 151–80. Cambridge, MA: The MIT Press.

Strange, Winifred (1995) Cross-language studies of speech perception: a historical review. In Winifred Strange (ed.) *Speech Perception and Linguistic Experience: Issues in Cross-Language Speech Research* 3–45. Baltimore: York Press.

Streck, M. (2003) *Die Akkadischen Verbalstämme mit ta-Infix*. Münster: Ugarit.

Suomi, K., J. M. McQueen and A. Cutler (1997) Vowel harmony and speech segmentation in Finnish. *Journal of Memory and Language* 36: 422–44.

Suzuki, K. (1998) *A Typological Investigation of Dissimilation*. PhD dissertation, University of Arizona.

Svantesson, J.-O. (1989) Tonogenetic mechanisms in northern Mon-Khmer. *Phonetica* 46: 60–79.

Svantesson, J.-O. and D. House (2006) Tone production, tone perception, and Kammu tonogenesis. *Phonology* 23: 309–33.

Takatori, Yuki (1997) *A Study of Constraint Interaction in Slavic Phonology*. PhD dissertation, Yale University.

Tersis, N. (1972) Le Zarma (République du Niger): étude du parler djerma de Dosso. *Société d'études Linguistiques et Anthropologiques de France* 33–34.

Tesar, Bruce (1998) Using the mutual inconsistency of structural descriptions to overcome ambiguity in language learning. In P. Tamanji and K. Kusumoto (eds) *Proceedings of NELS 28* 469–83. Amherst, MA: Graduate Linguistic Student Association.

Tesar, Bruce (2004) Using inconsistency detection to overcome structural ambiguity in language learning. *Linguistic Inquiry* 35: 219–53.

Tesar, Bruce (2005) Learning from paradigmatic information. In *Proceedings of NELS 36*. Amherst: Graduate Linguistic Student Association.

Tesar, Bruce (2006) Learning from paradigmatic information. In Eric Baković, Junko Ito and John McCarthy (eds) *Wondering at the Natural Fecundity of Things: Essays in Honor of Alan Prince*. Paper 14, eScholarship repository. Linguistics Research Center. http://repositories.cdlib.org/lrc/prince/14 [July 2006].

Tesar, Bruce (2007) Learnability. In Paul de Lacy (ed.) *The Cambridge Handbook of Phonology* 555–74. Cambridge: Cambridge University Press.

Tesar, B., J. Alderete, G. Horwood, N. Merchant, K. Nishitani and A. Prince, A. (2003) Surgery in language learning. In G. Garding and M. Tsujimura (eds) *Proceedings of the Twenty-Second West Coast Conference on Formal Linguistics* 477–90. Somerville, MA: Cascadilla Press.

Tesar, Bruce and Alan Prince (2007) Using phonotactics to learn phonological alternations. In J. Cilar, A. Franklin, D. Kaiser and I. Kimbara (eds) *CLS 39–2: The Panels: Papers from the 39th Annual Meeting of the Chicago Linguistic Society* 209–37. Chicago: Chicago Linguistic Society.

Tesar, Bruce and Paul Smolensky (1998) Learnability in Optimality Theory. *Linguistic Inquiry* 29: 229–68.

Tesar, Bruce and Paul Smolensky (2000) *Learnability in Optimality Theory*. Cambridge, MA: The MIT Press.

Tessier, Anne-Michelle (2004a) Input 'clusters' and contrast preservation in OT. In V. Chand, A. Kelleher, A. J. Rodríguez and B. Schmeiser (eds)

Proceedings of the West Coast Conference on Formal Linguistics 23 759–72. Somerville, MA: Cascadilla Press.

Tessier, Anne-Michelle (2004b) Root-restricted markedness and morpho-phonological domains. Paper presented at Montreal-Ottawa-Toronto Phonology Workshop, February 2004, University of Ottawa.

Tessier, Anne-Michelle (2006) *Biases and Stages in Phonological Acquisition.* PhD dissertation, University of Massachusetts Amherst. Rutgers Optimality Archive 883.

Thiry, Jacques (1989) Les consonnes faibles de l'arabe: maintiens et mutations. *Raport d'activites de l'institut de Langues Vivantes et de Phonetique* 23–24: 139–85.

Tracy, Frances (1972) Wapishana phonology. In Joseph E. Grimes (ed.) *Languages of the Guianas.* 78–84. Summer Institute of Linguistics Publications in Linguistics, 35. Norman: Summer Institute of Linguistics of the University of Oklahoma.

Trigo Ferre, Rosario Lorenza (1988) *On the Phonological Derivation and Behavior of Nasal Glides.* PhD dissertation, MIT.

Trubetzkoy, Nikolai S. (1939) *Grundzüge der Phonologie.* Güttingen: Vandenhoeck and Ruprecht.

Truckenbrodt, Hubert (2007) The syntax-phonology interface. In Paul de Lacy (ed.) *The Cambridge Handbook of Phonology* 435–56. Cambridge: Cambridge University Press.

Trudgill, Peter (1974) *The Social Differentiation of English in Norwich.* Cambridge: Cambridge University Press.

Uffmann, Christian (2003) A new look at intrusive [r]. Handout for a seminar at the University of Essex. http://www.staff.uni-marburg.de/%7Euffmann/essex-handout.pdf.

Uffmann, Christian (2005) Intrusive [r] and optimal epenthetic consonants. Unpublished ms, Marburg: Philipps-Universität Marburg. http://www.staff.uni-marburg.de/%7Euffmann/languagescience.pdf.

Urbanczyk, Suzanne (1995) Double reduplications in parallel. In Jill Beckman, Suzanne Urbanczyk and Laura Walsh Dickey (eds) *Papers in Optimality Theory* (University of Massachusetts Occasional Papers in Linguistics 18) 499–531. Amherst, MA: Graduate Linguistic Student Association.

Urbanczyk, Suzanne (2006) Reduplicative form and the root-affix asymmetry. *Natural Language and Linguistic Theory* 24: 179–240.

Ussishkin, Adam (1999) The inadequacy of the consonantal root: Modern Hebrew denominal verbs and output-output correspondence. *Phonology* 16: 401–42.

van Loon, J. (1981) Irreducibly inconsistent systems of linear inequalities. *European Journal of Operations Research* 8: 263–88.

Vendelin, I. and S. Peperkamp (2006) The influence of orthography on loanword adaptations. *Lingua* 116: 996–1007.

Vennemann, Theo (1972) On the theory of syllabic phonology. *Linguistische Berichte* 18: 1–18.

Vitevitch, Michael S. and Paul A. Luce (1998) When words compete: levels of processing in spoken word recognition. *Psychological Science* 9: 325–29.

Vitevitch, Michael S. and Paul A. Luce (1999) Probabilistic phonotactics and neighborhood activation in spoken word recognition. *Journal of Memory and Language* 40: 374–408.

Von Soden, W. (1952) *Grundriss der Akkadischen Grammatik*. Roma: Pontificium Institutum Biblicum.

Vossen, R. (1997) *Die Khoe-Sprachen: ein Beitrag zur Erforschung der Sprachgeschichte Afrikas*. Köln: Rüdiger Köppe.

Walker, Rachel (2000a) Long-distance consonantal identity effects. In R. Billerey and B. Lillehaugen (eds) *Proceedings of the West Coast Conference on Formal Linguistics 19* 532–45. Somerville, MA: Cascadilla Press.

Walker, Rachel (2000b) *Nasalization, Neutral Segments and Opacity Effects*. New York: Garland.

Walker, Rachel (2000c) Yaka nasal harmony: spreading or segmental correspondence? In L. J. Conathan, J. Good, D. Kavitskaya, A. B. Wulf and A. C. L. Yu (eds) *Proceedings of BLS 26* 321–32. Berkeley: Berkeley Linguistics Society.

Walker, Rachel and B. Feng (2004) A ternary model of morphology-phonology correspondence. In V. Chand, A. Kelleher, A. J. Rodriguez and B. Schmeiser (eds) *Proceedings of the West Coast Conference on Formal Linguistics 23* 773–86.

Wang, Jun and Guoqiao Zheng (1993) *An Outline Grammar of Mulao*. Canberra: National Thai Studies Center, Australian National University.

Warner, Natasha, Erin Good, Allard Jongman and Joan Sereno (2006) Orthographic vs. morphological incomplete neutralization effects. *Journal of Phonetics* 34: 285–93.

Warner, Natasha, Allard Jongman, Joan Sereno and Rachel Kemps (2004) Incomplete neutralization and other sub-phonemic durational differences in production and perception: evidence from Dutch. *Journal of Phonetics* 32: 251–76.

Watkins, L. J. (1984) *A Grammar of Kiowa*. Lincoln: University of Nebraska Press.

Weber, David and Wesley Thiesen (2001) A synopsis of Bora tone. In Stephen A. Marlett and J. Albert Bickford (eds) *Work Papers of the Summer Institute of Linguistics, University of North Dakota Session, 45*.

Wells, John C. (1982) *Accents of English*. Cambridge: Cambridge University Press.

Wells, John C. (1991) The Cockneyfication of RP? Unpublished ms, http://www.phon.ucl.ac.uk/home/estuary/cockneyf-sil.htm.

Werker, J. F. and R. C. Tees (1984) Cross-language speech perception: evidence for perceptual reorganization during the first year of life. *Infant Behavior and Development* 7: 49–63.

Werner, H. (1997) *Die Ketische Sprache*. Tungos Sibirica, Band 3. Wiesbaden: Harrassowitz.

Wheeler, Max (2005) *The Phonology of Catalan*. Oxford: Oxford University Press.

Wiese, Richard (2001) The structure of the German vocabulary: edge marking of categories and functional considerations. *Linguistics* 39: 95–115.

Wilson, Colin (2001) Consonant cluster neutralisation and targeted constraints. *Phonology* 18: 147–97.

Wilson, Colin (2003) Analytic bias in artificial language learning: consonant harmony vs. random alternation. Handout from a presentation given at the Workshop on Markedness and the Lexicon, Massachusetts Institute of Technology, 25 January 2003.

Wilson, H. I. (1972) *The Phonology and Syntax of Palauan Verb Affixes*. PhD dissertation, University of Hawaii.

Winslow, N. (2003) *Incorporating Exceptions in Optimality Theoretic Learnability*. Honor's thesis, University of Massachusetts Amherst.

Wolf, M. (2006) For an autosegmental theory of mutation. In L. Bateman, M. O'Keefe, E. Reilly and A. Werle (eds) *Papers in Optimality Theory III* (University of Massachusetts Occasional Papers in Linguistics 32). Amherst, MA: Graduate Linguistic Student Association.

Wolff, E. (1983) *A Grammar of the Lamang Language (Gwàɜ Làmàŋ)*. Glückstadt: J. J. Augustin GmbH.

Wright, R. (1996) Tone and accent in Oklahoma Cherokee. In Pamela Munro (ed.) *Cherokee Papers from UCLA* 11–22. Los Angeles: UCLA Department of Linguistics.

Wright, Richard (2004) A review of perceptual cues and cue robustness. In Bruce Hayes, Donca Steriade and Robert Kirchner (eds) *Phonetically Based Phonology* 34–57. Cambridge: Cambridge University Press.

Wright, Richard and Aaron Shryock (1993) The effect of implosives on pitch in SiSwati. *Journal of the International Phonetic Association* 23: 16–23.

Xu, C. X. and Y. Xu (2003) Effects of consonant aspiration on Mandarin tones. *Journal of the International Phonetic Association* 33: 165–81.

Xu, Y. (1997) Contextual tonal variations in Mandarin. *Journal of Phonetics* 25: 61–83.

Yip, Moira (1988) The Obligatory Contour Principle and phonological rules: a loss of identity. *Linguistic Inquiry* 19: 65–100.

Yip, Moira (1989) Feature geometry and cooccurrence restrictions. *Phonology* 6: 349–74.

Yip, Moira (1993) Cantonese loanword phonology and Optimality Theory. *Journal of East Asian Linguistics* 2: 261–91.

Yip, Moira (1995a) Repetition and its avoidance: the case of Javanese. In K. Suzuki and D. Elzinga (eds) *Proceedings of South Western Optimality Theory Workshop* 238–62. Tucson: University of Arizona.

Yip, Moira (1995b) Tone in East Asian languages. In J. A. Goldsmith (ed.) *The Handbook of Phonological Theory* 476–94. Cambridge: Blackwell.

Yip, Moira (1998) Identity avoidance in phonology and morphology. In S. LaPointe, D. Brentari and P. Farrell (eds) *Morphology and its Relation to Phonology and Syntax* 216–46. Stanford, CA: CSLI Publications.

Yip, Moira (2002) Perceptual influences in Cantonese loanword phonology. In H. Kubozono (ed.) *The Journal of the Phonetic Society of Japan. Special Issue on Aspects of Loanword Phonology* 6: 4–21.

Yip, Moira (2006) The symbiosis between perception and grammar in loanword phonology. *Lingua* 116: 950–75.

Yu, A. C. L. (2003) *The Morphology and Phonology of Infixation*. PhD dissertation, University of California, Berkeley.

Yu, A. C. L. (2004a) Infixing with a vengeance: Pingding Mandarin infixation. *Journal of East Asian Linguistics* 13: 39–58.

Yu, A. C. L. (2004b) Reduplication in Homeric Infixation. In Keir Moulton and Matthew Wolf (eds) *Proceedings of NELS 34*. Amherst: Graduate Linguistic Student Association.

Zamma, H. (2005) Predicting varieties: partial orderings in English stress assignment. Unpublished ms, Kobe City University of Foreign Studies/ University College London.

Zawaydeh, Bushra Adnan (1999) *The Phonetics and Phonology of Gutturals in Arabic*. PhD dissertation, Indiana University.

Zee, E. (1980) The effect of aspiration on the F0 of the following vowel in Cantonese. *UCLA Working Papers in Phonetics* 49: 90–97.

Zonneveld, W. (1978) *A Formal Theory of Exceptions in Generative Phonology*. Lisse: The Peter de Ridder Press.

Zonneveld, W. (1985) Environmental concerns in the study of phonology. *International Journal of American Linguistics* 51: 626–28.

Zuraw, K. (2000) *Patterned Exceptions in Phonology*. PhD dissertation, University of California, Los Angeles. Rutgers Optimality Archive 788.

Zuraw, K. (2002) Vowel reduction in Palauan reduplicants. *Proceedings of The Eight Meeting of the Austronesian Formal Linguistic Association* 385–98.

Zygis, Marzena and Jaye Padgett (to appear) A perceptual study of Polish fricatives, and its relation to historical sound change. *Journal of Phonetics*.

Index of constraints

Subject index

CPSIA information can be obtained
at www.ICGtesting.com
Printed in the USA
JSHW020320210120
3708JS00001B/3